Canada's Economic Apartheid

Canada's Economic Apartheid

The Social Exclusion of Racialized Groups in the New Century

Grace-Edward Galabuzi

Canadian Scholars' Press
Toronto

Canada's Economic Apartheid: The Social Exclusion of Racialized Groups in the New Century
by Grace-Edward Galabuzi

First published in 2006 by
Canadian Scholars' Press Inc.
180 Bloor Street West, Suite 801
Toronto, Ontario
M5S 2V6

www.cspi.org

Canadian Scholars' Press gratefully acknowledges financial support for our publishing activities from the Government of Canada through the Book Publishing Industry Development Program (BPIDP) and the Government of Ontario through the Ontario Book Publishing Tax Credit Program.

Library and Archives Canada Cataloguing in Publication

Galabuzi, Grace-Edward
    Canada's economic apartheid : the social exclusion of racialized groups in the new century / Grace-Edward Galabuzi.

Previous ed. published under title: Canada's creeping economic apartheid.
Includes bibliographical references and index.
ISBN 1-55130-265-9

    1. Race discrimination--Economic aspects--Canada. 2. Marginality, Social--Canada. 3. Discrimination in employment--Canada. 4. Canada- Race relations. I. Title. II. Title: Economic segregation and social marginalisation of racialised groups.

HD8108.5.A2G34 2005   305.8'00971   C2005-904578-7

Cover design by Aldo Fierro
Cover photo reprinted by permission of Emin Ozkan, from the stock.xchng web site,
    http://www.sxc.hu.
Page design and layout by Brad Horning

06   07   08   09   10   5   4   3   2   1

Printed and bound in Canada by Marquis Book Printing

Canadä

In memory of the late Margaret-Rose Namakula

and the late Gladys Nambuzi, my first teachers

Table of Contents

Acknowledgements

I am grateful to the Centre for Social Justice current and former staff members, especially John Anderson, and the CSJ equity committee members Maria Wallis, Ali Mallah, and Tariq Khan for the many hours they invested in some of the research on which this book is based. That research first appeared as a report titled *Canada's Creeping Economic Apartheid: The Economic and Social Marginalization of Racialized Groups.*

Many thanks to Roxana Ng, Michael Ornstein, JoJo Geronimo, Gerry Caplan, and Leah Vosko for their insightful reviews of that report, and to Victoria Smith, the copy editor.

Thanks to my editor, Megan Mueller, for proposing this project and for guiding me through it.

In solidarity, I thank the people behind the many stories and experiences depicted throughout this report that tell the tale of the racialized existence in this land. Many thanks for their and other people's continuing work of resistance. A luta Continua!

Finally, this is a work in progress and I want to thank my partner Shelina Kassam, and children Makula and Sanyu, who always pay the steepest price for the time and attention I devote to this work. This book is dedicated to them for their continued unconditional patience, love, and support.

Preface

Canada's Economic Apartheid: The Social Exclusion of Racialized Groups in the New Century calls attention to the growing social exclusion of racialized[1] group members in Canada, a process exemplified by the racialization of the gap between the rich and poor in Canadian society. This racialization is proceeding with minimal public and policy attention, despite the dire consequences for Canadian society. The book argues that the impact of neo-liberal global restructuring leading to the growth of precarious forms of work and declining power of labour, the retreat of the state from economic and social regulation, and the acceleration of South-North migration have combined with the historical processes of racialization in Canadian labour markets to render racialized groups more vulnerable to labour-market segmentation and declining social economic status. The consequence is the emergence of the racialization of poverty and other forms of social exclusion.

The book presents a picture of the experience of social exclusion in its various dimensions while challenging some common myths about the economic performance of Canada's racialized groups. Such myths are used to deflect public concern and attention from the condition of racialized communities and to mask the growing social crisis. The book points to the persistent role of historical patterns of racialization and systemic racial discrimination as key determinants of access to opportunity and livelihood for racialized group members, as demonstrated by their overrepresentation in low-paying occupations and low-income sectors, underrepresentation in high-income sectors and occupations, and their differential experience with higher unemployment, poverty, and social marginalization. Historical patterns of differential access to the country's resources mirror occupational segregation in the early 21st-century labour market. These patterns combine with intensified demands for flexible deployment of labour under conditions of neo-liberal restructuring, and neo-liberal state policies and practices to reproduce structures and outcomes of racial inequality in other areas of Canadian life. The overall impact is to rob racialized group members of the opportunity to participate fully in Canadian life and damn them to lives of exclusion.

While Canada embraces globalization and romanticizes the idea of multiculturalism and cultural diversity, persistent expressions of xenophobia and structures of racial marginalization suggest a continuing political and cultural attachment to the idea of a White-settler society. Canada has always imagined itself as a White immigrant nation, ignoring both the Aboriginal reality and the racialized immigrant population. This unresolved tension is reflected not only in racially segregated institutions such as the labour market and the subsequent unequal outcomes detailed below, but also in the quality of citizenship to which racialized group members can aspire. In recent years, racial and other forms of inequality have been exacerbated by the neo-liberal shift away from an active role for governments in responding to social crises, and towards a free-market approach.[2] This raises questions about Canada's commitment to the liberal democratic ideals of *equal* citizenship as enshrined in the Canadian Charter of Rights and Freedoms, and to its international obligations under the various United Nations human rights covenants and conventions.

Canada's racialized groups are set to become one fifth of the national population early in the new century. Yet even as they become demographically more significant, they continue to confront racial discrimination in many aspects of their everyday lives. Despite comparable educational attainment, their labour-market experience is one of limited access to and limited mobility in employment, and discrimination in the workplace. They confront a racially hierarchical and segmented labour market in which they are ghettoized into low-end jobs and low-income sectors. They are denied recognition of internationally obtained qualifications and skills, face questionable demands for Canadian experience, and sustain above-average unemployment and underemployment levels.

Canada's racialized groups (and particularly racialized women) bear a disproportionate burden of the demands for labour flexibility. Many end up in precarious employment — insecure and low-paying temporary, casual, contract, and home-based employment — and are often at the mercy of unscrupulous employers and employment agencies. Racialized groups thus provide a subsidy for the booming globalizing economy, drawing parallels to the contribution of free slave labour to the emergence of industrial capitalism. The resulting social crisis is what we document here: a persistent income gap, high levels of poverty, above-average levels of unemployment, and poor prospects in a segregated labour market. Racialized groups are disproportionately found in substandard housing, and increasingly in segregated neighbourhoods. They suffer high mental health and other health risks, while many are exposed to tense relations with the criminal justice system. Ultimately, entire segments of racialized groups experience heightened *social exclusion*.[3]

The book examines the socio-economic condition of racialized groups with particular emphasis on their experiences in Canada's urban centres, where over 75% of them live. It analyses their economic performance based on their employment income, patterns of labour-market participation, levels of unemployment, utilization of educational attainment, and incidence of low income (poverty). To varying degrees, it also reviews other indicators of socio-economic performance such as housing and neighbourhood selection, health, education, contact with the criminal justice system, representation in the media, and political participation. While we recognize that there are particular and differentiated experiences based on racial grouping, ethnicity, and gender, here we present a generalized picture of both the recent immigrant and Canadian-born segments of racialized communities.[4]

By choice, this book's reach is limited to the experience of non-Aboriginal racialized groups. Though we know well that the conditions under discussion are in many ways shared by members of Aboriginal communities, we are conscious of the specificity of the Aboriginal experience, which is rooted in the historical claim to first nationhood in Canada. While there is a time and place to collapse these experiences, this would be a different book if we were to do that.

This book captures some of the realities of life for racialized groups in Canada's urban centres, where most of these groups live, by looking at their socio-economic conditions and presenting some narratives and voices of members of racialized groups and of the organizations that advocate for them. We acknowledge the fact that statistical profiles and numbers do not fully express the extent and impact of the racialization and social exclusion that these communities face. Hearing some of the voices offers a broader and deeper understanding of the challenges faced daily by the racialized groups. These stories also speak to the challenge that Canada faces regarding the growing racialization of poverty, and the threat it poses to the country's stability and economic progress.

Persistent income and employment inequality, economic and social segregation, and political marginalization imply a looming crisis of social instability and political legitimacy for Canadian society. Social inequality exacerbates social instability and economic decline, and may even lead to violence as key institutions in society lose legitimacy among the affected communities. Further research is essential to deepen the analysis and develop more effective governmental and civil-society responses before these patterns mature into urban racial enclaves, complete with a subculture of underdevelopment. Such a development is increasingly common in other industrialized countries dealing with similar issues.

For now, it is imperative that governments and key institutions in Canadian society assume the responsibility of undertaking a comprehensive, multifaceted response founded on an anti-racist plan of action. The need for aggressive anti-racism cannot be overstated, given the social, cultural, and political nature of the problem of social exclusion. With the growth of the population of racialized groups far outpacing that of the rest of the Canadian population, Canadian society and the Canadian political class need to come to terms with the fact that while racialized assumptions inform a broad range of public, economic, and social-sector decisions, they are no longer sustainable. The contribution of Canada's racialized groups to Canada's gross domestic product is already disproportionately higher than that of other Canadians, making their economic performance an issue of survival for Canada.[5]

Combined, racialized population growth and the growth in racialized productivity represent an important source of social and economic vitality and security for an increasingly aging Canadian population. The sustainment of programs such as Canada Pension Plan, health care, and a host of social services, not to mention economic growth, rests increasingly on this population. A general awareness of this reality is essential, along with the necessary political commitment to implementing effective remedies for the growing social exclusion of racialized groups. Because of the threat this crisis represents to Canadian society, Canada's political, economic, and social leaders need to engage it with the same zeal they have brought to the recurring constitutional crises. In a chapter dealing with possible remedies, the book discusses the contours of an anti-racist plan of action needed to deal with the crisis outlined.

The term *economic apartheid* is adopted here from the historical use of "apartheid" to name a condition of racialized structural inequality in South Africa. In this case, it reflects the structuring of the Canadian economy, which is evolving a segregated labour market that consigns racialized group members to particular types of work, occupations, and sectors of the economy. The resulting system of racialized exploitation depends on the racialized undervaluing of human capital, racialized undercompensation for labour, and racialized income inequalities to benefit capital accumulation. The growing social exclusion is not limited to economic outcome but extends to other spheres of life as segregation in housing and neighbourhood selection, racialization of poverty, above-average contact with the law, and lower health status. All of these factors contribute to the characterization of "separate development" or "aparthood."

There is specific historical resonance in the concept of apartheid within Canada. Not only did Canadian immigration policy selectively encourage White settlement and prohibit immigration from racialized group members for many years, using a logic similar to that of the apartheid regime in South Africa, but also when the minority White South African regimes officially instituted the apartheid system of Bantustans or homelands for indigenous Africans, they looked to Canada's system of segregation of Aboriginal peoples and use of reserves to conceive the eventual model for their racist project. Further, while apartheid South Africa's use of domestic and migrant racialized labour was distinctive in the intensity of its exploitation, there are parallels to the historical exploitation of racialized labour in the Canadian labour market. The structural resonance leads to the disproportionate consignment of racialized groups to dead-end work (increasingly within precarious work — contract, casual, or contingent), with low wages and limited mobility. These conditions are complemented by increasingly segregated neighbourhoods, differential treatment by the criminal justice system, perpetuation of racist images by mainstream media, and cultural propagation of stereotypes about the groups. All of these factors further magnify the alienation and social exclusion of racialized groups.

The Organization of the Book

The book is organized as follows:

Chapter 1: Introduction: Emerging Realities and Old Problems identifies and introduces the patterns of growing social exclusion and racial inequities in the economic performance of Canada's non-Aboriginal racialized populations, both immigrant and Canadian-born, and the related socio-economic implications for the communities and the broader Canadian society. It situates the economic performance of Canada's racialized communities in a historical context, which has generated racially and gender-stratified labour markets, persistent barriers to socio-economic and political participation, and an increasingly segregated existence.

Chapter 2: Race and Racialization in Theory discusses the process of racialization from a theoretical perspective, and more specifically reviews the impact of the process of racialization on the integration of racialized groups into Canada's labour markets. The chapter includes some treatment of the theory of labour-market segmentation and the mainstream human-capital approach to explain unequal labour-market outcomes along racial lines.

Chapter 3: Social Exclusion in Historical Context examines the structures responsible for racializing the division of labour in a historical context. Beginning with colonization and racially selective immigration, it takes a historical sweep of the emergence of the hierarchical and racialized structures. Such structures, which generate racialized inequalities in access to the country and its resources, explain the multiple dimensions of the gap in income and employment between racialized groups and other Canadians.

Chapter 4: The Economic Exclusion of Racialized Communities — A Statistical Profile demonstrates that, according to income and employment indicators as well as other economic-performance measures, members of racialized groups are at a disadvantage in Canadian labour market. The significant employment, income, and occupational-status gap between racialized group members and the rest of the Canadian population renders racialized groups increasingly vulnerability to poverty. This gap implies increasing social exclusion as its various dimensions take on a systemic character.

Chapter 5: Beyond the Numbers: Dimensions of Economic Exclusion presents a portrait of the racialized existence in Canada's urban areas as one of growing social exclusion and multiple challenges. The experience of racialized group members goes beyond the exclusions in traditional workplaces. It is increasingly typified by Canada's fastest-growing forms of "flexible" work, especially precarious forms of work — contract, temporary, and contingent work arrangements brought on by the demands of globalization and economic restructuring for global competitiveness. This development both undermines the bargaining position of labour and disproportionately impacts racialized groups, particularly racialized women who experience both race and gender oppression. It also afflicts a less typical class of racialized men and women: those with international qualifications. Though often highly skilled, these individuals find that their lot is increasingly with those struggling to make a living in precarious environments. A broader process of exclusion extends to higher health risks, with racism as a social determinant of health. Also symptomatic of exclusion are disproportionate contact with the criminal justice system, criminalization, racial profiling, and the socio-cultural impact of negative media images. Specific attention is given to the experience of racialized women, because, along with racialized disabled people, they have to deal with a double oppression. A gendered income and poverty gap arises out of women's overrepresentation among those experiencing low income and bearing a disproportionate burden of the social reproduction of communities.

Chapter 6: Challenges to Conventional Explanations for Racial Inequality in Economic Performance — Myths and Facts acknowledges competing explanations for the racialized gap in economic performance and presents arguments and evidence to counter some of the often-used myths about racialized groups, especially recent immigrants. Such myths have become so commonplace that they have significantly influenced Canadian government policy-making. An attempt is made to intervene in the ongoing public debate about the declining socio-economic conditions of racialized group members, especially those with an immigrant background, by addressing head-on the conventional explanations for the growing gap in economic performance between the groups and the rest of Canadian society. The chapter concludes that race does indeed matter and is a determining factor in allocating access to the resources crucial to the pursuit of livelihood and life chances in late 20th- and early 21st-century Canada.

Chapter 7: Social Exclusion: Socio-economic and Political Implications of the Racialized Gap attempts a holistic approach to the study of the economic gap because, for many, the experience of differential treatment includes unequal access to the country, differential integration into the labour market, inequalities in labour-market participation, and unequal access to social goods such as housing, education, and health care. The continuum of inequality extends to contact with the criminal justice system, differential life chances, and unequal civic and political participation. The resulting conditions of social exclusion undermine the objective goal of full citizenship, and may lead to social instability in urban centres.

Chapter 8: The Role of the State in arresting social exclusion is crucial, as is the role of other key institutions in society, such as the labour movement on whom the communities will have to rely to organize the fight for better wages and working conditions. Other social justice organizations within civil society can support initiatives to empower racialized communities to assert their voices and full citizenship, as a basis for challenging government and private-sector practices, which perpetuate the structures of social exclusion. The chapter considers the need for effective full employment and legislated employment equity as well as effective policy and program responses to barriers to access to professions and trades. Such programs can begin to address the condition of social exclusion.

Chapter 9: A Program for Action offers some principles and ideas as a basis for building progressive policy and advocacy initiatives. The call for action is directed as much at governments as at Canada's key economic and social institutions. Such bodies must rise to the challenge to avert the adverse social and economic repercussions of persistent racial inequality and social exclusion. It is our hope that the book can also provide advocates for social justice in the racialized communities and in the broader community with another tool to use in their daily struggles to protect the economic and social rights of all of Canada's people.

Chapter 10: Conclusion returns to many of the main themes of the book, especially the patterns of growing inequities in the economic performance of Canada's non-Aboriginal racialized populations. We revisit the resulting social exclusion and its implications for the communities and the broader Canadian society in the early 21st century, a period of intensifying globalization. The book then issues a call for action that we hope will be heeded both by those in positions of power and privilege, and by the victims of social exclusion who can act to change the course of Canada's history.

Notes

1. The term "racialized groups" is used to describe non-Aboriginal people of colour, also referred to by Statistics Canada and in the *Federal Employment Equity Act* as visible minorities. Its use here and elsewhere suggests a discomfort with the official use of the term "visible minority" because it implies permanence of minority status that is imposed on the population. Racialized denotes that process of imposition, the social construction of the category, and the attendant experience of oppression as opposed to the seemingly

neutral use of the terms "visible minorities" or "racial minorities," which have the effect of masking the oppressions.

2. G. Galabuzi, "Racializing the Division of Labour: Neo-liberal Restructuring and the Economic Segregation of Canada's Racialized Groups." In *Challenging the Market: The Struggle to Regulate Work and Income*, edited by J. Stanford and L. Vosko (Montreal/Kingston: McGill-Queen's University Press, 2004), 175–204.

3. Social exclusion is used here to describe both the structures and the dynamic processes of inequality among groups in society, which, over time, structure access to critical resources. These resources determine the quality of membership in society and ultimately produce and reproduce a complex of unequal outcomes. In the Canadian context, social exclusion refers to the inability of certain groups or individuals to participate fully in Canadian life due to structural inequalities in access to social, economic, political, and cultural resources. This exclusion arises out of the often intersecting experiences of oppression relating to race, class, gender, disability, sexual orientation, immigrant status, and the like.

4. A variety of sources of data were used in this book. In particular, data were drawn from a special run of Statistics Canada's *Survey of Labour and Income Dynamics* for incomes during 1996, 1997, 1998, and 2001 (a period of relative prosperity), as well as 1996 and 2001 census data on selected industries and equity groups from the Labour Standards and Workplace Equity Branch of Human Resources and Skills Development Canada. It also drew from occupational data from the Government of Canada, *Report of the Taskforce on the participation of Visible Minorities in the Federal Public Service, 2000: Embracing Change in the Federal Public Service* (Ottawa: Supply and Services Canada, 2000).

5. See Conference Board of Canada, *Making a Visible Difference: The Contributions of Visible Minorities to Canadian Economic Growth. Economic Performance and Trends* (April, 2004). The Board estimates that between 1992 and 2001, despite the fact that racialized groups were 11% of the labour force, they accounted for a disproportionately high 0.3% of real gross domestic product growth. In contrast, the rest of the 89% of the labour force accounted for 0.6%. The Board projects an increase of $794.7 billion (in 1997 $), in GDP growth over the period 1992–2016, of which $302 billion will accrue to capital stock, $241 billion to technical efficiency, and $251.4 billion to labour force gains. Of that labour force gains figure, racialized groups will account for $80.9 billion. See also Statistics Canada, *Earnings of Canadians* (Ottawa: Statistics Canada, 2003).

A Note from the Publisher

Thank you for selecting *Canada's Economic Apartheid: The Social Exclusion of Racialized Groups in the New Century* by Grace-Edward Galabuzi. The author and publisher have devoted considerable time and careful development (including meticulous peer reviews) to this book. We appreciate your recognition of this effort and accomplishment.

Teaching Features

This book distinguishes itself on the market in many ways, including pedagogically rich chapters containing Critical Thinking Questions and Recommended Readings, which often include relevant websites; a high-quality Glossary; thorough Bibliography; and Index.

The art program includes provocative chapter-opening photographs as well as many tables and boxed inserts. The boxed inserts bring to life the topic at hand and add further insight. They include contemporary newspaper articles and key extracts or passages by leading Canadian scholars in the area, such as Peter Li and Frances Henry.

This book also features two appendices that are essential resources for students: Appendix A: Universal Declaration of Human Rights (United Nations, 1948); and Appendix B: Declaration on the Rights of Persons Belonging to National or Ethnic, Religious and Linguistic Minorities (United Nations, 1992).

Some Highlights

- The face of Canada is changing as its population distribution becomes more diverse racially and ethnically. The percentage of racialized minorities in the Canadian population reached 13.4% by 2001. The immigrant population accounted for 18.4% of the Canadian population in 2001. Those figures are projected to rise to 20% and 25% respectively by 2015. In the most recent census period, 1996–2001, while the general population grew by 3.9%, the growth of the racialized population was a remarkable 24.6%. Between 1996 and 2001, the male racialized proportion of the labour force grew by 28.7% (compared to 5.5% of total working male population) and the female racialized working group population grew by 32.3% (compared to 9.0% for the total working female population).
- According to a Conference Board of Canada study, this contribution to labour-market growth is significant. While racialized groups averaged less than 11% of the labour force between 1992 and 2000, they accounted for 0.3% of real gross domestic product growth (GDP). That contrasts with a contribution of 0.6% from the remaining 89% of the labour force. This disproportionately large contribution to GDP growth is likely to grow over the 2002–2016 period relative to the contribution of the rest of the population. The Board report concludes that in monetary terms, over the period 1992 to 2016, racialized groups will contribute $80.9 billion in real GDP growth. However, this productive capacity was not rewarded as the average wages for racialized groups over that period remained 14.5% lower than those of other Canadians.
- There is a persistent and sizeable (double-digit) gap between the economic performance of racialized group members and other Canadians over the period 1996–2001. According to income data, in 1998 there was a 24% gap in average before-tax income and a 20% gap in after-tax income. The gap grew from 1996 (23% on average before tax and 20% after tax). The median after-tax income gap grew from 23% to 25%, while the median before-tax gap remained statistically stagnant (29% in 1996 and 28% in 1998). The gap average before tax income fell back somewhat to 13% (2001) but remained

in double digits during a period of relative prosperity. Moreover, racialized groups experienced a lag in rewards from the improved economy, unlike their counterparts.

- Income, sectoral occupation, and unemployment data show that a racialized labour market is a feature of the Canadian economy. Characteristics of racial and gender labour-market segmentation include the overrepresentation of racialized (particularly women) members in low-paid, low-end occupations and low-income sectors, and also in temporary work. They are especially overrepresented in low-end service sector jobs and precarious and unregulated temporary or contingent work. Conversely they are underrepresented in high-paying occupations and high-income sectors.

- The racialized employment income gap is observable both among low-income earners and high-income earners. It persists among those with low and high educational attainment (among those with less than high school education and also among those with university degrees). It only diminishes to single digits when one compares racialized and non-racialized unionized workers.

- The demands for labour-market flexibility in the urban "globalized" economy have exposed racialized groups disproportionately to precarious forms of work—contract, temporary, part-time, and shift work with little or no job security, poor and often unsafe working conditions, intensive labour, excessive hours, low wages, and no benefits. Many are employed in exploitative environments in the textile and garment-making industries, in light manufacturing industries, and in the service sector. Many are on highly exploitative contracts by temporary agencies, with some assigned work based on racial stereotypes. Racialized women are particularly overrepresented in Canada's sweatshops—unregulated workplace and home work production. This labour is a subsidy for many employers at the expense of quality of life for these poorly paid workers.

- While the average educational attainment of immigrants has risen, partly due to strict skills-based immigration policy requirements, this has not translated into comparable employment and income opportunities. The human quality of many internationally trained professional and tradespeople is devalued, and many end up as part of an educated underclass even as their skills degrade. The condition has been referred to as "brain waste." Ironically, the federal government has invested more policy capital in resolving the problem of what is referred to as the "brain drain" to the United States of America, although Canada gains four skilled people for every one it loses, and the incoming group holds an educational advantage over the outgoing cohort. Today, over 60% of new immigrants are in the independent skilled-worker class, helping raise the level of education among racialized groups over that of the non-racialized cohort. Yet the racialized have lost ground in income and occupational status attainment, endure high levels of poverty, and are more likely to work in precarious job environments.

- Racialization diminishes the value of Canadian citizenship for racialized groups. While over a third of racialized group members are Canadian-born, assumptions of non-Canadian origins are common in public discourse, workplaces, and even employment interviews. Many racialized Canadians are left with a feeling of not belonging, and some choose to avoid civic or public service for fear of questions about their Canadian-ness.

- Immigration status has become a proxy for racial discrimination as employers insist on Canadian qualifications or Canadian experience despite operating in an increasingly globalized economy. While European immigrants' qualifications routinely go unchallenged, racialized Canadians often lose opportunities because of the perceived low value of their qualifications. As a result, racialized group immigrants have a longer immigration lag than non-racialized immigrants.

- Income inequalities are a significant contributor to racialized group members' persistent above-average poverty rates across the nation, and particularly in key urban areas where they are concentrated. The patterns suggest that a process of racialization of poverty is underway. These patterns are intensified among racialized women. The racialization of poverty is increasingly manifest in urban centres where racialized groups are concentrated, and in the emergence of racial enclaves and a growing racial underclass.

- This process is intensifying in increasingly racially segregated neighbourhoods. In an increasingly segregated housing market, racialized groups are relegated to substandard, marginal, and often overpriced housing. The growing social inequalities act as social determinants of health and well-being, with higher health risks, barriers to social services, and increased contact with the criminal justice system.

- Within the general framework of racialized labour markets, particular forms of racism have emerged directed at specific racialized communities. Anti-Black racism, anti-Chinese racism, anti-Asian racism, anti-Arab racism, and Islamophobia have proliferated in the post-September 11 period. Racial profiling intensifies the various experiences of racial discrimination, and group-based discourses of scapegoating and labelling further affect racialized groups in the workplace, in social settings, and in the community at large.

- Demographic data show that with current mobility trends, racialized groups will soon form economically disadvantaged majorities in some of Canada's major urban centres. These centres, which receive most new immigrants, are also the areas where most Canadian-born members of racialized groups reside. This raises issues of political representation as an expression of socio-political exclusion, as major decision-making structures remain overwhelmingly White.

- These developments have policy significance, especially because Canada increasingly relies on immigration to address labour-market shortages in the face of the competitive demands of globalization. An overwhelming majority of Canada's immigrants come from racialized countries, as the traditional sources countries for Canada's immigrants have changed over the last 30 years. Social exclusion leads to possible social instability, with many immigrants unable to translate their international qualifications and skills into comparable employment and compensation, and hence live lives of marginality. Canada's competitive position for the world's best and brightest immigrants becomes increasingly untenable. Canada will have difficulty meeting immigration targets, as some choose not to act on their immigrant visas, seek employment in the United States, or else choose to live in what are called "astronaut families," splitting the family so that they can continue to practice their professions in the "home" country.

CHAPTER 1

Introduction:
Emerging Realities and
Old Problems

Photo: Health Canada/Santé Canada

Canada's Economy and Changing Population across the Millennium Divide

Canada's population has become more ethnically and racially diverse in the late 20th and early 21st century. This follows key changes in the 1960s to an otherwise historically Eurocentric immigration policy. This Eurocentric bias was part of a nation-building project that traces its roots to Canada's original imaginary as a White-settler colony. This imaginary was sketched out in the early colonial contact with the Aboriginal nations, and continued through the period of colonization right into Confederation. But that picture's veracity was always suspect; in fact, Canada has always had a multicultural, multi-racial character. The "White nation" myth was achieved through a state-sponsored campaign of social exclusion of Aboriginal peoples and racialized groups throughout Canada's history.

The tension between myth and reality was suppressed for as long as the population profile could sustain the concept of Canada as a White nation. Immigration policy staunchly defended the socially constructed notion of Canada's character by encouraging and even recruiting European immigrants, while turning away formerly enslaved African Americans or Caribbeans, Middle-Easterners, Latin Americans, South Asians, and South East Asians. But that is fast changing and the raw nerves of the project are beginning to fray. Canada's population growth is now disproportionately dependent on immigration from source countries with racialized populations.

Box 1.1: *Emergence of "Visible Minorities" in Canada* by Peter S. Li

In Canada, the emergence of visible minorities to constitute a sizeable segment of the population is a rather recent phenomenon that resulted mainly from the changes in immigration regulations in 1967; historically, however, Canada had relied on waves of Oriental labour in the development of major industries and megaprojects in Western Canada (Li, 1998). The term *visible minority* received official recognition in 1984 when Rosalie Abella identified visible minority as one of the designated groups in the *Royal Commission Report on Equality in Employment* (Canada, Royal Commission on Equality in Employment, 1984). The subsequent *Employment Equity Act* of 1986 included visible minority as one of the target groups for which contract compliance in government-regulated businesses would be used to improve the employment opportunities of racial minorities (S.C. 1986, c. 31). The 1986 *Employment Equity Act* defines the four designated groups as "women, Aboriginal peoples, persons with disabilities and persons who are, because of their race or colour, in a visible minority in Canada" (S.C. 1986, c. 31, s. 3). In the 1986 Census of Canada, Statistics Canada defined visible minorities to include 10 origins: Blacks, Indo-Pakistani, Chinese, Korean, Japanese, South East Asian, Filipino, Other Pacific Islanders, West Asian and Arab, and Latin American, excluding Argentinean and Chilean (Statistics Canada, 1990: 71–72).

In the 1991 Census of Canada, slightly over 2 million people were classified by Statistics Canada as belonging to the visible minority, which was made up of largely immigrants from Third World countries. Members of the visible minority constituted 7.6% of the total population, or 10.7% of the population that declared a single origin only; they do not include the 470,615 individuals who chose Aboriginal origin as a single ethnic origin in the 1991 Census (Statistics Canada, 1993).

No doubt, the single most important factor contributing to the growth of the visible minority in Canada has been immigration since the 1970s. The changes in immigration regulations in 1962 and then in 1967 removed national origin as a consideration in selecting immigrants. Since 1967, immigrants have been able to enter Canada on the basis of educational and occupational qualifications, and of family ties with Canadians and permanent residents of Canada. Prospective immigrants from Asia, Africa, and other non-White regions that historically were restricted to enter Canada have been evaluated for admission under the same immigration regulations as applicants from Europe. The removal of racial or national barriers in immigrant selection has facilitated immigration from Third World countries.

As noted earlier, immigration statistics for the period after 1967 show that there has been an increase in the proportion of immigrants from Asia and Africa, and a corresponding decrease in the proportion of immigrants from Europe. In the five years after 1967, between 1968 and 1971, Canada admitted 737,124 immigrants, of which slightly over half came from Europe, 15.5% from the United States, and 15% from Asian countries. Thereafter, the proportion of immigrants from Europe continued to decline: from 38% for 1973 to 1977 to 22.6% for 1988 to 1992. In contrast, Asian immigrants increased from 25.4% for the period between 1973 and 1977 to 40% between 1978 and 1982, and then further to 51.8% between 1988 and 1992. Similarly, African immigrants, who made up only 5% of immigrants between 1973 and 1977, rose to 6.7% between 1988 and 1992.

In total, for the period of 25 years from 1968 to 1992, Canada admitted 3.7 million immigrants, of which 35.7% came from Asia, 4.8% from Africa, and 7.4 from the Caribbean. If immigrants from these regions were estimated to be members of racial minorities in Canadian society, then about 48% of the 3.7 million immigrants coming to Canada between 1968 and 1992 would have been members of the visible minority. In addition, if some of the immigrants from Central and South America were also counted as members of racial minorities, then the proportion of the visible minority among immigrants to Canada between 1968 and 1992 would exceed 50 per cent. For the same period, European immigrants made up 33.9% of all immigrants entering Canada, and immigrants from the United States accounted for 9%.

The immigration statistics suggest that about 1.8 to 1.9 million members of the visible minority were added to the Canadian population between 1968 and 1992. In view of the fact that in the 1991 Census about 2 million individuals belonged to the visible minority in Canada, then it is clear that most of the growth in the population of the visible minority took place in the period from the late 1960s to the 1990s. The immigration pattern also means that most members of the visible minority are first-generation immigrants born outside Canada, in contrast to most European-Canadians who, because of a historical immigration policy in favour of their admission, tend to be native-born in Canada.

By the time the 1996 Census was taken, the number of visible minority members in Canada had reached 3.2 million people, or about 11.2% of Canada's total population

(Statistics Canada, 1998). It is clear that the visible minority population grew at a faster rate than Canada's population, since the visible minority population increased from 6.3% of Canada's population in 1986 to 9.4% in 1991 and then to 11.2% in 1996. There is no doubt that immigration since the late 1960s has contributed principally to this growth. The increase in the visible minority population is more conspicuous in metropolitan areas, since immigrants have a tendency to move to large urban centres. Thus in 1996, British Columbia and Ontario accounted for three-quarters of the visible minority population in Canada, even though these two provinces accounted for only half of Canada's population. In particular, 42% of Canada's 3.2 million visible minority members resided in Toronto, and they accounted for 32% of Toronto's population. Visible minority members also made up 31% of Vancouver's population in 1996, and 17% of Calgary's (Statistics Canada, 1998b). It is this concentration of the visible minority population in some urban areas of Canada that gives the exaggerated impression that the immigration policy has substantially altered the cultural and racial composition of Canada.

References

Government of Canada. *Royal Commission on Equality in Employment.* Ottawa: Minister of Supply and Services Canada, 1984.

Li, P. *The Chinese in Canada,* 2nd edition. Toronto: Oxford University Press, 1998.

Statutes of Canada. *Employment Equity Act,* c. 31 (1986).

Statutes of Canada. *Employment Equity Act*, c. 31, s. 3 (1986).

Statistics Canada. *Public Use Microdata File on Individuals: Documentation and User's Guide* (1990): 71–72.

Statistics Canada. *Ethnic Origin: The Nation.* 1991 Census of Canada, Catalogue 93-315. Ottawa: Minister of Industry, Science, and Technology, 1993.

Statistics Canada. "1996 Census: Ethnic Origin, Visible Minorities." *The Daily.* (February 17, 1998).

Statistics Canada. *The Daily* (February 17, 2002).

Source: P.S. Li, *Destination Canada: Immigration Debates and Issues,* 33–36. Don Mills: Oxford University Press, 2003.

This reversal of earlier trends and policies assuring near-exclusive European or White immigration has less to do with political choice, and more with population pressures in Canada, global immigration trends and the process of globalization.[1] Yet debates on Canada's immigration policy continue to labour under a White-settler colony imaginary, betraying a persistent hostile sentiment toward racialized group settlement in Canada.[2]

The percentage of racialized groups in the Canadian population, under 4% in 1971, grew to 9.4% by 1991, then 11.2% by 1996, and had reached 13.4% by 2001. The immigrant population accounted for 18.4% of the Canadian population in 2001. Both racialized groups and immigrants are projected to rise to 20% and 25% respectively by 2015. Outside of Australia, this is the highest proportion of immigrants in any population, higher than the 9% in the United States. In a number of major Canadian urban centres, racialized group members and recent immigrants now make up majorities in the population.

Table 1.1: Total Population 15 Years and Over by Racialized Population, 2001 Census, Geography: Canada

	Total Population	Total Racialized Population	Percentage
Total—Both Sexes	29,639,030	3,983,845	13.4
Males	14,564,275	1,945,510	13.4
Females	15,074,755	2,038,340	13.5

Source: 2001 Census, Statistics Canada

The trend is more likely to grow than recede. In fact, in the most recent census period, 1996–2001, while the general population grew by 3.9%, the racialized population grew by a remarkable 24.6%. Between 1996 and 2001, the male racialized proportion of the labour force grew by 28.7% (compared to 5.5% of total working male population) and the female racialized working group population grew by 32.3% (compared to 9.0% of the total working female population). (See Tables 1.3 and 1.4.)

While the growth was highest in Ontario (28%), it was significant in British Columbia (26.6%), Alberta (22.5%), New Brunswick (18%), Quebec (14.7%), and Manitoba (12.6%) among others, only falling in Prince Edward Island (−22%) (see Table 1.2).

According to the 2001 Census, the largest number of racialized group members were to be found in Ontario (2,153,045), making up 19% of the population of Canada's largest province. That share is projected to rise to 25% by 2015. British Columbia had the highest proportion of racialized group members (836,445) in its population at 22%.

Much of that growth can be attributed to immigration, with significant increases from Asia and the Middle East, and some growth in Africa and Latin America as source areas too. Given Canada's continued reliance on immigration for population growth and labour-market needs, and the escalating process of globalization, these trends are likely to persist and even intensify.

Canada's racialized population is mainly concentrated in urban centres, with nearly three quarters (73%) living in Canada's three largest cities in 2001 and accounting for major proportions of the populations of those municipalities—Toronto (43%), Vancouver (49%), and Montreal (23%). Other municipalities with significant racialized populations include Calgary (18%); Edmonton (15%); Markham, Ontario (56%); and Richmond, B.C. (59%) (Statistics Canada, 2003).

While 68% of Canada's racialized group members are immigrants, a significant proportion, 32%, are Canadian-born. The size of the racialized population will continue to be an important consideration for public policy because it is concentrated in urban Canada, which, in the early 20th century, is the engine of Canada's economy.

**Table 1.2: Racialized Groups, 2001 Count and Percentage Change 1996–2001
Geography: Canada, Provinces and Territories**

	Total Population	Total Population % change (1996–2001)	Total Racialized	Total Racialized % change (1996 -2001)
Canada	29,639,030	3.9%	3,983,845	24.6%
Newfoundland and Labrador	508,075	−7.1%	3,850	0.9%
Prince Edward Island	133,385	0.4%	1,180	−22.6%
Nova Scotia	897,565	−0.3%	34,525	10.2%
New Brunswick	719,710	−1.4%	9,425	18.0%
Quebec	7,125,580	1.1%	497,975	14.7%
Ontario	11,285,550	6.0%	2,153,045	28.0%
Manitoba	1,103,700	0.3%	87,115	12.6%
Saskatchewan	963,150	−1.4%	27,580	2.4%
Alberta	2,941,150	10.2%	329,925	22.5%
British Columbia	3,868,875	4.9%	836,445	26.6%
Yukon Territory	28,520	−6.9%	1,020	2.5%
Northwest Territories	37,100	−6.0%	1,545	2.0%
Nunavut	26,665	8.1%	210	35.5%

Source: 2001 Census, Statistics Canada

**Table 1.3: Total Population in the Labour Force (15 Years and Over by Racialized
Groups)—Male Canada: 1996–2000**

	1996	2001	Percentage Change
Total Population	8,007,955	8,452,015	5.5
Racialized Population	817,955	1,052,965	28.7

Source: 2001 Census, Statistics Canada

**Table 1.4: Total Population in the Labour Force (15 Years and Over by Racialized
Groups)—Female Canada: 1996–2000**

	1996	2001	Percentage Change
Total Population	6,804,745	7,420,060	9.0
Racialized Population	720,805	953,330	32.3

Source: 2001 Census, Statistics Canada. http://www12.statscan.ca/english/census01/home/
index.cfm

Racialized Groups and Urban Canada

In 2001, racial minorities accounted for significant minorities of major urban populations. See Table 1.5 for details.

Table 1.5: Racialized Group Members Proportion of Population by City, 2001

City	Percentage of Population
City of Toronto	43%
City of Vancouver	49%
City of Montreal	22%
City of Calgary	21%

Source: 2001 Census, Statistics Canada

Immigrants and Urban Canada

Immigrants' share of the population makeup of urban Canada has been on the rise. Every year, over 75% of all immigrants end up in Canada's three biggest metropolitan centres, Toronto, Montreal, and Vancouver. However, immigration is also changing the population makeup of Canada's other urban centres (see Table 1.6).

Table 1.6: Immigrant Population by Census Metropolitan Area, 2001

Census Metropolitan Area	Percentage of Immigrants in Population
Toronto	43.7%
Vancouver	38%
Calgary	22%
Montreal	18%
Edmonton	18%
Winnipeg	17%
Halifax	7%

Source: 2001 Census, Statistics Canada

Racialized groups now represent a key source of human resources for the Canadian labour market. Already, according to Human Resources and Skills Development Canada (HRSDC), 70% of net new entrants into the labour force are immigrants, 75% of whom are racialized. By 2011, over 100% of net new entrants will come from this group. Resolving the issue of racial discrimination will be critical to their integration into the Canadian labour market and to the continued success of the Canadian economy (HRDC, 2002). According to a Conference Board of Canada study, while racialized groups averaged less than 11% of the labour force between 1992 and 2000, they accounted for 0.3% of real gross domestic product growth (GDP).

That contrasts with the remaining 89% of the labour force, which contributed 0.6%. This disproportionately large contribution to GDP growth is likely to grow over the 2002–2016 period as the contribution of the rest of the population falls. However, this productive capacity was not rewarded as the average wages for racialized groups over that period remained 14.5% lower than those of other Canadians. The Board report concludes that in monetary terms, over the period 1992 to 2016, racialized groups will contribute $80.9 billion in real GDP growth.[3]

The complex dynamics of population change are interwoven with the organization of the Canadian economy. Canada's economy has historically created social class hierarchies, which emphasize divisions such as gender and race. While race is a social construct based principally on superficial differences in physical appearance, it has always been an important part of Canada's population-economy complex. From early European attempts to take control of the land, resources, and trade from the First Nations, which involved restricting their economic participation, to the selective importation of African American, Asian, and Caribbean labour, and the more recent casualization of racialized immigrant labour, race has been and continues to be a major factor in determining access to economic opportunity in Canada. Late 20th-century intensification of racial segregation in the labour market is located within the context of the neo-liberal restructuring of the global economy. The shift toward neo-liberal forms of governance and labour market deregulation aimed at flexible labour deployment is calculated to achieve maximum exploitation of labour. Because of persistent historical structures of systemic discrimination, the growing dominance of flexible work arrangements in this liberalized environment, facilitated by the state deregulation of the labour market and the reversal of state anti-discriminatory policies and programs, has disproportionately impacted racialized groups.

Moreover, the cumulative impact of those processes suggests a redefining of other social hierarchies and social structures in Canadian society. The process of racial segmentation, underway in the Canadian labour market during this neo-liberal era, represents an intensification of the racialization of the process of class formation, as suggested by key structural patterns of income differentials, occupational concentration, and sectoral segregation in the Canadian labour market.[4] Racial segmentation in the labour market then leads to such social outcomes as differential access to housing, neighbourhood selection, contact with the criminal justice system, health risks, and political participation. The result is a deepening of the racialization of poverty and related conditions such as the racial segregation of low-income neighbourhoods, and the intensification of social exclusion for Canada's urban-based racialized group communities. These processes are central to the emergence of what Li (1998) has referred to as a social hierarchy of race, and what we refer to as the *colour-coded vertical mosaic*.[5] But while the racialization of class formation furthers the oppression of racialized groups by intensifying their social exclusion, it also makes it possible to engage in a racially conscious class-based struggle and workplace-based politics of resistance in response to the neo-liberal political project. Ironically, the racializing of the division of labour may serve to undermine the neo-liberal project by mobilizing racialized workers in solidaristic formations based in workplaces where they predominate, but share with other non-racialized workings, and by tapping into their shared experience of class-based social exclusion. The contradictions of the late 20th- and early 21st-century capitalist accumulation make possible a process of class formation rooted both in the common experience of precarious wage relations and in the cultural experience of racialization.[6]

Canada's Population Changes Driven by Labour Needs

As a resource-rich and labour-poor country, Canada has historically met its labour shortages by encouraging immigration, but within the framework of an assimilation policy aimed at maintaining a "White society," hence the official categories of "desirables" and "undesirables" that dominated immigration policy until recently. The demands of an expanding economy and the declining of interest in migration to Canada by different groups of Europeans led to a decision to remove the legal restrictions against non-European immigration in the 1960s. Even so, administrative restrictions continued to be enforced, demanding that only those with government designated "essential skills" qualify ahead of family members seeking reunification, as was previously practiced. Refugees had often cracked this carefully constructed shield, but those fissures were closed with a new stringent refugee determination system that ensured that a clear majority of applicants were denied asylum and either deported or descended into a non-status limbo. These measures, largely enacted as the source countries for immigrants became predominantly countries in the global South, served to manage the flow of immigrants so as not to threaten the Eurocentric nature of the country.

The outcome of the policies is a gender and racially stratified social profile, as manifested in the Canadian labour market today. From a gender standpoint, not only did racialized women face the racial structures in the workplace and society, but also they were incorporated into the "pink ghettos" where women are disproportionately represented. Beyond being imported into the lower ranks of the health-care sector, the textile and garment industry, the service sector and clerical ghettos, and disproportionately subjected to precarious forms of employment, many female immigrants from the global South were forced to apply as domestic workers, although many had professional and other qualifications.[7]

This book takes the position that the developments in the late 20th century and the related insights into the racialized nature of social hierarchies in Canada essentially update John Porter's concept of vertical mosaic based on the social stratification of Canadian society in the 1960s (Porter, 1965).[8] The idea of an ethnically defined Canadian vertical mosaic has lost some of its explanatory value and been updated by a racially distinct vertical mosaic on the grounds that while the association between ethnicity and inequality has weakened, the role played by race in stratifying Canadian society has increased.[9] These changes justify references to a colour-coded vertical mosaic (Herberg, 1990; Lian and Matthews, 1998; Li, 1998). This book is sympathetic to that characterization of late 20th-century and early 21st-century Canadian society. The growth of the racialized population makes the characterization more compelling than in years past. Much of the evidence presented in the book seeks to validate the concept of a colour-coded vertical mosaic.

Shifts in Canada's Immigration Policy

Canada's immigration policy shifted in the 1960s toward a more racially liberal skills-based points system that attracted many newcomers from outside Europe. Immigrants from the South with a broad range of skills arrived, only to face barriers to access in employment—as documented by a Royal Commission report in the early 1980s—or to be slotted into low-end job ghettos, as other research shows. The immigration data show that the increased numbers of skilled immigrants from the South have not experienced economic success comparable to that of European immigrants or Canadians of European heritage. Instead, in a departure from earlier patterns of immigrant economic performance, the lag in economic attainment has become a permanent income gap between racialized communities and the rest of the population. In a pattern that coincides with the influx of racialized immigrant groups, and seems to be holding both during and after the recession years of the late 1970s, 1980s, and early 1990s, immigrant economic performance has grown progressively worse over the last quarter century. So while Canada's population is becoming more racially diverse, the country's history of differential treatment of non-European peoples limits the life chances of racialized groups in a manner not experienced by previous waves of immigrants, who also came to seek a better life.

Racialized Immigration, Neo-Racism, and Competitive Racism

As we noted above, the political, economic, and social destabilization brought about by the processes of global restructuring, together with the growing inequality between the North and the South, have had a profound impact on the nature of population flows around the world. While the population movement during periods of colonialism were from North to South in order to establish settler colonies and to entrench structures of colonialism, the new movements are in reverse. Largely but not exclusively, they are movements of poor people from the South to the North. These "immigrants" come to seek both asylum and a better way of life. They are 138 million migrants, including part of the over 5 million documented refugees running from political conflict and economic displacement, and the many more millions who are internally displaced and cannot afford the means to make the trips North.[10] However, the influx of newcomers, combined with the unequal articulations of capitalist development, which force them into conditions of disadvantage, has created what is now called "South in the North" — communities and neighbourhoods whose conditions are more like those in the South than those generally found in the North. This phenomenon is characterized by the racialization of neighbourhoods and, in some cases, cities and regions.

These developments emerge within the framework of existing racialized social structures, prompting new forms of response within the host societies. Immigration has become one of the most contentious public policy areas. What has come to be known as *neo-racism* is said to explain the anti-immigrant discourses and policy actions of people in the North in response to the new migration unleashed by globalization's displacement of entire communities. Neo-racism represents a particular construction of race at the historical moment of 21st-century globalization. Like all other forms of racism, it utilizes the social construction of racial categories to demand limits on the numbers of certain racial groups allowed into the country and on racial mixing. Neo-racism's dominant theme is the insurmountability of cultural differences. It concentrates on the harm that can come out of abolishing borders, and on the incompatibility of social traditions and lifestyles. In an ironic twist, it uses the very defence of difference to justify its cultural segregationist position.[11]

In Europe as in North America, the term *immigrant* has been redefined to refer to non-Whites, especially Africans, Caribbeans, East Asian, South Asians, and Latin Americans, regardless of whether they are immigrants or born in that particular country. Immigrant status has been racialized, and the inferior status of racialized peoples is now extended to immigrants to the point where the quality of their human capital is called into question. The consequences are dire for those with international qualifications. Balibar has suggested that this category slippage is a form of racism particular to the period of globalization because it represents a response to the reversal of population movements, a phenomenon considered dangerous by increasingly insecure dominant populations. While this use of the term is more prevalent in Europe than in North America, there are signs, including the recent pronouncements by civic leaders, that attest to the phenomenon in Canada.[12]

Canada's Political Economy and the Racialized Growing Economic Gap

There is mounting evidence that the bouts of economic restructuring Canada has endured in the last two decades have intensified processes of racialization and feminization in the labour markets, leading to increased economic, social, and political inequality and immiseration of vulnerable populations of women, men, and children. The patterns of intensified inequality suggest that racialized groups, immigrants, refugees, and women have borne the brunt of economic restructuring and austerity. Global economic restructuring has not only encouraged the informalization of economies and the emergence of "precarious work"—temporary, part-time, contract, and casual work with low pay, no benefits, no job security, and poor working conditions—but also exacerbated previous fissures of racial and gender inequality based on systemic discrimination. A growing body of Canadian studies suggests that flexible work arrangements, facilitated by the state-mediated processes of deregulation and re-regulation of the labour market, have particularly disadvantaged racialized groups, and especially racialized women.[13] Adding to the problem are persistent discriminatory labour-market structures. The consequences are increased segmentation of the labour market along racial lines, the racialization of poverty, the racialization and segregation of low-income neighbourhoods, and intensified social exclusion.

Central to this phenomenon is the global restructuring that is taking place in Canada's economy and changing the nature of work on offer. This restructuring is disproportionately impacting racialized group members. The intensification of flexible accumulation on a global scale has created an increasingly transnational division of labour and unleashed new migrations trends that may partly explain Canada's increased absorption of new immigrants. But it has also ushered in a growing informalization of the economy, "normalizing" the shift to non-standard forms of work through labour market deregulation, as previously peripheral forms of work become increasingly dominant.[14] The disproportionate participation of racialized groups in these forms of work is an important part of their declining social economic status. While the racialization of production is obviously not new, recent patterns and size of migration from the South to the North, which reverse the colonial North-South patterns that ushered in industrial capitalism, have combined with persistent structures of systemic discrimination to disproportionately relegate racialized groups to non-standard forms of work.[15]

Accentuating the consequences of the flexible accumulation, informalization, and South-North migration discussed above is a shift toward neo-liberal forms of governance that has dismantled the key elements of the Welfare state in the North and many of its social protection mechanisms. This has increased intra-working-class tensions and competition for decent employment, which have unleashed expressions of overt racism. Some refer to these expressions of racism as "competitive racism within capitalist economies."[16] In this instance, racism arises out of competition brought on by the deregulation of work arrangements, which drives down wages and increases levels of exploitation and vulnerability. As we noted before, for racialized groups, this intensification of oppression ironically opens the door to a class-based yet racially conscious struggle against the articulations of global capitalism.

Given the nature of economic restructuring, the normalization of non-standard forms of work is central to understanding the present-day racialization of class formation, especially in Canada's urban areas. The racialization of class formation is an outcome of the impact of historical processes of flexible accumulation identified with capitalist restructuring on a global scale on Canada's labour market in the late 20th and early 21st centuries. It also reproduces pre-existing racial discriminatory structures in the labour market directed at racialized populations for the purposes of subsidizing global capital. The labour of racialized group members is devalued, with added significance because of their increased numbers in Canada's urban areas. The process of intensified exploitation is manifest even during a period of relative prosperity in Canada, and as we account in this book, between 1996 and 2001, the gap between rich and poor became not only wider, but also increasingly racialized.

While historically, the majority of immigrants have achieved some degree of economic success in the Canadian labour market, many immigrants started with wages and salaries lower than those of comparable Canadian-born workers. But as the length of residence in Canada increased, their earnings approached, and sometimes exceeded, those of Canadian-born workers. However, as we will see below, recent trends raise questions about this analysis of immigrants' economic integration. Since the beginning of the 1980s, immigrants' earnings have stalled and are no longer converging with comparable Canadian-born workers' (DeVoretz, 1995; Ley and Smith, 1997; Reitz and Sklar, 1997). National data show evidence of racialized workers, many of whom have arrived since 1980, stuck disproportionately at the bottom of the economic ladder in terms of income, employment, and access to high-paying sectors and jobs (Ornstein, 2000; Galabuzi, 2001; Lian and Matthews, 1998; Reitz, 1998; Smith and Jackson, 2002).

The Emergence of Precarious Work and the Racialization of the Labour Market

The neo-liberal global economic restructuring has left a mark on Canada's labour market, one felt intensely by racialized groups. This restructuring represents a qualitative shift in the way work is organized in Canada. Broad (2000) has suggested that five interrelated structural transformations have combined to create the conditions for the emergence of precarious work as a major feature of Canadian labour markets. These include the globalization of capitalist production, the emergence of the neo-liberal state, flexible production, the rise of the service economy, and the increased re-entry of women into the economy.[17] For our purposes, these combine with the phenomenon of increased flow of immigrants from the South to Canada's urban areas to create the conditions under which racial segmentation of the labour market is becoming normalized. For those concerned about the everyday life conditions of working people, it is clear that these processes, coupled with the dismantling of the Canadian welfare state, have created key deficits in social reproduction that help explain the racialization of poverty, which we will discuss in detail below. Cutbacks in social program spending, cuts to income transfers to individuals and families, a shift to the workfare program, deregulation, the lowering of employment standards and other forms of labour legislation have had a deleterious effect. Compounding this is the fact that the state has also retreated from anti-discriminatory policies and programs. The devaluation of racialized labour and the increased supply of low-end labour has allowed for greater employer latitude and has given currency to demands for Canadian experience, to rejection of skills gained in other countries, and to other forms of employment discrimination.[18]

Precarious work has become a major feature of the Canadian labour market at the beginning of the 21st century. By the end of the 1990s, a far greater proportion of people were either on contract, self-employed, or doing temporary work than at the beginning of the decade. While the form of work is not new, the levels depart from previous decades. Growth in full-time employment accounted for only 18% of new job growth between 1989 and 1998, compared to 58% during the preceding decade. Meanwhile, self-employment accounted for 58%, compared to 18% in the 1980s.[19]

The dramatic increase in temporary, contract, part-time, piece work, and self-employment has had a dramatic impact on racialized group members, especially racialized women. Not only do disproportionate numbers of racialized group members depend on precarious work, but also the work is largely unregulated, involving long hours and low pay. The effect is an intensification of work, with many either working longer hours or working multiple jobs. Many of the workers in the service sector and light manufacturing industries increasingly find themselves on temporary contracts from employment service agencies, which pay them a fraction of what they earn in the jobs to which they are assigned, and hold them to those contracts even when their employers require their services permanently.

Box 1.2: Globalization and Racial Discrimination Intensify Economic Exclusion

- Neo-liberal restructuring and demands for flexibility have made precarious employment the fastest-growing forms of work; contract, temporary, part-time, piecemeal, shift work, or self-employment are increasingly the norm in some sectors. Precarious employment has combined with historical racial discrimination in employment to make racialized groups more vulnerable to the vicissitudes of the global economy.
- Characteristics of these forms of employment include low pay, no job security, poor and often unsafe working conditions, intensive labour, excessive hours, and low or no benefits.
- Because of their vulnerability, racialized workers and new immigrants are disproportionately overrepresented in precarious work. This translates into lower incomes and occupational status than other Canadians have.

In material terms, the disproportionate concentration of racialized populations in part-time, temporary, and home work — particularly for racialized women — leads to low income, with consequences being their overrepresentation in substandard housing and increasingly segregated neighbourhoods, along with higher mental and other health risks, tensions between communities, and contact with the criminal justice system. There is heightened *social exclusion* of whole segments of racialized groups, some of whom have resorted to internecine violence.

Employment Income and Racialized Groups

A series of studies done in the late 1990s by economist Armine Yalnyzian for the Toronto-based Centre for Social Justice, titled *Growing Gap,* show that while the Canadian economy was growing faster in the late 1990s than at any time over the last 25 years, Canadian incomes were becoming more unequal. There was a generalized growing gap between the top 10% income earners and the rest of the population.[20] The gap between Canada's racialized groups and other Canadians also grew and became sustained in double digits. What we show here is that the income inequality in Canada was also increasingly along racial lines. Income inequality represents just one dimension of the socio-economic exclusion of racialized groups, which is manifested in their labour-market experiences of higher unemployment; overrepresentation in low-end occupations and low-income sectors; and underrepresentation in managerial, professional, and high-income occupations and sectors. The process of economic exclusion has also had broader effects such as higher poverty rates, lower civic and political participation, higher health risks, lower quality housing, intensified segregation of neighbourhoods, and more contact with the criminal justice system. It is important to note that these effects are not limited to immigrants or "newcomers," but are also experienced by many racialized group members who have either lived in Canada for extended periods of time or were born in the country.

Analysis of a special run of Survey of Labour and Income Dynamics (SLID) data for the CSJ Foundation for the period 1996–2001 show a sustained double-digit gap between the incomes of racialized group members and other Canadians. This being a period of relative prosperity suggests that the market-based approach to dealing with racial inequality has clearly failed. Based on individual earnings, racialized Canadians in 1996 earned a pre-tax average of $19,227, while non-racialized Canadians made $25,069, or 23% more. The median income (showing half earning more and half earning less) gap at 29% ($13,648 to $19,111) suggests an even more profound inequality. The gap grew in 1997 as the racialized group average pre-tax income increase of $19,558 did not keep pace with the $25,938 earned by other Canadians; the gap is 25%. The median before-tax income again betrays deeper inequality, with racialized earnings declining to $13,413, while others saw a modest increase to $19,602. The median income gap also grew from 1996 to 1997 to 32%. The growing economy improved the income position of racialized group members in 1998, but the gap did not diminish substantially over the three-year period. Data show an average before-tax income for racialized groups of $20,626, which accounted for 76% of the $27,174 the rest of the population earned, for a gap of 24%. The median racialized income increased to $14,507, compared to $20,517, leaving the gap at 28%.[21]

The tax effect was marginal in terms of closing the gap. The average after-tax income of the racialized groups in 1996 was $16,053, compared to $20,129 for other Canadians, a 20% gap. After-tax incomes grew for both groups in 1997 to $16,438, or 79% of the $20,793 for other Canadians, figures still showing a marginal growing gap. But while the median after-tax income for 1996 was $12,991 for racialized groups, compared to $16,922 for other Canadians, a gap of 23%, that gap grew in 1997 to 26% as racialized group members took home less at $12,895, while other Canadians increased their earnings to $17,320. In 1998, taking the tax effect into consideration, racialized groups earned an after-tax average of $17,376, i.e., 80% of the $21,694 for the rest of the population. The median racialized after-tax income was $13,561, compared to $18,146, for a still-high gap of 25%.[22]

In essence, analysis of the employment income data for this "economic boom" period (1996–1998) shows a growing gap that marginally levelled off in 1998, leaving a high income gap that, if one looks at median incomes for the three years, is as high as 32%.

Table 1.7: After-Tax Income of Racialized Persons, Canada, 1996

	Total Population	Racialized (a)	Non-racialized (b)	Difference $	%
Average	19,631	16,053	20,129	4,076	20.2
Median	16,394	12,991	16,922	3,931	23.2

Source: Statistics Canada, Income Statistics Division, Survey of Labour and Labour and Income Dynamics, Custom Tables, 1996–2002.

The situation did improve between 1991 and 2001 as there was a delayed benefit for racialized groups from the economic gains of the late 1990s. However, the gap remained double digit, and the time lag in acquiring the benefit suggests that structures exist that impede the allocation of rewards to certain groups in society.

During the period 1996–2001, racialized groups experienced a median after-tax income gap of 13.3% ($18,138 to $15,909), and an average after-tax income gap of 12.2% ($23,023 to $20,627). The gap is highest among male youth (average after-tax income gap 42.3% and median after-tax income gap 38.7%), as well as those with less than high school education (median after-tax income gap 20.6%) and those over 65 years (average income gap of 28% and median income gap of 21%).[23]

Table 1.8: After-Tax Income of Racialized Persons, Canada, 2000

	Total Population	Racialized	Non-racialized	Difference	
		(a)	(b)	$	%
Average	23,023	20,627	23,522	2,895	12.3
Median	18,138	15,909	18,348	2,439	13.3

Source: Statistics Canada, Income Statistics Division, Survey of Labour, and Labour and Income Dynamics, Custom Tables, 1999–2002

The gap was evident among those with higher education as well as among those with less than high school education, as was the time lag between non-racialized and racialized populations seeing the rewards of the improved economy (see Tables 1.9 and 1.10).

Table 1.9: After-Tax Income of Racialized Persons with University Degree, Canada, 2000

	Total Population	Racialized	Non-racialized	Difference (a-b)	
		(a)	(b)	$	%
Average	38,312	35,617	38,919	3,302	8.5
Median	32,832	28,378	33,230	4,852	14.6

Table 1.10: After-Tax Income of Racialized Persons with Less Than High School Education, Canada, 2000

	Total Population	Racialized	Non-racialized	Difference (a-b)	
		(a)	(b)	$	%
Average	15,125	11,958	15,444	3,486	22.6
Median	12,955	10,378	13,068	2,690	20.6

Source: Statistics Canada, Income Statistics Division, Survey of Labour, and Labour and Income Dynamics, Custom Tables, 1999–2002

Racialized Groups and Unequal Access to the Workplace

Numerous studies discuss the issue of unequal access to the workplace for racialized groups.[24] This is an important factor in explaining the double-digit racialized income gap. The employment gap between racialized groups and other Canadians dramatically demonstrates this unequal access to work opportunities. The unemployment rate for racialized group members in 1991 was 16%, compared to 11% for the general population.[25] The data show that the levels of unemployment were much higher among specific racialized groups, including women and youths. The 1995 rate for racialized women was 15.3%, compared to 13.2% for racialized men, 9.4% for other women, and 9.9% for other men.[26]

In 1991, the participation rate for the non-racialized group adult population was 78%, compared to 70.5% of the racialized adult population. The participation gap grew in 1996, with the participation rate for the non-racialized group adult population dropping to 75%, compared to 66% of the racialized adult population. While the participation rate for the total population improved to 80% in 2001, racialized participation rates lagged at 66%. Unemployment rate differentials were also evident, with the total population at 6.7% in 2001, and the racialized rate about twice as high at 12.6%. In 1996, unemployment rates were also higher among specific racialized groups, including women, youths, and those without post-secondary education; this difference levelled off in 2001, except among recent immigrants. The data show a relationship between systemic discrimination in access to employment and overrepresentation in low-income sectors and low-paying occupations, despite comparable educational levels. For many racialized group members, educational attainment has not translated into comparable compensation, labour-market access, or workplace mobility. Immigrants (68% of the racialized group) face structural barriers to recognition of their skills, demands for Canadian experience, denial by provincially regulated licensing bodies of accreditation for those with trade and professional qualifications, and the general devaluation of their skills. These factors in part account for immigrants' inability to translate qualifications — key to their selection in the immigration process — into comparable employment and compensation.

Both newcomers and other racialized group members experience differential treatment in the labour market. Consequently, the impact of systemic racial discrimination is crucial to understanding the emergence of the racialized income and employment gap. In most cases, this experience is shared by Canadian-born members of the groups.[27] The data show that immigrant members of racialized groups have more in common, in terms of unemployment and low income, with Canadian-born racialized group members than with immigrants from Europe arriving in the same period. In fact, the income gap between European immigrants and other immigrants is also growing; this suggests differential access to economic opportunity due to discriminatory structures in the labour market.

The impact of systemic discrimination in employment has been identified by a major Royal Commission and by numerous studies conducted in the 1980s and 1990s (see note 24). This research prompted some government policy responses, including federal employment equity legislation in 1986. Annual reports under the federal legislation show a continuing pattern of discrimination in employment both in the federal public service and in federally regulated sectors such as banking, telecommunications, and broadcasting.[28]

The Racialization of Poverty

According to 1995 Statistics Canada data, 35.6% of members of racialized groups lived under the poverty line, compared to 17.6% in the general Canadian population; the rate of poverty is thus twice as high.[29] In 1996, the rate of poverty among racialized group members in Canada's urban centres was 37.6%, compared to 20.9% for the rest of the population.[30] While we are not able to disaggregate the data further, the picture is even worse when one looks at particular racialized groups. Research has indicated that such is the case with racialized women, single-parent groups, and certain ethno-racial groups.[31] Other research — based on SLID special run data for the CSJ Foundation — which looks at after-tax family income shows that in 1998, some 19% of racialized community families lived in poverty, compared to 10.4% of other Canadians, i.e., almost double the poverty rate.[32]

Poverty rates were particularly high among recent immigrants, signalling the failure to translate internationally obtained skills into equivalent compensation. During the past two decades, low-income rates have increased among successive groups of newly arrived immigrants. In 1980, 24.6% of immigrants who had arrived during the previous five-year period lived below the poverty line. By 1990, the low-income rate among recent immigrants had increased to 31.3%. After peaking at 47.0% in 1995, the rate fell back to 35.8% in 2000. In 1995, four out of every 10 racialized immigrants who held less than a high school education were among the poorest 20% in the country.[33] Between 1980 and 2000, the full-time employment earnings of recent male immigrants fell 7% (from $40,600 to $37,900). This compares with a rise of 7% for the Canadian-born cohort ($45,600 to $48,600). Among the university-educated the drop was deeper (13% — $55,300 to $48,300, versus $69,100 to $76,000). The full-time employment earnings of recent female immigrants rose, but less than other female full-time earnings ($23,800 to $26,800 versus $28,800 to $34,400; $32,7000 to $34,7000, versus $45,200 to $50,000).[34]

According to 1995 Statistics Canada data, 35.6% of members of racialized groups lived below the poverty line. The developments described above point directly to a process of racialization of poverty. Key social and economic indicators like income, levels of unemployment, and sectoral participation patterns offer some insights into how economic globalization and the persistent legacy of racism have resulted in the growing patterns of low incomes among the racialized groups, income inequality between racialized group members and other Canadians, and the deterioration of the standard of housing available to racialized group members. Today, racialized group families are twice as likely to be poor as are other Canadian families. In some urban areas and among some groups of racialized group members, the rate is three to four times. The situation is particularly adverse with single-parent families, most of which are led by women.[35]

In urban centres like Toronto, Vancouver, Montreal, and Calgary, where racialized group populations are statistically significant, the normalization of racially segmented labour markets has an impact beyond the racialization of poverty. Racialized groups face other social patterns such as sustained school drop-out rates; the racialization of the penal system; the criminalization of the young; and the racial segregation of urban low-income neighbourhoods. These conditions have created a deepening social marginalization unprecedented in modern Canadian society. This is seen, for example, in a number of low-income neighbourhoods in Toronto where racialized group members are disproportionately represented as tenants of poorly maintained public and substandard private housing. In these neighbourhoods, the process of immiseration, desperation, hopelessness, and disempowerment has resulted in a level of violence that has claimed many young lives and threatens to spiral out of control.[36]

The experience of poverty has many implications for the life chances of individuals, families, or groups. Low incomes cut into basic-needs budgets, dooming many racialized people to substandard and increasingly segregated housing, poor-quality diets, reliance on food banks, and a decline in health status. Poverty imposes learning difficulties for the young; social and psychological pressures within the family; and increased mental and other health risks. It also imposes an array of symptoms of social exclusion, including increased contact with the criminal justice system, and an inability to participate fully in the civic and social life of the community or to exercise democratic rights such as voting and advocacy.

Why Conventional Explanations for Racial Inequality Don't Measure Up

Conventional explanations for the gap in the economic performance of racialized groups – the income gap, the gap in employment levels, overrepresentation in low-paid occupations, underrepresentation in high-income occupations and sectors, and disproportionate exposure to precarious work – tend to focus on three factors: recent immigration, lack of Canadian experience, and educational attainment differentials. It is commonly argued that, because of these three, recent immigrants initially lag behind other Canadians, but are able to catch up over time.

However, the experience of the last 25 years is one of sustained low relative economic performance for racialized immigrant groups. Both educational attainment and human capital data for immigrants after the 1970s, when the majority of immigrants to Canada were racialized, do not support the "low immigrant quality" contention. A number of recent studies refute the myth that the lower "human capital quality" of racialized job seekers and/or workers explains these differential experiences in the labour market. While Canadian experience should matter less and less in a globalized economy, it is often noted that in Canada's major urban centres, far too many cab drivers have professional and advanced degrees. Why are people who have previously enjoyed such high levels of success excluded from reasonable access to the labour market?

Racialized immigrant groups are increasingly better educated, yet they face longer immigration lag periods and relegation into casual and temporary work; Canadian-born group members are experiencing similar patterns in the labour market. Moreover, the gap in economic performance between racialized and non-racialized immigrants is growing, with an income gap as high as 28% over the period 1991–1995. The persistence of systemic discrimination, including the use of immigrant status as a proxy for "low human capital," conditions the patterns of underemployment of a labour force with above-average education. Even when dealing with segments not as well prepared for labour-market participation (as is often said of some refugee populations, for instance), there are unjustifiable levels of overrepresentation in low-income sectors and occupations, casual, contract, temporary, and piecemeal work.[37] These are better explained by differential access to the labour market, which in turn leads to the growing gap in economic performance, and the incidence of poverty along racial lines.

The Nature of State and Civil Society Responses to Racialization of the Economic Gap

While studies and reports show that conventional explanations are not sustainable, they nevertheless continue to be used in many Canadian jurisdictions to support a generalized policy of non-intervention by the different levels of government. Neither the alarming statistics about the socio-economic condition of whole segments of racialized communities nor the racialization of the growing income gap has mobilized government action beyond voluntary equity programs in select jurisdictions. The federal government's *Employment Equity Act* came into force in 1986. Most other jurisdictions rely on human rights codes to regulate racially discriminatory conduct. The federal government's anti-racism program is also governed by the federal Multicultural Policy, introduced in 1988 and administered by the Secretary of State for Multiculturalism. Provinces have jurisdictional responsibility for employment law, and regulate working conditions through employment standards acts.

Even these modest measures have met resistance. In Ontario in 1995, the Conservative government repealed the *Ontario Employment Equity Act* of 1994 as soon as it was elected to power. Recently, the Ontario government also gutted the *Employment Standards Act*, increasing the average number of work hours possible per week to 60 from 44. As documented by the participation of visible minorities in the Public Service Taskforce, the federal *Employment Equity Act*, which was amended in 1995, has not adequately addressed the problems of racialized groups in the federal public service. Not only are participation levels still chronically low (5.4%), but the enforcement regime that plagued the original legislation enacted in 1986 was not improved in the 1995 review. Canada is a signatory to various international covenants and conventions under the United Nations, including the United Nations Covenant on Social, Economic and Cultural Rights, and the Convention on the Elimination of All Forms of Racial Discrimination; however, the contradictions that Frances Henry and others have characterized as "democratic racism" have impeded progress in implementing those international obligations.[38]

Two key reasons may explain government non-action. One is the embrace of a market ideology by the different levels of government in the 1990s. The prevailing ideology of neo-liberalism considers the market the final arbiter of social justice and equality. The market determines what is fair compensation for labour, independent of the needs of the individual or family. The idea that the government should make up the shortfall to ensure that citizens have a living income is frowned upon as distorting market conditions. That logic renders the distribution of wealth of little consequence to social order. Increasingly, governments and representatives of big business define the problem of racism away in the same way they define away poverty: by shifting the focus to absolute levels of material well-being—the meeting of the most basic human needs—as opposed to an individual's or group's position relative to other citizens or groups.

The general response of the different levels of government has been to deny the impact of racialization in the workplace and in the public domain. When confronted with evidence of differential treatment leading to racial inequality in economic performance, officials insist that the solution is economic growth rather than government action. But while economic growth can be a solution to the problems of poverty and low incomes, the uneven distribution of its rewards still suggests a need for action on racial discrimination. Clearly, growth in the Canadian economy has not sufficiently addressed the racialized's higher-than-average levels of unemployment, income gap, or levels of poverty. Even within the logic of market supremacy, we are confronted with a case of market failure. But as Reitz and Breton have suggested, the government's failure to act seems to meet with Canadian public approval, making advocacy for state action quite a challenge.[39]

There are flaws in the economic-growth approach. For one, economic growth is uneven and does not benefit everyone or every group equally, so that structural inequities are simply reproduced by the changes in economic performance. Indeed, in recent years, economic growth has been associated with the immiseration of some groups of people. For instance, demands for flexibility and technological intensification have not led to an increase in full-time jobs but the growth of part-time, casual, and contingency work, with many racialized workers forced to accept less than minimum wages. It has also forced less-skilled workers right out of work. In addition, the argument that the distribution of income is irrelevant is not supported by evidence from around the world. Studies show that the relative economic position of individuals and communities does determine an individual's or a group's life chances.

On the other hand, the response from civil society organizations has lacked conviction. The reality of racism in Canada as a cultural force may explain the failure of social justice and labour organizations to mobilize effectively to respond to the crisis of racial inequality. As Henry and Tator (2000b) have remarked, too often myths about racism get in the way of action and replace collective action with strategies for denial.

Social Inequality: An Issue of Public Concern

Social inequality is both a social justice and an economic issue. It is also an issue of public and political concern because inequality leads to group tensions and social instability in society. Studies from around the world, as well as some recent Canadian studies, show that the most unequal societies are also the most unstable. The higher the level of inequality, the higher is the probability of violence and disorder within society. Inequality does in fact matter.

Health and well-being are heavily influenced by the distribution of economic resources, prestige, and social position. Studies show that quality of life appears to be lower in unequal societies, as such societies suffer illness-generating conditions. Socio-economic inequality is one of the most powerful influences on health and mortality rates. The greater the income differences within populations, the greater the health risks. There are risks arising from the conditions of work to which low-income earners are subjected, so that the disproportionate participation of groups in that type of work leads to greater exposure to health risks. This is clearly the case with racialized groups, especially women involved in garment work, domestic work, industrial cleaning, etc. The gender and racial stratification of the labour market definitely has implications for health and well-being.[40]

North American studies show that reducing income disparity decreases mortality rates. Other data show that income inequality is related to other social breakdowns, such as increase in homicide and violent crime.[41] A final observation relating to income distribution is that cities with greater inequality are less socially cohesive. The challenge of social harmony is likely greater if the inequality is along racial lines.

The Political Nature of the Problem of a Growing Racialized Gap

Ultimately racial inequality is a political problem, and solving it requires political commitments by governments and different sectors of society. An economy showing increasing levels of economic inequality along racial lines challenges the notion of a democracy-based equal citizenship. It not only devalues the citizenship of some groups in society, but also raises questions of political legitimacy; as those who are economically excluded become more politically assertive, they may seek to reverse the unjust outcomes of the market and government policy using means that may undermine societal stability. The rhetoric of multicultural harmony and embracing diversity that has been a prominent part of Canadian government policy over the last 20 years does not jibe with the reality of rising inequality between the racialized communities and other Canadians. The challenge falls on organizations in civil society to combat racial and other forms of inequality with a holistic political agenda that will shift public discourse away from criminalizing immigration, marginalizing racialized groups and the poor, and devaluing non-European human capital. Instead, we need to commit to using governments as a positive instrument to respond to social problems. The need is urgent to build a progressive coalition that will engage both governments and other actors in society in a meaningful debate about the nature of Canadian society and the place of racialized groups in it. We need to challenge the denial that too often accompanies the discussion of racial inequality, and adopt an aggressive anti-racist approach to designing new institutions, policies, and programs. Only through such measures can we forge a 21st century that will bear witness to our aspirations to be a diverse and multicultural/multiracial society.

Conclusion

This book calls attention to the deepening processes of social exclusion faced by racialized groups in Canada in the early 21st century. These processes are intensified by the restructuring of the Canadian economy, away from a regulated environment and toward state deregulation and market regulation. Historical forms of racial discrimination and racial hierarchies in the Canadian labour market are being reproduced. The book calls for urgent action by the various levels of government and key institutions in society to address the resulting socio-economic exclusion of Canada's racialized population, and the impact that the growing income, employment, and quality of life gap between that population and other Canadians is having on their full participation in Canadian society.

While specific policies and programs are needed to address this racialized gap, the gap in citizenship can be bridged only if all Canadians come to terms with the tension between the commitment to the ideals of equality as enshrined in the *Canadian Charter of Rights and Freedoms*, and the reality of a persistent nostalgia for a "White supremacist" society. Eurocentric and Euro-dominant nostalgia informs far too many decisions in the labour market, in governments and public institutions, in the social sector, and in cultural institutions such as the mass media. Racialized group members recoil when they are confronted with the stereotypes the mainstream media peddles about them. Media distorts reality through inaccurate or sensationalized reporting focusing on crime and sports, or through omissions and erasures. Racialized groups in Canadian society face greater peril from the everyday discounting of their human capital and value in the workplace, in public institutions, in the social service sector, in civil society organizations, in the arts, in the media, and in government than they do from cross-burning, swastika-wielding Heritage Front members, whose form of aggressive racism Canadian society has already marginalized.

The book attempts to make a constructive contribution by naming the problem and by presenting some ideas for policy and program responses. Some have been widely articulated elsewhere, among them employment equity, remedies to ensure fair access to professions and trades, improvements in employment standards legislation, and measures to strengthen equitable access to services like health care, education, training, and housing. However, they remain vital to the response because they have not been adequately tried or implemented.

The book looks to social institutions such as organized labour to make a more concerted effort to empower the affected communities in the workplaces and in the sectors in which they are overrepresented or underrepresented. Organized labour played a crucial role in raising the wages of Canadian workers in the post-Depression era through effective collective bargaining. While union density has diminished in the era of global neo-liberalism, it remains imperative that workers be mobilized to fight for better working conditions, wages, transparency in employment practices, and mobility in the workplace through collective bargaining given that they have very low union density and high proportions of racialized group members: sectors such as the textile and garment-making industry, light manufacturing and assembly, and the services sector should be the focus of new efforts at unionization. Organized labour needs to extend the union advantage to the workers in precarious work environments. There is also a need to review barriers to unionized sectors and occupations that pay well. Unions can also extend their advantage to racialized workers by bargaining employment equity provisions into their collective agreements. Finally, further research is needed into ways in which systemic racial discrimination and social exclusion are manifested in various sectors of society, such as housing, education, the political and judicial systems, social sectors, the media, and Canadian culture. Such research would inform appropriate public policy and effective action by social justice movements.

Notes

1. However, the change in immigration policy in the 1960s coincided with the Canadian government's enactment of the *Bill of Rights* and Canada's prominent role in the creation of the international human rights regime, developments that probably had some impact on the immigration policy debates at the time.

2. An Ekos/*Toronto Star* poll conducted in June 2000 found that 30% of those surveyed believed that there were too many immigrants of colour in Canada. See also, P. Li, *Destination Canada: Immigration Debates and Issues* (2003); D. Palmer, "Determinants of Canadian Attitudes towards Immigration: More Than Just Racism?" *Canadian Journal of Behavioural Sciences* 28 (1996): 180–192. The Ekos/*Toronto Star* poll results reflect this sentiment, as does some of the discourse on immigration. Both the discourse and public attitudes have had an impact on Canadian immigration policy, leading to key changes aimed at stricter selection rules and dramatically lower refugee admission rates.

3. Conference Board of Canada, "Making a Visible Difference: The Contributions of Visible Minorities to Canadian Economic Growth," *Economic Performance and Trends* (April, 2004).

4. See Creese (1999); Das Gupta (1996); de Wolff (2000); Galabuzi (2001); Hiebert (1997).

5. The idea of a colour-coded vertical mosaic updates John Porter's concept of an ethnically defined vertical mosaic based on the social stratification of Canadian society in the 1960s (Porter, 1965). It suggests the emergence of a racially defined stratification of Canadian society, with a hierarchical social structure where racialized groups are located at the bottom and non-racialized groups at the top. In this formulation, race is said to be a determinant of access to opportunities in a variety of sectors of life including income (and protection against poverty), employment, health care, political participation, neighbourhood selection, and, in general, a group's life chances. While not fully formed, the various indicators of social economic status that we review in this book suggest a resonance with such a hierarchical ordering of Canadian society. See also, P. Li, "The Market Value and Social Value of Race," in *Racism and Social Inequality in Canada: Concepts, Controversies and Strategies of Resistance*, edited by V. Satzewich (Toronto: Thompson Educational Publishing, 1998), 115–130; J. Lian and D. Matthews, "Does a Vertical Mosaic Really Exist? Ethnicity and Income in Canada, 1991," *Canadian Review of Sociology and Anthropology* 35, no. 4 (1998): 461–481.

6. See G. Galabuzi, "Racializing the Division of Labour: Neo-Liberal Restructuring and the Economic Segregation of Canada's Racialized Groups," in *Challenging the Market: The Struggle to Regulate Work and Income*, edited by J. Stanford and L. Vosko (Montreal: McGill-Queen's University Press, 2004), 175–204; P. Daenzer, *Regulating Class Privilege: Immigrant Servants in Canada, 1940–1990s* (Toronto: Canadian Scholars' Press, 1993).

7. T. Das Gupta, "The Political Economy of Gender, Race and Class: Looking at South Asian Immigrant Women in Canada," *Canadian Ethnic Studies* XXVL, no. 1 (1994): 59–73; D.

Brand, "Black Women and Work: The Impact of Racially Constructed Gender Roles on the Sexual Division of Labour," *Fireweed* 25 (1987): 35.

8.   Porter's concept of a vertical mosaic differentiated the dominant or privileged social status of what he called the Charter class — the English and the French — from that of groups that had immigrated after the establishment of the modern Canadian nation. These were a range of ethnic groups mostly from Northern, Eastern, and Southern Europe, as well as racialized groups. The concept of the mosaic refers also to the power relations that maintained that status. More recently, though, some of the then-underprivileged groups have been able to acquire "White" status, making the analysis less compelling.

9.   See Glossary for distinction between ethnicity and race.

10. H. Zlotnik, "Trends of International Migration Since 1965: What Existing Data Reveal," *International Migration* 37, no. 1 (1999): 21–61.

11. E. Balibar, "Is There a Neo-Racism," in *Race, Nation, Class: Ambiguous Identities*, edited by E. Balibar and I. Wallerstein (London: Verso, 1991).

12. See comments by Mississauga Mayor Hazel McCallion (2001); Deputy Mayo Bell of Markham, Ontario, and Winnipeg School Trustee, Betty Granger (2000). A popular CNN program that previously focused on business affairs has had a segment on illegal immigration for months now — detailing the threat immigration poses to American workers. In 2000, an EKOS/Istar survey of supporters of the then official opposition reform party showed 40% agreed with the statement that there were too many immigrants in Canada (see Note 2).

13. See literature review by I. Zeytinoglu and J. Muteshi, "Gender, Race, and Class Dimensions of Non-Standard Work," *Industrial Relations* 55, no. 1 (Winter, 2000): 133–166; J. Badets and L. Howatson-Leo (1999); L. Vosko, *Temporary Work: The Gendered Rise of a Precaurious Employment Relationship* (Toronto: University of Toronto Press, 2000); A. de Wolff, *Breaking the Myth of Flexible Work* (Toronto: Contingent Workers Project, 2000); B. Fox and P. Sugiman, "Flexible Work, Flexible Workers: The Restructuring of Clerical Work in the Large Telecommunications Company," *Studies in Political Economy* 60 (Autumn, 1999): 59–84; M. Ornstein, *Ethno-Racial Inequality in Toronto: Analysis of the 1996 Census* (Toronto: Access and Equity Centre of Metro Toronto, 2000); G. Galabuzi, *Canada's Creeping Economic Apartheid: The Economic Segregation and Social Marginalization of Racialized Groups* (Toronto: Centre for Social Justice, 2001); K. Hughes, *Gender and Self Employment: Assessing Trends and Policy Implications* (Ottawa: Canadian Policy Research Network, November, 1999).

14. J. Stanford, "Discipline, Insecurity and Productivity: The Economics behind Labour Market Flexibility," in *Remaking Canada's Social Policy: Social Security in the Late 1990s*, edited by J. Pulkingham and G. Ternowetsky (Halifax: Fernwood Publishing, 1996), 130–150. Stanford argues that there has been a "substantial weakening of a whole range of institutional and social controls over labour market outcomes." The result is the proliferation of non-standard forms of work.

15. A. Jackson and D. Robinson, *Falling Back: The State of Working Canada 2000* (Ottawa: Canadian Centre for Policy Alternatives, 2000); Vosko (2000); de Wolff (2000); Fox and Sugiman (Autumn, 1999): 59–84; Ornstein (2000); Galabuzi (2001).

16. B.S. Bolaria and P. Li (eds.), *Racial Oppression in Canada* (Toronto: Garamond Press, 1988); V. Satzewich (ed.), *Racism and Social Inequality in Canada: Concepts, Controversies and Strategies of Resistance* (Toronto: Thompson Publishing, 1998); R. Miles, *Racism* (London: Routledge, 1989).

17. D. Broad, *Hollow Work, Hollow Society: Globalization and the Casual Labour Problem in Canada* (Halifax: Fernwood Publishing, 2000).

18. S. McBride and J. Shields. *Dismantling a Nation: The Transition to Corporate Rule in Canada* (Halifax: Fernwood, 2000).

19. G. Picot and Heisz, *The Performance of the 1990s Canadian Labour Market*, Paper no. 148 (Ottawa: Statistics Canada, April, 2000).

20. A. Yalnizyan, *The Growing Gap* (Toronto: Centre for Social Justice, 1998).

21. Based on a special run of Statistics Canada's *Survey of Labour and Income Dynamics (SLID)*, 1996, 1997, 1998, 1999, 2000, for the Centre for Social Justice.

22. Ibid.

23. Statistics Canada, Income Statistics Division, *Survey of Labour and Labour and Income Dynamics*, "Custom Tables, 1999–2002." See C. Teelucksingh and G. Galabuzi, *Working Precariously: The Impact of Race and Immigrants Status on Employment Opportunities and Outcomes in Canada* (Toronto: Centre for Social Justice/Canadian Race Relation Foundation, 2005).

24. The list of reports and studies dealing with racial inequality in employment runs from the 1981 study by J. Reitz, L. Calzavara, and D. Dasko, *Ethnic Inequality and Segregation in Jobs* (Toronto: Centre for Urban and Community Studies, University of Toronto, 1981) through to that of the Canadian Parliamentary Taskforce on the Participation of Visible Minorities in Canada titled *Equality Now* (1984); also, the Abella Commission report *Equality in Employment* (1984), the reports *Who Gets the Job* (Henry and Ginsberg, 1985) and *No Discrimination Here* (Billingsley and Muszynski, 1985); the Urban Alliance on Race Relations and Social Planning Council of Metro Toronto report *A Time for Change* (1990), and the most recent *Report of the Taskforce on the Participation of Visible Minorities in the Federal Public Service* (Government of Canada, 2000). These, and many more, all conclude that racial discrimination was pervasive in Canada's employment systems. Further, that, as Judge Abella remarked, "Strong measures were needed to remedy the impact of discriminatory attitudes and behaviour."

25. R. Dibbs and T. Leesti, "Survey of Labour and Income Dynamics: Visible Minorities and Aboriginal Peoples" (Ottawa: Statistics Canada, 1995).

26. J. Chard, "Women in Visible Minorities, in Women in Canada: A Gender Based Statistical Report" (Ottawa: Statistics Canada, 2000).

27. Some exceptions exist, though. Japanese Canadians are often cited as one. For comparison, according to 1996 Census data, two out of every three Japanese Canadians (44,000) are Canadian-born, while the ratio among African Canadians is two out of every five African Canadians (241,000). That is closer to the racialized group average of 68% (immigrants) to 32% (Canadian born).

28. Various Annual Reports, *Employment Equity Act*; see also *Taskforce on the Participation of Visible Minorities in the Federal Public Service* (Government of Canada, 2000).

29. Statistics Canada, "1996 Census: Sources of Income, Earnings," *The Daily* (May 12, 1998).

30. K. Lee, *Urban Poverty in Canada* (Ottawa: Canadian Council on Social Development, 2000).

31. Ornstein (2000).

32. R. Dibbs and T. Leesti, *Survey of Labour and Income Dynamics: Visible Minorities and Aboriginal Peoples* (Ottawa: Statistics Canada, 1995).

33. A. Jackson, "Poverty and Immigration" *Perception* 24, no. 4 (Spring, 2001): 6–7.

34. Statistics Canada, "Low-Income Rates among Immigrants, 1980–2000," *The Daily* (June 19, 2003).

35. Ornstein (2000).

36. J.D. Hulchanski, "Immigrants and Access to Housing: How Welcome Are Newcomers to Canada?" *Proceedings of the Second National Conference, Seminar on Housing and Neighbourhoods* (Montreal, November 23-26, 1997): 263; S. Novak, J. Darden, J.D. Hulchanski, A.-M. Seguin, "Housing Discrimination in Canada: What Do We Know About It?" *University of Toronto Research Bulletin #1* (2002), Centre for Urban and Community Research; K. Dion, "Immigrants' Perceptions of Housing Discrimination in Toronto: The Housing New Canadians Study," *Journal of Social Issues* 57: 523-539.

37. J. Anderson and J. Lynam, "The Meaning of Work for Immigrant Women in the Lower Echelons of the Canadian Labour Force," *Canadian Ethnic Studies* XIX, no. 2 (1987): 67–90; Vosko (2000); T. Das Gupta, *Racism and Paid Work* (Toronto: Garamond Press, 1996).

38. F. Herny, C. Tator, W. Mattis, and T. Rees, *The Colour of Democracy: Racism in Canadian Society* (Toronto: Harcourt Brace, 2000). The authors suggest that the concept of democratic racism explains the co-existence of the principles of liberal democracy, such as equal rights for all, and the reality of racial discrimination in Canadian society.

39. J. Reitz and R. Breton, "Prejudice and Discrimination in Canada and the United States: A Comparison," in *Racism and Social Inequality in Canada*, edited by V. Satzewich (Toronto: Thompson Educational Publishing, 1998), 47–68. The authors cite a 1987 survey of attitudes about the *Canadian Charter of Rights and Freedom* in which 63.3% of those surveyed agreed that it is not the government's job to guarantee equal opportunity to succeed.

40. L.Yanz, B. Jeffcott, D. Ladd, and J. Atlin, *Policy Options to Improve Standards for Women Garment Workers in Canada and Internationally* (Ottawa: Status of Women, Canada, 1999); Vosko (2000); Das Gupta (1996); R. Sennett and J. Cobb, *The Hidden Injuries of Class* (New York: Knopf, 1973).

41. R. Wilkinson, *Unhealthy Societies: The Afflictions of Inequality* (New York: Routledge, 1996); G.B. Rodger, "Income and Inequality as Determinants of Mortality: An International Cross-Section Analysis," *Population Studies* 33 (1979): 343–351; J. Bartley, "Ethnic Inequality and the Rate of Homicide," *Social Forces* 69 (1990): 53–70; J. Blau and P. Blau, "The Costs of Inequality: Metropolitan Structure and Violent Crime," *American Sociological Review* 47 (1982), 114–129; A. Glyn and D. Miliband, "Introduction," in *Paying for Inequality: The Costs of Social Injustice*, edited by A. Glyn and D. Miliband (London: Rivers Oram Press, 1994).

Questions for Critical Thought

1. What are some of the major trends in Canada's population growth?
2. What are the social and economic implications of Canada's population makeup?
3. What is the impact of population change on the competitiveness of the labour market?
4. What other forces are driving the process of change in the Canadian labour market?
5. What significance do these forces have for racialized groups in the Canadian economy?
6. What are the implications for the place of racialized groups in Canadian society?

Recommended Readings

Bolaria, B.S., and P. Li (eds.). *Racial Oppression in Canada*. Toronto: Garamond Press, 1988.

Broad, D. *Hollow Work, Hollow Society: Globalization and the Casual Labour Problem in Canada*. Halifax: Fernwood Publishing, 2000.

Glyn, A., and D. Miliband (eds.). *Paying for Inequality: The Costs of Social Injustice*. London: Rivers Oram Press, 1994.

Li, P. *Destination Canada: Immigration Debates and Issues*. Toronto: Oxford University Press, 2003.

Pendakur, R. *Immigrants and the Labour Force: Policy, Regulation and Impact*. Montreal: McGill-Queen's University Press, 2000.

Satzewich, V. *Racism and Social Inequality: Concepts, Controversies and Strategies of Resistance*. Toronto: Thompson Educational Publishing, 1998.

Vosko, L. *Temporary Work: The Gendered Rise of a Precarious Employment Relationship*. Toronto: University of Toronto Press, 2000.

Wilkinson, R. *Unhealthy Societies: The Afflictions of Inequality*. New York: Routledge, 1996.

CHAPTER 2

Race and Racialization in Theory

"Capital works through ... the culturally specific character of labour power, or to put it another way, class and race are mutually constitutive and shaping forces." (Loomba, 1998:30)[1]

"The ideologies that ... gain currency in society reflect and reproduce the interest of the dominant classes." (Loomba, 1998:25)

Introduction

Classifications like race, ethnicity, and gender are socially constructed, and imbued with social value and meaning that differ in historical and contemporary usage. Historically, Canada's diversity in race, ethnicity, gender, and class has been used to establish government policies and programs that benefited certain groups and disadvantaged others. These policies help entrench positions of privilege and majority status for some, and disadvantage and minority status for others. There are many such examples of racially motivated government policies before and after Confederation in 1867. While early exclusions of First Nations peoples were founded on a colonial invasion and the establishment of a White-settler colony, they were easily extended to Black Loyalists who immigrated to Nova Scotia and Lower and Upper Canada in the late 1700s. The promises of rewards for loyalty to the British crown in the American War of Independence did not translate into freedom and fertile land with which to begin new lives; unlike their White counterparts, Black Loyalists found that marginal land and differential wages awaited them north of the border, forcing many to flee to Jamaica and Sierra Leone. Race proved more determinant than commitment to the enduring political ideas of "order and good government" that separated the Canadian formative experience from the American one.

Race would continue to be a defining factor of the Canadian reality once the Canadian state took form, with racial hierarchies codified in law through the establishment of such instruments as the *Indian Act* of 1876, the imposition of the Chinese head tax under the *Chinese Immigration Act* of 1885, and the *Chinese Exclusion Act* of 1923, which banned Chinese immigration until 1947. There were also various prohibitions against South Asian immigration, the immigration of freed African slaves from the United Slaves, the segregated school systems in Ontario, the denial of voting rights to Chinese immigrants in British Columbia, the differential wage rates for South Asian and Chinese workers in British Columbia and the internment of Japanese Canadians during World War II. These evoked experiences similar to those of freed slaves in Nova Scotia in the late 1700s and early 1800s.

Race and racial categories took on particular prominence in policies that reinforced the idea of Canada as a White nation. Racist immigration policies maintained an external "pecking order"' that labelled as undesirables African Americans, East Asians, South Asians, and other racialized peoples. Jews and Southern Europeans were also placed in this category from time to time. Complementing these immigration policies was an internal infrastructure that ensured that racial hierarchies defined the Canadian idea and experience: workplace regulation, citizenship rule, access to education, and social prohibitions amounting to segregation.

Within that historical context, race, while a powerful tool of state formation, was conceived ambiguously, and the categories of race and ethnicity were sometimes collapsed and used synonymously. In the 1960s, John Porter's groundbreaking work on the vertical mosaic suggested that ethnicity was more important than race as a determinant of social, political, and economic class location in Canada. For many years after, race remained undertheorized as a determinant of socio-class status in Canada. More recently, though, scholarship on race as a socio-economic and political category has become more prominent, even as racial categories have received official and constitutional recognition in the *Charter of Rights and Freedoms*, and in human rights legislation. State and institutional diversity and employment equity programs have adopted the concept of racial categories for remedial purposes. Because race is socially constructed, much of this historical reality is made possible by *essentializing* the concept of race. Powerful groups in society suggest that differences based on superficial physical (and cultural) attributes transcend the common membership or citizenship in society, and hence entrench their own positions of political, social, economic, and cultural advantage.

Essentializing race draws exclusionary boundaries, allowing the privileged to pursue specific interests at the expense of the broader society, and particularly of the groups that are depicted as outsiders. The social construction of race and ethnicity, like other socially constructed categories such as gender, serves to distinguish between groups for the purpose of creating or maintaining an advantage for the dominant group. This is especially the case in a society that has adopted the capitalist mode of production and its emphasis on competition for resources. The power of race consists in the adaptive capacity to define population groups and by extension social agents as self and "other" at key historical moments.[2] These categories are then used by those with power to differentiate labour value for the purposes of ensuring differential exploitation of labour and of undermining working class solidarity. The dominant group uses the process of group differentiation to impose minority or inferior status on the group defined as the subordinate "other." In other words, the process of minority creation is central to the race-based stratification of the Canadian political economic order that we discuss in this book.

This process has acquired special social value at key moments in the history of Canada, one of them being the early 21st century. Balibar has suggested that at such moments, concepts such as competitive racism gain special relevance by creating divisions within the ranks of those who would otherwise be candidates for working-class solidarity within nations.[3] Ideology plays a key role in reproducing the logic of differentiation and in justifying the injustices that arise from it. It also helps undermine efforts to create solidarity across race and gender. At both the national and global levels, organizing a working-class movement to respond to the demands of global capitalism is rendered impossible unless these forms of differentiation and their purposes are confronted and overcome. This chapter introduces the key processes of race, racialization, racial discrimination, minority construction, and the dynamics of social and economic exclusion, which we discuss in the rest of the book.

The Imperative of Minority Construction

Canadian official records refer to racialized peoples as visible minorities or racial minorities. This raises the obvious questions of what we mean by minorities, and why they are accorded that status. Minorities are socially constructed entities in societies, and the label implies the imposition of an inferior status. They are often set apart by the majority group as incompetent, abnormal, or dangerous because of differences pertaining to race, gender, culture, and religion. Majority or dominant groups use these differences to distance themselves from minorities for the purpose of acquiring or maintaining privilege and power. In the process, the minority group becomes the "other," an outsider, sometimes dangerous and sometimes a pariah. Although in the Canadian case some argue that minority refers to the numerical status of the groups, the concept of minority is often extended to numerical majorities such as women (or with the majority Black population in South Africa under the apartheid regime). In the case of race, as a determinant of minority status, imposing the label suggests that race is the most important distinguishing feature in the experience of racialized people in Canada—not class or gender or religion. It also fixes their identity for all time within that imposed silo, suggesting that the racialized groups will always be the "other" in Canadian society.

Once the status of "other" is imposed, the majority group is freed from moral obligation against acts of oppression and discrimination directed toward the minority group, and feels justified in carrying out acts of aggression in defence of the interests of the dominant group. This ideological position by the majority groups is then reinforced by such cultural institutions as the media and educational institutions, as well as by discourses that maintain "invalidating myths" about the minority group.[4] These in turn reinforce public policy and inform decisions about access to resources and opportunity.

Again, minority status is not dependent on numerical inferiority. References will likely not change if, as trends suggest, racialized groups soon become the numerical majority in a number of Canada's urban centres. Women are numerically superior to men but endure minority status because of the unequal relations of power between men and women; similarly, the inferior socio-economic and political position of racialized groups ensures their minority status regardless of their numbers. Unsubstantiated assumptions about the inferiority of their attributes and competencies will continue to be the basis for their oppression. Their impeded access to economic, social, political, and cultural resources have historically been rationalized and institutionalized as normal.[5]

The development of minority status is central to the stratification of Canadian society along racial and gender lines. It secures and reinforces access to privilege, power, and resources for some groups at the expense of others. In the Canadian context, that process has come full circle with the official adoption of the category "visible minority."[6] The category has been normalized on the basis that it identifies those whose colour differs markedly from that of the majority population for the purpose of addressing their disadvantage; however, it also has the effect of reinforcing the very status of disadvantage and socio-economic and political inferiority assigned to racialized groups in Canada.

The Colour of the Vertical Mosaic

The context within which social stratification in Canadian society has been studied was set by the work of John Porter in the 1960s. His observations about minority construction provided the basis of his groundbreaking analysis of Canadian society, which he described as a vertical mosaic.[7] According to his model, Canadian society is stratified along ethnic lines into three fairly distinctive groups of people, with the "founding ethnic groups" — the French and English — accorded the highest status as the charter class. Along with them were groups of Northern Europeans who could easily acculturate and acquire charter status. In the middle he put those, especially from Eastern and Southern Europe, whose bio-cultural characteristics diverged somewhat from those of the dominant groups. At the bottom were racialized minorities, particularly the Aboriginal peoples who were most economically, socially, and politically disadvantaged, but also racialized refugees and immigrants of various generations.

The idea of the vertical mosaic based on ethnicity has been challenged and updated to accommodate the reality of mobility across strata; the variations in the ability of the groups to harness economic, social, or political power; and the role of structural factors such as racial discrimination in determining economic mobility (Darroch, 1979; Lautard and Guppy, 1990; Herberg, 1990; Isajiw, 1999). Moreover, ethnicity as a category has also come into some disrepute as a descriptor of an entity based on a set of attributes that are not fixed, such as culture and language. More recently, it has been suggested that while the ethnic dividing line has become blurred, a racial basis for socio-economic stratification is increasingly discernable.

A growing body of literature analyzing the socio-economic performance and the political status of racialized groups has concluded that they are subject to structural disadvantages that confirm their place at the bottom of the mosaic. Processes of social exclusion and the growth in the size of the groups help reinforce the structural tendencies toward maintaining and reproducing the existing order. New immigrants are incorporated into the mosaic often in total disregard of their socio-class position in the country of origin — a process referred to elsewhere as class shifting.[8] The emergence of race as a key constitutive feature of socio-stratification in Canada has prompted debate about the existence of a *colour-coded mosaic*.[9]

Race

Race is a difficult concept to define because it is more a social construction than an essential biological concept. Earlier attempts at biological definition have largely been abandoned.[10] Since human beings have more similarities than differences in their biological makeup, arbitrary physical and social traits are often used to denote race. The most common are superficial physical traits such as colour and hair texture. Nonetheless, advocates of racial ideologies use categories based on race to attribute competencies and deny opportunities to certain "races." In fact, it is for social, economic, or political utility that the project of socially constructing race employs the biological distinctions.[11] There was a time when race was considered a natural phenomenon to which essence was assigned and whose meaning was fixed.

Increasingly, the concept of race has come into disrepute as its theoretical coherence has been challenged. However, because it continues to serve a socio-political purpose, proponents of racial ideologies continue to essentialize the category based on these superficial physical differences. Again, the purpose is to entrench a racial hierarchy for the purpose of exploiting certain groups, and to subject them to oppression or differential treatment for the benefit of others.[12] But recognizing its social significance, the victims of racial categories have also used it to mark common experiences and to crystalize identities of resistance. References to their particular group as black, brown, or yellow are common among racialized peoples. On the basis of the common experience that comes from the oppressive structures of race and racism, they seek to construct identities as a platform for organizing anti-racism responses. Ironically, these days they are likely confronted with a claim that the processes they oppose are colour blind.[13]

Henry and Tator (2000b) have provocatively suggested that race is an ideological construct used to reconcile the tension between the liberal democratic ideals Canadian society espouses and the reality of persistent racial discrimination. This argument is in line with one advanced by Fields (1990) in the American context. Fields suggests that race as an ideological construct emerged as a prop for the ideological need to justify the existence of slavery in a society that claimed to be founded on the idea of liberty and freedom. Once formed, the concept of race took on a life of its own beyond justifying social inequality and oppression. Fields argues as follows:

> Since race is not genetically programmed, racial prejudice cannot be genetically programmed either, but must rise historically.... having arisen, race then ceases to be a historical phenomenon and becomes instead an external motor of history ... [that is] ... it takes on a life of its own.[14]

While Fields is compelling in her argument, at least in relation to the emergence of racism in period, the genesis of race as a concept traces back to a more ancient time. In other words, the genesis should not be located within the historical context of capitalism and slavery as she suggests. Though the application of the concept of race varied, its use to establish a category of "other" is time-worn. Through history, the category of "race," like those of gender and class, has been used to delineate privilege and domination for some, and oppression for others. It is important to note that such categories are products of, and represent complex interactions with, the socio-economic, political, and cultural makeup of various societies and periods in history.

In Canada, whose original mission was to build a White-settler colony, a deterministic form of race construction provided the basis for systematic policies of economic exclusion and segregation. The aim was to subordinate first the Aboriginal population, and later other people of colour. These policies validated the little-talked-about Canadian legacy of slavery. They also determined the "undesirability" of the immigration of Blacks, South Asians, East Asians, and Jews at key moments in Canadian history. They provided the rationale behind the restrictions against Black farmers from the United States at a time when the Canadian government was, at its own expense, recruiting farmers from Europe to settle the West. In the contemporary period, numerous studies have identified processes of racialization as central to the differential treatment of racialized peoples in the economy, in the education system, in the criminal justice system, and in social-sector institutions. Racialized peoples experience the complex interactions of race and power when the category of race intersects with the other hierarchical categories such as gender and class, as is the case in the life experiences of racialized women in particular.[15]

Racialization

In the process of racialization, race first acquires social significance as certain biological features become the basis for designating distinct groupings. The social process of racialization then imbues the categories with value, leading to socio-economic practices that reflect and reinforce those values. These practices are responsible for the differentiation in individual behaviour and institutional practices, policies, treatment, and the emergence of hierarchical structures that privilege some and oppress other members of society.[16]

The process of racialization therefore involves the construction of racial categories as real, but also unequal, for purposes that impact the economic, social, and political composition of a society. While the emphasis has largely been on physical traits, ethnicity, culture, place of birth, and other social characteristics have also been used as the basis for defining race and determining racial treatment. Giving race social, economic, cultural, and political significance has led to differential treatment and outcomes in Canada. Racialization translates into actions and decisions within social systems that lead to differential and unequal outcomes, and the entrenchment of structures of oppression. The influence of negative race-based judgements on decision-making at different levels of society produces racial inequality. The growing inequality between racialized groups in Canada and other Canadians has its systemic origins in the racial inequalities that racialization produces and perpetuates.

Box 2.1: *The Social Value of Race* by Peter S. Li

For much of Canada's history, Canada has maintained discriminatory policies and practices towards people of certain racial origins. The result is that in the racial origin of members of such groups and their social conditions have defined their place in society. In this way, race was given social importance in that it provided the grounds for segregating people for differential treatment as well as for justifying such actions. The history of Canadian Aboriginal peoples, for example, was characterized by the domination of Europeans, which led to the destruction of their livelihood and the loss of autonomy (Patterson, 1972). The Indian Act of 1876 legalized the distinction between Indians and the rest of the population, since the Act formally established what Indian status was, and placed Indians under the legislative and administrative control of the state. With the decline of the fur trade and agricultural expansion into western Canada, the Aboriginal peoples lost further control over their land, their livelihood, and their political future. Even today, the marginal social and economic position of Aboriginal peoples in Canadian society makes them dependent on the state for survival (Frideres, 1993; Satzewich and Wotherspoon, 1993). Thus, the term *Indians* or *Native peoples* becomes associated not only with a racial origin of a remote past, but also signifies a contemporary people which is economically deprived, socially marginal and politically militant. Canada's past policies and treatment of Asian Canadians also reflect how the public and the state resorted to using the notion of a foreign race to manage and control a marginalized segment of the population (Li, 1998). Throughout the latter half of the nineteenth century and early twentieth century, Asians in Canada were viewed as an inferior race, with loathsome values, customs and behavioural standards that would corrupt the morality and culture of Europeans (Anderson, 1991; Li, 1998; Roy, 1989; Satzewich, 1989). By the early part of the twentieth century, the notion of Asians in general, and Chinese in particular, as racially distinct and culturally inferior was well entrenched in the ideology and practice of Canada; as well, the view of a racial hierarchy that favours Occidental culture and the White race was prevalent in Canadian society (Anderson, 1991; Berger, 1981; Li, 1998). Canada's historical treatment of racial minorities has imputed many deep-seated symbols and meanings to the notion of race in Canadian society. However, in the decades after the Second World War, Canada also developed legal protection and public policies to safeguard basic human rights. Some of the major statutes include the Canadian Charter of Rights and Freedoms in Part I of the Constitution Act of 1982 (Statutes of Canada 1982, c. II), the Employment Equity Act of 1986 (Statutes of Canada 1986, c. 31) and the Multiculturalism Act of 1988 (Statutes of Canada 1988, c. 31). These statutes in particular formally affirm the fundamental rights of the individual to equality without discrimination; the Multiculturalism Act endorses the policy of the federal government to recognize and to promote cultural and racial diversity of Canadian society as the individual's freedom of choice. At the same time, there are some indications that racialized minority groups, such as the Chinese and Japanese, which historically were marginalized and discriminated, have been upwardly mobile in terms of educational level and occupation status (Li, 1990). As well, the First Nations became more assertive in their claims of Aboriginal recognition and constitutional entitlement in the post-War decades; consequently, they have gained some political concessions from both federal and provincial governments when it comes to Aboriginal title and Aboriginal rights (Boldt, Long, and Little Bear, 1985). On the surface, it would appear that the post-War social conditions are more favourable towards racial minorities than the historical ones. As a result, the social import of race may have receded as human rights are entrenched in Canadian society.

Some authors have argued that despite the legal protection of human rights and the general acceptance of the principle of equality in Canadian society, racism continues to be manifested in the ideas of people and in practices of social institutions (Henry et al., 1995; Li, 1995; Zong, 1994). Henry et al. (1995:17) use the term *democratic racism* to refer to the contradictory way in which racist ideologies are articulated in Canadian society, which also upholds egalitarian values of justice and fairness. Democratic principles and racist ideologies can co-exist, especially when some people rely upon their stereotypes of race to make sense of their everyday experiences, since they provide the grounds for simplistic but convenient explanations of complex economic and social problems. Ironically, the entrenchment of individual rights and freedoms in Canadian society in the post-war decades also gives added legal ammunition to extremists to advocate racial supremacism in the name of freedom of speech (Li, 1995). As Canadians face an uncertain future due to economic re-structuring, it is appealing to accept a rationale which allows those who feel their traditional economic and social security being eroded to blame racial minorities and immigrants for their woes (Li, 1995). In this way, the historical construction of race in Canada is given a contemporary reality, as it offers a simplistic but meaningful solution to people in dealing with the hardships and contradictions they face (Li, 1995).

There is substantial empirical evidence to indicate that Canadians continue to attribute unequal social worth to people of different racial origin despite the public's awareness and general acceptance of democratic principles of equality and justice. For example, Berry, Kalin and Taylor (1976) reported data from a 1974 national survey to show that Canadians tended to rank people of European origin much higher than racial minorities in terms of whether they were considered "hardworking," "important," "Canadian," "clean," "likable," "interesting" and other qualities. Among the groups with the lowest ranking were "Chinese," "Canadian Indian," "Negro," and "East Indian" (Berry, Kalin, and Taylor, 1976:106).

Other studies have also produced evidence to show that Canadians tend to project a lower social image on racial minorities (Driedger and Peters, 1977, Filson, 1983; Li, 1979; Pineo, 1997; Richmond, 1974). For example, Pineo (1977) reported findings from a national study to show that English Canadians regarded "Negroes," "Coloureds," "Canadian Indians," "Chinese" and "Japanese" to have the lowest social standing, while French Canadians gave "Chinese," "Negroes," "Coloureds," and "Japanese" the lowest social ranks. Filson (1983) indicated that Canadian respondents in a 1977 national survey showed most hostility towards immigrants from India and Pakistan, followed by those from the West Indies; in contrast, British and American immigrants received the least hostility. Foschi and Buchan (1990) studied perceptions of university male subjects to see how much they perceived their partner as competent to perform a task on the basis of the racial origin of the partner, and found that the subjects were more influenced from a partner portrayed as White than from one portrayed as East Indian.

References

Anderson, K.J., *Vancouver's Chinatown: Racial Discourse in Canada, 1875–1980.* Montreal-Kingston: McGill-Queen's University Press, 1991.

Berger, T.R. *Fragile Freedoms: Human Rights and Dissent in Canada.* Toronto: Clarke, Irwin and Company Limited, 1981.

Berry, J.W., R. Kalin, and D. Taylor. *Multiculturalism and Ethnic Attitudes in Canada.* Ottawa: Minister of Supply and Services Canada, 1976.

Boldt, M., J.A. Long, and L. Little Bear. *The Quest for Justice: Aboriginal Peoples and Aboriginal Rights.* Toronto: University of Toronto Press, 1985.

Filson, G. "Class and Ethnic Differences in Canadian's Attitudes to Native People's Rights and Immigrants." *Canadian Review of Sociology and Anthropology* 20, no. 4 (1983): 454–482.

Foschi, M., and S. Buchan. "Ethnicity, Gender and Perceptions of Task Competence." *Canadian Journal of Sociology* 15, no. 1 (1990): 1–18.

Frideres, J.S. *Native Peoples in Canada: Contemporary Conflicts.* 4th edition. Toronto: Prentice-Hall, 1993.

Henry, F., C. Tator, W. Mattis, and T. Rees. *The Colour of Democracy: Racism in Canadian Society.* Toronto: Harcourt Brace, 1995.

Li, P.S. *The Chinese in Canada.* 2nd edition. Toronto: Oxford University Press, 1998.

Li, P.S. "Racial Supremacy under Social Democracy." *Canadian Ethnic Studies* 27, no. 1 (1995): 1–18.

Li, P.S. "The Emergence of the New Middle Class among Chinese in Canada." *Asian Culture* 14 (April, 1990): 187–194.

Patterson, E.P. II. *The Canadian Indian: A History Since 1500.* Toronto: Collier-Macmillan of Canada, 1972.

Pineo, P., 1997. "The Social Standings of Racial and Ethic Groupings," *Canadian Review of Sociology and Anthropology* 14, no. 2 (1997): 147–157.

Roy, P.E., *A White Man's Province: British Columbia Politicians and Chinese and Japanese Immigrants, 1958–1914.* Vancouver: University of British Columbia Press, 1989.

Satzewich, V., and T. Witherspoon. *First Nations: Class, Race, and Gender Relations.* Toronto: Nelson, 1993.

Satzewich, V. "Racism and Canadian Immigration Policy: The Government's View of Caribbean Migration, 1962–1966." *Canadian Ethnic Studies* 21 (1989): 229–241.

Statues of Canada. *Canada Act,* c. 11 (1982).

Statutes of Canada. *Employment Equity Act,* c. 31 (1986).

Statites of Canada. *Canadian Multiculturalism Act,* c. 31 (1988).

Zong, L. "Structural and Psychological Dimensions of Racism: Towards an Alternative Perspective." *Canadian Ethnic Studies* 26, no. 3 (1994): 122–134.

Source: P.S. Li. "The Market Value and Social Value of Race." In *Racism and Social Inequality in Canada,* edited by V. Satzewich, 117–119. Toronto: Thompson, 1988.

Not an autonomous process, racialization often evolves in tandem with processes of class formation and the minority construction of groups on the basis of gender. There is a form of oppression specific to racialized women called *gendered racism.* Gendered racism has always been embedded in the Canadian society and manifested in a variety of ways. One important one for our purposes is the creation of a gendered and racialized division of labour, which leaves racialized women vulnerable to a double disadvantage as victims of both racism and sexism.

Racial Discrimination

As a system in which one group exercises power over others on the basis of skin colour and other superficial traits, racial discrimination has had many persistent effects in Canadian history. Racial discrimination shaped the early relationships between European settlers and Aboriginal peoples. For decades it defined immigration policies as well as patterns of settlement. It informed educational policies in many of the provinces. Among other factors, it explains the denial of civil and political rights to Japanese Canadians in British Columbia during World War II, the imposition of the head tax on Chinese immigrants, the denial of landing for the *Komagata Maru*, a ship carrying South Asians off the coast of Vancouver at the turn of the century, the race riots in Nova Scotia in the late 1800s, the segregation of African Canadians in the educational system in Ontario until the 1960s, the treatment of nurses from racialized groups in the 1970s and 80s, the denial of employment opportunities for racialized peoples, the documented overrepresentation of racialized group members in the prison system in Manitoba, Nova Scotia, and Ontario, persistent differential access to services such as housing, health care, social assistance, recreational facilities, imposition of limits on access to property, and differential treatment in the criminal justice system.

Box 2.2: *Everyday Racism* by Frances Henry, Carol Tator, Winston Mattis, and Tim Rees

Everyday racism involves the many and sometimes small ways in which racism is experienced by people of colour in their interactions with the dominant White group. It expresses itself in glances, gestures, forms of speech, and physical movements. Sometimes it is not even consciously experienced by its perpetrators, but it is immediately and painfully felt by its victims—the empty seat next to a person of colour, which is the last to be occupied in a crowded bus; the slight movement away from a person of colour in an elevator; the over-attention to the Black customer in the shop; the inability to make direct eye contact with a person of colour; the racist joke told at a meeting; and the ubiquitous question "Where did you come from?"

From a research perspective, these incidents are difficult to quantify because they are only revealed in the thoughts, feelings, and articulations of victims:

It is very difficult to determine "objectively" the nature of everyday interaction between Whites and Blacks ... a variety of studies have shown that those who are discriminated against appear to have more insight into discrimination mechanisms than those who discriminate .... Blacks have a certain amount of expertise about racism through extensive experience with Whites. The latter, conversely, are often hardly aware of the racism in their own attitudes and behaviour. (Essed, 1990)

And, although people of colour are often sensitive to everyday racism, it may be so subtle that they are unaware of it. Research on racism has therefore tended to focus on what is more immediately visible and measurable. Thus racial discrimination in employment, in the media, and other more visible manifestations of racism have been studied.

In analyzing everyday racism, a further important distinction can be made between active and passive racism. Active racism includes:

all acts that—consciously or unconsciously—emerge directly from the motivation to exclude or to inferiorize Blacks because they are Black. Passive racism is complicity with someone else's racism. Laughing at a humiliating joke ... and "not hearing" others' racist comments are passively racist acts. (Essed, 1990)

Reference

Essed, P. *Everyday Racism: Reports from Women of Two Cultures.* Alameda: Hunter House, 1990.

Source: F. Henry et al., *The Colour of Democracy: Racism in Canadian Society*, 2nd edition. Toronto: Harcourt Brace, 2000, p. 55.

Racial discrimination is systemic, institutional, and cultural. It is sustained by practices of racial superiority and structures of social exclusion. More important for our purposes here, numerous studies have documented that because of its systemic nature, racial discrimination determines the differential experience of racialized groups in economic performance, in the educational system, in the criminal justice system, and in access to social services.[17]

Absence of motives is no defence for the impact of differential outcomes. As Canada's Supreme Court has stated, it is impact, not motive or intent, that is the proper test of unequal treatment.[18]

The Supreme Court of Canada has also ruled that:

Discrimination may be described as a distinction, whether intentional or not but based on grounds relating to personal characteristics of the individual or group, which has the effect of imposing burdens, obligations, or disadvantages on such individual or group not imposed upon others, or which withholds or limits access to opportunities, benefits, and advantages available to other members of society. Distinctions based on personal characteristics attributed to an individual solely on the basis of association with the group will rarely escape the charge of discrimination, while those based on an individual's merits and capacities will rarely be so classed.[19]

Further, the Supreme Court Justice Madame L'Heureux-Dube clarified the point that:

A distinction is discriminatory within the meaning of section 15 (of the Canadian Charter of Rights and Freedom) where it is capable of either promoting or perpetuating the view that the individual adversely affected by this distinction is less capable, or less worthy of recognition or value as a human being or a member of Canadian society, equally deserving of concern, respect and consideration.[20]

In her Royal Commission on Equality report, Judge Rosalie Abella concludes as follows:

Discrimination in this context means practices or attitudes that have, whether by design or impact, the effect of limiting an individual's or group's right to the opportunities generally available because of attributable rather than actual characteristics. What is impeding the full development of the potential is not the individual's capacity but an external barrier that artificially inhibits growth.

It is not a question of whether this discrimination is motivated by an intentional desire to obstruct someone's potential, or whether it is an accidental by-product of innocently motivated practices or systems. If the barrier is affecting certain groups in a disproportionately negative way, it is a signal that the practices that lead to this adverse impact may be discriminatory. This is why it is important to look at the results of a system. [21]

Abella's points of reference are the ideals of equality entrenched in the *Canadian Charter of Rights and Freedoms*, which provide a basis for challenging such discriminatory outcomes as racialized poverty. The *Charter of Rights and Freedoms* sets the stage for raising questions about both public policy, and the practices and policies of major institutions in society with regard to their efforts to remedy this persistent form of systemic discrimination that denies many Canadians full participation in Canadian society. Some have argued that it suggests a positive duty on the part of the state to deal with these structural disadvantages in Canadian society.[22] On that point, Abella suggests that:

It is not that individuals in the designated groups are inherently unable to achieve equality on their own, it is that the obstacles in their way are so formidable and self-perpetuating that they cannot be overcome without intervention. It is both intolerable and insensitive if we simply wait and hope that barriers will disappear with time. Equality in employment will not happen unless we make it happen.[23]

Abella's findings of the persistence of racial discrimination in employment are consistent with the findings of Canadian studies and reports that have documented discrimination in employment, in education, in social-service delivery, in the criminal justice system, in the media, and in housing, to name but a few areas.

Racial Discrimination in Employment

Differential outcomes in employment have been attributed to racially discriminatory systemic practices such as:

- Differential treatment in recruitment, hiring, and promotion;
- Extensive reliance on non-transparent forms of recruitment, such as word of mouth, which reproduce existing networks;
- Differential valuation or effective devaluation of internationally obtained credentials;
- Demands for Canadian experience;
- Use of immigrant status as a proxy for lower quality of human capital.[24]

Historical structures of racial discrimination have influenced the incorporation of racialized immigrants into the Canadian labour market. It can be speculated that without major interventions, Canadian labour markets will continue to show patterns of racial and gender stratification. The continued racial segregation in the labour market is compounded by a key phenomenon of globalization: the emerging dominance of precarious or non-standard forms of work. Modern-day processes of social exclusion recall past labour-market displacement and exclusion, especially during tough economic times, which are widely documented.[25] Today's racialized immigrants fit into a hierarchy of stratification of labour that imposes differential levels of exploitation in support of capitalist accumulation. The system generates a form of "racial dividend" from racially defined labour-market differentiation.

Racial discrimination in employment has been documented for over a century, especially in the United States of America, yet the study of racial discrimination in employment in Canada is a more recent enterprise. It was not until the 1984 Parliamentary Committee report "Equality Now" that racial discrimination in employment became a prominent part of contemporary scholarship.[26] In the Report of the Equality in Employment Commission (1984), which identified racial discrimination as part of the phenomenon of discrimination in employment in Canada, Judge Rosalie Abella defined discrimination in employment as "practices or attitudes that have, whether by design or impact, the effect of limiting an individual or group's right to opportunities generally available because of attributed rather than actual characteristics."[27]

According to the Commission Report, discrimination represents an arbitrary barrier standing between a person's ability and his or her opportunity to demonstrate it. While discrimination occurs in different ways at different times and in different places, there is one constant: the persistence of barriers that disproportionately affect certain groups. All things being equal, in a market economy, the value of labour should be derived from its marginal productivity, and equally productive persons should both be compensated equally and have equal opportunities for mobility. Yet the reality is that, in the Canadian labour market, there are widely documented differential outcomes that occur along racial and gender lines, suggesting a more complex, differentiated, and even hierarchical labour market.

Box 2.3: Racial Discrimination in Employment

- Economic discrimination is said to occur when employers make generalized assumptions about the employment capacity of members of a group, either willfully or because they are unable to assess ability, as may be the case when the value of qualifications from a certain country or region is unclear.
- Exclusionary discrimination occurs when members of a group are not hired or paid commensurate wages, or once hired, not promoted regardless of their skills and experience.
- Both forms have been documented among racialized group members and may explain the congruence between the economic performance of foreign-trained and Canadian-trained racialized members in the Canadian labour market.

Racial discrimination occurs in a variety of ways. Racial discrimination in employment refers to two practices that deny racialized group members equality of opportunity in the Canadian labour market and secure an advantage for non-racialized groups. *Economic discrimination* is said to occur when employers, unable to assess the ability of members of a group, make generalized assumptions about the worth of their human capital, as may be the case when the value of qualifications from a certain country or region is considered unclear. *Exclusionary discrimination* occurs when members of a group are not hired or paid commensurate wages, or once hired, not promoted regardless of their skills and experience. In both cases, it is the outcome, not the intent, that is the standard as established by the Supreme Court of Canada. In *Andrews* v. *Law Society of British Columbia*, the Court clearly identified discrimination as:

> distinction which, whether intentional or not but based on grounds relating to personal characteristics of an individual or group, has an effect which imposes disadvantages not imposed upon others or which withholds or limits access to other members of society. (*Andrews* v. *Law Society of British Columbia*, [1989] S.C.R. 144).

In emphasizing the negative impact of discrimination, the Court seemed to depart from the then-conventional approaches to labour-market discrimination. In much of the human resource management discourse of the time, discrimination was considered a function of the free exchange of labour and wages, subject to competitive market forces, to the exclusion of influences from other institutions in society. This was especially true of what is known as the human-capital approach, popular with neo-classical economists, who are more comfortable talking about statistical discrimination than systemic discrimination. Yet these practices have never been innocuous or without consequence for individuals, communities, and the Canadian nation.

Human-Capital Theories of Differential Outcomes in Employment: Becker's "Taste for Discrimination"

The study of discrimination in labour markets has its international roots in the United States, where Becker's 1957 study of economic discrimination led to an explosion of interest in racial and gender discrimination in the labour market.[28] Becker's groundbreaking study compared the experiences of male and female employees as well as mostly White employers/employees and Black workers shunned by the former group. In typical neo-classical economics fashion, Becker's work assumes that the labour market is made up of free agents, potential employers and employees, with workers trading their labour to the highest bidder, recreating a situation similar to free trade among nations. However, given the evidence of differential wages and occupational concentration between Black and White workers, Becker was compelled to offer an explanation that would account for the anomaly, within the conventional neo-classical model. Using both macro and micro economic analyses, Becker identified the existence of "taste"-driven preferences in decisions made by employers and employees relating to choices of employees and fellow workers. To maintain the integrity of the neo-classical model, he suggested that acting upon such exclusionary tastes meant many were prepared to incur costs to assert their preferences.

Becker then extrapolated this condition to the general labour market, and used what he called the "taste for discrimination" to explain the persistence of acts of discrimination in the labour market, reconciling it to the profit motive. Subsequent scholarship either supported Becker's supply-side approach, suggested modifications that addressed its flaws, or responded to it critically from the demand side. Becker's theory has proven empirically invalid, partly because its neo-classical bias limits his exploration of the socio-cultural basis for the "taste of discrimination" he identifies and so fails to address the dynamics of discrimination.

Becker was boxed into an analytical corner because he defined the complex phenomenon of labour-market discrimination as purely economic; he was forced into the absurd assertion that the discriminators were the real victims because they incurred pecuniary costs (as opposed to benefiting from the process of discrimination). Becker maintained his position in the face of widespread evidence to the contrary. He also held to the assertion that the labour market is a highly competitive, highly efficient, integrated mechanism for allocating human resources, again a position that is unsustainable given the evidence to the contrary, as we will see later in the book. Lastly, the ahistoric nature of his formulation could not satisfactorily explain a process that clearly builds over time and whose historical basis is important in understanding the structural outcomes in modern labour markets.

Following Becker, some public-choice theorists attempted to address some of the weaknesses in his approach. According to these theorists, it was possible to maintain both a competitive labour market and racially differential outcomes; they suggested that the differentials were inherent in the quality and quantity of the subject labour — in essence assigning the difference to female or racial inferiority. Kenneth Arrow (1972) attributed the racial and gender differences in wages to adjustment costs related to the hiring, recruitment, and training of racialized and female labour.[29] He maintained the position that there exists a single free market of labour in which decisions are made by free agents seeking to maximize their benefits, uninfluenced by institutional imperatives that go beyond the functioning of the ideal type free market. Yet even Arrow could not convincingly explain away the mounting empirical evidence that while some forms of discrimination could be said to impose a cost on those who practice them, the most prominent feature of discrimination in employment was the costs imposed on the victims. The privileged group, the discriminators, drew a social and economic benefit, which in fact was the material basis sustaining discrimination.

A number of Arrow's critics suggested that in an economy creating more wealth than ever, the persistence of a "return to human capital investment gap" can best be explained by the disproportionate return that some groups in society achieved at the expense of others. This suggested the existence of a structurally determined economic benefit for some and cost for others that sustained racial discrimination. Nevertheless, the neo-classical school stood its ground. It extended its influence into the Canadian debate via the "human capital" approach, whose claims that the inherent lower quality of racialized labour explained its lower compensation and occupational segregation echoed those of the American school (DeVoretz, 1995; Economic Council of Canada, 1991; Stoffman, 1992).

Box 2.4: *The Market Value of Race* by Peter S. Li

The social importance of race is manifested in many facets of life in Canadian society. One such facet is in the labour market, where race affects the opportunities and economic outcomes. Many studies have found that there are differences in occupation and earnings associated with the racial and ethnic origin of Canadians. Historically, members of racialized minorities, such as the Chinese, were systematically paid less than White workers, and they were hired in labour-intensive projects when White workers were hard to find (Li, 1998). But as soon as White workers became readily available, Chinese labourers became the targets of racial exclusion and were blamed for taking away the jobs of White Canadians and depressing their wages (Li, 1998).

Table 2.1: Ranking of Selected Immigrant Ethnic Groups and Canadian-Born Ethnic Groups According to the Percent of Respondents Who Indicated Having the Highest Comfort Levels Being around Individuals from Each Group

Origin Being Evaluated	Respondents Indicating the Highest Comfort Levels toward:	
	Immigrant Ethnic Group (%)	**Canadian-Born Ethnic Group (%)**
British	83	86
Italian	77	83
French	74	82
Jewish	74	78
Ukrainian	73	79
German	72	79
Portuguese	70	76
Chinese	69	77
Native Canadian	...	77
West Indian Black	61	69
Moslem	49	59
Arab	52	63
Indo-Pakistani	48	59
Sikh	43	55

Source: *Multiculturalism and Canadians: Attitude Study 1991 National Survey Report*, submitted by Angus Reid Group, Inc. to Multiculturalism and Citizenship Canada, August, 1991, p. 51.

Porter's systematic study (*The Vertical Mosaic*) of the relationship between ethnic origin and occupational status shows that certain racial and ethnic groups were underrepresented in professional, managerial, and technical occupations, but overrepresented in labouring jobs, and that the occupational disadvantages associated with racial and ethnic origins persisted from 1931 to 1961, the period being studied (Porter, 1965). A number of people have reconsidered Porter's thesis and have since found that he overstated the magnitude of the relationship between ethnic affiliation and social class (Brym with Fox, 1989; Darroch, 1979). However, despite disagreements over the precise magnitude of influence of ethnic origin on socio-economic performance, many studies have shown that race affects one's market outcomes such that non-Whites are often disadvantaged in occupational status and earnings.

For example, using data from the 1981 Census, Li (1988) showed that Canadians of European origin had an income advantage over those of Black origin or Chinese origin, even after differences in education and other factors had been taken into account. Data from the 1986 Census also indicated that an earning disadvantage was associated with non-White origin, while an advantage was linked to White origin, despite controlling for social class, and adjusting for differences in education and other variables (Li, 1992). Non-White women in particular were most affected by income disadvantage that could be attributed to race and gender (Li, 1992). These studies show that there is a market value being attached to racial origin, and that people of different origins are being remunerated in unequal terms in the Canadian labour market.

The 1991 Census provides further evidence for estimating the market value of race. The 1991 Census allowed respondents to be classified according to whether or not they belong to the visible minority category. A person is defined as belonging to the visible minority category if he or she claims a single or multiple origin of the following groups: Black, South Asian, Chinese, Korean, Japanese, South East Asian, Filipino, Other Pacific Islanders, West Asian and Arab, and Latin American (Statistics Canada, 1994b:56). On the basis of the 1991 Census data on origin, respondents can be classified as White Canadians, visible minority and Aboriginal peoples.

The 1991 Census shows that White Canadians account for 87% of the total population, Aboriginal peoples, 3.7%, and visible minorities, 9.3 %. White Canadians and visible minorities can be further classified into those born in Canada (native-born) and those born outside of Canada (foreign-born).

References

Brym, R.J. and B. Fox. *From Culture to Power: The Sociology of English Canada*. Toronto: Oxford University Press, 1989.

Li, P.S. *Ethnic Inequality in a Class Society*. Toronto: Thompson, 1988.

Li, P.S. "Race and Gender as Bases of Class Fractions and Their Effects on Earning." *Canadian Review of Sociology and Anthropology* 29, no. 4 (1992): 488–510.

Li, P.S. *The Chinese in Canada*. Toronto: Oxford University Press, 1998.

Porter, John. *The Vertical Mosaic*. Toronto: University of Toronto Press, 1965.

Statistics Canada. *Public Use Microdata File on Individuals: Final Edition*. Catalogue 48-039E. Minister of Industry, Science, and Technology, 1994b.

Source: P.S. Li. "The Market Value and Social Value of Race." In *Racism and Social Inequality in Canada*, edited by V. Satzewich, 120–122. Toronto: Thompson, 1988.

The Canadian Dimension

The 1980s and 90s saw a growing body of literature dealing with the experiences of racialized and immigrant populations in the Canadian labour market. This coincided with the shift in the source countries of most immigrants, from Europe to countries in the global South. The studies represent part of a debate in which the "structural barriers" analysis of the differential economic performance of racialized group members and particularly recent immigrants is set against the "human capital" approach to racially differential outcomes in the labour market. This latter approach was represented by the 1991 Economic Council of Canada report titled "Economic and Social Impacts of Immigration," which argued that immigrants (and refugees), most of whom were now racialized, had lower human capital quality; this explained their difficulty in "integrating" into the Canadian labour market and their experience of differential outcomes.[30] The "diminishing returns to human capital" school became especially prominent in the late-1980s and early-1990s debates about immigration, and had a significant impact on Canadian immigration policy, leading to limits in refugee approvals and a shift toward the selection of independent-class immigrants over family reunification. However, it did not address the evidence of differential outcomes that went beyond the experience of recent immigrants and were shared by the Canadian-born racialized group.

As in the United States, the limits of the human-capital approach have drawn critics arguing for a broader, institutional framework for explaining racial inequality in the labour market. Boyd's (1985) study of immigrant women's wages identified gender and racial discrimination as the cause of their experience of inequality. A study by Christofides and Swindinsky in 1994 pointed to racial discrimination as explaining the wage gap between racialized and non-racialized workers. Henry and Ginsburg's 1985 workplace audit of prospective employers found that equally qualified Black applicants received one offer for every three that White applicants received. More recently, findings from Harvey, Siu, and Keil's (1999) studies have suggested that "[t]he race 'factor' appears to have implications on how severe, extensive and persistent immigrants' socio-economic disadvantage is."[31] Data show that non-racialized Canadians realize higher earnings and occupational status, despite having average educational attainment rates lower than their racialized counterparts.

A plausible explanation consistent with Harvey et al.'s findings is that many employers use racial status (and immigrant status) to determine employability and estimate productivity and compensation—perhaps to compensate for their inability to gauge the quality of the human capital of racialized workers, whom most assume are immigrants (32% are not). The practice is what the neoclassical school terms "statistical discrimination."[32]

The structural school takes a different approach, which leads it to identify a manifestation of systemic discrimination. This school claims race is used as a surrogate for measurable human capital quality. In the absence of verifiable evidence, a socially constructed group is believed to inherently possess certain set levels of productivity. The structuralist school thereby rejects the position that the differential compensation is market generated and focuses on an alternate pecuniary factor: race.

Structural Theories of Labour-Market Discrimination

Structural theories present alternative explanations that attempt to address the flaws in the neo-classical economic framework by identifying labour markets as social institutions embedded in particular societies in time and space. They are hence subject to the structural pressures of dominant social relations in the particular societies.

The "structural factors" approach suggests that racial discrimination in the labour market is an important factor in the discriminatory outcomes documented in this book and elsewhere. Variants of the structural approach use the concept of labour-market segmentation to explain these differential outcomes. Proponents of this approach identify a market split into multiple spheres or multiple labour markets on the basis of race, gender, and other such structures that determine differential access and outcomes.[33] On the basis of this observation, they challenge the assertion that occupational and earnings differentials pertain solely to differences in education quality, language skills, or cultural differences as claimed by the "human capital" school. Instead they attribute the occupational and earnings inequality between racialized and non-racialized groups to factors imposing structural barriers to access to the labour market, such as racial discrimination.

Split Labour Market

The idea of segmented labour markets draws from the work of Edna Bonacich on split labour markets as a source of conflict, and differential pricing of labour among ethnic groups in the American labour market. Bonacich noted that under certain circumstances, two or more groups, distinctly identified by race or ethnicity, are thrown into conflict when the compensation for similar work is not equivalent. The labour price differentials derive from assumptions about a group's human resources quality being correlated to their ethnicity, as well as to the motives of the employer. What results is a three-way conflict between the employer and the two groups as the employer seeks to displace the higher-paid group in favour of the lower-paid. The group holding the income advantage is at a job security disadvantage so it responds by creating a form of exclusive labour system—a type of "closed shop"—to ensure its job security.[34]

The idea of exclusionary social closure processes helps explain discriminatory practices in employment because it speaks to the benefit that the discriminator derives from discrimination, as opposed to Becker's human capital theory, which attributes disadvantage to the discriminator.[35] In general, the social-closure explanation suggests that status groups create and preserve their identity and advantages by reserving certain opportunities for group members. In other words, exclusionary practices reserve the best positions and most desirable opportunities in the labour market for members of more powerful status groups. An important implication of the social-closure argument is that advantaged White male employees benefit from and therefore act to maintain exclusionary practices.

Bonacich argues that racially defined competition leads to four possible outcomes: (1) displacement of higher-paid workers, (2) exclusion of racialized workers, (3) a submerged system with barriers to mobility for racialized workers, (4) or a radical coalition between majority and minority labour (Bonacich, 1972, 1976). [36]

According to Bonacich, split labour markets exist where the cost of labour differs along racial or ethnic lines for the same or similar work. This analysis rings true for Canada with its historical and current accounts of lower wages for the same work by Chinese and South Asian workers in British Columbia, Black workers in Halifax in the 1800s, Black railway porters across Canada, domestic Filipino workers, racialized nurses in Ontario, and the ever-growing ranks of precarious workers in many of Canada's urban areas. Examples of displacement and exclusion, especially during tough economic times, are also widely documented, particularly in the literature dealing with the economic impact of immigration. In present-day Canada, there are observable signs of exclusion, but also the potential for a class-based response to intensified exploitation (Galabuzi, 2004a). Writing about a similar phenomenon in Europe, Balibar suggested in 1991 that "neo-racism" is a phenomenon of late 20th-century neo-liberal globalization, representing a response to the reversal of historic population movements southward and heightened vulnerability for workers in the global North. Neo-racists have been documented to engage xenophobic responses and attempts at closure. At the national level, they often demand an end to immigration.

A well-known organizational closure argument is associated with the dual economy theory.[37] In general, the argument is that high-resource organizations can afford to employ higher-paid White male labour. Racialized peoples, and often enough women, are systematically denied access to the most favourable employment organizations. They are relegated to a secondary labour market. The dual labour market approach presents discriminatory behaviour by employers as a way of preserving privilege enjoyed by one group over another. In essence, employers are responding to pressures from advantaged employees or to their own discriminatory preferences when they refuse to hire women or members of racialized groups. So employers discriminate in hiring, generally with encouragement of advantaged employees; and employers allocate to women and racialized group members jobs that require skills lower than those they may actually have. The more highly skilled and better-paying jobs are reserved for the advantaged group.

Labour Market Segmentation

A related structuralist approach that addresses the experience of racially segregated labour markets is presented by those who use the segmented labour market approach. According to this approach, here, jobs and industries are divided into primary and secondary (or peripheral) sectors and occupations on the basis of differentials in wages, employment stability, potential for promotion, working conditions, unionization, and job rights. These patterns of segmentation extend to mobility both within sectors, and from sector to sector. While the primary sector has higher wages, employment stability, and mobility, the secondary sector work is marginal, low-paying with little protection, often seasonal, and dead-end. Workers in the secondary sector confront a reality of intensified exploitation and have little or no bargaining power.[38]

Updated variants of the segmented labour market approach present employers as participating in a more systemic process of discrimination through the differential evaluation of the skills and productive potential of workers based on their race or gender. In addition, kin and friendship networks ensure that the flow of jobs remains largely within certain social circles, thereby reproducing the racial composition of the segments. The radical version suggests that employers act in concert with such institutions as the state in order to maximize exploitation for the purposes of capitalist accumulation and the subjugation of the victim group of workers. It is assumed that the labour market is an extension of social structures; society and the social relations and relations of power in the society also structure the labour market and access to employment, compensation, and mobility.[39]

A popular critique of the theory is that it divides work into good and bad jobs, a position that is controversial and contested. There is a healthy debate as to what constitutes a good job and a bad job. Moreover, the idea of creating a hierarchy of jobs undermines worker solidarity. As well, the idea that the labour market is so firmly divided into either primary and secondary sectors or core and periphery industries strikes many as too rigid to describe the labour markets in capitalist societies, where class formation is more volatile.

However, the segmented labour market approach helps identify the racialized patterns of labour-market participation. Not only are racialized groups incorporated into the low end of the labour force, but also they are disproportionately exposed to low-skill work in many of the low-wage sectors. They are also last hired and first fired, and many find themselves in contract, temporary, and part-time work.

In the Canadian context, most of the structuralist approaches build on the insights from Porter's vertical mosaic analysis. Proponents of the structural approaches focus on the structural imperatives and the demand-side barriers to employment, mobility, and compensation that determine the "place" of racialized workers in the Canadian labour market.[40]

Critical Anti-Racism Theory

Finally, critical race theory is growing in popularity because of its capacity to explain the dynamics of racial discrimination.[41] Critical anti-racism has been used to explain the processes of racialization in institutions such as labour markets. The approach presents a structural explanation of how class, gender, and other forms of oppression intersect with race to create the exclusion experienced by racialized group members in a capitalist society. As Winant (1994) has remarked, this approach views race as a "fundamental organizing principle of contemporary life" — organizing work without priorizing race over class or gender. In other words, race determines access to the labour market while reinforcing the overarching profit-maximizing logic of capital (Calliste, 2000).[42] As Loomba puts it:

> Critical anti-racism interrogates the historical institutionalization of racial discrimination through legal and customary sanctions which uphold the economic

supremacy of one group or groups in society over another or others. The group(s) benefiting from this institutionally imposed privilege defend those institutionalized or normalized rules and sanctions by perpetuating them through systemic processes, policies and practices. The resulting structures reproduce themselves and ensure that the processes of privilege production endure. (Loomba, 1998:120)

The historical dimension is important in understanding the unequal distribution of institutional privilege. Historically, the incorporation of racialized groups into the Canadian economy has been subject to their racialized status, whether one is looking at enslaved Blacks; largely segregated "free" Blacks in Nova Scotia, New Brunswick, Quebec, and Ontario; Chinese railway workers in British Columbia; South Asian businessmen seeking government contracts; Japanese professionals (denied accreditation and working as apprentices); Caribbean and Filipino domestics; Caribbean farm workers; or, more recently, immigrants from Africa, the Caribbean, Latin America, the Middle East, South Asia, China, Vietnam, and the Philippines. The organization of labour deployment under Canadian capitalism seeks to guarantee cheap sources of labour. In the case of racialized groups it sees an opportunity to produce a "racial" dividend for those who own the means of production.

A fundamental contribution to critical anti-racism theory has been made through the work of Frances Henry, Carol Tator, Winston Mattis, and Tim Rees. Their work includes the introduction of the groundbreaking concept of democratic racism, which aims to explain the co-existence of egalitarian values and racist ideologies in the same society. (See Box 2.5.)

Box 2.5: *The Concept of Democratic Racism* **by Frances Henry, Carol Tator, Winston Mattis, and Tim Rees**

The primary characteristic of democratic racism—the most appropriate model for understanding how and why racism continues in Canada—is the justification of the inherent conflict between the egalitarian values of justice and fairness and the racist ideologies reflected in the collective mass-belief system as well as the racist attitudes, perceptions, and assumptions of individuals.

Racist beliefs and practices continue to pervade Canadian society. Attitude surveys have found that many Canadians hold racist views. In the first such survey carried out in Canada, about 16% of Canadian adults were found to be confirmed bigots, while a further 35% held somewhat intolerant views. Another 30% leaned toward tolerance, and the remaining 20% were extremely tolerant (Henry, 1978). Later surveys and polls support these findings. Most Canadians therefore hold some degree of racist attitudes. But, living in a society that believes in democracy, most Canadians also recognize that these attitudes are socially unacceptable. In order to maintain their racist beliefs while championing democratic values, Canadians have developed the ideology of democratic racism—a set of justificatory arguments and mechanisms that permit these contradictory ideologies to coexist.

> Democratic racism, therefore, results from the retention of racist beliefs and behaviours in a "democratic" society. The obfuscation and justificatory arguments of democratic racism are deployed to demonstrate continuing faith in the principles of an egalitarian society while at the same time undermining and sabotaging those ideals.
>
> **Reference**
>
> Henry, F. *The Dynamics of Racism in Toronto*. Toronto: York University, 1978.
>
> Source: F. Henry et al., *The Colour of Democracy: Racism in Canadian Society*, 2nd edition. Toronto: Harcourt Brace, 2000, p. 19.

In the end, most recent research dealing with the experience of racialized groups and their incorporation in Canadian society and the Canadian labour market suggests a persistence of structural inequalities in access to and mobility in the labour market. The various structuralists seek to explain the evidence of unequal incomes and labour market segregation defined by concentrations in certain sectors and occupations. Unlike the largely ahistorical human-capital school, the analysis here is founded on the empirical observations of unequal outcomes informed by historic restrictions in access to opportunities.

Dynamics of Racial Discrimination in the Canadian Labour Market

The position of racialized groups in Canada's labour market has been a growing area of study in the last 25 years. Much of it has occurred under the rubric of racial discrimination in employment and racial inequality in incomes. Among others, Gillian Creese's (1991) study of Chinese workers in Vancouver before World War II found patterns of structural segregation similar to those that exist today. Adrienne Shadd (1985) and Agnes Calliste's (1987) work on sleeping car porters early in the last century documents structures of segmentation in the labour market that consigned Blacks to low-end jobs in low-wage sectors of the economy. Das Gupta's study of South Asian immigrant workers focused attention on the racialized structures through which racialized labour was incorporated into the Canadian labour market throughout history. A 1981 study by Reitz, Calzavara, and Dasko on *Ethnic Inequality and Segregation in Jobs* concluded that, despite higher levels of education, members of the racialized minority groups received lower compensation on average than other Canadians. The report of the Parliamentary Taskforce on the status of racialized groups found that racial discrimination was pervasive in Canadian employment systems. Studies done by Henry and Ginsberg (1985), titled *Who Gets the Job*, and by Billingsley and Musynski (1985), titled *No Discrimination Here*, demonstrated through field research the extent of discrimination in employment in Canada's biggest urban centre, Toronto. Henry and Ginsberg found that Whites got three job offers for each one a Black applicant got when they sent out actors with matched resumes and backgrounds to meet with employers.[43]

Box 2.6: Racial Discrimination in Employment

- Historical racism and gendered racism in access to employment practices
- Most jobs filled through word of mouth, reproducing existing networks and privileged access
- Barriers to occupational mobility in workplace and among sectors

Barriers to access to professions and trades
- Non-recognition of international credentials
- Devaluing human capital on basis of source country
- Demands for Canadian experience

A study by Harish Jain (1985) identified barriers in employment systems, including limited recruitment procedures such as word of mouth, biased testing, stereotypical decision-making in the interview process, promotions, transfers, and salary increases. In the late 1980s, a study by Vorst and others documented the marginalization and segregated participation of racialized women in the public service, and concluded that a disproportionate number of them worked as cleaners, cafeteria workers, nurses' aides, and low-level clerical workers. In the private sector, they observed that racialized women were largely ghettoized in private domestic service, light manufacturing, and the low-paying service industry. Barriers were also documented in Brand's 1980s study of the race and gendered division of labour in Canada, in Tania Das Gupta's study of the experience of racialized nurses and garment workers, in Agnes Calliste's documentation of racialized nurses in segmented labour markets and railway porters, and in a 1989 Urban Alliance on Race Relations study titled "Canada's Employment Discriminators."[44]

A series of studies by the Canadian Civil Liberties Association (1975, 1976, 1980, 1991) targeting employment agencies in Ontario found that many maintained a "Whites only" policy for employers who wanted a screen for race when referring temporary workers. In one case, a review of practices at 15 agencies showed that only three were unwilling to accept discriminatory job orders.[45]

A 1989 Ontario government taskforce report on the situation of foreign-trained professionals and tradespeople, titled *Access! Report*, echoed the finding of a study in British Columbia by Fernando and Prasad (1986) that many faced barriers in getting credentials to practice in their fields of training and experience, and in converting their educational attainment into economic compensation. Among the many immigrants whose university education and trades training went unrecognized by Canadian authorities were doctors, teachers, lawyers, social workers, engineers, nurses, technicians, plumbers, accountants, and mechanics.[46] In the 1990s, according to a department of Employment and Immigration Canada annual employment equity report, the average salaries in the federal public service for racialized group members in management were about 18% lower than those of the Canadian population. Among manual workers, group members earned 10% less than the rest of the population.[47]

A 1995 study of racialized men's incomes by Pendakur and Pendakur, titled *The Colour of Money,* found that racialized men earned significantly less than White immigrant men. They concluded that the differences could not be accounted for by educational, occupational, or place-of-training differentials. They also found differences of up to 10% between Canadian-born visible minority men and White men.[48] More recently, a series of studies of ethno-racial inequality in Metro Toronto by Ornstein (1996, 2000) shows that racialized group members suffer higher-than-average unemployment rates (up to three times higher for most groups) and higher levels of poverty (again up to three times higher). According to the reports, racialized women fare even worse, with some groups sustaining poverty rates as high as 60%.[49]

Yet another study focusing on the trends in education, employment, and earnings for racialized groups was done by the Canadian Council on Social Development for the Canadian Race Relations Foundation in 2000. Some of its key findings confirm those in many of the other studies and reports. They speak to unequal access to employment despite higher educational attainment among racialized groups, barriers to commensurate employment and compensation for those with international training and experience, overrepresentation in low-income groups, and underrepresentation in high-income groups. These patterns hold even among immigrant populations, with non-racialized immigrants outpacing racialized immigrants in income and access to employment. Focus group research done across the country for the report also confirmed the persistence of racial discrimination in employment.[50] Finally, a recent taskforce report on the participation of racialized group members in the federal government acknowledged that 15 years after the introduction of federal employment equity legislation, racialized groups members make still make up less than 5% of the public service; this should be compared to their numbers in the population (11%).[51]

Box 2.7: Key Patterns of Racialized Participation in Canada's Labour Market

- The gap between the employment income of racialized and non-racialized groups.
- The differential labour market participation of groups based on unequal employment and unemployment rates.
- The racially defined sectoral distribution of groups in the labour market.
- The failure of racialized groups to convert their education into occupational status and income.
- The differential experience of recent immigrants with access to professions and trades.

Conclusion

A historical approach to understanding the place of racialized groups in Canada begins with the study of the processes of racialization. This is particularly important because patterns of racialization tend to reproduce themselves. Present-day Canadian institutions such as the labour market manifest the outcome of historical processes of minority construction, racialization, and social exclusion. These processes lead to what we have suggested is a colour-coded form of social stratification in Canadian society.

As a central activity in our lives, work ensures livelihood and defines our identity, making it a key site for the manifestation of these processes and the struggles they provoke. Sectoral and occupational segregation, which in part explains the earnings differentials between racialized and non-racialized group, is part of a much longer historical process. Racialized groups' concentration in low-paying, low-status, and precarious jobs suggests that race is a key feature of the economic, social, cultural, and political structures and processes that form the foundation of the modern Canadian nation. Both Canadian state and institutional policies and practices are rooted in these processes and structures.

It is not enough to say that the processes of racialization reinforce the idea of Canada as a White nation even as the political elites make new claims about the multicultural, multi-racial character of Canada and its commitment to diversity. The challenge is to understand how this occurs. In the chapters that follow, we present empirical evidence about how the various aspects of racialization in the Canadian labour market help explain the social exclusion of racialized groups.

Notes

1. A. Loomba, *Colonialism/Postcolonialism* (London: Routledge, 1998).
2. M. Omi and H. Winant, "On the Theoretical Status of the Concept of Race," in *Race, Identity and Representation in Education,* edited by C. McCarthy and W. Crichlow (New York: Routledge, 1993), 3–10.
3. E. Balibar, "Is There a Neo-Racism?" in *Race, Nation, Class: Ambiguous Identities,* edited by E. Balibar and I. Wallerstein (London: Verso, 1991), 17–28.
4. E. Kallen, *Ethnicity and Human Rights in Canada* (Toronto: Oxford University Press, 2003).
5. Ibid; P. Li, *Ethnic Inequality in Canada* (Toronto: Thompson Educational Publishing, 1988); P. Li, "The Market Value and Social Value of Race," in *Racism and Social Inequality in Canada: Concepts, Controversies and Strategies of Resistance,* edited by V. Satzewich (Toronto: Thompson Educational Publishing, 1998), 115–130; F. Henry, C. Tator, W. Mattis, and T. Rees, *The Colour of Democracy: Racism in Canadian Society* (Toronto: Harcourt Brace, 2000).
6. Visible minority is used for Canadian Census purposes and by federal government departments such as Statistics Canada to describe non-Aboriginal people of colour. Visible minority is also identified in the *Federal Employment Equity Act* as a broad category for most non-Caucasian, non-Aboriginal people in Canada. The term remains in wide use even outside the federal government.

7.   J. Porter, *The Vertical Mosaic* (Toronto: University of Toronto Press, 1965).

8.   G. Galabuzi, "Racializing the Division of Labour: Neo-liberal Restructuring and the Economic Segregation of Canada's Racialized Groups," in *Challenging the Market: The Struggle to Regulate Work and Income*, edited by J. Stanford and L. Vosko (Montreal: McGill-Queens University Press, 2004): 175–204.

9.   J. Lian and D. Matthews, "Does a Vertical Mosaic Really Exist? Ethnicity and Income in Canada, 1991," *Canadian Review of Sociology and Anthropology* 34, no. 4 (1998): 461-481; E. Herberg, "The Ethno-racial Socio-economic Hierarchy in Canada: Theory & Analysis of the New Vertical Mosaic," *International Journal of Comparative Sociology* 31, no. 3–4 (1990): 206–221.

10. M. Banton, *Racial Theories* (London: Cambridge University Press, 1987).

11. R. Miles, *Racism* (London: Routledge, 1989).

12. B. Bolaria and P. Li, *Racial Oppression in Canada* (Toronto: Garamond Press, 1985); Miles (1989); M. Omi and H. Winant, "On the Theoretical Status of the Concept of Race," in *Race, Identity and Representation in Education*, edited by C. McCarthy and W. Crichlow (New York: Routledge, 1993). 3–10.

13. The Canadian Ethno-Cultural Council (CEC), the National Anti-Racism Coalition of Canada (NARCC), and the National Coalition of Immigrant and Racial Minority Women are such examples. See also P.J. Williams, *Seeing a Colour-Blind Future: The Paradox of Race* (New York: Noonday Press, 1997).

14. B.J. Fields, "Slavery, Race and Ideology in the United States of America," *New Left Review* 181 (May/June, 1990): 95–118.

15. A. Calliste and G. Sefa Dei, "Anti-Racist Feminism: Critical Race and Gender Studies," in *Anti-Racist Feminism*, edited by A. Calliste and G. Sefa Dei (Halifax: Fernwood Publishing, 2000), 11–18; Bolaria and Li (1985); Li (1999).

16. P. Essed, *Everyday Racism: Reports from Women of Two Cultures* (Claremont: Hunter House, 1990); Henry and Tator (2000b).

17. See R. Abella, *Equality in Employment: A Royal Commission Report* (Ottawa: Supply and Services Canada, 1984); *Equality Now! Report of the Special Committee on Visible Minorities in Canadian Society* (Ottawa: Supply and Services Canada, 1984); *Report of the Royal Commission on the Donald Marshall, Jr. Prosecution* (Halifax: Province of Nova Scotia, 1989); *Report of the Aboriginal Justice Inquiry of Manitoba* (Winnipeg: Province of Manitoba, 1991); *Report of the Commission on Systemic Racism in the Ontario Criminal Justice System* (Toronto: Province of Ontario, 1995); *Report of the Canadian Task Force on Mental Health Issues Affecting Immigrants and Refugees* (Ottawa: Supply and Services Canada, 1988); *A Time for Change: Moving beyond Racial Discrimination in Employment* (Urban Alliance on Race Relations and the Social Planning Council of Metropolitan Toronto, 1990).

18. *Ontario Human Rights Commission v. Simpson-Sears, Ltd.* (1985) 2 S.C.R. 536 (S.C.C.): 549.

19. *Andrews v. Law Society of British Columbia* (1989) 56 DLR 1 (S.C.C.), p. 18, as cited in C. Eboe-Osuji, "Ferrel and Others v. Attorney General of Ontario, Factum," (1996):12.

20. *Egan Versus Canada* (1995) 124 DLR 609 (S.C.C.), p. 638, as cited in C. Eboe-Osuji, "Ferrel and Others v. Attorney General of Ontario, Factum," (1996):12.

21. Abella (1984: 2).

22. Eboe-Osuji (1996).

23. Abella (1984: 254).

24. Various reports speak to the prevalence of these practices. See Abella (1984); C. Agocs and C. Burr, "Employment Equity, Affirmative Action and Managing Diversity: Assessing the Differences" *International Journal of Manpower* 17, no. 4–5(1998); Alliance for Employment Equity, "Charter Challenge—The Case for Equity" (Spring, 1998); Bakan and Kobayashi (2000); Billingley and Musynski (1985); Equality Now (1984); Henry and Ginsberg (1985); Jain (1985), (1988); Kunz et al. (2001); NARC (2002); *Report of the Federal Taskforce on the Participation of Visible Minorities in the Federal Public Service* (2000).

25. Anderson and Lynam (1987); Brand (1987); Calliste (1991); Creese (1991); Daenzer (1993); das Gupta (1996); Reitz (1981).

26. *Equality Now: Report of the Special Committee on the Participation of Visible Minorities in Canadian Society* (Ottawa: Queen's Printer, 1984).

27. Abella (1984: 2).

28. G. Becker, *The Economics of Discrimination* (Chicago: University of Chicago Press, 1957). Becker's study was predated by some early debates on gender discrimination to which Sidney Webb's 1891 study, "The Alleged Differences in the Wages Paid to Men and to Women for Similar Work," was most notable. In the 1940s, Gunnar Myrdal's *An American Dilemma: The Negro Problem and American Democracy* (New York: Harper and Row, 1944) focused more directly on the racial divide. Like Becker, much of this work was situated in the microeconomic framework, with basic assumptions about free markets. Only Myrdal departed somewhat from the neo-classical assumptions in dealing with the "Negro problem in America" by identifying a cause and effect relationship betweeen the labour market experiences of Blacks and the other institutions in society that reinforced the disadvantages in income and occupation he observed.

29. K. Arrow, "Models of Job Discrimination," in *Racial Discrimination in Economic Life*, edited by Anthony Pascal (Lexington: D.C. Heath, 1972), 187–203.

30. Economic Council of Canada, *Economic and Social Impacts of Immigration* (Ottawa: Supply and Services Canada, 1991).

31. E.B. Harvey, B. Sin, and K. Reil, "Ethnocultural Groups, Periods of Immigration and Social Economic Situation," *Canadian Ethnic Studies* 30, n. 3 (1999): 95–103.

32. K. Arrow, "What Has Economics to Say About Racial Discrimination?" *Journal of Economic Perspectives* 12, no. 2 (1998): 91–100.

33. D. Hiebert, "The Colour of Work: Labour Market Segmentation in Montreal, Toronto and Vancouver, 1991," Working paper No. 97-02. (Vancouver: Research on Immigration and Integration in the Metropolis, 1997). Hiebert argues, after Doeringer and Piore (1971), that the labour market is effectively split into jobs in which workers receive substantial rewards for their human capital and those where they don't.

34. E. Bonacich, "A Theory of Ethnic Antagonism: The Split Labour Market," *American Sociological Review* 37 (October, 1972): 547–559.

35. The notion of social closure can be traced to back to Max Weber's *Economy and Society* (1968), with contemporary treatments by Parkin (1979) and Murray (1988).

36. E. Bonacich, "Advanced Capitalism and Black/White Relations in the United States: A Split Labour Market Interpretation," *American Sociological Review* 41 (1976): 34–51.

37. Hiebert (1997); Calliste (2000).

38. R. Edwards, *Contested Terrain* (New York: Basic Books, 1979); For further discussion and critique of segmented labour market theories, see T. Das Gupta, *Racism and Paid Work*

(1996); D. Hiebert, "The Colour of Work: Labour Market Segmentation in Montreal, Toronto and Vancouver, 1991," Working Paper No. 97-02 (Vancouver: Research on Immigration and Integration in the Metropolis, 1997); L. Vosko, *Temporary Work: The Gendered Rise of a Precarious Employment Relationship* (Toronto: University of Toronto Press, 2000).

39. Hiebert (1997).

40. These include but are not limited to: Akbari (1989); Boyd (1985); Christofides and Swindinsky (1994); Henry and Ginsburg (1985); Hiebert (1997); Jain (1985); Lian and Matthews (1998); Pendakur and Pendakur (1998); Reitz et al. (1981); Reitz (1990).

41. Representative texts include: A. Calliste and G. Sefa-Dei (eds.), *Anti-Racism Feminism: Critical Race and Gender Studies* (Halifax: Fernwood Publishing, 2000); T. Das Gupta, *Racism and Paid Work* (Toronto: Garamond Press, 1996); P. Li, *Ethnic Inequality in a Class Society* (Toronto: Thompson Educational, 1988); H. Winant, *Racial Conditions* (Minneapolis: University of Minnesota Press, 1994); R. Miles, *Racism and Migrant Labour* (London: Routledge and Kegan Paul, 1982); V. Satzewich and P. Li, "Immigrant Labour in Canada: The Cost and Benefits of Ethnic Origin in the Job Market," *Canadian Journal of Sociology* 12 (1987): 229–241.

42. H. Winant, *Racial Conditions* (Minneapolis: University of Minnesota, 1994); A. Calliste, "Nurses and Porters: Racism, Sexism and Resistance in Segmented Labour Markets," in *Anti-Racist Feminism*, 143–164, edited by G. Dei and A. Calliste (Halifax: Fernwood, 2000).

43. J. Reitz, L. Calzavara, D. Dasko, *Ethnic Inequality and Segregation in Jobs* (Toronto: Centre for Urban and Community Studies, University of Toronto, 1981); *Equality Now: Report of the Parliamentary Taskforce on the Participation of Visible Minorities in Canada* (Ottawa: Queen's Printer, 1984); F. Henry and E. Ginsburg, *Who Gets the Job? A Test of Racial Discrimination in Employment* (Toronto: Urban Alliance on Race Relations and Social Planning Council of Metro Toronto, 1984); B. Billingsley and L. Musynski, *No Discrimination Here* (Toronto: Social Planning Council of Metropolitan Toronto and Urban Alliance on Race Relations, 1985).

44. H. Jain, *Anti-Discrimination Staffing Policies: Implications of Human Rights Legislation for Employers and Trade Unions* (Ottawa: Secretary of State, 1985); J. Vorst et al., *Race, Class, Gender: Bonds and Barriers* (Toronto: Between the Lines, 1989); D. Brand, "Black Women and Work: The Impact of Racially Constructed Gender Roles on the Sexual Division of Labour," *Fireweed* 25 (1987): 35; T. das Gupta, *Racism and Paid Work* (Toronto: Garamond Press, 1996); A. Calliste, "Anti-Racism Organizing and Resistance in Nursing: African-Canadian Women," *Canadian Review of Sociology and Anthropology* 33, no. 3 (1996): 361–390; A. Calliste, "Nurses and Porters: Racism, Sexism and Resistance in Segmented Labour Markets," in *Anti-Racist Feminism*, edited by A. Calliste and G. Sefa Dei (Halifax: Fernwood Publishing, 2000), 143–164; UARR, "Canada's Employment Discriminators," *Currents: Readings in Race Relations* 5, no. 2 (1989): 18–21; G. Creese, "Organizing against Racism in the Workplace: Chinese Workers in Vancouver before World War II," in *Racism in Canada*, edited by O. McKague (Saskatoon: Fifth House, 1991). 33–44.

45. Canadian Civil Liberties Association, *Survey of Employment Agencies* (Toronto: CCLA, 1991).

46. P. Cummings, et al., *Access! Report of the Taskforce on Access to Trades and Professions* (Toronto: Ministry of Citizenship, 1989); T. Fernando and K. Prasad, *Multiculturalism and*

Employment Equity: Problems Facing Foreign-Trained Professionals and Trades People in British Columbia (Vancouver: Affiliation of Multicultural Societies and Services of British Columbia, 1986).

47. Employment and Immigration Canada, *Annual Report: Employment Equity* (Ottawa: Ministry of Supply and Services, 1992).

48. K. Pendakur and R. Pendakur, *The Colour of Money: Earnings Differentials among Ethnic Groups in Canada* (Ottawa: Department of Canadian Heritage, 1995).

49. M. Ornstein, *Report on the Ethno-racial Inequity in Metropolitan Toronto: An Analysis of the 1991 Census Data* (Toronto: Access and Equity Centre of Metro Toronto, 1997); *Ethno-Racial Inequality in Toronto: Analysis of the 1996 Census* (Toronto: Access and Equity Centre of Metro Toronto, 2000).

50. J.L. Kunz, A. Milan, and S. Schetagne, *Unequal Access: A Canadian Profile of Racial Differences in Education, Employment and Income. A Report for the Canadian Race Relations Foundation by the Canadian Council on Social Development* (Toronto: CRRF, 2000).

51. Taskforce on the Participation of Visible Minorities in the Federal Public Service, *Embracing Change in the Federal Public Service* (Ottawa: Supply and Services Canada, 2000).

Questions for Critical Thought

1. What do we mean when we say that race is a social construct?
2. How and why do classifications of humans such as race come about?
3. Why are processes of social stratification relevant to contemporary Canadian society?
4. How can we understand the existence of racial inequality in a democratic society like Canada?
5. Does the test established by the Supreme Court of Canada for discriminatory action seem reasonable?
6. Describe some of the approaches used to explain the existence of unequal outcomes in the labour market.
7. Why do processes of exclusion persist even when they are exposed as creating inequality in a society committed to equality of citizenship?

Recommended Readings

Abella, R. *Equality in Employment: A Royal Commission Report.* Ottawa: Supply and Services Canada, 1984.

Becker, G. *The Economics of Discrimination.* Chicago: University of Chicago Press, 1957.

Calliste, A., and G. Sefa-Dei (eds.). *Anti-Racism Feminism: Critical Race and Gender Studies.* Halifax: Fernwood Publishing, 2000.

das Gupta, T. *Racism and Paid Work.* Toronto: Garamond Press, 1996.

Edwards, T. *Contested Terrain.* New York: Basic Books, 1979.

Essed, P. *Everyday Racism: Reports from Women of Two Cultures.* Claremont: Hunter House, 1990.

Henry, F., C. Tator, W. Mattis, and T. Rees. *The Colour of Democracy: Racism in Canadian Society*. Toronto: Harcourt Brace, 2000.

Li, P. *Ethnic Inequality in a Class Society*. Toronto: Thompson Educational, 1988.

Miles, R. *Racism and Migrant Labour*. London: Routledge and Kegan Paul, 1982.

Omi, M., and H. Winant. "On the Theoretical Status of the Concept of Race," in *Race, Identity and Representation in Education*, edited by C. McCarthy and W. Crichlow. New York: Routledge, 1993. 3–10.

Winant, H. *Racial Conditions*. Minneapolis: University of Minnesota Press, 1994.

CHAPTER 3

Social Exclusion in Historical Context

Introduction: Canada's Changing Population Confronts an Historic Racial Divide

In the last two decades, we have witnessed the fastest growth in the size of the racialized group in Canada's history. Much of that growth has been achieved through immigration, as over 75% of new immigrants are members of racialized groups. The racialized proportion of the Canadian labour force will continue to grow, with trends showing increases in full-time participation of both male and female racialized workers between 1996 to 2001 far outpacing those of other Canadians. While this development is to be celebrated as an affirmation of Canada's multicultural reality, in the early 21st century, the growth of the racialized population is prompting new questions about some old assumptions regarding Canadian society.

What are the implications of the growth of a population that has historically been the victim of racial discrimination? Concerns about the hierarchical structures that determine the distribution of opportunity in the labour market, structures responsible for the inequalities in employment and other institutions of Canadian society, are likely to intensify. In a modern liberal democratic society such as Canada, racial discrimination is an affront to the principle of equality for all its citizens. It also represents an inefficient way to allocate scarce human resources and imposes an economic cost both on racialized groups and on the Canadian economy as a whole. It robs the economy of a valuable resource in a competitive global environment. It undermines the competitiveness of Canadian business at home and abroad. At the same time, those whose talents are improperly deployed see their skills degrade along with their self-esteem. The result is social, economic, and psychological hardship for individuals, families, and communities. This scenario often leads to poverty, and hence increases the national and provincial cost of dealing with poverty and its impacts on health and social well-being.

A related concern deals with the aspirations of thousands of highly qualified newcomers to Canada, many of them professionals and tradespeople, whose lives and participation in the Canadian economy have been disrupted by the devaluation of their human capital. While these skilled immigrants are attracted from their home countries by an aggressive immigration policy that promises to improve their lives and to let them contribute to a modern economy and multicultural society, many find themselves relegated to precarious employment in low-wage sectors and low-end occupations. Barriers in the Canadian economy deny them the opportunity to use their skills and be compensated in a manner commensurate with their training and experience.

As old as Canada itself, these experiences of exclusion are a recurring and salient feature of the Canadian labour market. What Kallen (2003) has referred to as the techniques of domination and social control have been with us since the origin of the idea of Canada. They have always involved practices of institutionalized racism and legal racism, and from the beginning provided the most effective instruments of colonization and creation of racial hierarchies in Canadian society and the Canadian labour market. These included majority or dominant group control over access to land, denial of educational opportunities, denial of the franchise, denial of employment and wages, denial of adequate housing and access to certain neighbourhoods, and control and denial of immigration and expulsion.[1] We now turn to this historical record to give us a better understanding of why we are where we are in the early 21st century.

Canada's Changing Demographic Makeup

Canada's population and economy are changing, prompting new questions about some old assumptions regarding Canadian society. Canada's welfare state has undergone massive restructuring as the country's economy has become more integrated into the global economy. The ethnic and racial composition of the labour force is changing even more rapidly, thanks in part to conditions of heightened globalization. In 1961, over 95% of Canada's population was of European heritage, largely due to a history of racist immigration policies. But a demographic shift began to occur in the 1970s with the increase in immigrants from Asia, Africa, the Caribbean, and Latin America. Over the last 30 years, Canada's population has become increasingly ethnically and racially diverse, as the source countries of Canada's immigrants have changed from Europe to countries dominated by people of colour.

In 2001, Canada was home to about four million racialized group members, or 13.4% of the Canadian population, a 24.6% increase since 1996. This increase far outpaced the overall Canadian rate of 3.9% over the five-year period. The racialized share of the population is projected to rise to 20% by 2016. Much of that growth is due to immigration. Canada welcomed an annual average of close to 200,000 new immigrants and refugees over the 1990s. Immigration accounted for more than 50% of the net population growth and 70% of the growth in the labour force over the first half of the 1990s (1991–1996). According to a study by the Human Resources and Skills Development Canada, it is expected to account for virtually all of the net growth in the Canadian labour force by the year 2011 (HRDC, 2002). According to the 2001 census, immigrants made up 18.4% of Canada's population, projected to rise to 25% by 2015; this 18.4% is the largest share in more than 50 years. Of note is the fact that, since the 1970s, increasing numbers of immigrants to Canada have come from Asia and the Middle East. Asian-born immigrants accounted for more than half (57%) of the immigrants who arrived since 1991.[2] In Toronto, Canada's largest city, over 25% of the students in the school system have arrived in Canada in the last 10 years.

Box 3.1: *Starting Life Poor* by Margaret Philp

Troy Fraser looks like a young, Black, hip answer to the cardigan-clad Mr. Rogers, sitting in a rocking chair, a gaggle of small children scattered on the rug at his feet listening to the book he reads on the miracle of life in a seed.

This is science class in his Grade 1 classroom, cluttered with pint-sized metal desks and children's clumsy artwork taped to the walls, where struggling immigrants from the shabby high-rises that surround the school send their children.

Mr. Fraser was one of these children two decades ago, born in a nearby hospital and raised in the Jane-Finch corridor, a north Toronto neighbourhood that has become more notorious for gangs, drugs, and guns than for the abundance of hard-scrabble immigrants and second-generation single mothers assigned to life on Canada's bottom rung.

The social-housing project where he lived as a child with his single mother and older siblings is in plain view from the front door of the school where he works. Twenty years ago, when he was in Grade 1, he sat in a classroom like this one, just blocks away.

As a university graduate with a respectable salary, a man who packs his three children into a minivan, he could live anywhere. He has made it.

But he stays. Mr. Fraser and his like-minded wife, Joesie Nelson, chose to raise their family here, even if that means living next door to poor neighbours who begrudge their good fortune. He deliberately chose to work in a school where White children are the lone, visible minority and nearly two in three students speak a language other than English at home.

"My whole drive was to work in this community," he says. "Me giving back to what has shaped me. I wanted to be a positive role model—male, Black, young—for a kid. The kids need me here."

Poverty is a legacy handed down through the generations. It starts with children who tend to be sicker, earn lower grades in school, and suffer from more behavioural problems. In later years, many will repeat family history.

But not always. Poverty is not a life sentence.

Canadians have wrung their hands over a child-poverty rate that has remained as stubborn as a stain over the past two decades, at nearly one in five children. It's only in the past few years that social scientists have found that a surprising four in 10 Canadians who start life at the bottom rung rise to the top half of the income ladder.

Mr. Fraser, 25, and Ms. Nelson, 26, belong with those who seize the opportunity to climb. Among the roughly 200,000 Canadians now in their twenties who grew up poor in the 1980s—when the poverty rate never slipped below 15%—they broke with tradition as teenagers in the 1990s to chase higher education.

What set them apart from neighbours, also raised by single mothers in dilapidated apartments, who became pregnant as teenagers, quit school, and now collect welfare or juggle low-wage jobs? Why were they running for election to their high-school student council when neighbours Jen McKenzie and Maxine Cadogan were dropping out and pushing baby strollers?

"It's got something to do with education policy and access to postsecondary education in a big way," said Miles Corak, director of family and labour studies at Statistics Canada. "And it's got something to do with early childhood investments and how you get those kids into a situation that they're able to choose whether they're going to have a postsecondary education or not."

*****

Mr. Fraser is on recess duty.

Here in the Topcliff Public School playground, the demographics of the school are laid bare. Most of the faces in the crowd are shades of brown, the children of parents who hail from India, Africa, and the Caribbean, from Vietnam, China, and the Philippines. Most live in four nearby apartment high-rises.

Mr. Fraser sees himself in these children whose futures are still blank slates. He understands the powerful imprint he can leave, standing before them as a second-generation Black immigrant from the neighbourhood.

"Even in Grade 1," he said, "these kids know that I went to university. They know I went to York. They know that this is a place that is accessible to them. I still say, 'When you graduate from high school,' and 'When you go on to postsecondary,' so that it's not foreign to them."

University was always a prospect for Mr. Fraser. He was raised by a tireless mother who returned to college in her forties, after her divorce, to become a nurse. He became close to a couple of teachers. One urged him to run for student council. Another enrolled him in a program that pairs Jane-Finch students with faculty at nearby York University. He would later land a scholarship at York that covered his tuition for the first few years.

He started to hang out with the strait-laced crowd in his grungy, 25-storey apartment building. It was there he met Joesie, the daughter of a struggling single mother from Jamaica, whose ambition to climb from the poverty of welfare matched his own.

She has a harder time tracing her rise. Her mother was laid-back; her father was absent. None of her teachers inspired her. But after years of skipping classes, hanging with the bad crowd, and dabbling in drugs and booze, she remembers acing a tough geography test in Grade 10. Suddenly she was basking in the realization she possessed the stuff of academic success.

She remembers going to a youth group in her apartment building. The group leader showed the children an article titled "Trapped in Poverty," suggesting that was their lot in life. Ms. Nelson recalls thinking, "That's not going to be me."

When she found herself pregnant in her first year of university, she suddenly saw her brilliant future falling to pieces. Back at her old high school, the grapevine hummed with news that the stellar student had fallen from grace.

"I'd made it that far," she said, "and was going to have to drop out and look after the child and repeat the cycle and be another poverty statistic."

But her mother would have none of it. Though she had never pushed her daughter to attend university—no one in the family had ever graduated with a degree—she was not about to watch her slip into that trap. She quit her job to care for her granddaughter.

"She knew I had the potential," Ms. Nelson said. "My mother would sacrifice anything for her kids."

She became so smitten by the academic life that her sights are set on studying for a PhD, although for now she is consumed with her job as a community-development worker. Like her husband, she works in their old neighbourhood.

*****

A handful of young women sit on lawn chairs in the backyard of a row of Jane-Finch townhouses, keeping an eye on their children who run back and forth from the kitchen to the playground.

Jen McKenzie, 23, suffers the late-afternoon heat. Seven months pregnant with her third child, she leans back in her chair to ease the weight of the bump under her red T-shirt and tucks into a cheese sandwich.

She collects welfare and has never worked. By the time she was a teenager, she was spending far more time with boys than books. "Boys and sex were my drugs," she said simply.

In Grade 9, she became pregnant. Since her daughter Tymika was born eight years ago, she has returned to school a few times to try to finish her high-school diploma. It never lasts long.

"Every time I try to go to school, I get pregnant," said the blunt Ms. McKenzie, whose children are fathered by different men. "I was supposed to go to school this year, but I got pregnant with this one." She patted her belly.

Her Jamaican-born mother raised the family without a father, sometimes collecting welfare, other times working odd jobs in a store, a hotel, an old-age home. Ms. McKenzie still lives with her in the same subsidized apartment.

Her mother, who now collects social assistance, would like her to leave, finish school, find a husband and get a house with a white picket fence. While she resents the pressure, Ms. McKenzie confesses that she aspires to leave the neighbourhood that has trapped her mother. It is as if leaving Jane-Finch is a life's ambition on its own—a notch on the barometer of success, like a university degree or a lucrative job.

"When I get a good job," she said dreamily, "I'm out of here. I've been here for 23 years, and I don't need to stay here for the next 23. I don't want that for my kids."

Unlike her childhood friend Jen, Maxine Cadogan returned to high school a few years after her teen-age pregnancy, dragging a baby, a stroller, and a two-year-old toddler on the bus every morning for two years.

"I was tired of staying at home," said Ms. Cadogan, 25. "I was tired of waking up in the morning with nothing to do. I mean I was raising my kids, of course. But I wanted more for myself."

Her mother, an immigrant from Barbados whose husband left when his daughter was six years old, had worked a handful of jobs at a time, often as a hotel chambermaid and a nursing assistant. She was seldom home to watch her two sons and wild daughter.

They lived across the street from a school, but her mother insisted Ms. Cadogan commute to one outside the confines of Jane-Finch to avoid unsavoury influences. It didn't work.

"I grew up in the 'hood. Of course I got into trouble," said Ms. Cadogan, a striking woman with enormous brown eyes and meticulously manicured nails. "I hung out with the wrong crowd. Basically it was boys. I wasn't into drugs."

By Grade 10, she was pregnant with her elder son, Trayvon, 9, whose name is tattooed down her left arm. Her mother was "heart-broken."

"It hurt her because she wanted me to go to school and get an education and do better," she said.

A second son, Demar, arrived two years later. Ms. Cadogan now lives several blocks outside the projects in the basement of a house that her mother bought with savings from years of working night and day.

Ms. Cadogan graduated from high school three years ago and landed a job as a receptionist at a medical clinic. She quit a few months ago and has started to upgrade her marks at a local high school; she wants to apply to college to study nursing.

"Eventually, I want to go on to better. I don't want to stay here forever," she said. "There's so much more out there for me, so why should I stay at this level?"

*****

It was not until Mr. Fraser and his wife reached university, outside the confines of their neighbourhood, that they realized how poor they were. Growing up, they had few possessions. But neither did anyone else.

Now that they are close to being middle-class parents, they are lavishing toys and clothes on their three children—Brianne and her two-year-old twin brothers, Brayden and Jayden—that they themselves were blissfully unaware of as children.

Their daughter tears along the street on a Barbie bicycle and a scooter that are the envy of her poor friends. Some of the children are so jealous that they refuse to play with her. Their parents accuse Mr. Fraser and Ms. Nelson—whose salaries are far from lucrative and whose student loans are the size of a mortgage—of being rich and no longer belonging.

But a nagging sense that their affluence is a passing phase—a fleeting stroke of luck that could turn sour in an instant—pushes Ms. Nelson to buy her daughter all that her heart desires while she can.

"I always live with this fear of what happens if we lose it all. I wasn't born with money, so I know what it's like not to have it."

Moving up
Who remains at the bottom and who rises? What pushes Troy Fraser and Joesie Nelson on to a university campus when most of their high-school classmates have barely graduated?

Statistics Canada's Miles Corak spent several years trying to peg a number to the likelihood that children raised in poverty will themselves be poor as adults. He and a colleague studied 400,000 tax files, comparing fathers' incomes in the late 1970s and early 1980s with those of their children more than a decade later.

They discovered that only some of the parents' socioeconomic disadvantage is passed down to the children. A young man raised at the bottom 10 percent of Canadian incomes stands less than a one-in-six chance of remaining there, and one-in-17 odds of reaching the very top of the ladder.

"What we're saying is that more than a quarter of people who start out at the bottom won't get higher than the [middle]," Dr. Corak said. The other part of the story is a lot go beyond that. They found Canada to be more a land of equal opportunity than either the United States or Britain, where child poverty is close to the same level as in Canada but children born to poor fathers have twice the chance of remaining poor. A college or university degree has become the ticket to a fatter paycheque in Canada.

> The research uncovered a few other distinctions. The children of fathers who collected employment insurance tended to have lower incomes as adults than those whose fathers never relied on that form of assistance. So did children from poorer neighbourhoods.
>
> But children whose fathers collected income from investments—even those at the bottom with little to invest—reported an average of $3,000 more in yearly income: "You don't have to have a lot," Dr. Corak said.
>
> "It could even be interest from a savings account. But broadly, it signals that you're thinking ahead."
>
> Source: Margaret Philp, "Starting Life Poor," *The Globe and Mail* (June 26, 2003), A6.

The percentage of racialized minorities in the Canadian population, which was under 4% in 1971, grew to 9.4% by 1991, hit double digits (11.2%) by 1996, and 13.4% in 2001. It is now projected to be 20% by 2016. With Canada's continued reliance on immigration for population growth and with globalization escalating, these trends are likely to continue.[3] Canada's racialized groups are mainly concentrated in urban centres, with Toronto, Vancouver, and Montreal accounting for about 75% of the total racialized population (Toronto 42%, Vancouver 18%, and Montreal 13%).

In 2001, racialized groups accounted for an increasing number of people in the major Canadian urban centres as well as the most populous provinces (see Table 3.1).

Overwhelmingly, the changes in immigration composition have been felt most by Canada's three biggest urban areas — Toronto, Vancouver, and Montreal. The cumulative increase in the number of racialized group members over the last 30 years is most noticeable in the major urban areas, where, in the 1990s, more than 80% chose to settle. They have transformed these areas into diverse cultural centres, and their increased contributions to the life and economies of cities like Toronto have led many Torontonians to proclaim diversity as their city's strength. In 1996, the Toronto Census Metropolitan Area (CMA), which roughly covers the Greater Toronto Area (GTA), was home to 1.3 million racial minorities, who constituted 32% of its total population. That number had risen to 1.7 million by the year 2001. Five out of every 10 recent immigrants settled in the Toronto CMA, and 60% of them were from Asia and the Middle East. The other big magnet for recent immigrants is Vancouver, which received 18% of all recent immigrants to Canada between 1991–1996, 80% of whom were Asian-born.[4]

As indicated earlier, during much of the 1990s, over 75% of Canada's newcomers were members of the racialized group communities. This shift in the composition of population change in Canada has had implications in a number of areas, not the least of which is the economy. Already, with that shift has come a noticeable lag in economic attainment among members of the immigrant groups. It is a lag that increasingly defies conventional explanation, given that the recent emphasis on a skills-based points system for immigrants and an increase in "independent class" and "economy class" immigration were supposed to raise the skill level of those migrating to Canada.

Table 3.1: Racialized Group Population as Percentage of Total Canadian Population, 2001

	Total Population	Racialized Population	Racialized Group Share of Total Population (%)	Regional Racialized Population as Share of Canada Total (%)
Canada	30,007,094	3,983,845	13.4	100
Newfoundland	512,930	3,850	0.8	0.1
P.E.I	135,294	1,180	0.9	0.0
Nova Scotia	908,007	34,525	3.8	0.9
New Brunswick	729,498	9,425	1.3	0.3
Quebec	7,237,479	497,975	7.0	12.5
Ontario	11,410,046	2,153,045	19.1	54
Manitoba	1,119,583	87,110	7.9	2.1
Saskatchewan	978,933	27,580	2.9	0.7
Alberta	2,974,807	329,925	11.1	8.2
B.C.	3,907,738	836,440	21.6	20.9
Yukon	28,674	1,025	3.6	0.0
N.W.T.	37,360	1,545	4.2	0.1

Source: *Census 2001*, Statistics Canada

Between 1991 and 1996, about 34% of recent immigrants aged 25–44 had completed university, compared to 19% in the rest of the Canadian population. In 1996, 43% of all recent immigrants aged 25 to 44 were post-secondary graduates (university or college).[5] Patterns of high educational attainment and poor economic performance seem to be holding both during and after the recession years of the late 1980s and early 1990s. While most groups did better during the period of recovery in the late 1990s, recent racialized immigrants (10 years or less) did at best only marginally better, and many are still struggling with high unemployment, low incomes, and family and child poverty.

The complex dynamics of population change are interwoven into the organization of the Canadian economy and into the quality of life both in Canada's urban centres, where the new immigrants have chosen to build new lives, and in the rural areas where many first sought job opportunities.[6] In the early 21st century, these changing dynamics affect the role of governments and their responsibility for the provision of public services such as welfare and settlement services. While previously it was assumed that governments can exert a positive influence on the political, economic, and cultural makeup of society, increasingly policy-makers are sceptical about the role of government in the lives of citizens, if not downright hostile. The laissez-faire attitude toward government intervention does not extend to those responsible for Canadian immigration policy, who for decades insisted, first officially and later administratively,

Table 3.2: Racialized Group Population as a Percentage of Census Metropolitan Areas (CMA), 2001

CMA	Racialized Groups as Share of CMA Population (%)
Canada Total	13.4
Vancouver	36.9
Toronto	36.8
Calgary	17.5
Edmonton	14.6
Ottawa-Hull	14.1
Montréal	13.6
Windsor	12.9
Winnipeg	12.5
Kitchener	10.7
Hamilton	9.8
London	9.0
Victoria	8.9
Halifax	7.0
Oshawa	7.0
Saskatoon	5.6
Regina	5.2
Kingston	4.7
St.Catharines-Niagara	4.5
Saint John	2.6
Sherbrooke	2.6
Thunder Bay	2.2
Greater Sudbury	2.0
Québec	1.6
St. John's	1.4
Trois-Rivières	0.9

Source: 2001 Census data, Statistics Canada

on racially based hierarchical classifications that would ensure European dominance.[7] That may be because concern about the impact of immigration-induced population change has been expressed by members of the public, who in recent opinion surveys have been showing a growing intolerance for racialized immigrants. While a majority of those surveyed did not believe that Canada's changing demographic makeup posed a danger to the country, other research into the attitudes of Canadians regarding recent immigration, which was conducted by Palmer (1996), supports the contention that many Canadians are concerned at least about the economic consequences of immigration, if not about issues of integration.[8]

The areas of the country most affected by the massive demographic changes brought about by recent immigration are Ontario, British Columbia, Quebec, and perhaps Alberta. The impact goes beyond sheer numbers to issues of public policy and identity. Ontario has 37% of Canada's population, but 54% of the immigrant population. Over 26% of the province's people are immigrants, and over the first five years of the 21st century, the province accounts for 57% of the annual inflow into the country. Michael Ornstein's recent analysis of the 1996 census data, funded by the City of Toronto, showed that racialized group members living in Toronto, Ontario's capital and biggest city, are three times as likely to live in poverty and twice as likely to be unemployed as other Torontonians.

This poses a challenge in terms of both economic and social public policy.[9] Immigration from Asia was key to helping British Columbia's economy outperform other provinces during the recession in the early 1990s, but it has also been speculated that fear of immigration made many traditional New Democratic Party voters into instant Reformers, and led the party to an electoral breakthrough in 1993.[10]

British Columbia (whose population is 25% immigrant, and which is the destination of 21% of new immigrants), chose Canada's first premier from a racialized group, Ujjal Dosanjh, in the mid-1990s. In Quebec, whose population is 10% immigrant, some in the sovereignty movement have fingered "ethnic communities" for the razor-thin win by the "No" side in the last referendum, suggesting that ethnic communities have an inordinate influence on Quebec politics.[11] We do not accept this assertion as fact, given the variation of opinion on sovereignty within the racialized communities. However, the ethnic communities, of which recent immigrants form a sizeable part in Quebec, are said to be on average more sympathetic to the Canadian federation than those of French-Canadian heritage.

Systemic Racism and the Canadian Immigration Policy in Historical Perspective

As we saw in the last chapter, race and racism have been central to the development of Canadian society. Canada's first settlers were its First Nations peoples, arriving here over 11,000 years ago.[12] However, it is the more recent immigrations that have defined the nation, largely led by Europeans and much more recently by Asians, Africans, Caribbeans, Latin Americans, and Americans. The Europeans who began migrating to Canada in earnest in the 1600s came with a mission to establish a White-settler colony upon their arrival. In a process that involved war, conquest, and treaty-making, they took control of land, resources, and the fur trade from the First Nations. This was followed with systematic policies of economic exclusion, genocide, and segregation aimed at subordinating and eliminating the Aboriginal population. At the same time, other policies aimed at assimilating the Aboriginals. The policy of systemic denial of access to resources aimed at Aboriginal nations defined the nature of the country that was to emerge, creating a race and class complex that resulted in and of the racialized unequal social and economic outcomes. In a then largely agrarian and mercantile society, the policies that reserved economic opportunity for Europeans created the first racialized economy in Canada, one in which differential access to resources led to improvements in the economic performance of European settlers at the expense of First Nations peoples.

Box 3.2: *Biases in Public Discourse on Immigration* **by Peter S. Li**

Public discourse on immigration is often coloured by the race question, especially in view of the changing composition of immigration since the late 1960s that involves the decline of immigrants from Europe and the United States to Canada and the corresponding rise of non-White immigrants from what comes to be known as "non-traditional" source countries(1). The assessment of immigration by the Canadian public is not necessarily based on scientific findings, but often premised on subjective experiences and partial interpretations. In the end, it is difficult to segregate the immigration debate from the race question, since the "colour" of immigrants becomes a key component of the discourse even though it is articulated subtly and indirectly. Thus, the value of immigrants may be discounted or distorted in the immigration debate simply on the basis of the changing racial composition of immigrants.

There is substantial evidence from opinion surveys to indicate that some segments of the Canadian public are unhappy about the growing number of non-White immigrants coming to Canada, and consequently are reluctant to support a more liberal immigration policy to enlarge the intake of immigrants. The reluctance is premised on the view that non-White immigrants represent unbridgeable differences that would undermine the social landscape, the normative order, and the European tradition of Canada. From this vantage point, the reservation towards immigration is to a large degree a reservation towards people of colour. Mercer (1995: 171) made a similar point when he wrote, "Canadians have chiefly interpreted themselves and the immigration experience from a Eurocentric perspective ...; in racial terms, Canadians have seen themselves as white."

The racial message of the immigration discourse is often formalized and indeed legitimized in opinion polls seeking to find out what Canadians think about immigration as well as in media reports analyzing these results. Government departments frequently use public opinions to solicit citizens' views regarding social issues and to measure their support of government policies(2). In discussions and consultations about immigration, the government is particularly interested to find out from Canadians the level of immigration and the type of immigrants that are acceptable to them. The media and polling companies also support public opinion surveys about immigration because the topic is sensational, controversial, and newsworthy. It is in seeking Canadians' views on "diversity" in opinion polls that the racial subtext of the immigration discourse becomes most apparent (Li, 2003).

Certain standard questions have been routinely used in such polls as a means to gauge what is often referred to as the "tolerance" level of Canadians towards "diversity." For example, in a national immigration survey conducted in January 2000 by Ekos Research Associates for the federal government, the following question was asked:

"Forgetting about the overall number of immigrants coming to Canada, of those who come would you say there are too many, too few or the right amount who are members of visible minorities?" (Ekos Research Associates, 2000: 6). The same question had been asked in earlier polls. A news report on the survey was widely printed in several major newspapers (see, for example, *Globe and Mail,* 2000; *Vancouver Sun,* 2000). Reporter Nahlah Ayed revealed that 27% of the respondents in the 2000 survey indicated that there were "too many" visible minority immigrants, compared to 25% who said so in 1999, and 22% in 1998. The *Vancouver Sun* used the headline "Survey Finds Less Tolerance for Immigrants" to highlight the story (*Vancouver Sun,* 2000). It becomes clear that the view of visible minority immigrants being too numerous, which was given by a quarter of the survey respondents, is elevated to the level of Canadians' tolerance of diversity, and the minute change of percentage of this segment over time (from 25% in 1999 to 27% in 2000) is given the scientific stature in revealing "Canadians becoming less tolerant."

There is a clear racial message that can be ascertained in the way the survey question is framed and interpreted, even though the words *race* or *non-White* are not used. First, the wording of the question indicates that pollsters and interest groups funding the survey can legitimately ask the general public to consider "race" as a factor in immigration, and to assess the social worth of "non-Whites" in terms of whether there are too many or too few of them, provided a term like *race* or *colour* is avoided. The term *visible minorities* replaces a racially charged term such as *coloured people,* but the pollsters framing the question as well as respondents answering it are clear about what the term *visible minorities* means. Another phrase that has been used in polls to substitute for *coloured people* is *people who are different from most Canadians.* Pollsters sometimes use this codified phrase to ask respondents to indicate whether they think such people should be kept out of Canada (see *Globe and Mail,* 1992). The attractiveness of a term like *visible minorities* is that its softer appearance and its use in the *Employment Act* (S.C. 1986, c. 31) make it a convenient label that can be innocently adopted to discuss the social worthiness of "race" and "non-Whites" without running the risk of being branded "racist." Most Canadians would probably find it objectionable if asked to express an opinion about whether there are too many or too few "non-Whites" in a situation in which they participate, such as a school, a corporation, or a social occasion, in part because this is too racially blatant, and in part because the principle of racial equality is clearly defined in the *Charter* and the Canadian tradition (3). Yet, when the question about visible minorities is asked in a public poll, it appears to be much more acceptable, and indeed neutral, as a tool to find out how far Canadians are prepared to accept non-Whites or coloured races. In short, opinion polls sanctify the racial phenomenon by giving Canadians a public forum to evaluate the "coloured" segment of the population as "too many" or "too few" purely on the basis of "race," as though such an evaluation is natural and proper in itself (4). The way the "colour" question is camouflaged in opinion polls reifies the notion of "race" by legitimizing the right of Canadians to pass judgment on newcomers based on their superficial features. Furthermore, Canadians' opinions on immigrants' race are not seen as a social problem that has to be addressed; rather, they are presented as a democratic choice of citizens regarding how many "diverse" elements in Canadian society they are prepared to "tolerate."

There is further evidence to suggest that pollsters and interest groups actively pursue the question about opinions regarding immigrants' "race" in opinion surveys, and then present such opinions as citizens' intolerance of "diversity" or their "cultural insecurity" that should be taken into account in policy formulation. For example, in an immigration consulting meeting organized by Citizenship and Immigration Canada in Montebello, Quebec, on 6–7 March 1994, results of a public opinion survey conducted by Ekos Research Associates were presented, and it was reported that "growing intolerance appears to have a racial dimension (since) 87% of respondents who believe that too many immigrants are drawn from visible minorities also believe that immigration levels are too high … , (and that) Canadians are concerned about a 'slipping away of our values' and a loss of Canadian identity" (Public Policy Forum, 1994) (5). Shortly after, in an article in the *Globe and Mail* on 28 March 1994, it referred to the finding in the Ekos survey that showed "most Canadians believe there are too many immigrants, especially from visible minorities," and used it to explain how "cultural insecurity" amid change fuels resentment among a majority of Canadians towards Asian, African and Arab migrants' (Sajoo, 1994). It is clear from the prevailing interpretation that respondents' opinions on "race" are not considered "racist" in the public immigration discourse, but rather, they are regarded as Canadians' genuine expression of "growing intolerance" or "cultural insecurity" based on a legitimate concern that too many "non-Whites" would render Canadian values "slipping away." Furthermore, the message is clear that Canadians' reservations over too many immigrants is misunderstood when in fact they are only concerned about too many "non-White" immigrants and not immigrants *per se* (6). In this way, the racial message in the immigration discourse is covered up as non-racist, and indeed elevated to the level of noble concerns by citizens who only want to protect Canada's ideological tradition and the national unity.

The fact that the racial message in the immigration discourse is typically regarded as legitimate concerns of citizens also implies that polling results have a substantial influence on the outcomes of the immigration debate. Lucienne Robillard, then minister of citizenship and immigration, made this point clear when she announced in 1996 the government's intention not to increase the immigration level because "the Canadian population is divided, according to the last poll we had" (Peirol, 1996). Often, Canadians' reservations over admitting more immigrants and their opinions regarding too many "non-White" immigrants are treated by the media as an indication of a public "backlash," and not a problem of Canadian society that has to be addressed (Peirol, 1996) (7). The term backlash implies a public disapproval of a policy direction that produces a widely perceived undesirable social change.

The public immigration discourse in Canada is in a difficult epistemological position. On the one hand, the discourse has legitimized the importance of public opinions in assessing the value of immigration; on the other hand, it has racialized the immigration question in allowing the colour of immigrants to be used as an acceptable basis for assigning a value to immigrants. The public discourse on immigration illustrates that subjective perceptions and normative values about race can distort the tone and the tenor of the immigration debate, and that such distortion can also affect the way objective facts and scientific findings are gathered and presented.

Notes

1. This section and the next are mainly based on materials in Li (2003).

2. Government-funded opinion polls are routinely conducted, but the results are not always released publicly. For example, in an internal report written for Citizenship and Immigration Canada, the author states that the report is based on surveys collected by Ekos in November 1996, Environics in December 1996, and Angus Reid in February 1997, which include "questions asked specifically on behalf of CIC (Citizenship and Immigration)" (Palmer, 1997:1). In a news story reported by *Toronto Star* on 19 Aug. 1996, the paper said it had to use the *Access to Information Act* to obtain results of a public opinion poll on immigration commissioned by the federal government (*Toronto Star,* 1996c).

3. Section I5 of the Canadian *Charter of Rights and Freedoms* states: "Every individual is equal before and under the law and has the right to the equal protection and equal benefit of the law without discrimination and, in particular, without discrimination based on race, national or ethnic origin, colour, religion, sex, age or mental or physical disability" (S.C. 1982, c. 11).

4. It is sometimes pointed out that Canada has a right to choose its immigrants, and Canadians have a say in exercising this right. Advocates of immigration restriction also suggest that Canadians do experience problems caused by immigrants coming from a different background; an often-cited problem has to do with public schools being overwhelmed by immigrant children not speaking the official languages, resulting in non-immigrant parents worrying about declining educational quality (see *Globe and Mail,* 1994c). My argument is not about whether Canada has a right to choose its immigrants or not, or whether there are problems of adjustment for immigrants and Canadian society. The simple fact remains that the *Charter* guarantees the equality of rights and non-discrimination for all, and the choice of preferred immigrants cannot be based on "race" or "colour" in violation of the *Charter,* in the same way that immigrant selection cannot be based on "gender." In asking respondents to indicate their "racial preference" of immigrants and in giving a "racial preference" as the answer, Canadians are in fact using "race" or "colour" as a criterion in choosing their preferred immigrants.

5. Michael Valpy, a well-known columnist, was sympathetic to the dominant interpretation of "cultural insecurity" in the immigration discourse. He wrote: "Ekos found that opposition to high immigration levels does not rest primarily on economic insecurity—the traditional blue-collar fears of immigrants-are-taking-our-jobs. Rather it rests most of all on cultural insecurity. The cultural fear is a product of resurging anxieties—particularly anglophone anxieties—about eroding Canadian identity. It is about the lack of sufficient Canadian homogeneous tribalness to form national consensuses on public policy direction" *(Globe and Mail,* 1994a: A2). Some readers expressed different views, but these opposition voices were ineffective to influence the dominant perspective in the immigration discourse. For example, a reader wrote: "I expected Canadians to regard freedom, honesty, hard work, personal accountability and tolerance as their most cherished values. I am not aware of any immigrant group not subscribing to these ideals. However, I am definitely aware of the millions who cheat on taxes, engage in UT and welfare fraud, expect 42 weeks' government handout after 10 weeks' employment, indulge in cross-border shopping with false customs declarations ... and [are] intolerant to and unwilling to respect the culture of Aboriginals (the 'true' Canadians), and these millions are mostly members

of Mr. Valpy's 'old Canada'" (*Globe and Mail*, 1994d: A26). Such opposition voices are largely ignored in the immigration discourse.

6. The corollary of this argument is that some Canadians are concerned over too many "non-White" immigrants and that they would probably not have said that there are too many immigrants if these immigrants were "White."

7. Alan Li, President of the Chinese-Canadian National Council, argued for the need to regard negative public opinions on immigration as a social problem in itself: "Unless the government takes a more proactive stance on immigration, public perceptions will not change. These are misconceptions that the government hasn't taken steps to correct" (Peirol).

References

Ekos Research Associates. *National Immigration Survey.* Presentation to the Hon. Elinor Caplan, Minister of Citizenship and Immigration Canada, 2000.

Li, P.S. "The Racial Subtext of Canada's Immigration Discourse." *Journal of International Migration and Integration* 2, no. 1 (2001): 77–97.

Mercer, J. "Canadian Cities and Their Immigrants: New Realities." *Annals of the American Academy of Political and Social Science* 538 (March 1995): 169–84.

Peirol, Paulette. "Immigration Levels Reflect Backlash." *The Globe and Mail* (October 30, 1996): A1, A6.

"Poll Showed Hostility to Immigrants." *The Globe and Mail* (September 14, 1992): A4.

"Poll Shows Opposition to Minorities Rising." *The Globe and Mail* (March 11, 2000): A8.

Public Policy Forum. *Developing a Ten-Year Strategic Framework for Canadian Citizenship and Immigration Policy and Programs: Finding the Right Consultative Process.* Ottawa: Public Policy Forum, 1994.

Sajoo, Amyn B. "Canadians Should Shake Off Their Insecurity." *The Globe and Mail* (March 28, 1994): A13.

Statutes of Canada. *Employment Equity Act*, c. 31 (1986).

"Survey Finds Less Tolerance for Immigrants." *The Vancouver Sun* (March 11, 2000): A11.

Source: P.S. Li. *Destination Canada: Immigration Debates and Issues*, 171–174. Don Mills: Oxford University Press, 2003.

Canada's political and economic development was similar to that of other colonized societies in that it involved the subordination of indigenous peoples; the suppression of their civil, political, and cultural rights; and often the forced use of their labour to extract their natural resources. The historic development of the capitalist economy laid the foundation for the policies of slavery, marginalization, and socio-economic exclusion of racialized immigrants. Historical structures of racial discrimination influenced the incorporation of racialized immigrants into the Canadian labour market, leading to a labour market stratified along racial lines. In earlier periods of immigration, many potential immigrants from the global South could work only as domestics and labourers despite their professional and other qualifications. Today's racialized immigrants, most selected on the basis of their skills, often end up with similar labour-market participation patterns — in sectors with largely casualized employment and low-end jobs.[13] They fit into a hierarchy of labour that imposed differential levels of exploitation for capitalist accumulation and a type of "racial dividend" from labour-market differentiation.

Slavery of Aboriginal and subsequently African peoples was a part of European settlement from the 16th and 17th centuries. French settlers owned both Aboriginal and African slaves. The graves of hundreds of Pawnee First Nation slaves have been uncovered in Quebec. Slavery was also legal in British North America until 1837. There was widespread slave ownership by White Loyalist settlers and others in the colony of Nova Scotia. In Upper Canada, slavery was widespread and many of the leading British families of the colony, such as the Russells and the Jarvises (after whom a major Toronto street is named), owned slaves even after the first governor of Upper Canada, Lord Simcoe, outlawed the slave trade in 1837. Children born to slaves were to be free, yet slavery continued in Upper Canada and in all of British North America after it was abolished in the British Empire in 1832.

The political system and economy that emerged in Canada were based on the concept of a White-settler society: the building of an "overseas replica of British society," complete with dominant culture, values, and institutions that "mimicked" those of the "home" country and an internal colonial economy.[14] These patterns persisted even as the population changed to include significant numbers of Blacks from the United States, who arrived as part of the Loyalist immigration after the American war of independence as freed slaves, or as fugitives through the Underground Railroad. When free Black Loyalists began to arrive in Canada after 1783, they were given only a fraction of the land given to White Loyalists, despite promises of equal treatment (100 acres for Whites and one acre for Blacks).[15] Whether as Black slaves or "freemen," as Chinese railroad workers, or as South Asian farm workers in the 19th and early 20th centuries, racialized workers fit into a hierarchy of labour that imposed the level of exploitation needed to ensure the accumulation of capital for the purpose of industrial development and nation-building.

Other racialized non-Aboriginal groups such as the East Asians and South Asian immigrants began to arrive in Canada in larger numbers in the late 1800s. They found that institutionalized structures of preferential access impeded their participation in the economy, limiting them to low-paying, dead-end, mostly unskilled jobs, even though some of them were artisans. Many toiled as cheap labour, laying tracks on the railroad going west, others mining the rocks with dynamite to clear the route for the railroad. It is an enterprise in which many lost their lives. The threat of an influx of Asian immigrants led to racist immigration policies such as the head tax, which was aimed at keeping the "hordes" out. These policies were the product of a systemic form of racism aimed at maintaining Canada as a White-settler colony.[16] It involved a social, cultural, economic, and political process whose purpose was to ensure that Canadian society was re-created in the image of European society.[17] There was a consensus shared by politicians across the spectrum of ideological opinion, including such progressives as J.S. Woodsworth, who would later become the leader of the CCF.[18] For instance, J.S. Woodsworth suggested that Asians and Blacks were "essentially non-assimilable elements [that] are clearly detrimental to our highest national development, and hence should be vigorously excluded."[19]

An important part of the Canadian national project was the determination to institutionalize European culture in all facets of Canadian life. As Balibar (1991) has suggested, social construction of the nation state tends to articulate both nationalism and racism. The "imagined community" fixes on what the ideal population should be, along with its cultural makeup, economic mode of production, and sometimes its religious composition. Immigrants are recruited to fit that constructed reality and to further that nationalist project as well as to support the mode of production.[20] There is a contradiction between the general thrust of this project and the claim that these modern states are founded on liberal democratic values—something that Henry (2000) has referred to as democratic racism (see boxed insert in Chapter 2). In the case of Canada, the social construction of the nation was premised on the suitability of Whiteness and European culture. The racial differentiation of peoples on the basis of socially selected physical traits served to normalize the European character of the settler colony through the discourses of racial purity as well as justify persistent forms of slavery. European immigration, which was predominantly White, brought with it cultural and social values that became the dominant cultures, as well as an economic mode of production that commodified the land, and in the process subordinated or erased Aboriginal cultures. Even when labour shortages forced the acceptance of racialized migration, racialized immigrants were incorporated into the economy in a way that posed the least risk to the character of the nation. In other words, they were incorporated into the labour market in a manner that produced and reproduced racial inequality. Their allocation to unequal sites engendered the establishment of racial hierarchies in the economy and social life that were then used to justify acquiring or maintaining an advantage for one group or other.[21]

The process of racialization in the Canadian imaginary also took on a gender dimension. Dua (2000) has suggested that the absence of women in much of the historical accounts of immigration shows the masculinized nature of the Canadian nation-building project. The immigration exclusions specific to racialized women were aimed at protecting the Canadian nation from the "nation reproductive" role women play. The concern was that while racialized male labour was considered transient, racialized women represented the establishment of community and roots. In analyzing the debates on "Hindu question" in the late 19th and early 20th centuries, Dua shows how the Canadian state gendered its immigration policy to forestall the possible emergence of a racialized community in Canada. In essence, the South Asian woman became a dangerous and subversive presence because of her assumed specialization in community-building. The popular debates and discourses about the threat posed by "peoples from the far east and west" very often led to public policies of exclusion. Dua quotes an ex-British army officer, an immigrant himself, as a representative voice:

> The admittance of the wives of Hindus into the province must be prohibited at any price .... if British Columbia allows Hindu women to come their presence will create a sociological problem which will be well nigh impossible of solution. If they are allowed in, the immigration of them will be impossible to control or stop. (*Victoria Daily, Colonist*, February 20, 1912). (Dua, 2000:61)[22]

South Asian women were considered dangerous because they were bearers of tradition and social values, and because they were believed to possess "extraordinary fertility." This fertility threatened to overwhelm the Canadian nation, and to alter its White character and European social values. South Asian women also represented the emergence of racialized communities with alternative forms of social organization. In that sense, they were a "plague," just as Chinese immigration was considered a "peril" to Canadian society. These debates—especially the gender debate and the concern about the potential reproduction of racialized labour force—represent an acknowledgement of the extent to which the Canadian nation has always been racialized.

The Intersection of Canadian Political Economy and Immigration Policy

[That] Canada should desire to restrict immigration from the Orient is natural; that Canada should remain a White man's country is believed to be not only desirable for economic and social reasons, but highly necessary on political and national grounds. (Excerpt from Report of W.L. Mackenzie King, C.M.G, 1908)

Canada is an underpopulated country by most standards of measurement ... there is little dissent from the proposition that Canada needs immigrants .... without a substantial continuing flow of immigrants, it is doubtful that we can sustain the high rate of economic growth and the associated cultural development which are essential to the maintenance and development of our national identity beside the economic and cultural pulls of our neighbour to the south[23]

Canada's labour-market policies correspond to the complex dynamics of population change that drive the organization of the Canadian economy. The historical demand for labour either in the urban industrial heartland, the resource-extraction hinterland, or the farming rural regions accounts for the successive waves of immigrants from around the world who have made Canada their home over the decades. Canadian immigration policy has traditionally focused on issues of labour-market demand and related dynamics (especially ensuring that the inflows do not represent a hardship to the existing workforce), total reunification and humanitarian consideration. Immigrant selection was concerned with categories of desirables and undesirables, with the assimilation of immigrants, and more recently with consideration of skills and labour-market criteria such as choice of occupations in determining eligibility.

Racial and ethnic considerations have always been key elements of Canada's immigration policy. While its primary task was always to meet the country's human-resource needs, Canada's immigration policy emerged within the context of the White-supremacist culture that informed the founding and development of the Canadian nation. At key moments in Canada's history, immigration policy clearly manifested an embedded racism perpetuated by the dominant group against those both within and without its borders.

Since 1994, Ekos Research Associates has been polling Canadians about the acceptability of racialized immigrants. In its June 2000 survey, it found that 30% of those surveyed and 45% of those intending to vote for the Alliance party felt there were too many racialized immigrants in Canada. As Li (2000) has suggested, the blatantly racist premise of the question is justified on the basis of the need to collect information about the challenge of integration for newcomers to Canada.[24] The surveys represent a continuation of racialized discourses that inform immigration policy and the debate about the nature of immigration.

What emerges then is a labour market that is not only based on social class, but is also racially stratified as a result of racially motivated policies that determine access to the Canadian labour market both for immigrants and those within Canada. Given the stated commitment by the federal government to continue labour-market-based immigration policy, it is important that we understand the place of immigration in shaping not only the Canadian political economy, but also the country itself.

As early as 1784, racial tensions and discrimination against Black workers, who objected to earning a quarter of the wages of their White counterparts, led to racial riots in the towns of Shelbourne and Birchtown in Nova Scotia, and to the exodus of over 1,200 Blacks to Sierra Leone.[25] After Confederation in 1867, many racially motivated immigration policies defined the composition of Canada's labour force for years to come. While Chinese immigrants were welcome to work on the building of the railway between 1881–1885, in 1885 the Canadian government passed the *Chinese Immigration Act*, which established the Chinese head tax. Its objective was "stemming the tide" of Chinese immigrants, who were suddenly seen as competitors for jobs performed by White workers. The amount demanded was increased to a prohibitive $500 in 1903.[26]

Additional restrictions were slapped on other racialized immigrants with a federal order-in-council in 1907 that imposed an entry minimum of $200 on South Asian immigrants. The 1908 *Continuous Passage Act* sought to further impede the immigration of South Asians, whose immigration status was superior to that of the Chinese, since they were from a country in the British Commonwealth. The act required non-stop journeys from India to Canada and nullified the right of entry to East Indians if their ship either stopped at a port en route to Canada, or if the tickets were not issued in India. An agreement between the Canadian and Japanese governments stipulated that the former would not discriminate against Japanese immigrants already in Canada if the latter restricted further immigration from Japan. These measures effectively halted the flow of immigrants from Asia.[27] Other prohibitions were imposed on Black farmers from the United States even as seasonal migrant farm workers were being routinely imported from the Caribbean in the early 1900s.

The 1910 *Immigration Act* created a class of undesirables on the basis of perceived inability to successfully integrate, because of low educational attainment, or the Canadian climate or social, educational, and labour force requirements. The administration of the act relied on the existence of a preferred-nations list, and targeted people from racialized countries and warm climates for exclusion. These considerations were clearly proxy to a racialized policy that aimed to keep Canada "White." In 1923, having failed to achieve the goal of slowing Chinese immigration through earlier legislation that imposed the head tax, the *Chinese Exclusionary Act* was enacted, prohibiting Chinese immigration to Canada until 1947. In the post-World War II era, the changes to the *Immigration Act* of 1953 still maintained demands for successful integration in Canada that were based *less* on educational attainment, and more on assumptions of inability to adjust to the Canadian climate, and on social and labour force requirements. The administration of the policy continued to rely on the existence of a preferred-nations list and particularly targeted people from racialized countries in Asia, Africa, and Latin America and the Caribbean for exclusion.[28]

The 1962 *Immigration Act* was a milestone in recent Canadian immigration history. Promulgated under the Conservative government of Prime Minister Diefenbaker, the act shifted the focus from the racially discriminatory policy of country preference to a policy of admission for skilled immigrants and reunion for families. The new policy divided immigration into three categories, removing reference to ethnicity, race, or geographical areas, although the minister retained the right to use ethnicity-based criteria. Independent-class immigrants (and accompanying family) were admitted on the basis of education, training, skills, or other such qualifications. Family class involved sponsored immigrants, with sponsors of immigrants from the United States and Europe allowed a broader range of possible relatives than those from Asia and Africa. There was also the nominated class, a hybrid of the two classes above. Immigrants in the nominated class had to have skills and qualifications in demand in the Canadian economy and also be sponsored by a relative living in Canada who promised to provide some degree of support. Because of that family support, they were evaluated against lower criteria on labour-market requirements.

The change occurred during a period of decline in immigrants from Europe, partly because of growing prosperity in European source countries. It also coincided with a time of relative international scarcity of highly trained manpower and decolonization in the global South. With economic indicators in Canada suggesting that the postwar economic boom was over — unemployment was high and investments down — Europeans were further discouraged from leaving their prosperous countries for North America. Added to that was domestic pressure to reconcile the immigration policy with human rights legislation — especially the *Canadian Bill of Rights*, 1960 — as well as come into conformity with the international recognition of human rights enshrined in the United Nations Universal Declaration of Human Rights and the various conventions and covenants of the UN Human Rights Charter.

Canada responded by opening the door to immigrants and refugees from areas outside Europe; as a result, the immigrant pool became more ethnically diverse in composition than ever before.[29] The independent category increasingly gave access to those who had skill qualifications, but were not from the preferred source countries. A growing number of talented women and men from the southern countries began to choose Canada as their new home.

In 1967, in response to the findings of the White Paper on Immigration released in 1966, the policy shift was institutionalized through the adoption of a nominally colour-blind "points system."[30] The government's introduction of the "Global Concept" regulations removed explicit racial and national preference; emphasized labour market requirements, family reunification, and humanitarian issues; and expanded the "independent or unsponsored" class through a skills-based "colour-blind" points system. Under the points system, admission is granted on the basis of an objective assessment of individual attributes, rather than on race or nationality. Two objectives of the new system were to increase the average skill level of new arrivals and to bring the immigration policy into compliance with national and international human rights regimes. The changes in policy marked an end to the country-of-origin-based admissions policy.

Since then, the ethnic and racial profile of immigrants arriving in Canada has dramatically changed. The composition of the contemporary immigration group changed partly because of the abandonment of official racist immigration policy in the 1960s. The changing global economic economy, coupled with the recovery and stability of European economies, meant that Europeans were now choosing to stay home and participate in the fruits of their reconstruction efforts. Europe's economy presented would-be migrants with real prospects, while the impact of changes in the global economy and political instability forced people from outside Europe to consider immigration to and asylum in Canada. The source countries shifted from Europe to Asia, Africa, Latin America, and the Caribbean.[31]

Between 1967 and 1974, the policy change led to a high (74%) acceptance of immigrants in the independent class—the skills-tested group. Public opinion in the 1970s prompted a shift toward a humanitarian element in the policy, which led to an increase in the family and refugee categories from 24.7% and 1.3% during 1970–1974, to 33.8% and 16.6% respectively during the 1990–1994 period. The move achieved its objective of insulating Canada from international criticism about the racial and geographical specificity of the immigration policy, which was becoming increasingly anachronistic.[32] Those changes were reflected in the passage of the *Immigration Act*, 1978, which marked an important moment in recent Canadian immigration history. Canada embraced a more open policy toward asylum seekers, which led to a substantial increase in the number of refugees admitted into the country each year. The policy had an effect on the proportion of assessed immigrants each year. Furthermore, the post-1978 regulations also eased entry requirements under family class by awarding 15 points for the presence of relatives in Canada. The changes were especially significant because the setting of the levels of family class and refugee immigrants remained independent of the needs of Canadian labour markets. The composition of the immigrant pool shifted somewhat toward what some have characterized as a less-skilled or "lower quality" pool.[33]

The recession pressures of the early 1980s forced the federal government to cut immigration levels drastically for the year 1983 and to require independent-class immigrants to present a validated job offer before their applications could be considered. The government introduced a new category of "business class" immigrants as part of the independent class in 1986; applicants under the category were required to demonstrate potential for establishing a business in Canada that would hire local Canadians.

As the economy improved, the federal government announced another significant change in 1988: the expansion of the definition of family class to include never-married sons and daughters of immigrant Canadian residents, regardless of age. However, this short-lived change was reversed in 1992 in response to a perceived drop in the skill level of immigrants.[34]

Table 3.3 summarizes the effects of the above changes on the class composition of immigrant inflows to Canada over the period 1970–1994. Changes in Canadian immigration policy have resulted in the two classes of immigrants noted below: the economically assessed classes (independent, business, and assisted relatives), and the non-economically assessed group (family class and refugees). The changing proportions and assumptions about the human capital quality of different groups are an important part of the debate over the efficacy of Canadian immigration policy.[35]

Table 3.3: Distribution of Immigrant Landings by Class, 1970–1993

	Economically Assessed Classes		Non-economically Assessed Classes	
Period of Immigration	Independent	Assisted Relatives	Family	Refugee & Designated
1970–1974	74.0	NA	24.7	1.3
1970–1974	51.0	24.4	24.6	NA
1975–1978	32.2	24.2	43.7	NA
1975–1979	47.8	NA	42.8	9.4
1980–1984	34.7	10.0	37.2	18.1
1985–1989	36.4	9.3	36.4	17.9
1990–1994	33.8	10.0	39.6	16.6

Source: Akbari (1999); de Silva (1992)

The data used here are drawn from available Department of Immigration data on immigrant arrivals by classes since 1980. For the pre-1980 period, data were taken from two different sources with slightly different groupings of immigrants in each class: pre-1979 sponsored or nominated categories. NA signifies data "not available."

In the late 20th and early 21st century, the political, economic, and social destabilization brought about by global restructuring has had a profound impact on the nature of population flows around the world. These are movements of largely but not exclusively of people from the global South to the global North. These immigrants come to seek both asylum and a better way of life. The asylum seekers are but a fraction of the over five million documented refugees running from political conflict and economic displacement and even the many more millions who are internally displaced and cannot afford the means to make the trips North. But often enough they cause waves in the receiving country. And their arrival is transforming parts of the societies in the global North. A combination of the exodus of newcomers and the unequal articulations of capitalist development that force them into conditions of disadvantage have created what are now called South in the North—mostly communities and neighbourhoods whose conditions are increasingly more like those in the South than what we have come to accept as generalized conditions in the North.[36] It has created a phenomenon that can be characterized as the racialization of neighbourhoods, and in some cases cities and regions.[37]

These developments emerge within the framework of existing racialized social structures, prompting new forms of response within the host societies. Immigration is again one of the most contentious public policy areas. Scholars have used the term *neo-racism* to explain the anti-immigrant discourses and policy actions of people in the North in response to the new migration unleashed by the displacement of entire communities by the processes of globalization. It represents a particular construction of race at the historical moment of C21 globalization and like all other forms of racism, it utilizes the social construction of racial categories to demand limits on the numbers of certain racial groups allowed into the country and on racial mixing. It describes a form of racism whose dominant theme is the insurmountability of cultural differences. It concentrates on the harmfulness of abolishing borders, the incompatibility of traditions and lifestyles. In an ironic twist, it uses the very defence of difference to justify its cultural segregationist position.[38]

In Europe as in North America, the term *immigrant* has been redefined to refer to non-Whites, especially Africans, Caribbeans, East Asian, South Asians, and Latin Americans, regardless of whether they are immigrants or born in that particular country. Immigrant status has been racialized, and the inferior status that is imposed on racialized peoples is now extended to immigrants. In consequence so much so that the quality of their human capital is called into question, with dire consequences for those with international qualifications. Balibar has suggested that this category slippage is a form of racism particular to the period of globalization because it represents a response to the reversal of population movements, a phenomenon considered dangerous by dominant populations. While its usage is more prevalent in Europe than in North America, there are signs here that confirm the prevalence of the phenomena in Canada. The spectre of competitive racism hangs over the labour market. What was old is new again.

In the early 21st century, neo-liberal restructuring of the global economy and the shift toward neo-liberal forms of governance have intensified the impact of racial hierarchies. This is compounded by labour-market deregulation, aimed at flexible labour deployment, which provokes new forms of competitive racism rooted in the historical forms of employment discrimination. Globalization has a particular impact on the experiences of racialized groups because of the growing dominance of flexible work arrangements, facilitated by the state deregulation of the labour market and the reversal of state anti-discriminatory policies and programs. This means that restructuring imposes disproportionately impact on racialized groups. The emerging prevalence of precarious forms of work in sectors where racialized groups are disproportionately employed has meant that, despite higher levels of educational attainment, disproportionate numbers of racialized workers are confined to unstable forms of work in either low-wage sectors of the economy or low-wage occupations. This has amplified racial segmentation in the labour market and racialized income inequality and poverty.

Racial segmentation in the labour market also represents an intensification of the racialization of class formation, represented by such structural patterns as income inequality and occupational segregation in the Canadian labour market (Creese, 1999; Das Gupta, 1996; Li, 1998). These processes of labour market segmentation then determine such social outcomes as differential access to housing, neighbourhood selection, contact with the criminal justice system, health risks, political participation, and other outcomes. The result is the now well-documented deepening of the processes of the racialization of poverty, and the attendant racial segregation of low-income neighbourhoods and the intensification of social exclusion, especially in Canada's urban-racialized group communities. Despite its liberal democratic traditions, these development lead to a denial of racialized men, women, and immigrants full participation in Canadian society and Canada of the full benefit of the potential of a growing proportion of Canadians.

Conclusion

Canada's population makeup is changing, and with this change arise questions about the place of racialized groups in Canada. During much of the 1990s, over 75% of Canada's newcomers were members of the racialized group communities. This shift in the composition of population change has had implications for Canada in a number of areas, not the least of which is the economy. The complex dynamics of population change are interwoven into the organization of the Canadian economy. The political economy that emerged in Canada was based on the concept of a "White-settler society." The immigration policies aimed both to maintain a viable capitalist economy as well as the "White" character of the nation. From early European attempts to take control of the land, resources, and trade from the First Nations, which involved restricting the economic participation of Aboriginal peoples, racial exclusion could be discerned from the selective importation of African American, Asian, and Caribbean labour, and continues to be a major factor in determining access to economic opportunity in Canada. Racial hierarchies became more prominent in the organization of the Canadian economy in the 1970s, as the numbers of racialized immigrants from the South became more significant.

In the early 21st century, racialized groups continue to confront a historical enemy with a new twist. Racialized communities in Canada's urban areas have grown in size. Globalization has had a particular impact on the experiences of racialized groups because of the growing dominance of flexible work arrangements, facilitated by the state deregulation of the labour market and the reversal of state anti-discriminatory policies and programs. New forms of competitive racism have emerged, along with amplified racial segmentation in the labour market and increased racialized income inequality in neighbourhood selection. Racialized Canadians have seen the impact in their ability to participate fully in Canadian life.

Notes

1. E. Kallen, *Ethnicity and Human Rights in Canada* (Toronto: Oxford University Press, 2003).

2. Statistics Canada, *2001 Census data* (2003).

3. Statistics Canada, *The Daily* (February 17, 1998). Canada Census data (Statistics Canada) since 1991 provide the most comprehensive information about the racial breakdown of Canadian society. Previous censuses asked a variety of related questions, either about ethnicity or about the ancestral country of origin. We have used all these sources to offer approximate numbers of racialized group members in the Canadian population at different times in history.

4. Statistics Canada, *The Daily* (November 4, 1997).

5. Statistics Canada, *The Daily* (April 14, 1998).

6. V. Satzewich, *Racism and the Incorporation of Foreign Labour: Farm Labour Migration to Canada Since 1945* (London: Routledge, 1991).

7. D. Stasiulis and R. Jhappan, "The Fractious Politics of a Settler Society: Canada," in *Unsettling Settler Societies*, edited by D. Stasiulis and N. Yuval-Davis (London: Sage Publications, 1995), 55–131; D. Stasiulis, "The Political Economy of Race, Ethnicity and Migration," in *Understanding Canada: Building on the New Canadian Political Economy*, edited by W. Clement (Montreal: McGill-Queen's University Press, 1997), 141–171; B.S. Bolaria and P. Li (eds.), *Racial Oppression in Canada* (Toronto: Garamond Press, 1988); J. Kage, "On the Eve of a New Canadian Immigration Act" (Toronto: Jewish Immigrant Aid Services, 1974).

8. An Ekos/*Toronto Star* poll conducted in June 2000 found that 30% of those surveyed believed that there were too many immigrants of colour in Canada; D. Palmer, "Determinants of Canadian Attitudes towards Immigration: More Than Just Racism?" *Canadian Journal of Behavioural Sciences* 28 (1996): 180–192.

9. M. Ornstein, *Ethno-Cultural Inequality in Toronto: Analysis of the 1996 Census* (Toronto: Access and Equity Unit, City of Toronto, 2000).

10. See L. Soberman, "Immigrants and the Canadian Federal Elections of 1993," in *Ethnicity, Politics and Public Policy*, edited by H. Troper and M. Weinfeld (Toronto: University of Toronto Press, 1998), 253–281.

11. Speech by Jacques Parizeau on referendum night in 1995 in which he blamed money and ethnic groups for the sovereignty loss.

12. D. Stasiulis and R. Jhappan, "The Fractious Politics of a Settler Society: Canada," in *Unsettling Settler Societies*, edited by D. Stasiulis and N. Yuval-Davis (London: Sage Publications, 1995), 55–131.

13. There is a substantial body of literature dealing with the experience of racialized minorities and their incorporation into Canadian society and into the Canadian labour market. Historically—from enslaved Blacks or largely segregated "free" Blacks in Nova Scotia, New Brunswick, Quebec, and Ontario, to Chinese railway workers in British Columbia, South Asian businessmen seeking government contracts, Japanese professionals (denied accreditation in medicine, law), Caribbean and Filipino domestics, Caribbean farm workers, and more recently immigrants from Africa, Caribbean, Latin America, Middle East, South Asia, China, Philippines—the incorporation of these groups in the Canadian

economy has been subject to their racialized status in Canada. The phenomenon speaks to the organization of the labour deployment under Canadian capitalism in ways that assure cheap sources of labour and produce a "racial" dividend for capital (Anderson and Lynam, 1987; Brand, 1987; Calliste, 1991; Daenzer, 1993; Das Gupta, 1996; Reitz, 1981, 1998).

14. Stasiulis and Jhappan (1995) suggest that the White-settler society construct may not be applicable to Canada because of the ethnic and racial diversity of the immigrant population, a diversity that prompted the construction of the racial/ethnic hierarchy. Yet it seems a European dominant variation may have been the compromise the British were prepared to live with, given the French presence and ethnic European diversity. What is clear is that the early and persistent rejection of Blacks, South Asians, East Asians, and Jews as candidates for immigration, even as the government was actively recruiting immigrants in Northern Europe, suggested a commitment to a Eurocentric settler colony.

15. Winks (1971). The outcome of this unequal treatment was desperation, destitution, race riots (which burned down the Black community quarters), and immigration for some back to Africa. The economic and social vulnerability of African Canadians in Nova Scotia to this day can be traced to those initial racist actions.

16. Systemic racism refers to the creation and use of racial categories for the purpose of engendering differential treatment and decisions that have the impact of unequal outcomes. The process involves the social construction of races as different and unequal, followed by the institutionalization of norms, processes, and a social system that generates actions and decisions that produce racial inequality.

17. R. Ng, "Racism, Sexism and Canadian Nationalism," in *Race, Class and Gender: Bonds and Barriers*, edited by J. Vorst (Toronto: Between the Lines, 1988), 10–25; D. Stasiulis, "The Fractious Politics of a Settler Society: Canada," in *Unsettling Settler Societies*, edited by D. Stasiulis and N. Yuval-Davis (London: Sage Publications, 1995), 95–131; F. Henry, C. Tator, W. Mattis, and T. Rees, *The Colour of Democracy* (Toronto: Harcourt Brace and Company, 2000).

18. See J.S. Woodsworth, *Strangers within Our Gates or Coming Canadians* (Toronto: University of Toronto Press, [1909]1972).

19. Ibid.

20. E. Balibar, "Racism and Nationalism," in *Race, Nation, Class: Ambiguous Identities*, edited by E. Balibar and I. Wallerstein (London: Verso, 1991), 37–67.

21. P. Li, "Race and Ethnicity," in *Race and Ethnic Relations in Canada*, edited by P. Li (London: Oxford University Press, 1999), 3–20; E. Dua, "The Hindu Woman's Question: Canadian Nation Building and Social Construction of Gender for South Asian Women," in *Anti-Racist Feminism*, edited by A. Calliste and G. Sefa Dei (Halifax: Fernwood Publishing, 2000), 55–72; M. Omi and H. Winant, "On the Theoretical Status of the Concept of Race," in *Race, Identity and Representation in Education*, edited by C. McCarthy and W. Crichlow (New York: Routledge, 1993), 3–10.

22. Dua (2000).

23. Government of Canada, "The White Paper on Immigration: Canadian Immigration Policy (Ottawa: Department of Manpower and Immigration, 1966).

24. Ekos Research/*Toronto Star* Survey, June 2000.

25. J. Walker, *The History of Blacks in Canada* (Ottawa: Minister of State for Multiculturalism, 1980); R. Winks, *Blacks in Canada* (New Haven: Yale University Press, 1971); B. Sheppard, "Plain Racism, the Reaction against Oklahoma Black Immigration to the Canadian Plains,"

in *Racism in Canada*, edited by O. McKague (Saskatoon: Fifth House, 1991), 15–31; V. Satzewich, *Racism and the Incorporation of Foreign Labour: Farm Labour Migration to Canada Since 1945* (London: Routledge, 1991).

26. P. Li, *The Chinese in Canada* (Toronto: Oxford University Press, 1998).

27. T. Cohen, *Race Relations and the Law* (Toronto: Canadian Jewish Congress, 1987); R. Sampat-Mehta, "The First Fifty Years of South Asian Immigration: A Historical Perspective," in *South Asians in the Canadian Mosaic*, edited by R. Kanungo (Montreal: Kala Bharati, 1984), 13–31 ; K. Ujimoto, "Racial Discrimination and Internment: Japanese in Canada," in *Racial Oppression in Canada*, edited S. Bolaria and P. Li (Toronto: Garamond Press, 1988), 126–160. These policy decisions reflected a pattern that was to become prevalent in Canadian immigration policy. As Bloom et al. have observed, Canada's immigration policy has traditionally accommodated public opinion. See D. Bloom, G. Grenier, and M. Gunderson, "The Changing Labour Market Position of Canadian Immigrants," Working paper No. 4672 (National Bureau of Economic Research, Inc., 1994).

28. D. Stasiulis and R. Jhappan, "The Fractious Politics of a Settler Society: Canada," in *Unsettling Settler Societies*, edited by D. Stasiulis and N. Yuval-Davis (London: Sage Publications, 1995), 55–131; F. Henry, C. Tator, W. Mattis, and T. Rees, *The Colour of Democracy: Racism in Canadian Society* (Toronto: Harcourt Brace, 1995); M. Weinfeld and L. Wilkinson, "Immigration, Diversity, and Minority Communities," in *Race and Ethnic Relations in Canada*, 55–87, edited by P. Li (1999).

29. Li, (2003); M. Kalbach and W. Kalbach, "Demographic Overview of Ethic Origin Groups in Canada," in *Race and Ethnic Relations in Canada*, edited by P. Li (Oxford: Oxford University Press, 1999), 21–49; M. Weinfeld and L. Wilkinson, "Immigration, Diversity, and Minority Communities," in *Race and Ethnic Relations in Canada*, edited by P. Li (Toronto: Oxford University Press, 1999), 55–87.

30. "The White Paper on Immigration: Canadian Immigration Policy" (Ottawa: Department of Manpower and Immigration, 1966).

31. D. Bloom and M. Gunderson, "An Analysis of the Earnings of Canadian Immigrants," in *Immigration, Trade, and the Labour Market*, edited by J. Abowd and R.B. Freeman (Chicago: University of Chicago Press, 1991), 321–342; C.J. Bruce, *Economics of Employment and Earnings* (Toronto: Nelson Canada, 1995); D. Bloom, G. Grenier, and M. Gunderson, "The Changing Labour Market Position of Canadian Immigrants," Working Paper No. 4672 (Ottawa: National Bureau of Economic Research, 1994); A. De Silva, *Earnings of Immigrants: A Comparative Analysis* (Economic Council of Canada, 1992).

32. A. Akbari, "Immigrant 'Quality' in Canada: More Direct Evidence of Human Capital Content, 1956–1994," *International Migration Review* 33, no. 1 (Spring 1999): 156–175.

33. A. Green and D. Green, "Canadian Immigration Policy: The Effectiveness of the Point System and Other Instruments," *Canadian Journal of Economic* 28 (1995): 1006–1041; F. Hawkins, *Critical Years in Immigration: Canada and Australia Compared* (Montreal: McGill-Queen's University Press, 1991).

34. Akbari (1999).

35. Akbari (1999); Baker and Benjamin (1994); Green and Green (1995); D. Bloom, G. Grenier, and M. Gunderson, "The Changing Labour Market Position of Canadian Immigrants," *Canadian Journal of Economics* 28, no. 4 (1995): 987–1005; A. de Silva (1992); S. Laryea,

"Economic Participation: Unemployment and Labour Displacement (Vancouver: CIC, Metropolis Project, 1998).

36. Sassen (1998).

37. A. Kazemipur and S. Halli, *The New Poverty* (Toronto: Thomson Educational Publishing, 2000).

38. E. Balibar, "Is There a Neo-Racism," in *Race, Nation, Class: Ambiguous Identities*, edited by E. Balibar and I. Wallerstein (London: Verso, 1991), 17–28.

Questions for Critical Thought

1. Historically, how have government policies such as immigration been used to create different classes of citizenship in Canada?
2. Was Canadian immigration policy racist? What are some of the events that support that contention?
3. What was the major motivation behind the shift to a skill-based immigration system?
4. What are some examples of how anti-immigration debates influence Canada's immigration policy?
5. Historically, how have racialized groups been incorporated into the Canadian labour market?
6. How would you describe the concept of a colour-coded vertical mosaic?

Recommended Readings

Daenzer, P. *Regulating Class Privilege: Immigrant Servants in Canada, 1940–1990s.* Toronto: Canadian Scholars' Press, 1993.

Government of Canada. *The White Paper on Immigration: Canadian Immigration Policy.* Ottawa: Department of Manpower and Immigration, 1966.

Li, P. *The Chinese in Canada.* Toronto: Oxford University Press, 1998.

Ng, R. "Racism, Sexism and Canadian Nationalism," in *Race, Class and Gender: Bonds and Barriers*, by R. Ng. Toronto: Between the Lines, 1988.

Ornstein, M. *Ethno-Cultural Inequality in Toronto: Analysis of the 1996 Census.* Toronto: Access and Equity Unit, City of Toronto, 2000.

Ranumgo, R. (ed.). *South Asians in the Canadian Mosaic.* Montreal: Kala Bharati, 1984.

Satzewich, V. *Racism and the Incorporation of Foreign Labour: Farm Labour Migration to Canada Since 1945.* London: Routledge, 1991.

Schecter, T. *Race, Class, Women and the State: The Case of Domestic Labour.* Montreal: Black Rose Books, 1998.

Stasiulis, D., and R. Jhappan. "The Fractious Politics of a Settler Society: Canada," in *Unsettling Settler Societies*, edited by D. Stasiulis and N. Yuval-Davis. London: Sage Publications, 1995, 55–131.

Ujimoto, K. "Racial Discrimination and Internment: Japanese in Canada," in *Racial Oppression in Canada*, edited by S. Bolaria and P. Li. Toronto: Garamond Press, 1988, 126–160.

Walker, J. *The History of Blacks in Canada*. Ottawa: Minister of State for Multiculturalism, 1980.

Winks, R. *Blacks in Canada*. New Haven: Yale University Press, 1971.

CHAPTER 4

The Economic Exclusion of Racialized Communities— A Statistical Profile

Introduction

We now turn our attention to the statistical profile of the racialized gap in social economic status. Economic exclusion can be discerned using a variety of indicators. Here we focus on two concepts central to understanding the process and its outcomes: access to work and compensation for work. These translate into three variables — income attainment, unemployment, and labour-market participation.

Wage rate differentials are considered the summary statistics that best characterize the labour-market disadvantages of paid workers in an identifiable group. Most studies that have dealt with the racialized income differentials have tended to use market income or wage rates of immigrant and racialized groups for their analysis. Included here are two important literature reviews by De Silva (1992) and Akbari (1989).[1] More recent work includes studies by Akbari (1992, 1999); Anisef, Sweet, James, and Lin (1999); Beach and Worswick (1993); Christofides and Swidinsky (1994); Baker and Benjamin (1994); Hou and Balakrishnan (1996); de Silva (1997); Kunz et al. (2000); Pendakur and Pendakur (1996, 1998); Ornstein (1996, 2000); and Stelcner (2000).[2]

In this chapter we use three important measures of economic performance for racialized groups, both immigrant and Canadian-born: unemployment, labour-market participation, and employment income. This approach gives a fuller picture of the condition of racialized group members in the Canadian economy. It also allows us to shift the emphasis away from the debate about measures of discrimination in income and toward a more rounded assessment of the contribution of structures of racial discrimination to the disadvantaged position of the racialized group in the labour market and ultimately in society. The approach also acknowledges other complex factors responsible for the disadvantage, including prolonged periods of economic downturn, mismatched skill sets, and length of stay in the country. These factors are also likely to be experienced by non-racialized group members, although not necessarily in the same way. The other benefit of this approach is that it allows the analysis to draw from broader research done on the employment barriers faced by racialized group members and the income implications of those barriers.

Using both the income and employment measures, we identify a gap between the economic performance of the racialized communities and the rest of the Canadian population. In fact, some data show that among some groups the income gap is growing and income inequality in Canada is increasingly along racial lines. The 1995 Statistics Canada for individual earners data show that about 10% of all people who reported employment income in 1995 (about 1.5 million individuals) were members of the racialized population. According to that data, in 1995 racialized group members' employment income was $22,498, 15% lower than the national average. Employment earnings of immigrants arriving from 1986 to 1990 were $21,538, or 18% of the earnings of non-immigrants. For more recent immigrants, coming after 1990, the employment income was $16,673, or 36% of that of non-immigrants. This gap also coincided with general cutbacks in the levels of government transfers, either in federal employment insurance benefits or provincial social assistance benefits, during much of the 1990s.[3] For racialized women, average earnings were $16,621 in 1996, compared to $23,635 for racialized men, $19,495 for other women, and $31,951 for other men.[4]

Table 4.1: Canada: Income of Racialized Group Individuals, 1995

	Total Population	Racialized Group	Difference %
Average	$27,170	$22,498	18%

Source: Statistics Canada, 1996 Census data, available at www12.statscan.ca/english/
    census01/home/index.cfm.

Racialized Groups as a Statistical Category[5]

The members of a racialized group correspond to the group defined as such in Statistics Canada data, using the term *visible minority*, as defined by the *Employment Equity Act* of 1986. The act defines "visible minorities" as "persons, other than Aboriginal peoples, who are non-Caucasian in race or non-white in colour." Under this definition, the act's regulations specify the following groups as visible minorities: Chinese, South Asians, Blacks, Arabs and West Asians, Filipinos, Southeast Asians, Latin Americans, Japanese, Koreans, and Pacific Islanders. In the 1996 census, the identification of the racialized group population was achieved using a new census question that asked respondents whether they were members of one of the population groups defined as a visible minority under the provisions of the *Employment Equity Act*. In previous censuses, this information had been derived primarily from responses to the question on ethnic or cultural origin. In this report, we have supplemented some of that data by looking at source-country data as it relates to immigrant populations, especially after 1970.

Data Confirms Unequal Employment Income of Racialized Group Members

Based on a set of special runs of Survey of Labour Income Dynamics data done for the Centre for Social Justice for 1996–1998, we conclude that racialized groups suffer a considerable disadvantage in employment income in the Canadian labour market.[6] This data, based on individual earnings before taxes, shows that in 1996, racialized Canadians earned an average of $19,227; non-racialized Canadians made $25,069, or 23% lower. The 1996 median before-tax income gap at 29% ($13,648 to $19,111) shows an even more profound inequality because it factors out the highest and lowest earners. This gap grew in 1997 as earnings of racialized individuals increased slightly to $19,558, a gap of 25% when compared to the $25,938 earned by other Canadians. The median before-tax income again betrays a widening inequality, with earnings of $13,413 for racialized groups and $19,602 for others, or a gap of 32%. The tax and government transfers' effect was marginal in terms of closing the gap. The average after-tax income of the racialized groups in 1996 was $16,053, compared to $20,129 for other Canadians, a 20% gap. After-tax incomes grew for both groups in 1997 to $16,438 for racialized individuals, or 79% of the $20,793 for other Canadians, with incomes still showing a marginal growing gap. The median after-tax income for 1996 was $12,991 for racialized groups compared to $16,922 for other Canadians, a gap of

23%. That gap grew in 1997 to 26%, as racialized group individuals took home less at $12,895, while other Canadians increased their earnings to $17,320.[7]

On average, the improving economy resulted in only a marginal change, with 1998 figures showing an average before-tax income for racialized groups of $20,626, which accounted for 74% of the $27,174 for the rest of the population. The median incomes of $14,507 (racialized) compared to $20,517 (non-racialized) left the gap at 30%. Taking the tax and government transfers into consideration, racialized groups

Table 4.2: Canada: Income of Racialized Persons, 1996, before Tax

	Total Population	Racialized Group (a)	Non-racialized Group (b)	Difference (a/b) $	%
Average	24,254	19,227	22,092	2,865	23
Median	18,304	13,648	19,111	5,463	29

Source: Centre for Social Justice special run of data, Statistics Canada, *Survey of Labour and Income Dynamics, 1996–2000,* 2001.

Table 4.3: Canada: Income of Racialized Persons, 1996, after Tax

	Total Population	Racialized Group (a)	Non-racialized Group (b)	Difference (a/b) $	%
Average	19,631	16,053	20,129	4,076	20
Median	16,394	12,991	16,922	3,931	23

Source: Centre for Social Justice special run of data, Statistics Canada, *Survey of Labour and Income Dynamics, 1996–2000,* 2001.

Table 4.4: Canada: Income of Racialized Persons, 1997, before Tax

	Total Population	Racialized Group (a)	Non-racialized Group (b)	Difference (a/b) $	%
Average	25,126	19,558	25,938	6,380	25
Median	18,762	13,413	19,602	6,189	31.5

Source: Centre for Social Justice special run of data, Statistics Canada, *Survey of Labour and Income Dynamics, 1996–2000,* 2001.

Table 4.5: Canada: Income of Racialized Persons, 1997, after Tax

	Total Population	Racialized Group (a)	Non-racialized Group (b)	Difference (a/b) $	%
Average	20,224	16,438	20,793	4,355	21
Median	16,756	12,895	17,320	4,425	25.5

Source: Centre for Social Justice special run of data, Statistics Canada, *Survey of Labour and Income Dynamics, 1996–2000,* 2001.

Table 4.6: Canada: Income of Racialized Persons, 1998, before Tax

	Total Population	Racialized Group (a)	Non-racialized Group (b)	Difference (a/b) $	Difference (a/b) %
Average	26,323	20,626	27,174	6,548	26
Median	19,700	14,507	20,517	5,650	28

Source: Centre for Social Justice special run of data, Statistics Canada, *Survey of Labour and Income Dynamics, 1996–2000,* 2001.

Table 4.7: Canada: Income of Racialized Persons, 1998, after Tax

	Total Population	Racialized Group (a)	Non-racialized Group (b)	Difference (a/b) $	Difference (a/b) %
Average	21,114	17,376	21,694	4,318	20
Median	17,501	13,561	18,146	4,585	25.3

Source: Centre for Social Justice special run of data, Statistics Canada, *Survey of Labour and Income Dynamics, 1996–2000,* 2001.

earned an after-tax average of $17,376, 80% of the $21,694 for the rest of the population. The median after-tax income was $13,561, compared to $18,146, or 25% lower.

Some have speculated that the income gap is a function of low educational attainment. However, an analysis of the 1998 high school and post-secondary educational levels shows that the gap between low and highly educated groups is similar, ranging from 22–24%. From the employment income data for the year 1998, we are also able to deduce that the proportion of the university-educated racialized population in the top 10% of earners is also much lower, 20.6% compared to 31% for the non-racialized population.

Tables 4.8 and 4.9 seem to confirm the structural nature of these income inequalities. Racialized group members are consistently overrepresented in the lower-income percentiles and underrepresented in the higher-income percentiles. Clearly the gap between racialized groups' incomes and those of non-racialized groups is an ugly reality of Canadian life.

A decile analysis of the income data confirms the racial stratification by income. With minor variations, racialized groups are disproportionately concentrated in the lower five income deciles (61.1%) as compared to the rest of the population (49%). The income gap is largely maintained when one considers disposable (after-tax) income, suggesting that the tax effect has not sufficiently compensated for the inequality generated in the market. These patterns are repeated for racialized groups in 1997 (60.5%) and 1998 (60.5%). The lowest decile also represents the highest single number of racialized group members: 15.9% in 1996, 15.9% in 1997, and 15.4% in 1998. The figures also hold true for highly educated groups, varying only slightly.

Table 4.8: Canada: Average Income of Persons by Educational Levels, 1998

Educational Level	Total Population	Racialized Group (a)	Non-racialized Group(b)	Difference (a/b) $	%
Less than high school	14,171	11,341	14,447	3,106	22
University degree	31,408	24,484	32,074	7,590	24

Source: Centre for Social Justice special run of data from Statistics Canada, *Survey of Labour and Income Dynamics, 1996–2000*, 2001.

Table 4.9: Canada: Median Income of Persons by Educational Levels, 1998

Educational Level	Total Population	Racialized Group (a)	Non-racialized Group(b)	Difference (a/b) $	%
Less than High School	12,414	9,727	12,666	2,939	24
University degree	31,408	24,485	32,074	7,589	24

Source: Centre for Social Justice special run of data from Statistics Canada, *Survey of Labour and Income Dynamics, 1996–2000*, 2001.

Table 4.10: Canada: Income of Racialized Persons by Select Deciles, 1996. Before Tax—1 is the Lowest and 10 the Highest

Deciles	Total Population	Racialized Group (a)	Non-racialized Group (b)	Difference (a/b) %
1st	10	15.9	9.2	6.7
2nd	10	12.8	9.6	3.2
3rd	10	11.3	9.8	1.5
4th	10	10.2	9.9	0.3
5th	10	10.9	10.0	−0.9
6th	10	8.5	10.1	−1.6
7th	10	9.1	10.0	−0.9
8th	10	8.3	10.3	−2.0
9th	10	7.1	10.4	−3.3
10th	10	5.8	10.6	−5.8

Source: Centre for Social Justice special run of data from Statistics Canada, *Survey of Labour and Income Dynamics, 1996–2000*, 2001.

Table 4.11: Canada: Income of Racialized Persons by Select Deciles, 1996, after Tax

Deciles	Total Population	Racialized Group (a)	Non-racialized Group (b)	Difference (a/b) %
1st	10	15.9	9.2	6.7
2nd	10	12.8	9.6	3.2
3rd	10	11.4	9.8	1.6
4th	10	10.2	9.9	0.3
5th	10	10.5	10.0	−0.5
6th	10	8.9	10.1	−1.2
7th	10	8.2	10.2	−2.0
8th	10	8.3	10.3	−2.0
9th	10	7.6	10.3	−2.7
10th	10	6.4	10.5	−4.1

Source: Centre for Social Justice special run of data from Statistics Canada, *Survey of Labour and Income Dynamics, 1996–2000*, 2001.

Table 4.12: Canada: Income of Racialized Persons by Select Deciles, 1997, before Tax

Deciles	Total Population	Racialized Group (a)	Non-racialized Group (b)	Difference (a/b) %
1st	10	15.4	9.3	6.1
2nd	10	13.6	9.6	4.0
3rd	10	12.9	9.6	3.3
4th	10	9.7	9.9	−0.2
5th	10	8.9	10.1	−1.2
6th	10	8.6	10.1	−1.5
7th	10	9.4	10.0	−0.6
8th	10	8.0	10.3	−2.3
9th	10	6.9	10.5	−3.6
10th	10	6.6	10.5	−3.9

Source: Centre for Social Justice special run of data from Statistics Canada, *Survey of Labour and Income Dynamics, 1996–2000*, 2001.

A labour-market structure with an overrepresentation of racialized groups in low-income occupations and sectors, and underrepresentation in highly paid occupations and sectors is bound to produce the documented gap in employment income. Any explanation of the income gap needs to address these racialized labour-market inequalities.

Table 4.13: Canada: Income of Racialized Persons by Select Deciles, 1998, before Tax

Deciles	Total Population	Racialized Group (a)	Non-racialized Group (b)	Difference (a/b) %
1st	10	14.8	9.1	5.7
2nd	10	12.7	9.7	3.0
3rd	10	12.7	9.7	3.0
4th	10	10.6	9.9	0.7
5th	10	9.7	10.0	−0.3
6th	10	9.1	10.0	−0.9
7th	10	8.3	10.3	−2.0
8th	10	8.2	10.3	−2.1
9th	10	7.1	10.4	−3.3
10th	10	6.8	10.5	−3.7

Source: Tables 4.10–4.13, Centre for Social Justice special run of data from Statistics Canada, *Survey of Labour and Income Dynamics, 1996–2000,* 2001.

Racialized Group Earnings and Unionization

As Table 4.14 shows, the only category with a single-digit gap between racialized and non-racialized employee incomes is the unionized sector. The average wages of racialized unionized workers are also comparable to those of employees with university degrees, suggesting that unionization is a serious non-governmental option to deal with the income gap between Canadians of colour and those of European origin. Yet the challenge there is significant too, given that racialized group members are underrepresented in unionized work. Of the 2,905,100 unionized workers in Canada, only 203,100 are racialized group members, or 7% of the union population (as compared to 11.4% in the population).

Table 4.14: Employment Income of Full-Year/Full-Time Racialized Persons in Unionized Workplaces before Taxes, 1998

	Total Population	Racialized Group (a)	Non-racialized Group (b)	Difference (a/b) $	%
Average	44,451	41,253	44,919	3,666	8%
Median	41,450	38,755	42,000	3,245	7%

Source: Centre for Social Justice specially run of data from the Statistics Canada, *Survey of Labour and Income Dynamics, 1996–2000,* 2001.

In a broader framework, what is the impact of unionization on access to the labour market for racialized group members, both Canadian-born and immigrant? A study by Reitz and Verma (2000), dealing with the union coverage of racialized group members based on an analysis of 1994 Survey of Labour and Income Dynamics data, concludes that racialized men have much lower levels of unionization than other men while the levels for women were only marginally lower. Controlling for such factors as gender, recent immigration, education, and occupation, they suggest that employment discrimination affects access to union jobs, especially in certain occupations and industries. The result is a lower unionization rate among racialized group members.[8]

While Reitz and Breton conclude that unionization may not mitigate racial discrimination in the workplace, the findings presented here suggest otherwise. The segregated nature of racialized group participation in the labour market, the overrepresentation in certain sectors, industries, and occupation (many non-unionized and lower paid), would suggest potential improvements of wage levels should those sectors be unionized. Similarly, increased access for racialized group members to sectors, industries, and occupations that are heavily unionized should improve their employment income. Even Reitz and Breton cite studies in the United States that suggest that unionization benefits workers from vulnerable groups like young people and low-skilled people, including African Americans. While their study is not conclusive as to whether that would be the case in Canada (they looked only at 1994 data), it can be speculated that unionization would indeed help workers in precarious forms of work like garment-making, harvesting, kitchen and food service, and some retailing.

Another related issue regards union rules dealing with entry into unionized workplaces; such provisions as seniority represent a barrier to access to and retention of regulated, well-paid work. Reitz and Breton's research would suggest that such barriers do exist, but that the level of impact is unclear. It is also the case that those last hired are usually the most vulnerable, having the least job security. However, labour-market regulation and union rules also protect workers from employers' arbitrary exercise of power, and would benefit racialized group members as their levels of unionization improve.

Making Sense of the Numbers

Regarding the observable income differentials between racialized and non-racialized groups, a Statistics Canada analysis concluded that compensating for the key differences between racialized and other Canadian-born earners, such as age, frequency of work, and patterns of labour market participation, reduces the gap between their average employment income from about 30% to 4%.[9] The conclusion raises as many questions as it attempts to answer. It is not clear that we can "compensate" for many of the differences because that assumption ignores the reality that racialized groups experience those variables because of discriminatory structures in the labour market that impede access to full-time, permanent employment. Those variables may reflect the discriminatory effect. From their study, Christofides and Swidinsky (1994) concluded that "raw, unedited evidence" supports the contention that racialized group members, like women, Aboriginal peoples, and people with disabilities, are disadvantaged in the Canadian labour market. These disadvantages derive from discriminatory treatment and account for a significant portion of their inferior income.

Their research, using Employment and Immigration data from 1990 and Statscan Canada Labour Market Activity Survey (LMAS) data from 1989, confirms that racialized group members were more likely, on average, to be paid less than other comparable employees.[10] A further analysis, using the Ordinary Least Squares (OLS) wage regression, demonstrated that "substantial portions of the observed differentials cannot be explained by productivity differences alone." According to Christofides and Swidinsky, these account for 30% of the wage gap. They attribute the unexplained residuals to labour-market discrimination.[11] These findings are consistent with those in a number of other studies, including Li (1988), Reitz and Breton (1994), Gosine (2000), Hou and Balakrishnan (1996), and Wanner (1998).[12]

Their research indicates that the labour-market disadvantages of racialized women are especially acute. It also suggests that racialized group members not engaged in regular paid employment routinely face particularly low wage offers—a condition confirmed by anecdotal evidence from those working for temporary employment agencies. A report by the Toronto-based Contingent Worker Project found that close to 70% of those surveyed from a pool of temporary agency workers, most of whom were racialized minorities, earned less than $1,500 a month.[13] These findings are consistent with Fernando Mata's work, which shows that "Immigrants, visible minorities and Aboriginal groups are experiencing great difficulty in terms of socio-economic integration. They are affected by higher unemployment rates, lower incomes and are more likely to be concentrated in manual jobs than other groups."[14] Akbari's (1989, 1999) examination of discrimination in employment experienced by racialized immigrants confirms these findings, as do numerous studies, some quoted above, dealing with inequality in employment.

The Income Gap between Racialized and Non-racialized Immigrants Is Growing

Fully 80% of racialized community earners were immigrants, most having arrived after 1965. For the racialized immigrant population, except for the immigrants who arrived in the period between 1956 and 1965, average employment income was lower than that of other immigrants, and the gap grew. More recent immigrants, a majority of whom are racialized group members, have significantly lower earnings. According to 1996 Census data, the average employment income of immigrants who came between 1986 and 1990 was 18% lower than that of non-immigrants. The average employment income of the most recent immigrants, those who came after 1990, was 36% lower than the average earnings of non-immigrants.[15] It is clear that, within almost every period of immigration, this gap grows, from about 2% for 1966–1975 immigrants to 28% for the most recent immigrants. Given the debate outlined previously about the immigration factor in explaining income differentials, it is instructive that the income differential extends to immigrant groups (see Table 4.25).

The Racialized Gap in 2000

There have been some changes since the late 1990s. An analysis of employment income for the year 2000 shows that while racialized group members made gains towards the end of the century, the patterns of inequality persists. In 2000, there was a significant increase in the median before- and after-tax income of racialized persons – 25.1% and 22.5% respectively (average after-tax increase 28.5%), an increase significantly above that of the non-racialized median before- and after-tax income at 7% and 8.4% respectively (average after-tax increase 16.9%).

While the income gap between racialized and non-racialized individual earners diminished over that period, it remained at significant levels and continues to be an important indicator of racial inequality in the Canadian labour market. While the median after-tax income of racialized persons was 23.2% lower than that of non-racialized persons in 1996, the gap fell to 13.3% in 2000 (Table 4.15). The median before-tax income gap fell from 28.6% in 1996 to 16.5% in 2000. While the size and persistence of the gap suggest a continuing problem with income inequality in the Canadian labour market for racialized groups, the higher rates of increase among racialized groups in 2000 point to a time lag in access to the benefits of the expansion of the Canadian economy over that period, an indicator of structural discrimination in employment. Some of that time lag can be explained by the "immigration effect," yet its size compares unfavourably to previous immigration periods.

Table 4.15: After-Tax Income of Racialized Persons, Canada, 2000

	Total Population	Racialized (a)	Non-racialized (b)	Difference $	Difference %
Average	23,023	20,627	23,522	2,895	12.3
Median	18,138	15,909	18,348	2,439	13.3

Source: Statistics Canada, Income Statistics Division, *Survey of Labour and Labour and Income Dynamics, Custom Tables, 1999–2002,* 2001.

There were also patterns of income disparity observable among cohorts with post-secondary education, who have an average after-tax income gap of 8.5%, and a 14.6% median after-tax income gap as well as among cohorts with less than high school education, who have average after-tax income gap of 22.6%, and a 20.6% median after-tax income gap (see Tables 4.16 and 4.17).

Time-lag trends are also observable among both the low-skilled and high-skilled groups. The increase in median after-tax incomes for university-educated racialized group members was 17.0% compared to 7.6% for non-racialized. Average after tax increases were 38.2% for racialized compared to 14.2% among non-racialized university educated (1997 and 2000 SLID data).

A decile breakdown confirms that racialized persons are overrepresented in the lower-income deciles, while non-racialized persons are overrepresented in the upper-income deciles (see Table 4.18).

Table 4.16: After-Tax Income of Racialized Persons, University Degree, Canada, 2000

	Total Population	Racialized (a)	Non-racialized (b)	Difference (a-b) $	%
Average	38,312	35,617	38,919	3,302	8.5
Median	32,832	28,378	33,230	4,852	14.6

Source: Statistics Canada, Income Statistics Division, *Survey of Labour, and Labour and Income Dynamics, Custom Tables, 1999–2002*, 2005.

Table 4.17: After-Tax Income of Racialized Persons, Less Than High School, Canada, 2000

	Total Population	Racialized (a)	Non-racialized (b)	Difference (a-b) $	%
Average	15,125	11,958	15,444	3,486	22.6
Median	12,955	10,378	13,068	2,690	20.6

Source: Statistics Canada, Income Statistics Division, *Survey of Labour, and Labour and Income Dynamics, Custom Tables, 1999–2002*, 2005.

Table 4.18: After-Tax Income of Racialized Persons by Select Deciles, Canada, 2000—1 Is the Lowest and 10 Is the Highest

Deciles	Total Population	Racialized (a)	Non-racialized (b)	Differences (a-b) %
1st	10	15.4	9.3	6.1
2nd	10	11.4	9.7	1.7
3rd	10	11.4	9.7	1.7
4th	10	8.7	10.1	−1.4
5th	10	9.9	10.0	−0.1
6th	10	8.8	10.2	−1.4
7th	10	9.7	10.1	−0.4
8th	10	8.6	10.2	−1.6
9th	10	8.4	10.3	−1.9
10th	10	7.7	10.4	−2.7

Source: Statistics Canada, Income Statistics Division, *Survey of Labour, and Labour and Income Dynamics, Custom Tables, 2002*.

There is some convergence between racialized and non-racialized female incomes, although racialized female-led families show a greater number of earners per household. See Table 4.19.

Table 4.19: After-Tax Income of Racialized, Female Persons, Canada, 2000

	Total Population	Racialized (a)	Non-racialized (b)	Difference $	Difference %
Average	18,267	17,250	18,476	1,226	6.6
Median	14,495	14,534	14,543	9	0.1

Source: Statistics Canada, Income Statistics Division, *Survey of Labour, and Labour and Income Dynamics,* Custom Tables, 2002.

While the inequalities occur in all age groups, they are especially deep among the male youth cohort (16–24 years) where the median after-tax income gap in 2000 was 38.6% and the average income was 42.3%, an increase from the 1997 rates of 37.2% and 32.2% respectively (Table 4.20). While not as high, it was also significant among the over-65 group at an average of 28.5% and a median of 21.2% (Table 4.21).

Table 4.20: After-Tax Income of Racialized, Male Persons (Ages 16–24), Canada, 2000

	Total Population	Racialized (a)	Non-racialized (b)	Difference $	Difference %
Average	9,564	6,165	10,036	3,871	38.6
Median	7,434	4,314	7,477	3,163	42.3

Source: Statistics Canada, Income Statistics Division, *Survey of Labour, and Labour and Income Dynamics,* Custom Tables, 2002.

Table 4.21: After-Tax Income of Racialized, Male Persons Age 65 and over, Canada, 2000

	Total Population	Racialized (a)	Non-racialized (b)	Difference (a-b) $	Difference (a-b) %
Average	23,458	17,191	24,060	6,869	28.5
Median	19,669	15,626	19,841	4,215	21.2

Source: Statistics Canada, Income Statistics Division, *Survey of Labour, and Labour and Income Dynamics,* Custom Tables, 2002.

On the other hand, the gap among females aged 16–24 years was more modest at 15.4% median after tax and 5.8% average after tax (Table 4.22).

Again in 2000, a key area of convergence is among unionized workers, where the median before- and after-tax income gap is minimal, although the racialized population is still underrepresented in the ranks of unionized workers (see Table 4.23).

Table 4.22: After-Tax Income of Racialized, Female Persons Age 16–24, Canada, 2000

	Total Population	Racialized (a)	Non-racialized (b)	Difference $	Difference %
Average	8,509	8,057	8,552	495	5.8
Median	6,739	5,705	6,743	1,038	15.4

Source: Statistics Canada, Income Statistics Division, *Survey of Labour, and Labour and Income Dynamics,* Custom Tables, 2002.

Table 4.23: After-Tax Income of Persons with Full-Year/Full-Time Unionized, Canada, 2000

	Total Population	Racialized (a)	Non-racialized (b)	Difference $	Difference %
Average	35,851	33,780	36,038	2,258	6.3
Median	34,360	33,040	34,418	1,378	4.0

Source: Statistics Canada, Income Statistics Division, *Survey of Labour, and Labour and Income Dynamics,* Custom Tables, 2002.

Immigration and Income Differentials

According to the 1996 census, in 1995, four of every five racialized group earners were immigrants, with almost all arriving after 1965. Of the 2.8 million immigrants who reported employment income, 1.5 million identified as members of racialized groups. While it is still the case that immigrant earnings vary according to period of immigration, there are troubling signs when racialized immigrant earning patterns are considered. Compared to non-racialized immigrants, and also considering compensation in relation to educational attainment, there are significant differentials suggesting the impact of racial discrimination in job attainment and compensation. The overall 1996 immigrant income average was reported at $27,684, which is 5.7% higher than that of non-immigrant Canadians, at $26,193. Much of the positive differential is attributed to higher educational attainment than that of non-immigrants, and a higher average of older earners (42 years to 36 years). An important part of this picture is the earnings of the mostly European pre-1976 immigrants group. Key differences begin to emerge when one focuses on racialized immigrant group employment income. While for the total immigrant population, the average income was $23,928, the racialized immigrant population earned only $18,044.[16]

Tracking immigrant income by period indicates the extent of the racialization factor. Looking at a period during which racialized group immigration has intensified, i.e., post-1986, we find that the employment income for immigrants arriving between 1986 and 1990 was $21,538, or 18% lower than the income of non-immigrants. The employment income level falls further for those arriving between 1990–1995, to $16,673, or 36% of the non-immigrant income. While it can be argued that the key variable here is period of stay, there are two reasons why that explanation is inadequate. First, the average income of racialized immigrants is lower than that of non-racialized immigrants during both the pre-1986 and post-1986 periods. The critical periods for our purposes are 1986–1990 and 1991–1995. The employment incomes of non-racialized immigrants for the periods 1986–1990 and 1991–1995 were $24,533 and $20,809 respectively, compared to $19,960 and $15,042 respectively for racialized immigrants. The second reason is that these patterns of difference are consistent with those of racialized non-immigrants, i.e., Canadian-born racialized earners. Their employment income for 1995 was $18,565, or 30% lower than that of other Canadian earners.[17]

Table 4.24 shows the decline in income attainment over the last 10 years among university-educated immigrants, for both the most recent immigrants as well as the 10-year resident, relative to a similarly educated Canadian population over the same period. According to the data, after one year in Canada, in 1990, a male immigrant with a university degree earned 55.8% ($33,673) of his male Canadian-born counterpart's income, while a female immigrant earned 56.6% ($21,059) of her female counterpart's. By 2000, that amount had fallen to 47.3% ($31,460) and 48.3% ($19,829) respectively. For those who had lived in the country for 10 years, the gap had not closed as was the case in the pre-1980s immigration class; rather, immigrants still lagged behind at 86.2% ($52,060) for males and 87.3% ($32,522) for females in 1990. Even more importantly, by 2000, the gap had grown to 28.6% among males and 20.9% among females. In both cases, while the incomes of immigrant graduates declined, those of the Canadian-born cohort grew, from $60,375 for males in 1990 to $66,520 in 2000, and from $37,235 for females in 1990 to $41,062 in 2000.

Table 4.24: Average Earnings of Immigrants and Canadian-Born with University Degree, in '000

	Male		Female	
	1990	2000	1990	2000
1 year in Canada	$33	$31.5	$21	$19.8
10 years in Canada	$52	$47.5	$32.5	$32.4
Canadian-born	$60	$66.5	$37	$41

Source: Statistics Canada, "Earnings of Canadians: Making a Living in the New Economy," 2001 Census analysis series (March 11, 2003).

Table 4.25 shows the extent to which the income gap is racialized. Among immigrants of comparable stay in the country, there is a growing gap between the racialized and non-racialized.

Canadian-Born Racialized Group Earners

According to Statistics Canada data, in 1995, just over 253,000 earners in the racialized group population were born in Canada. Their average employment income of $18,565

Table 4.25: Canada: Number and Average Earnings of Racialized and Non-racialized Immigrants by Period of Immigration

Number and average earnings of visible minority immigrants aged 15 and over by period of immigration, Canada 1995

Period of Immigration	Immigrant Earners		Average Earnings		% Difference
	Visible Minority Population	Others	Visible Minority Population	Others	
	Number		Dollars		
TOTAL	1,247,940	1,570,080	23,298	31,170	−25.3
Pre-1956	6,715	213,380	28,378	34,350	−17.4
1956–1965	28,360	341,155	36,910	34,011	8.5
1966–1975	293,485	488,160	32,852	33,399	−1.6
1976–1985	331,970	260,640	24,279	29,286	−17.1
1986–1990	264,420	139,365	19,960	24,533	−18.6
1991–1995	322,990	127,375	15,042	20,809	−27.7

Source: Statistics Canada, *The Daily* (May 12, 1998).

was almost 30% below the level reported by all other earners who were Canadian-born. Statistics Canada suggests that age distribution is a possible factor explaining the differential. However, while the median age of the Canadian born racialized group was lower by more than 11 years, the educational attainment of the racialized group earners was higher than that of other Canadian-born earners and should act as a compensatory factor. This is perhaps true only to a point. Some 45% were under the age of 25, while the figure was 18% for other Canadian-born earners. Less than 10% were between 45 and 64, compared with 25% for other Canadian-born earners. The argument is that older people earn more on average than younger earners, despite educational differentials. Statistics Canada also offered another explanation, that only one third of Canadian-born racialized group members were employed full time for the full year in 1995, compared with one half of other Canadian-born earners. However, it seems disingenuous to use this as an explanation for lower average incomes without commenting on the discriminatory nature of work attainment, especially barriers to full-time work. The higher levels of part-time, contractual, and precarious work that racialized group members experience are not natural phenomena. The explanation overlooks racial discrimination as a factor, which other studies have cited as an important contributor to both work attainment and lower incomes generally.[18] The Statistics Canada position also fails to acknowledge structural causes of the income gap such as the disproportionate participation in low-income sectors and occupations which, as discussed above, many studies have identified as a function of employment discrimination.

The higher levels of unemployment and their implications in terms of disproportionate impacts from cuts to Employment Insurance (EI) benefits contribute not just to the income gap but also to higher-than-average levels of low incomes among the racialized Canadian-born group. Limiting the explanation of the income gap to age and full-time employment differentials therefore fails to deal with the key implications of this finding, which include a high incidence of poverty, especially child poverty, an issue that should be the focus of government policy. In the final analysis, the dispute regarding the factors contributing to the employment-income gap does not negate its existence. This gap is growing and demands public attention.

Racialized Group Families' and Non-racialized Families' Earnings

According to census data for 1996, racialized husband-and-wife families earned a median income of $38,308, compared to $52,066 for non-racialized families, or an average of $13,758 (26%) less per year. Interestingly enough, this 26% disadvantage does not occur when the couple is mixed (one racialized group member and one not).[19]

This inequality is quite consistent across most of the major racialized groups. The three largest racialized groups, Chinese, South Asian, and Black, all earn roughly the same average. The fourth largest group, Arab/West Asian, is even lower.[20] However, there are variations within the groups themselves, as some subgroups (both gender and ethnic) sustain lower-than-average incomes and higher-than-average unemployment rates.

By 2000, however, the family income situation had changed dramatically. The gap diminishes when one considers family income (see Table 4.26). The higher average and median incomes for racialized families reported in Table 4.26 may be explained by the higher on-average number of wage earners in racialized families (in many cases three to four wage earners). In 2000, there was a gap in the percentage change in the median after-tax income gap among families with no employment-income earners, from 31.% and 20.1% to 18.6% and 19.35% among families with one income earner; 16.5% and 15.6% among families with two income earners, and 1.5% and 5.5% among families with three income earners. This suggests the significance of the multiple-earner effect among racialized families.

Table 4.26: After-Tax Income of Families, Canada, 2000

	Total Population	Racialized (a)	Non-racialized (b)	Difference (a-b)	
				$	%
Average	53,083	61,266	52,381	−8,885	−17.0
Median	43,265	50,912	43,080	−7,832	−18.2

Source: Statistics Canada, Income Statistics Division, Survey of Labour, and Labour and Income Dynamics, Custom Tables, 1999–2002, 2005.

Part of what accounts for this is the increase in average after-tax income of 40.1% between 1997 and 2000 (20.2% median after-tax income increase). Likely because they experienced a benefit from the improved-economy time lag, racialized families experienced the highest average and median after-tax increases between 1997 and 2000.

Inequality in Racialized Group Access to Employment: Unemployment

The disadvantages experienced by racialized groups and the gap in economic performance become clearer when we focus on the actual employment experience. The labour-market participation patterns reflect the racial differentiation observed in the income data. There are also differentials in unemployment levels. For instance, while racialized groups made up 11% of Canada's population in 1996, they had an average unemployment rate of 16%, compared to 11% for the general population in 1995. The labour-market participation of recent immigrants differs from that of the Canadian population as a whole. In 1996, processing and manufacturing accounted for 15.5% of the recent immigrant population's jobs, compared with 7.6% for the total Canadian population. A third of recent immigrants were in sales and service jobs, compared with just over a quarter of all Canadians.

Historically, racial discrimination in employment has been perpetuated in many ways. With a racialized labour market, racialized group members are often trapped in the low-end jobs and occupations. They are ghettoized in sectors of the economy that pay the least and have the worst workplace conditions. As a group, they continue to be vulnerable to precarious employment. This condition is often multiplied for racialized women, who face a double negative effect.[21] Historically, the dangerous work Chinese immigrants did on the building of the trans-Canada railway westwards typified racialized group work. Blacks were often restricted to occupations such as sleeping car porter.[22] In the early 20th century, South Asian and Japanese immigrants were restricted to such occupations as labourer or domestic under contracts with fixed quotas; they were denied fishing licenses or access to farmland.[23] To this day, the number of racialized group members working in low-paid occupations is disproportionately higher than their numbers in the population. Various reports dealing with the issue of racial inequity in employment present conclusive evidence to suggest that racial discrimination is not only an endemic feature of the Canadian labour market, but also pervades many of the policies and practices in Canadian workplaces.[24]

An analysis of the unemployment data from the 1996 Census shows the higher levels of low income and unemployment experienced by racialized groups. Statistics Canada shows that in 1996, 36.8% of women and 35% of men in racialized communities were low-income earners compared to 19.2% of other women and 16% of other men.[25] This trend is confirmed by other research. A recently completed study by Edward Harvey and Kathleen Reil titled "Poverty and Unemployment Patterns Among Ethnocultural Groups" compares the socio-economic status of 46 different ethnocultural groups in Canada, including a wide range of racialized ethnocultural groups, for 1986 and 1991. The study considers such socio-economic factors as employment income, unemployment, and incidence of low income as measured by Statistics Canada's Low Income Cut-off (LICO). The study supplemented the census data for 1986 and 1991 with a wide range of Canadian studies of ethnocultural groups and immigrants, the International Migration Data Base (IMDB), maintained by Citizenship and Immigration Canada, as well as three broadly representative focus groups organized by COSTI in Toronto and conducted by Harvey and Reil in June 1998.[26]

The study presented three key findings. First, when 1986 and 1991 data are compared, twice as many ethnocultural groups have higher unemployment rates in 1991. In 1986, 46% of the 46 ethnocultural groups had unemployment rates higher than the national average. In 1991, 76% of the 46 ethnocultural groups (35 groups) had unemployment rates higher than the national average. Second, although the overall national poverty level decreased in 1991 compared with the 1986 level, an increased number of the 46 ethnocultural groups experienced poverty in 1991 (contrary to the national trend). Third, the same ethnocultural groups remain consistently disadvantaged (compared with the national average) when 1986 and 1991 data are compared on the unemployment and poverty dimensions. The study identified a problem of persistent disadvantage for the ethnocultural groups.

In another paper titled "Ethnocultural Groups, Period of Immigration and Socio-economic Situation," Edward Harvey, Bobby Siu, and Kathleen Reil consider the socio-economic situation of immigrants in 17 ethnocultural groups. Immigrants are compared across five periods of immigration: before 1961, 1961–1970, 1971–1980, 1981–1987, and 1988–1991. Taken into account is the fact that of the immigrants coming to Canada, over 70% are members of racialized groups. In this study, both racialized and non-racialized ethnocultural groups are represented across the 17 groups.[27] Their findings confirm studies by the Economic Council of Canada that indicate that more recent immigrants have higher unemployment rates than their Canadian counterparts. The paper assesses the socio-economic situation of immigrants using measures for poverty, employment income, and unemployment, and concludes that:

- Employment experiences of recent immigrants are more diverse than their earlier immigrating counterparts.
- The socio-economic experience of different ethnocultural groups is not homogeneous. Immigrants of visible minority groups experience greater socio-economic disadvantage compared with immigrants of non-visible minority ethnocultural groups.
- Compared with immigrants who immigrated to Canada prior to 1981, immigrants who came to Canada after 1981 have higher unemployment rates, lower employment incomes, and greater incidence of low income.

Data show that despite variations within communities, racialized groups have higher unemployment rates. These findings are similar to ones reported earlier in this book. They represent a growing understanding of the congruence of the phenomenon of racialization and poverty, prompting an increasing number of analysts to draw parallels to the feminization of poverty. In this case, the racial factors disproportionately correlate to the incidence of low income to suggest a racialization of poverty.

More recent data confirms the patterns. As Table 4.27 shows, both the racialized group members and recent immigrants have been losing ground, with their unemployment rates almost twice those of the Canadian labour force by 2001.

Table 4.27: Unemployment Rates for Immigrants, Non-immigrants, and Racialized Groups (%)

	1981	1991	2001
Total labour force	5.9	9.6	6.7
Canadian-born	6.3	9.4	6.4
All immigrants	4.5	10.4	7.9
Recent immigrants	6.0	15.6	12.1
Racialized groups	n/a	n/a	12.6

Source: Statistics Canada, 2001 Census Analysis Series. *The Changing Profile of Canada's Labour Force*, February 11, 2000; Human Resource and Development Canada, *2001 Employment Equity Act Report* (Ottawa: HRSDC, 2001).

Inequality in Racialized Group Access to Employment: Labour Force Participation

According to Karen Kelly's analysis of 1991 census data, the labour-force participation rate for racialized women was (59%), lower among West Asian and Arab group (50%), while South Asian and Latin American women were at 52%. 1991 census data show that the unemployment rate of racialized groups was 13% (before and after age standardization) higher than that of other adults (10%). The Latin American and Southeast Asian groups, with the lowest labour force participation rates, also had the highest age standardized unemployment rates (19% and 17%, respectively). Unemployment was also high among West Asians and Arabs, and South Asians (each 16%).[28]

Jennifer Chard shows that by 1996, only 53% of racialized women were employed or self-employed, compared to 63% of non-racialized women.[29] Among racialized men, 65% were employed, compared to 74.1% for other men. It is among youth that the figures are the worst: only 36% of women and 36.4% of men aged 15–24 in racialized communities are employed, compared to 52% for other women and 54% for other men. The overall unemployment rates in 1996 were 13.2% for men and 15.3% for women in racialized communities, compared to 9.4% for women and 9.9% for men in other communities.[30]

According to Harvey et al.'s study discussed above, once the labour force participation rate of the racialized group population is age-standardized, its members have a 66% rate of labour-force participation, lower than that of the non-racialized population. The findings also suggest that immigrants from racialized ethnocultural groups experience economic disadvantage that is persistent over the 30-year period covered during this study. This is also demonstrated by the data in Table 4.27, which shows that racialized groups and immigrants have a persistent labour-market participation disadvantage that grows over the 20-year period analyzed, culminating in the 66% to 80.3% for non-racialized groups.

Table 4.28: Labour Force Participation Rates for Immigrants, Non-immigrants, and Visible Minorities (%)

	1981	1991	2001
Total labour force	75.5	78.2	80.3
Canadian-born	74.6	78.7	81.8
All immigrants	79.3	77.2	75.6
Recent immigrants	75.7	68.6	65.8
Racialized groups	n/a	70.5	66.0

Source: Statistics Canada, *2003: The Changing Profile of Canada's Labour Force*, 2003; Conference Board of Canada, *Making a Visible Difference: The Contribution of Visible Minorities to Canadian Economic Growth* (April, 2004).

Explaining the Disadvantage: Racialized Groups, Human Capital and Educational Attainment

Various contending explanations have been advanced for the inequalities facing racialized groups in the Canadian labour market. Derek Hum and Wayne Simpson have attempted to show that discrimination is, with one exception, statistically significant only when we examine the case of foreign-born racialized group men. They claim that all racialized group members who are Canadian-born, except Blacks, and all racialized women earn less, but do not suffer from discrimination.[31] This view of course presupposes that factors such as unemployment, the kind of employment, education, and experience, which are used as criteria to measure and examine the differences, are not themselves the product of discrimination! Others explain away the differences using educational achievement. The concept of low quality of human capital among racialized group members remains a persistent explanation for the inequalities.[32] But this is not borne out by analysis of the educational attainment of racialized group members, a key factor for evaluating the quality of human capital. As a recent study by Fernando Mata shows, racialized group members, both Canadian-born and immigrants, do not obtain "fair economic and occupational returns from their educational attainments."[33] This is particularly the case for immigrant and Canadian-born racialized women. Data show that racialized group members under 44 are more likely to have a higher educational attainment than other Canadians.

Hou and Balakrishnan's study also concludes that while racialized group members are more likely to have a higher level of education, they are underrepresented in "high status" occupations and have lower incomes than their educational counterparts.[34] Karen Kelly's work shows that "in 1991, some 18% of the racialized group population aged 15 and over had a university degree, compared with 11% of other adults. As well, while the percentage of those with less than high school education was 33% for racialized groups, it was 39% for other adults." Yet even among those aged 25 to 44 with a university degree, "adults in a racialized groups are less likely than others to be employed in professional or managerial occupations. Instead, many are concentrated in lower-paying clerical, service and manual labour jobs."[35] In 1996 17% of visible minority women had a degree, compared to only 12% for the non-racialized communities.[36] It is important to note that the structures of racial discrimination that generate these inequalities in the workplace also impact access to educational opportunity.

More recent data shows clearly that racialized groups have an educational advantage when one considers average levels of educational attainment based on years of schooling and post-secondary certificates granted. Table 4.29 shows a higher-than-average concentration in the university certificate (19.5%), Bachelor's degree (19.5%), Master's degree (20.1%), and PhDs (22.5%), all compared with their proportion of the population (13.4%).

The advantage that racialized groups have in educational attainment appears to be growing. Tables 4.29 and 4.30 show an increase in the numbers of degree holders in medicine, dentistry, veterinary science, and PhDs. The percentage growth among racialized groups in the two categories far outpaces the Canadian average (37.79% to 16.64% and 49.5% to 23.5%), suggesting that the advantage is likely to be maintained. Yet this advantage has had no significant impact on income attainment, suggesting an x factor responsible for the inability to translate the human-capital advantage into wages and occupational status. We suggest that that x factor is the devaluation of the human capital of racialized group members, resulting from racial discrimination in the labour market.

Educational attainment patterns are similar among the recent immigrant group. Table 4.32 below shows a steady improvement in educational attainment among immigrants arriving over a 30-year period from 1970 to 2001. While 22.5% of immigrants arriving in 1970 held university degrees and 26.10% had trades and college education, for a total of 48.4%, of those arriving in 1990, 40.7% had university degrees and 20.2% had trade and college education, for a total of 60.9%. That compares with the Canadian average of 22.2% with a university degree and 31.7% with a college and trade education, for a total of 53.4%. As the immigrant cohort has become more racialized, the immigration selection process has ensured that the group's educational attainment is greater than that of the Canadian-born group.

Racialized Groups and a Segmented Labour Market

An analysis of HRDC 1996 employment equity data shows that racialized group members were underrepresented in many highly paid occupations, and overrepresented in low-paying sectors of the economy and underrepresented in the

Table 4.29: Population Showing Representation by Highest Levels of Schooling
Geography: Canada

Educational Attainment	Males		Females		Visible Minorities	
	No.	%	No.	%	No.	%
Total—Highest Levels of Schooling	11,626,700	48.6	12,274,500	51.4	3,041,650	12.7
Less Than Grade 9	1,103,985	47.0	1,246,505	53.0	285,305	12.1
Grade 9–13 Without Secondary Certificate	2,558,290	49.9	2,568,120	50.1	567,665	11.1
Grade 9–13 With Secondary Certificate	1,520,080	45.1	1,847,820	54.9	379,235	11.3
Trades Certificate or Diploma	1,643,455	63.2	955,470	36.8	201,830	7.8
Some Other Non-university Without Certificate	714,270	46.5	823,350	53.5	186,210	12.1
Other Non-university With Trades or Certificate	1,166,035	40.1	1,742,155	59.9	287,855	9.9
Some University Without Univ. Cert./Degree	813,835	47.2	908,920	52.8	299,210	17.4
University certificate, degree or diploma	2,106,840	49.1	2,182,230	50.9	834,350	19.5
University Cert./Diploma Below Bachelor Level	242,160	40.3	359,260	59.7	117,490	19.5
Bachelor's Degree(s)	1,150,585	47.7	1,260,890	52.3	471,415	19.5
Degree in Medicine, Dentistry, Veterinary ...	79,970	65.3	42,570	34.7	28,605	23.3
University Cert./Diploma Above Bachelor Level	180,660	47.2	202,295	52.8	59,055	15.4
Master's Degree(s)	359,520	56.0	282,535	44.0	128,790	20.1
Earned Doctorate	93,945	73.0	34,680	27.0	28,995	22.5

Source: Human Resources and Skills Development Canada, *2001 Employment Equity Data Report* (March 2004).

Table 4.30: Degree in Medicine, Dentistry, Veterinary, Canada

	1996	2001	Percentage Change
Total Population	105,050	122,535	16.64
Male Population	73,790	79,970	8.38
Female Population	31,255	42,570	36.20
Visible Minority Population	20,760	28,605	37.79

Source: Human Resources and Skills Development, 2001. Employment Equity Data Report, March 2004.

Table 4.31: Doctorate, Canada

	1996	2001	Percentage Change
Total Population	103,860	128,625	23.5
Male Population	79,560	93,945	18.1
Female Population	24,300	34,680	42.7
Visible Minority Population	19,385	28,995	49.5

Source: Human Resources and Skills Development Canada based on 1996 and 2001 Census. Employment Equity Data Report (March 2004).

Table 4.32: Post-secondary Education among Immigrants and Canadian-Born (%)

Group	University	College	Trades	Total
Immigrated since 1970	22.5	12.1	14.0	48.4
Immigrated since 1980	25.5	12.5	10.9	48.6
Immigrated since 1990	40.7	12.7	7.57	60.9
Total Canada, 2001	22.2	17.9	12.9	53.4

Source: Statistics Canada, *Education in Canada: Raising the Standard*, 2001 Census analysis series (March 11, 2003).

higher-paying jobs in those sectors.[37] The sectoral segregation is a major reason for the lower incomes of the racialized group. The underrepresentation in many higher-paid occupational categories, though not in every category, is a key contributor to the racialized income gap.[38] An analysis of a cross-section of key industries confirms the structural nature of the systemic discrimination that racialized groups endure in Canada's workplaces. Industries like clothing and textile (36.2%), and banking services (15%), show the overrepresentation discussed above. On the other hand, racialized minorities are underrepresented in the motor vehicle industry (7%), primary steel (4.2%), and the federal government (5.6%).

Another dimension of the inequality is seen in the occupations within the different industries, especially the ones in which racialized minorities are overrepresented. As an example, in banking, where racialized group members are overrepresented at 15%, and 7% in senior management.

One key category is public-sector employment. As the industry-wide profiles below indicate, in key institutions in the public service, racialized groups are significantly underrepresented. The analysis shows that the importance of these discriminatory patterns goes beyond income. It is directly related to the limited participation of racialized groups in the administration of the Canadian state. Indeed it speaks to the social exclusion that these groups suffer in Canadian society.

Underrepresentation in key public-sector institutions has implications that go beyond compensation inequity. Broad public-sector occupations, such as police officer and judge, are well-paid jobs in Canada. These jobs are concentrated in the major urban areas where most racialized group members live, so that the effect of underrepresentation is magnified. Police officers, for instance, serve a key role in the administration of justice—often mediating the integration of various immigrant communities into the mainstream of Canadian life. They are at the centre of the tensions that often arise between marginalized groups and dominant cultural groups. The seemingly chronic underrepresentation of racialized groups can only exacerbate the tensions, often leading to charges of racial profiling and racially targeted policing.[39]

Based on 2001 employment equity HRDC data, while some 13.4% of the population are racialized group members, only 10 out of 2,080 fire chiefs are from racialized groups, a percentage of less than 0.5%! Only 2.2% of fire fighters across the country are from racialized group communities (500 out of 25,275). In Ontario, there were 75 racialized commissioned police officers out of 1565, or 4.8%, while in Alberta, there were 230 racialized police officers out of 5,465, or 4.2%.

Another major category in the administration of justice is judging. While figures show a higher-than-average level of contact with the criminal justice system for racialized group members in 2001, only 40 judges out of some 965 are from racialized groups members in Ontario, constituting less than 4% of the total.

Occupations with Underrepresentation of Racialized Groups

Table 4.33 shows a list of some well-paying occupations in which racialized group members are underrepresented. Racialized groups accounted for 11% of Canada's total population in 1996.

Select Occupations with Comparable or Overrepresentation of Racialized Groups

In contrast with the above, Table 4.34 shows an overrepresentation of racialized groups in lower-paying jobs.

The segregation effect is compounded by gender discrimination for racialized women, as Table 4.35 shows. Racialized women are at least twice as likely as racialized males to work in clerical and sales positions, while racialized males are three times as likely as racialized women to work as senior managers.

Table 4.33: Racialized Group Population Aged 15+ Lowest Representation in Occupation Groups and Unit Groups, 2001
Geography: Canada

Occupational Groups and Employment Equity and Occupational Groups and Unit Groups (NOC)	Male Population		Females		Visible Minorities	
	No.	%	No.	%	No.	%
Fire Chiefs and Senior Fire-Chiefs	2,035	97.8	45	2.2	10	0.5
8442 Trappers and Hunters	1,360	82.9	285	17.4	10	0.6
8241 Logging Machinery Operators	15,915	97.4	430	2.6	130	0.8
7436 Boat Operators	1,175	94.8	70	5.6	10	0.8
8211 Supervisors, Logging and ...	5,425	94.1	340	5.9	50	0.9
8231 Underground Production and ...	10,270	98.0	200	1.9	100	1.0
8411 Underground Mine Service and ...	2,200	95.4	100	4.3	25	1.1
8221 Supervisors, Mining and ...	4,810	95.6	220	4.4	55	1.1
8615 Oil and Gas Drilling, Servicing ...	12,115	95.7	550	4.3	245	1.9
8222 Supervisors, Oil and Gas	7,185	96.5	260	3.5	145	1.9
8262 Fishing Vessel Skippers and ...	28,860	86.7	4,420	13.3	650	2.0
6262 Firefighters	24,605	97.3	670	2.7	500	2.0
7382 Commercial Divers	965	95.5	45	4.5	20	2.0
8441 Fishing Vessel Deckhands	5,880	80.9	1,380	19.0	145	2.0
7421 Heavy Equipment Operators ...	78,515	97.7	1,870	2.3	1,700	2.1
0011 Legislators	5,585	63.5	3,210	36.5	195	2.2
6272 Funeral Directors and ...	3,535	75.3	1,155	24.6	105	2.2
8232 Oil and Gas Well Drillers ...	8,005	96.0	325	3.9	195	2.3
9464 Tobacco Processing Machine ...	445	52.7	395	46.7	20	2.4

Source: Human Resources and Skills Development Canada, Employment Equity Data, 2001; CSJ analysis, 2005.

(Partial: Complete table in appendix.)

Table 4.34: Racialized Group Population Aged 15+ Highest Representation in Occupation Groups and Unit Groups, 2001
Geography: Canada

Employment Equity and Occupational Groups and Unit Groups (NOC)	Males		Females		Visible Minorities	
	No.	%	No.	%	No.	%
9451 Sewing Machine Operators	5,720	8.4	62,650	91.6	31,475	46.0
9483 Electronics Assemblers …	17,650	46.0	20,680	54.0	16,210	42.3
9616 Labourers in Textile Processing	6,770	45.0	8,275	55.0	6,110	40.6
6682 Ironing, Pressing and …	2,975	36.2	5,240	63.8	3,335	40.6
9452 Fabric, Fur and Leather Cutters	4,615	57.6	3,400	42.4	3,215	40.1
9444 Textile Inspectors, Graders …	1,065	27.7	2,785	72.4	1,475	38.4
9442 Weavers, Knitters and Other …	4,550	46.0	5,355	54.1	3,715	37.5
9422 Plastics Processing Machine …	16,825	64.8	9,150	35.2	9,555	36.8
7413 Taxi and Limousine Drivers …	37,055	91.9	3,285	8.1	14,760	36.6
2173 Software Engineers	23,155	81.6	5,230	18.4	10,295	36.3
9517 Other Products Machine …	10,635	63.5	6,125	36.6	5,980	35.7
9487 Machine Operators and …	1,930	60.3	1,265	39.5	1,075	33.6
9492 Furniture and Fixture …	25,975	79.0	6,915	21.0	10,535	32.0
9443 Textile Dyeing and Finishing …	2,940	66.6	1,480	33.5	1,390	31.5
9619 Other Labourers in Processing …	43,600	52.2	39,945	47.8	25,705	30.8
7344 Jewellers, Watch Repairers …	4,145	75.4	1,355	24.6	1,690	30.7
9498 Other Assemblers and …	9,395	55.2	7,625	44.8	5,220	30.7
9222 Supervisors, Electronics …	3,130	62.9	1,845	37.0	1,510	30.3
2147 Computer Engineers (Except …	25,160	85.1	4,385	14.8	8,900	30.1

Source: Human Resources and Skills Development Canada. Employment Equity Data 2001; CSJ analysis 2005.

(Partial: Complete table in appendix.)

Table 4.35: Workforce Population Showing Representation by Employment Equity Occupational Groups (2001 NOC) in Canada by Employment Equity Occupational Groups

Employment Equity Occupational Groups (NOC)	Male Population	%	Female Population	%	Males Visible Minority	%	Females Visible Minority	%
Total	8,942,050	52.7	8,019,025	47.3	1,116,680	6.6	1,027,640	6.1
Senior Managers	161,980	74.9	54,325	25.1	13,390	6.2	4,300	2.0
Middle and Other Managers	928,205	62.5	556,210	37.5	110,265	7.4	64,680	4.4
Professionals	1,221,240	47.2	1,366,920	52.8	196,275	7.6	160,675	6.2
Semi-professionals and Technicians	624,525	47.7	685,485	52.3	83,130	6.3	73,735	5.6
Supervisors	93,915	43.3	122,950	56.7	12,315	5.7	13,640	6.3
Supervisors: Crafts and Trades	425,595	80.4	103,530	19.6	19,645	3.7	5,595	1.1
Administrative and Senior Clerical ...	137,125	15.0	774,640	85.0	16,290	1.8	68,045	7.5
Skilled Sales and Service Personnel	391,075	55.7	310,930	44.3	61,515	8.8	36,875	5.3
Skilled Crafts and Trades Workers	1,277,140	94.1	80,220	5.9	97,255	7.2	12,945	1.0
Clerical Personnel	438,995	27.3	1,170,155	72.7	77,540	4.8	157,095	9.8
Intermediate Sales and Service	603,565	31.5	1,312,470	68.5	82,160	4.3	168,105	8.8
Semi-skilled Manual Workers	1,428,340	77.6	411,295	22.4	183,735	10.0	93,900	5.1
Other Sales and Service Personnel	713,490	44.1	903,005	55.9	113,430	7.0	129,210	8.0
Other Manual Workers	496,870	74.9	166,890	25.1	49,745	7.5	38,850	5.9

Source: Human Resources and Skills Development Canada. Employment Equity Data 2001; CSJ analysis 2005.

Racialized Occupational Differentials: Occupational Profiles by Industries

Data from a sample section of Canadian industry demonstrate the structural nature of labour-market discrimination against racialized group members. By examining a number of industries by job categories and classifications, we are able to show the effect of differential access to the labour market, which results in overrepresentation in certain sectors and underrepresentation in others, as well as overrepresentation in certain occupations – particularly low-paying occupations – and underrepresentation in well-paying occupations and management-level positions.

An examination of the banking, auto, and steel industries confirms the argument that there is an underrepresentation of racialized group members at the managerial and supervisory levels of important and well-compensated occupations and industrial sectors, and that this is a key contributing factor to the low rates of racialized group incomes and economic performance. Conversely, an examination of the labour structure in the retail and textile industries demonstrates the reverse problem: an overrepresentation of racialized group members in the low-paid occupations.

The discriminatory effect is evident in categories such as senior managers, supervisors of skilled trades, skilled trades, and senior administrative personnel. Figures for the other industries generally show a similar rate of underrepresentation at the management and skilled-trade levels. Some industries such as banking, and especially clothing and textile products, show a larger concentration of racialized group members than exists in the population, while others, such as primary textile and general retail, are about proportional in terms of overall numbers.

In terms of its importance to the socio-political fabric of the country, perhaps the most glaring example of structural employment discrimination is the public sector, and specifically the federal public service. A recent federal government report identified the 5.3% participation rate of racialized groups, less than 50% of their composition in the Canadian population, as indefensible.[40] This finding comes 15 years after the introduction of a federal employment equity program for women, racialized groups, Aboriginal peoples, and persons with disabilities. Perhaps most disappointing is the fact that the lack of progress denies the federal public service the moral authority to act as a leader in implementing employment equity among industries regulated by the federal government. It also rules out the possibility of redressing employment discrimination through making federal jobs available, a strategy that seemed very effective when francophone exclusion was targeted by the federal government.

Conclusion

The statistical profile of the social economic status of racialized groups shows that the process of economic exclusion persists even after the economic expansion effect is taken into account. There is a gap between the economic performance of racialized and non-racialized groups when one considers such indicators as income, unemployment, and labour-market participation. This inequality leads to increased likelihood of low income or poverty. According to Statistics Canada, the incidence of low income among racialized group members was significantly higher than the national average over the period 1993–1996. Low Income Cut Offs (LICOs) are used by the government to determine the level of income under which a family or an individual is considered to be living in poverty in Canada. Statistics Canada notes that the rate of poverty among racialized groups was 36% in 1995, compared to 19% for the general population. The rate for children under the age of six living in low-income families was an astounding 45%, compared to the overall figure of 26% for all children, a rate of child poverty almost twice that in the population. The poverty gap among those in the over-65 age group is also substantial, at 32% among the racialized groups compared to the national average of 19%.[41] Of those who immigrated to Canada after 1976, more than 15% experienced poverty for four years, compared with 4% of those who were Canadian-born. In Canada's urban centres, while racialized group members account for 21.6% of the population, they account for 33% of the urban poor. In fact, in some cities like Richmond and Vancouver in British Columbia; and Markham, Richmond Hill, Toronto, and Mississauga in Ontario, more than half of those living in poverty are racialized group members.[42]

An analysis of the 1996 data for the City of Toronto by Michael Ornstein breaks the economic performance of racialized groups down by national origin to identify deep pockets of low incomes and unemployment among some African and Caribbean groups, South Asian groups, East Asian groups, Arab and Middle Eastern groups, and Latin American groups in Canada's biggest and most prosperous metropolis. The levels of poverty are most acute among women.[43] Marie Drolet and Rene Morisette's (1999) findings also show that, while 73.1% of the racialized group members lived above the low-income cut-off during the previous four years, the number for non-racialized group members was 86%.[44]

More recent research shows that low-income rates among successive groups of immigrants almost doubled between 1980 and 1995, peaking at 47% before easing up in the late 1990s. In 1980, 24.6% of immigrants who had arrived during the previous five-year period lived below the poverty line. By 1990, the low-income rate among recent immigrants had increased to 31.3%. It rose further to 47.0% in 1995, but fell back somewhat to 35.8% in 2000 (Picot and Hou, 2003).[45]

The data on income attainment, unemployment, skill utilization, and rates of poverty demonstrate in compelling fashion the impact of racialization in the Canadian labour market, and the persistence of social exclusion experienced by racialized groups. In the next chapter, we will consider its impact on particular groups and the extent to which those experiences tell us something new about Canada in the early 21st century.

Notes

1.   A. Akbari, *The Economics of Immigration and Racial Discrimination: A Literature Survey, 1970–89* (Ottawa: Multiculturalism and Citizenship Canada, 1989). Akbari (1999) has updated his analysis to include actual income and educational attainment data; A. De Silva, *Earnings of Immigrants: A Comparative Analysis* (Ottawa: Economic Council of Canada, 1992).

2.   A. Akbari, "Ethnicity and Earnings Discrimination in Canadian Labour Markets: Some Evidence from the 1986 Census" (Ottawa: Multiculturalism and Citizenship Canada,

1992); P. Anisef, R. Sweet, C. James, and Z. Lin, "Higher Education, Racial Minorities, Immigrants and Labour Market Outcomes in Canada, " International Symposium on "Non-Traditional" Students, University of British Columbia, August 16 and 17, 1999; M. Baker and D. Benjamin, "The Performance of Immigrants in the Canadian Labour Market," *Journal of Labour Economics* 12, no. 3 (1994): 369–405; C. Beach and C. Worswick, "Is there a Double-Negative Effect on the Earnings of Immigrant Women?" *Canadian Public Policy* XIX, no. 1: 36–53; L. Christofides and R. Swindinsky, "Wage Determination by Gender and Visible Minority Status: Evidence from the 1989 LMAS," *Canadian Public Policy* XX, no. 1 (1994): 34–51; F. Hou and T.R. Balakrishnan, "The Integration of Visible Minorities in Contemporary Canadian Society," *Canadian Journal of Sociology* 21, no. 3 (1996): 307–326; J.L. Kunz, A. Milan, and S. Schetagne, *Unequal Access: A Canadian Profile of Racial Differences in Education, Employment and Income* (Toronto: Canadian Race Relations Foundation, 2000); K. Pendakur and R. Pendakur, *The Colour of Money: Earnings Differentials among Ethnic Groups in Canada* (Vancouver: Metropolis Project, 1996); A. de Silva, *Wage Discrimination against Visible Minorities Men in Canada* (Ottawa: Human Development Canada, 1997); M. Ornstein, *Ethno-Racial Inequality in Metropolitan Toronto: An Analysis of the 1991 Census* (Toronto: City of Toronto Access and Equity Unit, 1996); see also M. Ornstein, *Ethno-Racial Inequality in Toronto: An Analysis of the 1996 Census* (Toronto: City of Toronto Access and Equity Unit, 2000); M. Stelcner, "Earnings Differentials among Ethnic Groups in Canada: A Review of the Research" *Review of Social Economy* LVIII, no. 3 (September 2000).

3.   In 1993, government transfers represented 12.9% of family income in Canada. That was down to 11.7% by 1996. Statistics Canada Catalogue 13-207, as cited in A. Yalnyzian, *The Growing Gap: A Report on the Growing Income Inequality between the Rich and Poor in Canada* (Toronto: Centre for Social Justice, 1998), 64.

4.   J. Chard, "Women in a Visible Minority," in *Women in Canada: A Gender-Based Statistical Report* (Ottawa: Statistics Canada, 2000). Cat. No. CS86-503-XPE.

5.   The 1996 census uses the term *visible minority* to denote a group here referred to as a racialized group.

6.   Special run of Statistics Canada Survey of Labour and Income Dynamics (SLID) for the Centre for Social Justice, 2000; 2005. See Galabuzi (2000).

7.   Based on a special run of Statistics Canada Survey of Labour and Income Dynamics (SLID) for the Centre for Social Justice, 1996; 1997.

8.   J. Reitz and A. Verma, *Immigration, Ethnicity and Unionization: Recent Evidence for Canada* (Toronto: Centre for Excellence for Research on Immigration and Settlement (CERIS), May, 2000).

9.   Statistics Canada, *The Daily* (May 12, 1998).

10. L. Christofides and R. Swindinsky, "Wage Determination by Gender and Visible Minority Status: Evidence from the 1989 LMAS," *Canadian Public Policy* XX, no. 1 (1994): 34–51.

11. Ibid., 35.

12. See P. Li, *Ethnicity in Canada* (Toronto: Wall and Thompson, 1988); J. Reitz and R. Breton, *The Illusion of Difference: Realities of Ethnicity in Canada and the United States* (Toronto: C.D. Howe, 1994); K. Gosine, "Revisiting the Notion of a 'Recast' Vertical Mosaic in Canada: Does a Post-Secondary Education Make a Difference?" *Canadian Ethnic Studies* XXXII, no. 30 (2000), 89–104; F. Hou and T.R. Balakrishnan, "The Integration of Visible Minorities in Contemporary Canadian Society," *Canadian Journal of Sociology* 21, no. 3 (1996): 307–325;

R. Wanner, "Prejudice, Profit or Productivity: Explaining the Returns to Human Capital among Male Immigrants in Canada," *Canadian Ethnic Studies* 30, no. 3 (1998): 25–55; J. Torczyner, "Diversity, Mobility and Change: The Dynamics of Black Communities in Canada," in *Canadian Black Communities Demographic Project* (Montreal: McGill University Consortium for Ethnic and Strategic Social Planning, 1997).

13. A. de Wolff, *Breaking the Myth of Flexible Work: Contingent Work in Toronto* (Toronto: Continent Workers Project Report, September 2000).

14. F. Mata, "Intergenerational Transmission of Education and Socio-economic Status: A Look at Immigrants, Visible Minorities and Aboriginals" (Ottawa: Statistics Canada, 1997).

15. Statistics Canada, *The Daily* (May 12, 1998). The situation is different when you discount the variation in the average earnings of immigrants by period of immigration. The much higher incomes of pre-1976 immigrants push the overall average earnings to $27,684, which was 5.7% higher than for non-immigrants ($26,193).

16. Statistics Canada, "Survey of Labour and Income Dynamics: Encountering Low Income," *The Daily* (March 25, 1999).

17. Statistics Canada, "1996 Census: Sources of Income, Earnings and Total Income," *The Daily* (May 12, 1998).

18. Among others, Akbari (1989, 1999); Bloom, Grenier, and Gunderson (1995); L. Christofides and R. Swindinsky, "Wage Determination by Gender and Visible Minority Status: Evidence from the 1989 LMAS," *Canadian Public Policy* 20, no. 1 (1994), pp. 34–51.

19. Analysis from J. Anderson, "Notes on Visible Minorities and the Income Gap," unpublished paper (Toronto: Centre for Social Justice, 2000).

20. Ibid.

21. T. das Gupta, "Political Economy of Gender, Race and Class: Looking at South Asian Immigrant Women in Canada," in *Canadian Ethnic Studies* 26, no. 1 (1994): 59–73; see also, T. das Gupta, *Racism and Paid Work* (Toronto: Garamond Press, 1996); M. Boyd, "At a Disadvantage: The Occupational Attainment of Foreign Born Women in Canada," *International Migration Review* 18, no. 4 (1985): 1091–1119; C. Beach and C. Worswick, "Is There a Double-Negative Effect on the Earnings of Immigrant Women?" *Canadian Public Policy* XIX, no. 1 (1993): 36–53.

22. S. Grizzle, *My Name's Not George: The Story of the Brotherhood of Sleeping Car Porters in Canada* (Toronto: Umbrella Press, 1998).

23. Boralia and Li (1988); Adachi (1976); Henry et al. (1995).

24. See note 24 in Chapter 1.

25. Chard, op. cit.

26. E. Harvey, K. Reil, and B. Siu. "Ethnocultural Groups, Period of Immigration, and Socioeconomic Situation," *Canadian Journal of Ethnic Studies* 31, no. 3 (1999).

27. E. Harvey, B. Siu, and K. Reil, "Ethnocultural Groups, Period of Immigration and Socio-Economic Situation," *Canadian Journal of Ethnic Studies* 30, no. 3 (1999): 95–103.

28. K. Kelly, "Visible Minorities: A Diverse Group / Les minorités visibles: une population diversifiée," *Canadian Social Trends / Tendances sociales Canadiennes* 37 (Summer, 1995): 2–8. Published separately in English and French, Statistics Canada Catalogue no. 11008.

29. Chard (2000).

30. Chard, op. cit.

31. D. Hum and W. Simpson, "Wage Opportunities for Visible Minorities in Canada" (Ottawa: Statistics Canada, 1998).

32. Abbott and Beach (1993); Baker and Benjamin (1994); Chiswick and Miller (1988); De Voretz and Fagnan (1990); De Voretz (1995); Stoffman (1993); Beach and Worswick (1993); Collacott (2002).

33. Mata (1997).

34. F. Hou and T.R. Balakrishnan, "The Integration of Visible Minorities in Contemporary Canadian Society," *Canadian Journal of Sociology* 21, no. 3 (1996): 307–325.

35. Kelly (1995), op. cit.

36. Chard, op. cit.

37. Anderson (2000). The sectors chosen for the study were picked in conjunction with Maria Wallis.

38. For instance, university professors and the post-secondary research and teaching categories show a demographic overrepresentation of racialized group members.

39. See Ontario Commission on Systemic Racism in the Criminal Justice System Report (1995); Clare Lewis report (1989), Pitman report (1977), Marshall report (Hickman 1989), Manitoba Aboriginal Justice (1991), Committee to Stop Targeted Policing (2000).

40. *Report of the Taskforce on the Participation of Visible Minorities in the Federal Public Service 2000: Enforcing Change in the Federal Public Service* (Ottawa: Supply and Services Canada, 2000).

41. Statistics Canada, "1996 Census: Sources of Income, Earnings," *The Daily* (May 12, 1998).

42. K. Lee, *Urban Poor in Canada: A Statistical Profile* (Ottawa: Canadian Council on Social Development, 2000), 38.

43. Ornstein (2000). Some questions have been raised about the group categories used in the report, but these methodological concerns are unlikely to impact the report's major findings.

44. M. Drolet and R. Morisette, "To What Extent Are Canadians Exposed to Low Income?" (Ottawa: Statistics Canada, March 1999).

45. G. Picot and F. Hou. *The Rise in Low-Income Rates among Immigrants in Canada,* catalogue no. 11F0019M1E–no. 198 (Ottawa: Statistics Canada, 2003) ; M. Frenette and R. Morissette, *Will They Ever Converge? Earnings of Immigrants and Canadian-Born Workers over the Last Two Decades,* Analytical Studies paper no. 215 (Ottawa: Statistics Canada, 2003) ; G. Schellenberg, *Immigrants in Canada's Census Metropolitan Areas,* catalogue no. 89-613-MIE–no. 003 (Ottawa: Statistics Canada, 2004); Statistics Canada, Earnings of Immigrant and Canadian-Born Workers, 1980–2000," *The Daily* (October 8, 2003).

Questions for Critical Thought

1. Does racism matter in the allocation of job opportunities in Canada's labour market today?

2. What are some of the arguments for and against the relevance of racial categories in the labour market?

3. To what extent does race explain the condition of Canada's racialized groups in the Canadian labour market?

4. What evidence suggests that race influences decisions by employers?

5. What are the implications of the racialization of the labour market?
6. How does this racialization explain the gap in economic performance between racialized groups and other Canadians?
7. What are some of the other implications of inequality in income in terms of life chances?

Recommended Readings

Akbari, A. *The Economics of Immigration and Racial Discrimination: A Literature Survey, 1970–89*. Ottawa: Multiculturalism and Citizenship Canada, 1989.

Chard, J. "Women in a Visible Minority," in *Women in Canada 2000: A Gender-Based Statistical Report*, edited by J. Chard, J. Badets, and L. Howatson-Leo. Ottawa: Statistics Canada, 2000.

De Silva, A. *Wage Discrimination against Visible Minorities Men in Canada*. Ottawa: Human Development Canada, 1997.

Frenette, M., and R. Morissette. *Will They Ever Converge? Earnings of Immigrants and Canadian-Born Workers over the Last Two Decades*. Analytical Studies paper no. 215. Ottawa: Statistics Canada, 2003.

Hiebert, D. *The Colour of Work: Labour Market Segmentation in Montréal, Toronto and Vancouver, 1991*. Vancouver: RIIM, March 1997.

Kunz, J.L., A. Milan, and S. Schetagne. *Unequal Access: A Canadian Profile of Racial Differences in Education, Employment and Income*. Toronto: Canadian Race Relations Foundation, 2000.

Lee, K. *Urban Poor in Canada: A Statistical Profile*. Canadian Council on Social Development, 2000.

Ornstein, M. *Ethno-Racial Inequality in Toronto: An Analysis of the 1996 Census*. Toronto: City of Toronto Access and Equity Unit, 2000.

Pendakur, K., and R. Pendakur. *The Colour of Money: Earnings Differentials among Ethnic Groups in Canada*. Vancouver: Metropolis Project, 1996.

Picot, G., and F. Hou. *The Rise in Low-Income Rates among Immigrants in Canada*. Research Paper Series. Catalogue no. 11F0019MIE2003198. Ottawa: Statistics Canada, 2003.

Pitman, W. *Now Is Not Too Late: Report of the Metropolitan Toronto Task Force on Human Relations*. Toronto: Task Force on Human Relations, 1977.

Schellenberg, G. *Immigrants in Canada's Census Metropolitan Areas*. Catalogue no. 89-613-MIE-no. 003. Ottawa: Statistics Canada, 2004.

Statistics Canada. "Earnings of Canadians." Catalogue no. 11F0019M1E – no. 198. Ottawa: Statistics Canada, 2003.

Statistics Canada. "Earnings of Immigrant and Canadian-Born Workers, 1980–2000."

Statistics Canada. *The Daily* (October 8, 2003).

Stelcner, M. "Earnings Differentials among Ethnic Groups in Canada: A Review of the Research." *Review of Social Economy* LVIII, no. 3 (September 2000).

CHAPTER 5

Beyond the Numbers: Dimensions of Economic Exclusion

Introduction

The experience of exclusion differs according to the subgroup to which racialized members belong. In this chapter, we take a look at the picture behind the numbers of the social economic status of racialized groups by discussing the experiences of two groups of racialized workers—racialized women and internationally educated professionals and tradespeople. Sex and immigrant status are two important bases for differentiating the racialized experience. Of course these can also be further disaggregated, but for our purposes, we will use the experiences as largely representative. Gendered racism and racialized women's exposure to precarious work are represented in one experience. The other experience is that of skilled immigrants with differential access to professions and trades. These experiences demonstrate the depth of the impact of the racialized existence in important ways. The experiences exemplify both persistent and new forms of the manifestation of economic exclusion in the lives of members of the racialized groups.

The two groups share a common experience of disproportionate exposure to precariousness in work. Most precarious workers are low-income earners, many of them women, many skilled immigrants, and some asylum seekers running from regimes that routinely abuse their human rights and put their lives at risk. They are therefore prone to being exploited by temporary employment agencies and employers. Many tradespeople and professionals denied access to practice in their own fields resort to survival forms of employment, thereby descending into precariousness. Similarly, racialized women are often expected to accept unsafe work as garment-workers, domestics, or cleaners. Many others work in sweatshops or as home workers in the clothing and textiles industry. These groups are also highly vulnerable to racialized poverty.

With limited job prospects and insecure work arrangements, many racialized group members also suffer disproportionately when governments decide to remove income and other supports that would compensate for low or limited incomes. Many fall victim to other socio-economic effects of living in poverty, such as higher health risks, marginal or substandard housing, family violence, and contact with the criminal justice system. Suffice it to say that their voices need to be heard today by many of us who don't appreciate the depth of their exclusion. We need to hear their stories of struggle and resistance in response to oppression and exploitation.

For a few years, Canada celebrated its United Nations Human Development Index (UN-HDI) status as "the best country to live in." The HDI methodology leaves the impression that average indicators apply to all peoples and communities. The impact of such assumptions is to erase from Canada's record the reality of the poor, the homeless, and those dealing with gender and racial discrimination and its socio-psychological and health impacts.

Two key principles are ignored by such indices. One is that poverty is first and foremost a household and community characteristic—a fact easily lost in national-average indices. It would be more accurate to measure how well the country or province succeeds in dealing with specific barriers that constrain poor households and poor communities. To the extent that the "best-country" label detracts from a societal commitment to fight against poverty and racism, it does the country a disservice. The second principle is that we must hear what the victims of poverty and racial discrimination themselves are saying about their condition. Here we attempt to include some voices of the people who live the experience of exclusion, and of their advocates.

Racism and Racialized Women's Experiences in the Workplace

The experience of racialized women (in the workplace) has been described as one of "double jeopardy." They have to contend not only with racism, but also with sexism in employment, both of which impose their burdens. Numerous studies have exhaustively dealt with this complex experience of double oppression. While some research approaches it by looking at the experience of immigrant women, others have studied the experiences of racialized women workers as domestics, community workers, nurses, garment-workers, workers in the hospitality industry, teachers, etc. Most, however, confirm the dual oppressions of race and gender discrimination.[1]

Racialized women increased in total numbers over a decade by 50% from 1986 (800,000) to 1996 (1.6 million). In 1996, they accounted for 11% of all women in Canada and 51% of all racialized group members. They come from various backgrounds, with Chinese (27%), South Asian (20%), and Black (18%) making up the three biggest groups. Other groups are Filipina (8%), Arab or West Asian (7%), Latin American (6%), South East Asian (2%), Japanese (2%), and Korean (2%); the rest made up another 2%. Sixty-nine percent were immigrants arriving after 1981 (22% arrived before then) while 28% were Canadian-born. In 1996, 17% of racialized women aged 15 and over had university degrees, compared to 12% of other Canadian women. In addition, 13% had some form of university education, compared to 10% of other women. However, this relatively high level of educational attainment did not translate into well-paying employment, and too often led to no employment at all. According to the 1996 Census data based on 1995 figures, 15% of racialized women aged 15–64 were unemployed, compared to 9% of other Canadian women. The rates of unemployment were highest among West Asians and Arabs (22%), Latin Americans (22%), Blacks (20%), South East Asians and South Asians (19%), and lowest among Japanese and Filipinas (8%). The unemployment rate for racialized women was higher than that of racialized men, at 13% compared to 11%. Racialized women were also more likely to be employed in administrative, clerical, sales and service jobs: 36% employed in sales and service, 24% in administrative or clerical jobs. Of those with paid employment, 13% were manual workers. In the ranks of management, 5% of employed racialized women held managerial or supervisory roles. But fully 44% of those racialized women who held a university degree worked in clerical, sales, or service jobs (compared to 24% for racialized men), while 4% were doing manual labour. While 36% of racialized women with degrees worked in professional occupations, the number for other women was 55%.[2]

In terms of income, in 1995 on average, racialized women aged 15–65 earned $16,600, compared to $19,500 for other women and $23,600 for racialized men. The highest earners among racialized women were those aged 45–54 at $22,400, compared to $25,000 for other women. Those aged 65 and over earned the lowest at $12,200, compared to the other women at $17,100. Finally racialized women were more likely than other women to live in poverty. In 1995, 37% of racialized women lived below the low-income cut-off, compared with 19% for other women and 35% for racialized men.[3]

Gendered racism has always been embedded in the Canadian labour markets and manifested in many ways. It reflects the persistent racist and sexist conceptions of gender-determined roles in the economy. Racialized women are often portrayed as less competent, less skilled, less disciplined (one assumption being that they take too much time off work to fulfil parental duties), and mainly secondary wage earners. All these conceptions go against empirical evidence that clearly documents racialized women as increasingly more educated than racialized men; working longer hours than men and with greater responsibilities; and working largely as "primary" wage-earners, many in single-family situations. Because of gendered racism, racialized women are subject to a higher level of marginalization and ghettoization. In predominantly female occupations like nursing, for instance, studies show persistent discrimination as racialized nurses face barriers to management positions, and find themselves overconcentrated in nurse's aide or orderly work, and other low-end positions.[4]

Racially segregated labour markets explain the segmentation of racialized women workers into the helping and nurturing occupations in which they are the victims of pay inequity for work of similar value. Racialized women in the workplace are excluded from secure, well-paid employment, and are often powerless to challenge the situation. Racism and sexism clearly interact with class to define the place of racialized women workers in the labour market, even in relation to other women workers. As the literature shows, this experience is evident in such occupations as nursing, garment-working, domestic work, community service, and such sectors as the health sector, human service, and the commercial service sector. These sectors are female-dominated, but within them racialized women have limited access to management, and find themselves disproportionately in low-skill, low-end jobs.

These structures tend to reproduce themselves, creating a gendered and racialized division of labour, with some employers insisting on particular racialized group workers on the assumption that they are naturally best suited to perform certain work functions. The documented requests made by employers to Employment Agencies for specific racial groups for specific jobs are further evidence of these racist preferences.[5]

In addition to the prevalent segmentation of racialized women workers into both health and social services and commercial service, racialized women are increasingly to be found in the precarious environments of contingent work—casual, part-time, contract work, often acquired through employment agencies, which pay exploitative wages on contracts that clearly disempower their employees.

Precarious Work: Temporary, Contract, and Part-time Work

Precarious work has become a major feature of the Canadian labour market at the beginning of the 21st century. By the end of the 1990s, a greater proportion of people were either contract-employed, self-employed, or doing temporary work than at the beginning of the decade. While the form of work is not new, it departs from previous decades. Full time employment growth in accounted for only 18% of new job growth between 1989 and 1998, compared to 58% during the preceding decade.[6]

The changing nature of the Canadian labour market is a response to the demands for increased flexibility, brought about by the intensified globalization of the Canadian economy. The dramatic increase in self-employment and contract work has had a dramatic impact on racialized group members, especially racialized women. Not only do disproportionate numbers of racialized group members depend on contract, part-time and contingency work, but the work is precarious, unregulated, involving long hours and low pay. Many of the workers in the service industry and light manufacturing are increasingly in temporary contracts from employment service agencies, which pay them a fraction of what they earn in the jobs they are assigned to and hold them to those contracts even when their employers require their services permanently.

Table 5.1: Employed in Canada by Class of Worker, 1989–1998 (in thousands)

	1989	1992	1997	1998	% increase 1989–1998	% new jobs
Total employment	13,086	12,842	13,941	14,326	9.5	
Self-employment total	1,809	1,936	2,488	2,525	39.6	57.7
S.E. no paid employees	822	904	1,282	1.351	64.3	42.6
Employees full-time	9,449	8,937	9,349	9.679	2.4	18.5
Employees part-time	1,828	1,969	2,103	2,122	16.1	18.8

Source: *Statistics Canada Labour Survey* quoted in A. Jackson, D. Robinson, B. Baldwin, and C. Wiggins, *Falling Behind: The State of Working Canada, 2000*, 56–60. Ottawa: Canadian Centre for Policy Alternatives, 2000.

A small number of self-employed workers earn enough to be above the Canadian average. However, in 1995, 45% of those listed as self-employed earned less than $20,000, while only 6.7% earned $100,000 or more. Non-permanent workers earned 82% of permanent workers' hourly wages, and 64% of their weekly wages.[7]

A report released recently by the Toronto-based Contingent Workers Project shows that the city's economy has consistently relied on underemployed and unemployed immigrant workers to fill contingency jobs because of the discrimination they face in regular work environments. In many respects, the city's recent boom has been subsidized by the access to this pool of cheap labour. The report claims that contingency workers often need multiple jobs to make ends meet, find it difficult to access Employment Insurance benefits, and are often forced to work at home doing piecemeal tasks. It claims that:

[There are] as many as 1,238,800 non-standard workers in the greater Toronto area. A large proportion is new immigrants who are being channelled into self-employment and temporary work. We are beginning to see that these forms of work play a key role in the creation and maintenance of ethno-racial segmentation in the city's workforce and an ethno-racial polarization income.[8]

Precarious workers are found in a variety of arrangements, most of which are largely exploitative. The concept of flexible work that has become popular with globalization has translated into new challenges for low-income workers, especially those with the most marginal and tenuous hold on the labour market. Not only are working conditions severe, but also the wages are often below the provincially mandated minimum wage. Many of the workers are considered self-employed or individual contractors and are contracted by temporary employment agencies which pick and choose, often based on racial categories, who will work where.[9]

Because racialized women suffer disproportionately high levels of unemployment, they tend to be overrepresented in temporary and casual work arrangements with low piecemeal and hourly payment. Many provide manual labour and deliver newspapers or food, while others clean dishes or buildings. Some have converted their own homes into sweatshops for the clothing industry. Many routinely suffer chronic limb and back injuries, while others are exposed to toxic cleaning substances without proper protection. These workers have little recourse since they are paid for the hours they work, and cannot afford to either complain, take time off for medical attention, or look for other employment. As a result, they are not only caught in a cycle of poverty, but also face higher health risks.

Racialized Women and Sweatshops

Along with the prevalent segmentation of racialized women workers into health and social service sectors and the commercial service sector, racialized women are increasingly to be found in the precarious environments of home work — casual, piece-meal, part-time, contract work, often acquired through employment agencies that pay exploitative wages on contracts that clearly disempower them. Racialized women are also increasingly being forced to work in their own homes, sewing clothes at a fraction of the wages in the communal workplaces. These "workplaces" are rarely subject to employment standards legislation, nor are any laws enforced to protect workers from extreme exploitation. Most work well below the minimum wage and for extremely long hours to meet the quota set for them. This is largely because the majority of the firms in the garment industry in the 1990s were small, non-unionized factories or sub-contractors. While in the 1970s, only 22% of the industry was made up of small firms, by the 1990s, 75% of the clothing was made in shops with fewer than 20 workers.[10]

Ng's 1999 study of garment workers in Canada described conditions of work that are typical of what we call sweatshops. Based on interviews of Chinese female garment-workers in the Greater Toronto Area, the study detailed hazardous work environments and low-paying piecemeal work, often done in the home. The study concluded that the majority of racialized immigrant women workers in the industry worked under conditions well below those prescribed by the *Ontario Employment Standards Act*. Many workers suffer physical and emotional ailments due to the long hours and repetitive forms of work, but do not claim compensation benefits because they fear that their employers will terminate them. While some received as little as $2 an hour in wages, paid on a per-item basis, most were not able to claim vacation pay although most worked longer than the mandated 44-hour week. Many of the women were also parents, some single mothers who had to accept this type of employment to provide for their families. While most held immigrant status, some were non-status residents or were yet to regularize their status, making it more difficult for them to challenge their conditions of work. According to Ng, the absence of legislative protection is a major contributor to the intense exploitation these women face. The lack of adequate enforcement of even the weak legislation in place allows unscrupulous employers and employment agencies to oppress these women with impunity.[11]

Box 5.1: Internationally Educated Professionals and Tradespeople and the Experience of Differential Access to Professions and Trades

The arrival each year of so many well-qualified immigrants could counteract the much-debated "brain drain" of Canadian educated workers to the U.S. if the credentialism policies were reduced. According to Dr. Ivan Fellegi, Chief Statistician of Canada: "University educated migrants coming to Canada outnumber those leaving for the US by four to one." (Fellegi,1999).

Evidently, there remains a massive disconnect between Canada's immigration program objectives and the reality facing many immigrants on arrival. This reality "makes a mockery of efforts by the immigration department to recruit well-educated immigrants." (Richmond 1994: 145)

Internationally Educated Professionals and Tradespeople (IEPs) represent another racialized subgroup whose socio-economic status reveals the experience of racialization and social exclusion. These highly skilled immigrants find themselves unable to convert educational attainment into comparable job status and labour-market participation rates. Because of their difficulty with the accreditation process in many of the provinces, many cannot practice in their field. They consequently experience relatively low incomes, are disproportionately engaged in precarious types of work, and report high levels of poverty.

In the early 21st century, IEPs represent an important part of the experience of racialized groups in the Canadian labour market. These individuals have been educated abroad but face numerous barriers in trying to convert their training into comparable occupational status and income. This category of racialized group members is referred to here as Internationally Educated Professionals and Tradespeople (IEPs).[12] It has been growing as Canada's immigration system has moved toward more stringent selection criteria, with emphasis on higher education and market-oriented skills. Because of IEPs' increasingly significant numbers as a proportion of the racialized cohort, their experience, while specific, in part explains the failure of racialized group members to translate educational attainment and experience into higher occupational status, intra- and intersectoral mobility and compensation.

IEPs' experience is an indictment of the major institutions responsible for ensuring access to trades and professions: governments, licensing bodies and other regulators, employers, educational institutions, and trade unions. They have failed to devise appropriate policy and program responses to address the problem of barriers to professions and trades, and to ensure a smooth transition for internationally trained professionals and tradespeople into their fields of expertise. The institutions have shown themselves unable to design a successful integration strategy that would focus on evaluating the competencies of trained immigrants rather than on validating demands for undefined Canadian experience. They have failed to match immigrant skills with the labour-market shortages that exist in Canada's industries, regions, provinces, cities, towns, and communities.

Historically, the Canadian government has supported past waves of immigration with such resources such as land for settlement. However, in the early 21st century, conditioned by the neo-liberal dogma of market regulation, governments have selected highly talented immigrants without assuming responsibility for their successful integration. The federal government does not track their progress as a basis for policy evaluation or decision-making. Instead, it has committed to a neo-liberal laissez-faire approach to immigrant integration, oblivious to the barriers in access to the Canadian labour market. At the same time, the government continues to "compete" for immigrants bearing similar skills.

Collaboration between the two federal departments that have a direct interest in this population—Citizenship and Immigration Canada (CIC) and Human Resource and Skills Development Canada (HRSDC)—is almost non-existent. Until recently there was almost no high-level inter-governmental coordination on access to professions and trades for immigrants. Ironically, the federal and provincial governments have responded to the debate on brain drain to the U.S. by implementing taxation and other policies measures aimed at discouraging skilled workers from emigrating to the United States. Yet, despite demands for action by racialized and immigrant communities and increasingly employers, the issue of access to professions and trades in Canada has remained on the policy back burner. This betrays great official negligence because in terms of numbers, Canada receives four skilled immigrants to every one migrant to the U.S. The incoming ones are as or even more highly skilled than the ones leaving—Canada attracts more master's and doctoral graduates than it loses. Additionally, these individuals have chosen to live and work in Canada.[13]

Barriers to Access to Professions and Trades

Internationally educated immigrants are supposed to be the future of Canada's increasingly labour-strapped economy. With massive baby boom retirements on the horizon, someone has to pay the boomers' pensions and keep the tax dollars flowing for the social programs they will need in their old age. Canada also promises the IEPs an opportunity to improve their lives and those of their families. It seems like a win-win proposition. But this depends on the relatively seamless integration of IEPs into their fields of expertise. Not unlike their predecessors, this group of largely racialized immigrants confront a Canadian labour market with racial hierarchies, and face institutional and attitudinal barriers to access to professions and trades. Yet, to date, the different levels of government have shown more commitment to deregulating than to intervening in failed labour markets to ensure the optimal allocation of this important pool of human resources.

From a historical standpoint, the changing racial composition of the immigration group in the 1980s coincided with a period during which the state and self-regulating professional and occupational bodies imposed strict administration of rules and regulations in the name of ensuring the public interest. This had the effect of erecting new barriers for many recently immigrated IEPs. While the labour-market conditions that precipitated the defensive actions have changed, the regulators have been slow to respond to the growing demands for licensing newcomers. And provincial governments, which have resisted the push by municipal governments for greater autonomy, are only too accommodating when it comes to another creation of theirs, the self-regulating bodies that run the professions and trades.

However, not all occupations or trades are regulated, and some are more regulated than others, which leaves the rest of the problem at the feet of the employers. Employers' attitudes toward internationally obtained skills and their bearers have been identified as part of the problem.[14]

There is some general agreement about issues that need to be addressed:

- Lack of adequate information about licensing process, pre- and post-arrival
- Paucity of reliable tools for assessing credentials and other prior learning
- Lack of competency-based licensing and language testing
- Inadequate bridging, supplementary training, and internship opportunities
- Limited transparency in the licensing process and lack of feedback or appeal process
- Limited coordination between stakeholders

A number of important Canadian studies dealing with the situation of internationally trained professionals and tradespeople in the Canadian labour market have come to a single conclusion: the failure to translate internationally obtained human capital and higher immigrant educational attainment into better labour-market performance can be partly explained by the existence of systemic barriers to the recognition of international qualifications and prior learning by regulators and employers.[15] Some argue that many immigrants require employment-related language training, sector-specific orientation, and labour-market information in order to be competitive in the labour market. Others acknowledge that immigrants face barriers to access to relevant information about licensing procedures both before and after arrival; barriers to obtaining equivalence, recognition, and certification of internationally acquired credentials; and barriers to obtaining employment in their fields of expertise because of employer attitudes. The experiences vary according to profession and trade as well as province and community. However, there are some common features across the country, which we will discuss below.

The findings of a recent study confirm the patterns identified in the previous studies. In the case of IEPs, barriers to access to professions and trades have contributed to higher levels of unemployment, lower levels of income, lower occupational status, and inability to convert prior learning into comparable job status.[16] According to the study, many of the settlement-sector officials interviewed suggested that the failure of the accreditation process amounts to the devaluing of IEPs' skills, to the detriment of both IEPs and their families, and the Canadian economy. More specifically, some pointed to the widely held view among the Canadian public, regulators, and employers that immigrants from "third-world countries" hold inferior "human capital."[17]

This characterization of skilled labour from the South and its implications fit in with the idea of Canada as an imagined "White-settler nation" that has historically defined the entry of racialized labour into the Canadian labour market. Some of those interviewed questioned the generalized attitude that Canadian credential standards and experience are superior to those of countries in the global South, where some of the immigrants may have been working with Canadian technology and producing products that, having met Canadian consumer standards, are consumed in Canada.[18]

I paraphrase a question that one advocate raised about the shifting standards:

> If products made by internationally trained engineers in Asia, Africa and Latin America increasingly dominate the Canadian commodity markets, how can the Canadian standard be so superior to those of the countries from which the products are made that the professionals who make them there cannot practice when they come to Canada?[19]

Many informants suggested that decisions regarding access to professional employment for the internationally trained are often based not on an objective assessment of their competency, but rather on outmoded attitudes held by regulators and employers about the general competencies of immigrants from certain countries. These negative attitudes are reinforced by the mass media, which tends to frame the immigration of racialized group members as representing an economic and social (and even security) concern for Canadian society. The media often presents a selective and negative portrayal of racialized immigrants; as has been documented, this results in the creation or entrenchment of negative stereotypes.[20] The effect is to undermine the seamless integration of recent immigrants into the Canadian labour market and to contribute to the increase in poverty among recent immigrants, and especially among university graduates.[21]

One of the outcomes of this form of economic exclusion is that many well-educated racialized job seekers settle for driving cabs or working as newspaper carriers after years of frustrating job searches. These exclusions contribute to emotional and psychological stresses that in some cases mature into mental health conditions.

Family life is also impacted, as families of skilled immigrants are increasingly prone to breakdown.[22]

A 1994 federal government study by Fernando Mata breaks down a number of significant human and social impacts resulting from Canada's failure to recognize the credentials of immigrants:

Ethnic/race relations impacts: Racialized immigrants who find themselves shut out of their occupations feel individually and collectively alienated as victims of institutional discrimination. This alienation results in mounting tensions between themselves and members of other groups who are not excluded. Moreover, as long as minority professionals continue to be barred from practising their professions, youths from those communities will lack effective role models, and this lack perpetuates the problem.[23]

Human rights impacts: Many foreign-trained professionals and tradespeople, as well as immigrant agencies, argue that policies and practices that limit access to accreditation and access to trades and professions contravene the protections accorded by the *Canadian Charter of Rights and Freedoms* and by provincial human rights legislation.[24]

Immigrant integration impacts: Lack of recognition of an immigrant's occupation often leads to underemployment and reduced income. In addition, "professional accreditation barriers for immigrant women and refugee groups are often insurmountable." For women, this lack of recognition arises from factors related to both their legal entry status and the added burden many of them face due to gender and family roles. For refugees, having to present original certificates and documents in order to be accredited often makes the situation even worse. Because many such documents may have been destroyed or lost in their flight from persecution, and because they cannot return to their countries of origin to retrieve them or request new ones, refugees may simply abandon their hopes of achieving the recognition of their professional credentials in Canada.[25]

Mental health impacts: According to the report, these impacts "may be the most harmful to society. The 1988 Report of the Canadian Task Force on Mental Health Issues singled out the barriers to trades and professions as major factors leading to an erosion of skills, loss of technical idiom, and diminishing confidence in one's capabilities." Desperation has even driven affected immigrants to conduct hunger strikes to bring attention to their situation and to instigate change. The mental health problems often result in physical health problems related to stress.[26]

The Role of Regulators and Employers

Many professions, trades, and occupations are regulated to protect the public interest. They require prospective employees to meet set standards of performance or demonstrated ability to obtain a licence. In many cases, though, regulators are not very familiar with international educational, training, technological, or professional standards, although the responsibility to evaluate international credentials falls on them.

Studies done with regulators and employers see the problem differently. Many see it as a supply problem with the onus of the IEPs to take the necessary measures to compete in a free labour market. Because of their position of power, these "skateholders" largely influence government policy. According to professional regulators and employers, there is a mismatch between the skills, education, and experience of IEPs and the jobs and occupations on offer in Canada. They attribute it to such individual factors as the lack of familiarity with the Canadian labour market and occupational requirements, low official language skills, and the quality gap in higher education between countries of the South and industrialized Northern countries (Basavarajappa and Verma, 1985; Devoretz, 1998; Sangster, 2001).

Employers point to limited period of stay in country, lack of Canadian qualifications, and low language facility as limiting the attractiveness of immigrants as candidates for hire or promotion. Employers also insist that the skilled immigrants lack soft skills such as communication, occupational language facility, and the ability to "fit in."[27] These are concerns often heard from regulators too. They also note the difficulty of evaluating international credentials for equivalency without all the necessary information about the educational institutions and the conditions of practice in the IEP's home country. While most don't see it as their responsibility to do more than assess the cases that appear before them, some have called for bridging programs to address what they see as a competence gap between Canadian and home-country practice.

Responses from Advocates of Internationally Educated Professionals and Tradespeople

Naturally, the problem appears rather different to the advocates for the internationally trained professionals and tradespeople. Many IEP advocates respond to the regulators' characterization of the problem with dismay. They suggest that the focus of employers and regulators is disproportionately on the subjective attributes of IEPs, and that IEPs are vulnerable to prejudiced judgements.[28] Drawing on their experiences, they argue that soft skills can be acquired and should not be a basis for throwing the baby out with the bath water.[29] Advocates are concerned about a tendency among regulators to view such limitations as fixed and unchanging, so the strengths and competence of the IEPs are not considered. Appropriate human-resource planning would suggest that the starting point should be to accurately assess the IEPs' level of competence based on their training and experience in the field. The assessment of competence needs to take place in a work-related environment to ensure maximum assessment of equivalence. Then the soft skills can be acquired through supplementary training and or bridging processes.

The advocates also identify as barriers the high cost of credential assessments, licensing exams, and the various elements of the certification process, which vary from province to province; such costs are largely not recognized by the regulators and employers. Advocates express concerns about the fact that educational institutions such as medical schools play a gatekeeping role when it comes to selecting international medical graduates for residency positions. This role is not subject to any form of accountability or transparency, a process that frustrates many international medical graduates who have often completed all the requisite exams, but are denied access to residency without explanation or feedback.

The advocates are also concerned that the prior learning or skill assessment, whether by educational institutions, by assessment agencies, or by licensing bodies, does not focus on individual competencies. Instead the focus is on the credential-granting institution, or on such subjective issues such as the average literacy level in the source country. In some cases the assumption is made that the IEPs lack language proficiency and so cannot be competent professionally. The advocates suggest a competency-based evaluation of skills that would better identify individual IEPs' abilities by taking into account their experience after graduation. Finally, advocates are concerned about the lack of transparency on the part of the licensing bodies and the failure of governments to hold them accountable for managing access to professions and trades; advocates worry that licensing bodies may not be acting in the public interest.[30]

The racialized experience of barriers to professions and trades creates substantial costs — both to individual immigrants and their families, and to Canadian governments, businesses, and the economy. The costs to the individuals and their families are not only financial, but also emotional, undermining their sense of identity and their self-esteem. The result is a highly educated and experienced underclass of immigrant professionals and tradespeople who are unemployed or underemployed in Canada, many finding only low-end, low-skill, contract, temporary or part-time, casual employment. Many highly trained immigrants end up as newspaper carriers, janitors, taxi drivers, fast-food deliverers, or security officers in Canada's urban areas (de Wolff, 2001; Galabuzi, 2001; Jackson, 2002). Many are vulnerable to compromised health; recent immigrants have historically enjoyed higher health status because of the stringent health selection process, yet now they are losing ground over time under conditions of social exclusion (Hyman, 2001). Standard employer demands for "Canadian experience" often lead to professionals and tradespeople "falling" out of their field of training and seeing their skills degrade over time. Over 90% of those who fail to find work in their field in the first three years of immigration end up permanently in other sectors.

Given these conditions, immigrant professionals and skilled tradespeople have not translated their educational attainment and experience into high occupational status or income. Advocates for immigrants refer to this situation as a "brain waste." According to a Price Waterhouse report (1998) commissioned by the Ontario government, the systematic failure to recognize foreign credentials costs the Ontario economy by increasing costs to the welfare system, imposing losses on employers who are unable to find employees with the skills and abilities they desperately require, and necessitating unnecessary retraining for foreign-trained individuals.[31]

Employers' and regulators' failure to properly evaluate prior learning casts them in the role not of defenders of the public interest, but of gatekeepers. The lack of transparency in the application processes, along with the existence of closed trade-union shops, makes it difficult to review their exercise of discretion. The effect is to devalue and degrade the skills of vulnerable IEPs, contributing to documented occupational and wage inequality.[32] Although IEPs, immigrants, and racialized communities are organizing to challenge this exercise of power, they are often powerless to stop their victimization and require the governments to enforce a broader definition of the public interest. Many educated immigrants face major and sometimes insurmountable barriers to obtaining occupational licences.[33] As a result, many immigrants are forced into unskilled labour or less skilled work at wages well below their potential, leaving them vulnerable to low-income status and subject to social class shifting.

Conclusion

While racialized persons in general experience social exclusion, factors such as gender and immigrant status also structure access to opportunity and resources in specific ways. Racialized women and recent immigrants increasingly meet in workplaces defined by the prevalence of precarious forms of work. In both cases, intersections of race and other identities or status intensify the experience of racialization. Suffering a double disadvantage, these groups experience poverty and negative socio-psychological impacts, which show up in the decline of health status of immigrants over the time of their residence in Canada. In the next chapter, we will explore these outcomes of social exclusion in more detail.

Notes

1. T. Das Gupta, *Racism and Paid Work* (Toronto: Garamond Press, 1996); T. das Gupta, "Political Economy of Gender, Race and Class: Looking at South Asian Immigrant Women in Canada," *Canadian Ethnic Studies* 26, no. 1 (1994): 59–73; A. Calliste, "Resisting Exclusion and Marginality in Nursing: Women of Colour in Ontario," in *Race and Ethnicity in Canada*, edited by M. Kalbach and W. Kalbach (Toronto: Harcourt Brace, 2000), 308–328; R. Ng, *Politics of Community Services: Immigrant Women, Class and the State* (Toronto: Garamond Press, 1988); Immigrant Women of Saskatchewan, *Doubly Disadvantaged: The Women Who Immigrate to Canada* (Saskatoon: Immigrant Women of Saskatchewan, 1985); M. Boyd, "At a Disadvantage: The Occupational Attainment of Foreign Born Women In Canada," *International Migration Review*, 18, no. 4 (1985): 1091–1119; D. Brand, "Black Women and Work: The Impact of Racially Constructed Gender Roles on the Sexual Division of Labour," *Fireweed* 25 (1987): 35; among others.
2. J. Chard, *Women in a Visible Minority* (Ottawa: Statistics Canada, 2000).
3. Ibid.
4. A. Calliste, "Anti-Racism Organizing and Resistance in Nursing: African-Canadian Women," in *Canadian Review of Sociology and Anthropology* 33, no. 3 (1996): 361–390; A. Calliste, "Resisting Exclusion and Marginality in Nursing: Women of Colour in Ontario," in *Race and Ethnicity in Canada*, edited by M. Kalbach and W. Kalbach (Toronto: Harcourt Brace, 2000), 308–328; das Gupta (1996b); J. Reitz et al., *Ethnic Inequality and Segregation in Jobs* (Toronto: Centre for Urban Studies, University of Toronto, 1981); K. Flynn, "Proletarianization, Professionalization, and Caribbean Immigrant Nurses," *Canadian Women Studies* 18, no. 1 (1998): 57–60.
5. Canadian Civil Liberties Association, *Survey of Employment Agencies* (Toronto: CCLA, 1991).

6.   G. Picot and F. Hou, *The Performance of the 1990s Canadian Labour Market*, paper no. 148 (Ottawa: Statistics Canada, April 2000).

7.   Statistics Canada, "1995 Survey of Work Arrangements," as quoted in A. de Wolff, *Breaking the Myth of Flexible Work: Contingency Work in Toronto* (Toronto: Contingency Worker Project, 2000).

8.   de Wolff (2000).

9.   A series of studies done by the Canadian Civil Liberties Association in the 1980s and early 1990s surveying employment agencies in Ontario's urban centres found that many were willing to observe a "White only" policy in job referrals when the employer demanded it. A subsequent complaint to the Ontario Human Rights Commission led to a finding of discrimination. See T. Rees, "Racial Discrimination and Employment Agencies," *Currents: Readings in Race Relations* 7, no. 2 (1991): 16–19.

10.   L. Yanz, B. Jeffcoat, D. Ladd, J. Atlin, and Maquila Solidarity Network, *Policy Options to Improve Standards for Women Garment Workers in Canada and Internationally* (Ottawa: Status of Women Canada: January, 1999).

11.   R. Ng, *Home-Working; Home Office or Home Sweatshop? Report on Current Conditions of Home-Workers in Toronto's Garment Industry* (Toronto: NALL, OISE, 1999).

12.   Given the contentious nature of non-Canadian training and experience, there has been a move way from references to these skilled workers as "foreign trained" to less negative references such as "internationally educated professionals and tradespeople (IEPs)" or "internationally trained professionals and tradespeople." In specific fields, they are also referred to as International Medical Graduates (IMGs), International Trained Engineering Graduates (ITEGs), etc.

13.   Scott Murray, Presentation. "Brain Drain, Brain Gain." Sessional Proceedings (Toronto: Maytree Foundation, May 25, 2000).

14.   While professions and occupations in the health care, education, and engineering fields are largely self-regulated, there is less rigorous regulation in social work, accounting, and practically none in the information technology field. However, there are educational credentials that serve as benchmarks and to which employers look for assessing the skills of the prospective employees. Needless to say, this process is highly subjective and open to pre-judgement.

15.   The Toronto-based Policy Roundtable Mobilizing Professions and Trades (PROMPT) has identified five key reasons why IEPs face persistent barriers to fair access to trades and professions: Lack of policy coherence among levels of government in Canada; lack of accountability among stakeholders; and negative attitudes toward immigrants in Canadian society, regulatory bodies, and employers. (PROMPT Update — June 2003).

16.   See C. Teelucksing and G. Galabuzi, *Working Precariously: The Impact of Race and Immigrant Status on Employment Opportunities and Outcomes in Canada* (Toronto: Centre for Social Justice/Canadian Race Relations Foundation, 2005). In a qualitative study, telephone interviews were conducted by the authors with key informants from the settlement sectors in Vancouver, Calgary, Toronto, Montreal, and Halifax, in the spring and summer of 2004. The purpose was to determine the prevalence of systemic barriers to access to employment in regulated and unregulated trades and professions among internationally educated professionals and tradespeople; to assess its impact on the employment prospects of IEPs; and to determine what measures IEPs and other stakeholders were taking to address the issues raised. The results confirmed the findings of previous qualitative research reported

by Basran and Zong (1998) and McDade (1988), among others. The findings also speak to a heightened awareness of the issues at the policy-making levels of governments, among regulators and employers, as well as to a growing mobilization among IEPs and communities to advocate for change.

17. Ibid.

18. Ibid.

19. Interview with a provincial coordinator of an IEP association (name withheld upon request).

20. See F. Henry and C. Tator, *Racist Discourses in Canada's English Print Media* (Toronto: CRRF, 2000); A. Fleras and J.L. Kunz, *Media and Minorities: Representing Diversity in Multicultural Canada* (Toronto: Thompson Educational Publishing, 2001).

21. The growing poverty gap between post-1980 immigrants and Canadian-born is an outcome of the social economic factors discussed previously in this chapter. See M. Frenette and R. Morissette, *Will They Ever Converge? Earnings of Immigrants and Canadian-Born Workers over the Last Two Decades*, Analytical Studies paper No. 215 (Ottawa: Statistics Canada, 2003).

22. Teelucksingh and Galabuzi (2005).

23. F. Mata, "The Non-Accreditation of Immigrant Professionals in Canada: Societal Impacts, Barriers, and Present Policy Initiatives," paper presented at the Sociology and Anthropology Meeting of the 1994 Learned Societies Conference, University of Calgary, June 3, 1994, p. 8.

24. Ibid., 9. See also, A. Brouwer, *Immigrants Need Not Apply: Canada Barring Highly Skilled Immigrants from Practicing Professions and Trades* (Toronto: The Maytree Foundation, 2000).

25. Ibid., 10. A recent federal court decision in the *Ahmed v. Citizenship and Immigration Canada* case has set the parameters for what is reasonable in terms of the demands the department can impose on those who flee and seek asylum in Canada without identification. Previous to this arrangement, many refugees from countries like Somalia, without any central state authority, have had their status unresolved and been left in limbo for years.

26. Canadian Taskforce on the Mental Health Issues Affecting Immigrants and Refugees, *After the Door Has Been Opened: Mental Health Issues Affecting Immigrants and Refugees in Canada*, Report of the Canadian Taskforce on the Mental Health Issues Affecting Immigrants and Refugees (Ottawa: Supply and Services, Canada, 1988).

27. See D. Sangster, *Assessing and Recognizing Foreign Credentials in Canada: Employers' Views* (Ottawa: CIC/HRDC/Canadian Labour and Business Centre, 2001). The study, done for Citizenship and Immigration Canada (CIC) and the Canadian Chamber of Commerce, surveyed the opinions of employers regarding foreign-trained accreditation. While some claimed the licensing processes were too restrictive, many suggested that immigrants' lack of information about the fields in which they want to practice and poor language skills led to their failure to get accreditation, or that their qualifications did not meet Canadian standards. However, study results show that some regulators and employers were not aware of the government-mandated prior learning assessment services and others were wary of the government forcing them to accept their outcomes as a basis for certification or employment.

28. A recent Government of Ontario study of internationally trained professionals arriving after 1994 found that almost three-quarters of the internationally trained professionals who had their academic qualifications assessed after immigrating obtained equivalent academic qualifications to those granted by Ontario universities. Moreover, most immigrants

tested well on official language facility. See Ontario Ministry of Training, Colleges and Universities, *The Facts Are in* (Toronto: Queen's Printer, 2002), 16–19.

29. Many settlement sector agencies are involved in providing labour market information, language services, job search skills, job referrals, sector specific mentoring, and even loans to cover the cost of credential assessments and licensing exams.

30. Teelucksingh and Galabuzi (2005).

31. Other studies quantifying the economic loss of unrecognized credentials include one by Bloom and Grant (2001) for the Conference Board of Canada, which suggests that close to 540,000 Canadian workers, 47% of whom are racialized group members, lose $8,000 to $12,000 of potential income per year, or a total of between $4.1 and $5.9 billion annually. A study by Reitz put the figure at a much higher $55 billion (Siddiqui, 2001).

32. Teelucksingh and Galabuzi (2005); Cummings (1989); Brouwer (1999); Basran and Zong (1998); Reitz (2001).

33. These vary from profession to profession, but generally include: demands for Canadian experience; lack of information about credential assessments and licensing; assessments that don't establish equivalency of credentials; financial costs of credential assessment and federal and provincial examinations; licensing exams not being held regularly; separate federal and provincial credential assessment requirements; demands for documentation directly from the credential-issuing institution in the home country; slow licensing process and in some cases limited positions such as the case with medical residency; employer bias; sector-specific language facility; and lack of networks.

Questions for Critical Thought

1. Does the experience of precarious labour explain the racial inequality in income?
2. Describe some of the characteristics of precarious work.
3. Describe how the concepts of gendered racism and intersectionality apply in the workplace.
4. How does the non-recognition of the qualifications of internationally educated professionals and tradespeople impact the economy?
5. How does the demand for Canadian experience impact the perceived value of the human capital of internationally educated persons?
6. Describe some of the barriers that internationally educated professionals and tradespeople face in the Canadian labour market.
7. How and why do existing structures of power reinforce the casualization of skilled workers?
8. Why are skilled immigrants disproportionately represented in precarious work?

Recommended Readings

Anisef, P., R. Sweet, and G. Frempong. *Labour Market Outcomes of Immigrant and Racial Minority University Graduates in Canada.* CERIS Working paper no. 23. Toronto: CERIS, March 2003.

BC Internationally Trained Professionals Network. *Internationally Trained Professionals in BC: An Environmental Scan.* Prepared by CB Mercer and Associates, 2002.

Bloom, M., and M. Grant. *Brain Gain: The Economic Benefits of Recognizing Learning and Learning Credentials in Canada.* Ottawa: Conference Board of Canada, 2001.

Brouwer, A. *Immigrants Need Not Apply: Canada Barring Highly Skilled Immigrants From Practicing Professions and Trades.* Toronto: The Maytree Foundation, 2000.

Chard, J. "Women in a Visible Minority." Ottawa: Statistics Canada, 2000.

Cummings, P., et al. *Access! Report of the Taskforce on Access to Trades and Professions.* Toronto: Ontario Ministry of Citizenship, 1989.

Daenzer, P. *Regulating Class Privilege: Immigrant Servants in Canada, 1940–1990s.* Toronto: Canadian Scholars' Press, 1993.

de Wolff, A. *Breaking the Myth of Flexible Work: Contingency Work in Toronto.* Toronto: Contingency Worker Project, 2000.

Ontario Ministry of Training, Colleges and Universities. *The Facts Are In: A Study of the Characteristics and Experiences of Immigrants Seeking Employment in Regulated Professions in Ontario.* Toronto: Queen's Printer, 2002.

Preston, V., and G. Man. "Employment Experiences of Chinese Immigrant Women: An Exploration of Diversity." *Canadian Woman Studies / Cahiers de la femme* 19 (1999): 115–122.

Quinn, J. "Food Bank Clients Often Well-Educated Immigrants." *The Toronto Star* (March 31, 2002): A12.

Reitz, J.G. "Immigrant Skill Utilization in the Canadian Labour Market: Implications of Human Capital Research." *Journal of International Migration and Integration* 2, no. 3 (Summer 2001), 347–378.

Yanz, L., B. Jeffcoat, D. Ladd, and J. Atlin. *Policy Options to Improve Standards for Women Garment Workers in Canada and Internationally.* Toronto: Maquila Solidarity Network/Status of Women Canada, 1999.

CHAPTER 6

Challenges to Conventional Explanations of Racial Inequality in Economic Performance— Myths and Facts

Introduction

The conventional explanations for the gap in economic performance between members of racialized and non-racialized groups focus on a number of factors that merit discussion here. Chief among them is perceived educational gap, which along with the labour-market information and adjustment gap, constitute an "immigrant lag." It has been generally held that immigrants take up to 10 years to adjust to labour market conditions outside the host country. Only then do they "catch up" to other workers. The immigration lag is also attributed to the perceived lower quality of human resource capital due to training and experience obtained in Canada.[1] More recently, as the social economic performance of immigrants has declined even after the 10-year period, there is recognition that economic restructuring is also an important consideration, especially when it is used to reinforce explanations that acknowledge other factors.[2] For instance, economic restructuring is said to create demand for new "soft" skills, such as communication, which racialized groups are said to lack and need as part of their adjustment to the Canadian labour market.[3] Much of the debate has been captured in reports and articles that contrast the earnings of immigrants over the last 25 years with the earnings of those in previous periods, as well as with the earnings of Canadian-born cohorts. Of significance to the debate is the coincidence of the change in immigration patterns over the 1975–1996 period—from mostly European sources to countries in Asia, Africa, Latin America, and the Caribbean—and the decline in the documented economic performance of immigrants. However, similar low performance patterns are observable among Canadian-born racialized group members. Invariably, though, as the countries in the global South have become the primary source of immigration to Canada—representing 75% of newcomers in the post-1980 era—the discussion of immigrant income differentials has tended to become racialized, focusing on such issues as the economic and social conditions of the source countries of racialized groups and suggesting the perceived diminished immigrant "quality" is the primary explanation for the differences in economic performance.[4]

Most mainstream explanations for the gap in economic performance emphasize three factors: the perceived gap in educational attainment between immigrants and the Canadian-born, the period of stay of immigrants in the country, and immigrants' lack of Canadian labour-market experience.[5] These arguments largely fall in a neo-classical tradition as variations of the human-capital approach, which, as discussed in Chapter 2, has more recently come under challenge by the structural barriers approach.[6] The arguments have been sustained despite documented evidence of racially discriminatory barriers in employment as provided in a number of reports and studies, including the Commission on Equality in Employment in 1984.[7] When introduced, discussion of racial discrimination in labour markets has tended to be presented as a separate and non-determinant variable disconnected from other factors, including economic change. The intersecting and mutually reinforcing nature of these factors has gone unexplored.

In this chapter, we suggest that a complex of factors combine to create the conditions of inequality described in the book. Racial discrimination, a social condition that has been historically established in Canada, combines with other productivity-related variables to determine decision-making in the labour market. There is now ample research to show that only part of the racial or gender differentials in incomes can be attributed to productivity-related individual characteristics of the racialized group members. We would propose a research agenda informed by a holistic approach to the problem because there is a compelling need to review some of the commonly held notions about racialized immigrants' economic performance, given their impact on public policy.

The Immigration and Labour-Market Complex

As we observed earlier, Canadian labour-market policy has always been linked to Canadian immigration policy. It is little wonder that developments in immigration policy influence the debates about labour-market utilization of immigrants and those considered "outsiders." Peter Li (2003) has remarked that discourse and research on immigration is fairly contested. Historically, Canadian immigration policy and to a large extent the research related to it has focused on the question of *"Who gets in?"* This was the case whether the objective was meeting specific labour-market shortages, or counterbalancing low population growth with immigrant recruitment. But the answer to the question was predicated on the unsupported assumption that certain ethnic groups of immigrants are better able to integrate, assimilate, or contribute to Canadian society. Hence the racialized nature of the Canadian immigration system in historical context. Officially, until the 1960s, ethnicity and race were disproportionate determinants of how that question was answered, as well as the attendant question about the "quality of immigrants" and what contribution they could make or what threat they posed to the Canadian economy and society. Considerable intellectual and political capital was expended in seeking ways to limit access to Canada for certain ethnic groups with the mistaken view that they were less likely to assimilate and contribute to Canada, or that they would be a burden to society.

Box 6.1: *We are All Capable People* by Marina Jimenez

It is a great irony to many in the immigration field, and to newcomers themselves, a bitter joke. Canada has a shortage of skilled professionals, and yet thousands of internationally trained doctors, engineers, teachers and nurses are forced to deliver pizzas and drive taxis.

Some immigrants believe that this is intentional, that Canada wants them only for their genetic potential. They may sweep floors and clean offices, but their offspring will be intelligent and creative. Why else would the government accept them and then make it so very difficult to have their credentials recognized?

Citizenship and Immigration Canada bristles at such a suggestion, and advises immigrants to check the ministry's Website, which clearly warns newcomers there is no guarantee they will find work in their chosen profession.

Still, frustration is mounting: This week, a British-trained accountant and his bookkeeper wife launched a lawsuit against the federal government, alleging that they were misled by immigration officials who assured them they would find good jobs here. Instead, the couple—he is originally from Sri Lanka and she from Malaysia—have spent five years in Edmonton shovelling snow, cleaning toilets and borrowing money to support their teenaged son.

"What angers me is we are capable people. We have the credentials. We just can't get the jobs," complained Selladurai Premakumaran, who feels the government has shattered his hopes and dreams.

Last year, when Canada changed the way it selects immigrants, many were happy to see the end of the old system, which matched newcomers with worker shortages.

Critics had long complained that, by the time the physiotherapists and teachers arrived, those jobs had been filled and the labour shortages were in other fields.

Now, Canada chooses immigrants based not on their occupation, but on their education, skills and language abilities. Applicants must score 67 of a possible 100 points to be accepted. Ostensibly, being talented and smart should make them more employable.

But it isn't working out that way. Canada is recruiting the right kind of people, but they are stuck in a bottleneck, as the agencies and bodies that regulate the fields of medicine, engineering, teaching and nursing struggle to assess their qualifications.

"We have a disaster on our hands," says Joan Atlin, executive director of the Association of International Physicians and Surgeons of Ontario.

"There are thousands of un- and under-employed foreign professionals across the country. At the same time, we have a shortage of skilled professionals, especially in the health-care field. We don't so much have a doctor shortage as an assessment and licensing bottleneck."

About 1,300 doctors from more than 80 countries have joined the association she heads, but she estimates there are many more out there. Ontario alone may have as many as 4,000, most of them still trying to get their medical licences.

At the same time, there is a shortage of as many as 3,000 physicians across the country, especially in smaller communities in Alberta, British Columbia, Saskatchewan and Ontario (provinces that have been forced to recruit doctors from South Africa, whose medical training Canada considers acceptable).

A recent Statistics Canada study of 164,200 immigrants who arrived in 2000 and 2001 found that 70% had problems entering the labour force. Six in every 10 were forced to take jobs other than those they were trained to do. The two most common occupational groups for men were science (natural and applied) and management, but most wound up working in sales and service or processing and manufacturing.

As well as credentials, there is a problem with supply and demand.

Patrick Coady, with the British Columbia Internationally Trained Professionals Network, believes that far too many engineers are coming—as many as 60% of all those accepted each year. (In Ontario, from 1997 to 2001, nearly 40,000 immigrants listed engineering as their occupation.)

"When they arrive, the Engineering Council for Canada evaluates their credentials, which sets up the engineer to think there are opportunities here," Mr. Coady says. "Then they discover that each province has a body that regulates the industry. They need up to 18 months of Canadian work experience before they will get professional engineering status. And, there isn't a great need for consulting engineers. A lot of the infrastructure has already been built in this country."

Michael Wu, a geotechnical engineer from China, is a classic example of what's happening. Accepted as a landed immigrant last spring, he came here with his wife and child, leaving behind a relatively prosperous life in Beijing, and now works for $7 an hour in a Vancouver chocolate factory.

Back in Beijing, "I had a three-bedroom apartment and took taxis everywhere—the Chinese government sent me to build a stadium in St. Lucia," says Mr. Wu, who has a PhD. "Here, no-one will hire me. Many engineering companies think engineers make up false documents. They are suspicious of my qualifications. I never imagined I'd end up working in a factory. But I will keep trying. Every month I go to the Vancouver Geotechnical Society lecture."

Susan Scarlett of the Immigration Department points out that regulating the professions is a provincial, not federal, responsibility. "We advise people who are thinking of coming to Canada to prepare by really researching how their credentials will be assessed."

Ms. Atlin says that "Canada has been very slow to change. Our regulatory systems have not caught up with our immigration policies."

But some relief may be on the horizon because the issue has become such a political flashpoint.

A national task force is about to report to the deputy minister of health on the licensing of international medical graduates. And this month Denis Coderre, the federal Immigration Minister, announced that he wants to streamline the process of recognizing foreign credentials, and have provinces announce their inventory of needs so Ottawa can work to fill the shortages.

Source: *The Globe and Mail* (October 25, 2003), Focus Section, p. F9.

The tone of the debate is not always neutral or non-offensive, and some voices do arouse a xenophobic response.[8] Despite the ease with which immigrants are often impugned as a burden to Canada, the issue of the performance of the immigrants who are already here, as a basis for predicting future integration success, has always been largely secondary for policy-makers. More often, it has been raised as a way of blaming immigrants for the poor economy in periods of high unemployment when structural changes in the economy have led to significant job loss. Despite the paucity of research to resolve this debate one way or another, decision-makers have not been keen to do follow-up studies on newcomers — even those from the preferred skilled-immigrant categories — to confirm predictions of integration success. However, this has not stopped them from imposing new prohibitions on certain types of immigrants, while their provincial colleagues countenance actions by provincially mandated regulatory bodies and by employers to deny them access to professions and trades. Ironically, the immigration process selects immigrants on the basis of skills they are prevented from using. What makes these seeming contradictions "acceptable" is that racially and ethnically based assumptions about the "human capital quality" of certain immigrant groups had taken on an official aura.

While officially this position changed with the advent of the point system in the 1960s, it remains very much an unspoken reality in immigration policy-making. This is clear from Conservative and Liberal governments' responses in the 1980s and 1990s to criticisms of too many "wrong" immigrants coming into Canada and to numerous reports pointing to new immigrants' socio-economic struggles as evidence of their having being poorly chosen.[9] The government's response has been to "tighten" the selection criteria by introducing a new selection system that seeks to "identify" the perfect "culturally attuned and appropriately skilled" immigrant. This response is objected to by many new immigrant groups who claim that it belies racist attitudes toward the predominantly racialized immigrants in the post-1980 era. A country built on working-class immigrant labour — some of it racialized — now largely eschews racialized working-class immigration.

In the past, in a more stable economy, the discriminatory impact of the selection process seemed inconsequential in terms of policy-making. The most affected immigrants were relatively small in number. And with a healthy job market, many racialized immigrants were able to overcome steep odds, and over time even outperform their Canadian-born cohorts. However, in the post-1980s period, patterns of inferior immigrant performance began to persist, although minimal attention was still paid to these workers' condition in the labour market. Governments, regulators, and employers did not blame the economic circumstances within the country — such as economic restructuring and a shift from Fordist mode of production to flexible modes, followed by two bouts of free-trade-induced structural adjustment and economic liberalization. Rather, governments simply accepted the charge by researchers and some anti-immigrant advocates that there were too many newcomers in the family class, a class previously favoured for its reproduction of the largely European immigration population. These immigrants, along with refugees, were said to diminish the quality of immigrant labour.

The Diminishing-Returns Approach

Led by the 1991 Economic Council of Canada report titled "Economic and Social Impacts of Immigration," what is known as the "diminishing-returns" approach became so prominent in the 1980s and early 1990s that it had significant impact on Canadian immigration policy, for instance leading to limits in refugee approvals and the priorization of the selection of independent-class immigrants.[10]

A renewed emphasis on the point system implied objective human-capital valuations of internationally obtained skills, leading to a shift from family class to independent class as the dominant immigrant class. However, the shift has not resolved the issues identified. That is partly because little has been done to gauge how these policy changes and new expectations translate in the labour-market experiences of the new immigrants. The idea that if the country recruited "perfect" immigrants, these issues would disappear continued to compete for airtime with the claim that there were too many immigrants.

The voices of the people whose experiences are at the heart of the debate have been largely left out of the policy debate. That is, until relatively recently when immigrant community organizations have become more forceful in articulating the struggles new immigrants face. While a growing number of researchers has pointed to the discriminatory barriers in the labour market and the changing economy as key sources of immigrants' increasingly poor performance in the labour market — economic restructuring, deregulation, and globalization have led to fewer good jobs and more contingency work — governments' focus has remained on the "ineffectiveness" or "failure" of the selection system to identify high-quality candidates. This preoccupation with selection has persisted in the face of increased proportions of highly qualified immigrants who in turn have struggled to establish themselves economically (Akbari, 1989; Christofides and Swindinsky, 1994; Galabuzi, 2001; Li, 1998a; Lian and Matthews, 1998; Pendukar and Pendukar, 1998; Smith and Jackson, 2002; Ornstein, 2000).

Governments continue to largely ignore the impact of employment barriers on the successful integration of racialized immigrants in particular, and to insist on fine-tuning the selection system to minimize the chance of "low-quality" immigrants getting through. Yet in the real world, these preoccupations do not correlate to the experience of immigrants in the labour market. Highly qualified entrants from the independent class are struggling to navigate discriminatory barriers in much the same way that refugees and family-class immigrants are. These barriers in essence negate the value of human capital that is otherwise the basis for the selection of newcomers, leading to high levels of unemployment, low employment status, low incomes, and disproportionate representation of immigrants in low-income sectors and occupations. Finally, this all translates into high poverty rates for recent immigrants, a highly racialized category.

To make matters worse, the criminalization of immigration in the public discourse and, more recently, the national security concerns due to the threat of terrorism have helped nullify efforts to focus public policy attention on the inequalities immigrants face in the Canadian labour market. *"Who gets in?"* has been reinforced as the central immigration question. In the post-September 11 era, Canada's security concerns have overwhelmed questions relating to the immigrant experience in the Canadian society, especially those related to barriers to successful integration in the labour market. Yet post-immigration experiences require as much public policy attention as does appropriate immigrant selection. Research increasingly shows that post-selection state intervention is critical in ensuring successful integration in such areas as training, credential assessment, and bias-free employment practices.[11]

Challenges to the Diminishing-Returns Approach

As observed above, in the 1980s some researchers and policy advocates interpreted these observations as indicative of the diminishing quality of immigrants, arguing that there were flaws in the immigration system because of the high content of family-class immigrants and refugees. However, these observations persisted through the 1990s, when the independent skilled immigrant class became dominant. That class now represents over 60% of newcomers.[12]

There is now significant research challenging the logic of the diminishing-returns approach. The question of immigrant performance in the Canadian economy has begun to draw some interest, with a variety of studies and reports dealing with the economic performance of immigrants and their impact on the Canadian economy. Many of the studies examining immigrants' performance have focused on the relationship between immigration and income levels (Akbari, 1989; Anderson and Lynam, 1987; Baker and Benjamin, 1994; Bloom, Grenier, and Gunderson, 1995; Borjas, 1985; Boyd, 1984; Christofides and Swindinsky, 1994; Grant and Oertel, 1998; Li, 1988; Lian and Matthews, 1998; Pendukar and Pendukar, 1998). Many have found that there is a growing gap between the performance of the post-1980s immigrants, a highly racialized group, and their pre-1980s cohort. The historical trajectory shows immigrants catching up over a 10- to 12-year period, and in some cases surpassing the performance of native-born Canadians. Now, however, there is evidence of a growing disadvantage in income attainment.

Increasingly, studies are pointing to wage discrimination along racial lines as a key factor in immigrant income attainment. Over the last decade, a number of studies—including Li (1988); Akbari (1989); de Silva (1992); Christofides and Swidinsky (1994); Baker and Benjamin (1995); Gosine (2000); Hiebert (1997); Hou and Balakrishnan (1996); Ornstein (2000); Lian and Matthews (1998); Pendakur and Pendakur (1998); Harvey, Siu, and Reil (1999); Galabuzi (2001); and Smith and Jackson (2002)—have examined the income and occupational inequalities between recent immigrant populations and native-born cohorts.

Much of this research shows that recent immigrants, and more specifically racialized group immigrants, suffer lower earnings and occupational status than native-born Canadians after controlling for other factors such as age, education, language, and period of employment. They not only experience downward career mobility upon arrival, but also disproportionately occupy jobs in the lower echelons of the Canadian labour market for extended periods of time, unlike previous immigrants. They work disproportionately in domestic and janitorial jobs, the low-end service sector, and low-end manufacturing. The latter category includes light manufacturing and garment-working, often in piecemeal arrangements in the home; some have described this type of arrangement as the postmodern sweatshop.

Two thirds of racialized group members are immigrants, and racialized individuals make up 75% of the recent immigrant population. Research that disaggregates the two categories suggests similar trends. Ornstein's (2000) cross-ethnic report, based on 1996 Census data and examining ethno-racial socio-economic performance in Toronto, looks at the inequality between immigrants and racialized groups on the one hand, and other Toronto residents on the other. It documented gaps in income as high as 50% for some recent immigrated racialized groups, and pointed in particular to the disadvantages faced by racialized women. Racialized group unemployment rates are three times those of European descendants; poverty levels are three to four times the CMA average. While European immigrants suffer some disadvantage, it is not as severe, except perhaps among Eastern Europeans from the most recent immigration period (under five years).

Much of this research suggests that institutional or structural barriers to opportunities explain a significant part of the income inequality. However, it may serve to respond to each of the key arguments presented by the human capital school.

The Educational Attainment Gap Argument

Let us begin with the perceived educational gap. The standard argument, as presented by DeVoretz and others,[13] is that, although the Canadian government's stated objective in adopting the points-based immigration policy in the 1960s was to increase the proportion of skilled immigrants admitted into the country, newcomers under the family and humanitarian classes continue to predominate over independent-class entrants. Because these immigrants are not assessed according to their potential labour-market performance in Canada, the de racialization of immigration policy resulted in the admission of immigrants with lower educational attainment than those who had come in the past, and lower educational attainment than Canadian-born people. The shift in migrant flows from European source countries to countries with lower than average skill levels is assumed to imply lower levels of skills among the racialized newcomers. As a result, the argument goes, not only have the new immigrants had difficulty adjusting to the Canadian economy, but also their poor performance and the economic performance gap are inevitable. These groups of recent immigrants have thus been held responsible for an overall decline in economic returns from immigration.[14]

The Period-of-Stay Argument

Secondly, it is suggested that racialized immigrants have been in the country for only a relatively short period of time and so should expect a lower-than-average level of economic performance. This is the "rites of passage" argument, often used in reference to other immigration waves and to what are claimed to be historical income gaps between Canadian-born population and immigrants in general. It is consistent with a long-held notion that difficulties associated with immigration and settlement (the entry effect) account for an economic lag between immigrants and Canadian-born people, irrespective of educational attainment. However, while newcomers have lower earnings than the Canadian-born at the beginning because of the "assimilation effect," the former see an improvement in their income corresponding to the length of stay, and effectively close the gap in 10 to 15 years. Earlier analysis of census data by Kuch and Haessel (1979), Richmond and Kalback (1980), Carliner (1981), and more recently by Chiswick and Miller (1988) and Green and Green (1995), suggests that whatever earning differentials may occur at the beginning tend to disappear over time; in fact, immigrants end up outperforming their Canadian-born counterparts.[15] Others, such as Hiebert (1991), also suggest that the length of stay determines not just the level of performance but also the sector-to-sector mobility for immigrants, and so explains the concentrations in low-paid ghettos. Looking at ethnic and gender segmentation in the labour markets in Toronto, Vancouver, and Montreal, he concludes that immigrants who have been in Canada longer are more evenly distributed across occupations and sectors than are the newly arrived. Hierbert is therefore able to attribute the overrepresentation of racialized groups in secondary or non-professional, low-skilled occupations, and low-income sectors almost exclusively to the period of stay in the country.[16]

The Quality of Human Capital Argument

Thirdly, Green and Green (1995), Stoffman (1993), Baker and Benjamin (1994), Wright and Maxim (1993), and DeVoretz and Fagnan (1990), among others, have argued that members of the racialized groups lack the "quality" of human capital, sometimes expressed as Canadian experience, that employers consider necessary to the performance of duties in the Canadian economy.[17] Risk-averse employers are said to be less comfortable hiring newcomers because they lack certain intangibles related to job performance. The assumption is that a prospective employee's recent immigration indicates reduced suitability for the job and lower projected productivity beyond what the resume or interview is able to uncover. Because of the assumed lack of familiarity with the Canadian labour market, institutions, and labour processes, immigrant job seekers are assumed to be less productive on average than their Canadian-born counterparts, regardless of education. Rather than go through the process of assessing each individual's competence or "human capital quality," employers attribute a level of relative productivity to those who fall within the newcomer class.[18] In essence, immigrant status and related race and ethnicity become proxies for "low quality of human capital," leading to hiring and promotion decisions that reflect "economic" considerations.

Myth Busting: Responses to Conventional Wisdom on Racialized Economic Performance Differentials

As suggested earlier, the literature on the economics of immigration has been dominated by research on the immigrant/Canadian-born earnings differentials and the earnings adjustments of immigrants. This research has attempted to document whether immigrants catch up and eventually overtake their Canadian-born counterparts in terms of earnings performance. Beginning with the work of Chiswick (1978) and Borjas (1985), the empirical literature has typically dealt with this question by estimating age-earnings profiles. The available literature provides a mixed picture of the earnings performance of immigrants relative to their Canadian-born counterparts. Under an older methodology, the standard answer was that, after 10 to 15 years, the average immigrant overtook his Canadian counterpart and thereafter earned more.[19] More recent evidence offers a dissenting view. For example, Bloom, Grenier, and Gunderson (1995), using data from the 1971, 1981, and 1986 Canadian censuses, found that recent immigrants experience less earnings growth, and, for all post-1970 immigrant cohorts, earnings "assimilation" does not occur; that is, their earnings may never catch up to those of the Canadian-born. Bloom et al. attribute this earnings collapse to declining immigrant human capital and the recession of the 1980s, which reduced the absorptive capacity of the labour market. They also attribute the decline to discrimination, a factor others have dismissed or ignored in the past. Frenette and Morissette's study (2003), which looked at immigrant earnings between 1980–2000, also concludes that increasingly there is no convergence with the Canadian-born population.[20]

Myth Busting No. 1: Race Does Still Matter
Numerous studies have come to the conclusion that race matters, and continues to influence Canadian government policy and determine access to the labour market. For instance, according to a study by Edward Herberg, five of the six highest groups in rankings based on post-secondary educational attainment are racialized groups, and yet they have not been able to translate these skills into compensation, leading to a negative gap between their income and that of non-racialized Canadians.[21]

But not everyone agrees, and those who disagree tend to have the power to influence public policy. Daniel Stoffman's (1993) critique of Canada's immigration implied that Canada's reliance on immigrants of colour had led to a decline in the quality of immigrants coming to Canada, and so called for major changes in the immigration policy. The changes called for aimed at tightening access to Canada for immigrants from the South and were imposed soon after.[22] Conrad Winn (1985), in his critique of the Abella Commission on Equality in Employment (1984), argued that there was no empirical support for the premise that Canada's labour market is immobile and that visible minorities cannot make economic progress in it without government intervention.[23] Similar arguments have been advanced by others, including Collacot (2002), Stoffman (2002), DeVoretz (1995), and Borjas (1994).

Clearly some of the arguments presented above call for myth busting. To begin, many of the studies in question ignore the fact that the development of the Canadian economy, and especially the incorporation of immigrant labour in the economy, has historically been racialized. Official government policies clearly suggest as much. That should be the context within which the debate on the nature and causes of the gap in economic performance is. The outcome of various racially motivated institutional and government policies has been the racial stratification of the Canadian economy.

As discussed previously, many researchers have acknowledged the extent to which Canadian immigration policy is sensitive to socio-economic factors. The setting of annual targets often directly reflects the public mood about the economy and concerns relating to integration. Curiously, few account for the increased incidence of racial discrimination as a response by the host country to an influx of racialized group immigrants — incidences documented widely throughout Canadian history, in sociological studies looking at immigrant integration and settlement, and more recently in studies looking at ethno-racial relations. A few studies raise the issue directly, including the public opinion surveys that test for attitudes toward immigrants. Akbari (1989) has argued that the increase in migration from the South is inevitably bound to raise "fears," and that the incidence of racial discrimination is likely to rise as a consequence of international migration, given the historical racialized context of Canadian society.[24] That effect may be reflected in the income inequality gap identified in studies by Feng and Balakrishnan (1996), Galabuzi (2001), Gosine (2000), Grant and Oertal (1998), Preston and Giles (1995), Pendukar and Pendukar (1998), and Ornstein (2000), among others.

Others studies that consider such variables as gender and specific ethnic differentials—cross-referenced with education and ethnicity, length of stay, and income and occupational status returns to education—show a discrimination effect (Harvey, Sui, and Keil, 1999; Boyd, 1992; Das Gupta, 1994; Hiebert, 1997; Hou and Balakrishnan, 1996; Kunz et al., 2001; Li, 1998; Preston and Giles, 1995; Reitz and Sklar, 1997; Wanner, 1998).

A study conducted by Galabuzi (2001) for the Centre for Social Justice analyzing Statistics Canada data on racialized and non-racialized immigrant incomes for the period 1996–1998 shows a growing income gap along racial lines.[25] With minor differences, a recent Canadian Centre for Social Development (CCSD) study also shows persistent income gaps between recent immigrants and the Canadian-born (Smith and Jackson, 2002). A study comparing racialized group members in the U.S. and Canada concluded that even native-born racialized group members in the U.S. are better rewarded than their counterparts in Canada. This is consistent with Canadian research focusing on racialized group members. Findings published in a Canadian Race Relations Foundation/Canadian Centre for Social Development study profiling racial differences in education, employment, and income (both immigrant and native-born) come to similar conclusions about the socio-economic status of racialized groups.

Henry and Ginsberg's 1984 study, which examined access to employment by evenly matching Black and White job seekers for entry positions in a number of established companies, shows that White applicants received three job offers for every offer a Black applicant received. In additional field-testing using phone interviews, many callers of South Asian or Caribbean heritage were screened out before they even received in-person interviews.[26]

A follow-up study titled *No Discrimination Here* (Billingsley and Musynski, 1985) found that discrimination was demonstrated in recruitment, promotional, and termination practices. The study documented the perceptions of employers and personnel managers, about a third of whom felt that racial minorities did not have the abilities Whites had, even without interviewing them.[27]

A number of these studies, using regression analysis, control for a range of factors such as sex, length of employment, age, level of education, field of study, occupation, period of stay in country, province of residence, census metropolitan area, place of birth (Canada or abroad), and mother tongue. Their findings suggest that racial discrimination is a significant factor in income and occupational inequality. More recent studies focusing on recent immigrants have also reached similar findings (Baker and Benjamin, 1994; Grant and Oertel, 1998; Reitz, 2000; Smith and Jackson, 2002).

Increasingly, these studies show several trends. First, employment discrimination, income inequalities, and barriers to professions and trades are often cited to explain why racialized members are unable to translate educational attainment into commensurate income and occupational status. Second, they show that the association between ethnicity and immigrant performance has diminished, increasingly replaced by race as the key factor in predicting immigrant success in the labour market. There has been a corresponding shift toward studying race as a key variable in immigrant performance, given similar period of immigration, length of residence, and Canadian work experience. As Harvey, Siu, and Keil have suggested, "the race 'factor' appears to have implications on how severe, extensive and persistent immigrants' socio-economic disadvantage is" (1999). Many employers also use race to determine employability — a practice some researchers refer to as statistical discrimination and others as systemic discrimination.[28]

Apparently, as racialized nations become the dominant source of Canada's immigrants, race and its attendant socio-historical baggage have become a proxy for immigrant status. Negative assumptions associated with race are amplified further by the information gap created by the failure to appropriately assess internationally obtained qualifications. These two factors have become mutually, but negatively reinforcing when it comes to evaluating the human capital of immigrants and making labour-market decisions. The outcome is the devaluation of immigrant human capital, lower employment status, and differential access to employment and compensation.

The research shift toward race-based variables is informed by a growing awareness of racial discrimination in Canadian society, and by public policy responses such as multiculturalism, employment equity, and anti-racism programs. As well, increases in levels of immigration in the late 1980s and early 1990s (during periods of recession) sparked old questions about the absorptive capacity of an economy on the ropes, and about the ethnic makeup of the immigrant cohort. The research shift is also informed by findings of intra-group divergence in immigrant outcomes over time. For instance, immigrants who came to Canada before 1980 are performing better than their native-born Canadian counterparts, while the post-1981 group compares poorly; the latter group experiences higher unemployment rates, lower employment incomes, lower occupational status, and a higher incidence of low income or poverty. According to Lian and Matthews (1998), the ethnic vertical mosaic has metamorphosed into a "colour-coded" vertical mosaic.

Myth Busting No. 2: Educational Attainment of Immigrants Remains High

Claims about declining educational attainment and immigrant quality for recent immigration periods are found in many widely cited studies, necessitating a second look at the educational attainments of immigrant inflows into Canada. To start, these studies considered skills transfers of only those immigrants who declared their intention to practice as professionals. The studies assume that non-professional immigrants have "lower human quality," and that their arrival suggests that Canada has admitted less-educated immigrants since the mid-1970s. More accurate studies on immigrant "quality" have analyzed the economic performance of an average immigrant on the basis of a broader educational attainment standard without specific regard to their status as professionals. This is particularly important because of the barriers that professionals face in accessing employment in their fields, and also because of the demands for flexibility in the 21st-century economy. I include here a recent study by Akbari (1999) as well as an earlier one by Bankey Tandon (1978).[29] Akbari's study deals with the educational attainment of new arrivals in Canada from 1956 to 1994, and Tandon's deals with the Ontario labour market in 1977. Both report a discrimination effect demonstrated by the gap in economic performance between non-racialized Canadians and racialized immigrants, educational attainment notwithstanding. Tandon also identifies variation among earnings of immigrants from different countries, and a gap between Canadian-born people and immigrants from some areas, such as Asia, Latin America, Southern Europe, and the West Indies. This gap is narrowed but not eliminated by length of residence.[30]

Akbari's study is instructive because he uses a range of data covering the period 1956–1994 and uses census data as well as immigrants' landing documents to analyze educational attainment over a longer period of time than do most other studies. The data are then compared with the educational attainment of the Canadian-born group. Overall data show that the percentages of new immigrants with only high school education or less have been falling over the period of analysis, while percentages of immigrants with university degrees have been rising. These trends refute the generally held view that changes in immigrant admission criteria after the mid-1960s resulted in more admissions under family and refugee class schemes, causing a decline in immigrant "quality" as measured by immigrants' educational attainment. The period immediately after the 1978 *Immigration Act*, which resulted in a rise in refugee-class immigrants, did cause a rise in the percentages of those who arrived with lower schooling and a fall in the percentage of those who held university degrees. However, these percentages have improved since the early 1980s.

Let us compare the above figures with those of native-born Canadians. This comparison is important for at least two reasons. First, some recent writers have drawn this comparison in a way that may misinterpret the data. For instance, Stoffman (1993) wrote, "In 1971, immigrants were three times as likely to have a higher education as native-born Canadians, but by 1986 that advantage had disappeared." This statement gives the impression that (a) recent immigrants are less likely to have an educational level higher than that of native-born Canadians and (b) recent immigrants are less educated than earlier immigrants. In fact, Stoffman is referring to a decline not in immigrants' absolute amount of education, but in the extent of their education relative to that of the Canadian-born.

A second reason for comparing the absolute educational levels of immigrant inflows at their time of entry with the educational attainment of native-born Canadians is that the non-use of previously acquired education status, for instance professional qualifications, degrades, and immigrants cease to refer to it, especially if they are considered overqualified for the low-income jobs they are forced to seek for survival. However, these skills can be easily upgraded. According to Akbari, a 1951 Census publication (Statistics Canada, 1951) noted that among adults aged 35 and over who had arrived in Canada over the period 1946–1951, around 12.7% had 13 years or more schooling, while for the corresponding native-born population, this percentage was only 7.8%: "Thus, it would appear that the addition of immigrant residents of the 1946–51 period did not lower educational standards in Canada."[31] It is therefore important to establish that fact as a basis for evaluating which policy changes since the 1960s, which shifted the country-of-origin mix as well as the immigrant-class mix, adversely affected the "educational standards" in Canada.

Akbari used Census data on the educational attainments of native-born Canadians to compute percentages corresponding to those of immigrants in Table 6.1. These are reported for the Census years 1961, 1966, 1971, 1976, 1981, 1986, and 1991 in Table 6.2. For immigrants, these data are presented by their time of arrival, since they date back further (1956) than do the time-of-landing data. Furthermore, the immigrant data for the periods 1966–1968 and 1969–1970 are grouped into one interval (1966–1970); for the periods 1976–1978 and 1979–1980, data are grouped into one interval (1966–1980). This grouping eases comparison with data on the Canadian-born that are available for the Census years. It is observed that, over the entire period of analysis, immigrants arrived in Canada with higher educational levels than those of resident native-born Canadians. The percentages of immigrants arriving with high school education or less have always been lower than those of native-born Canadians, while the percentages of immigrants arriving with university degrees have always been higher.

The data indicate that, over time, the gap in the educational attainment levels of immigrants and Canadian-born has been narrowing. Some, for instance Stoffman (1993), misinterpret this narrowing of the gap in the case of university degree holders and suggest that recent immigrants are less educated than those who arrived in the past. However, data presented in Akbari's study clearly show that this narrowing of the gap is due not to a decline in the educational levels among immigrants, but to increasing education levels among Canadian-born people.

A comparison of immigrants' educational attainment data at the time of landing since the mid-1980s with the educational attainment of Canadian-born residents does not change the main conclusion obtained above. As the tables show, although the percentages of immigrants having only high school education or less at the time of landing since the mid-1980s have been remarkably similar to those of the Canadian-born, the percentages of university degree holders have been significantly higher for immigrants than for the Canadian-born.

In 1996, 53% of new entrants were either skilled immigrants (81%) or business-class immigrants (19%).[32] According to Statistics Canada data, immigrants are now more likely to have a university degree than Canadian-born people. Up to 34% of recent immigrants aged 25 to 44 had completed university, compared to 19% in the comparable Canadian-born population.[33] Moreover, beyond that group as a whole, the immigrant population is older and as such has a larger proportion in the working-

Table 6.1: Educational Levels among Immigrant Inflows to Canada

	High School or Less Education		University Degree (%)	
	By Period of Arrival (a)	By Period of Landing (b)	By Period of Arrival (a)	By Period of Landing (b)
1956–1965	89.3	NA	5.5	NA
1961–1968	79.3	NA	12.4	NA
1969–1970	70.2	NA	19.0	19.0
1971–1975	NA	NA	NA	17.3
1976–1978	47.6	NA	19.2	17.5
1979–1980*	55.1	62.5	15.9	12.3
1981–1985	47.4	56.4	20.6	15.8
1986–1990	NA	52.3	NA	19.0
1991–1994	NA	53.0	NA	20.3

* Note that the period immediately after the *Immigration Act* of 1978 resulted in a rise in refugee-class immigrants and caused a rise in the percentage of those with lower schooling. This has been the basis for a lot of speculation about immigrant quality. However, these percentages improved after 1980.

Source: Akbari (1999) data derived from Statistics Canada Census data: 1961, 1971, 1981, 1986, 1991, as well as landed-immigrant data from Citizenship and Immigration Canada. The difference between the two sets of flow figures is denoted by (a) and (b), where (a) represents data obtained from Census sources and (b) data from Citizenship and Immigration Canada. The objective is to have figures for periods not captured by one or the other source.[34]

Table 6.2: Educational Levels in the Canadian-Born Population, Aged 25 and Older

Period*	High School or Less Education (%)	University Degree (%)
1961	92.0	3.5
1966	91.1	4.7
1971	89.7	5.4
1976	69.1	7.5
1981	63.3	9.1
1986	56.3	10.5
1991	53.7	10.6

* See also R. Pendakur, *The Changing Role of Post-War Immigrants in Canada's Labour Force: An Examination across Four Census Periods*, Ottawa: National Library of Canada, 1995.

Source: Akbari (1999). Data for 1961 are based on 1961 Canadian Population Census and are reported in Pendakur (1995). Data for 1966 are based on Statistics Canada (1966). Data for 1976 are based on the 1976 Canadian Population Census, as reported in Statistics Canada (1976). Data for 1971, 1981, 1986, and 1991 are based on the respective years' Canadian population censuses, micro data.

age group. A larger share of the working-age population and participation rates comparable to the Canadian-born group would suggest a larger-than-average share of income. But despite these characteristics, immigrants arriving since 1986 experience some of the highest poverty rates. This reality suggests that racial barriers are playing a major role in creating these conditions of poverty.[35]

Low Returns to Educational Attainments Due to Racialization

The problem with racialized groups and particularly racialized immigrants is not one of low quality of human capital, but rather of immigrants' failure to achieve equivalent return in their investment in education and skill acquisition. As we indicated earlier, not only is there a significant gap in the return in investment, but also racialized group members are outperforming the Canadian-born cohort in terms of their contribution to the growth of real GDP. That is partly because they are increasingly a key source of labour in the Canadian economy. But it is also because they maintain an educational attainment advantage. The educational attainment among racialized group members and immigrants improved in the 1990s.[36] Between 1991–2000, 76% of new immigrants had at least one type of internationally obtained credential.[37] Among immigrants in the country five years or less, the level of higher education was as high as 62% compared to 23% in the general population. As Table 6.3 shows, racialized group members make up a higher proportion of those with some university education (17.4%); bachelor's degrees (19.5%); degrees in medicine, dentistry, and veterinary science (23.3%); master's degrees (20.1%) and Ph.Ds (22.5%) than their proportion in the population (13.4%). Their levels of lower education—less than grade 9 (12.1%), grade 9–13 without certificate (11.1%), and grade 9–13 with certificate (11.3%)—all fall below their proportion in the population. They fall well below that proportion in the trade-certificate category(7.8%), likely because of the bias in the immigration process against working-class immigrants.

The educational advantage that racialized groups hold can also be demonstrated by the increase in the numbers of degree holders in medicine, dentistry, veterinary science, and Ph.Ds. As tables 6.4 and 6.5 show, the growth among racialized groups far outpaces the Canadian average (37.79% to 16.64% and 49.5% to 23.5%), suggesting that the advantage is sustained and growing.

Table 6.6 below shows a steady improvement in educational attainment among immigrants arriving from 1970 to 2001. While 22.5% of immigrants arriving in 1970 held university degrees and 26.1% had trades and college education, for a total of 48.4%, of those arriving in 1990, 40.7% had university degrees and 20.2% had trade and college education, for a total of 60.9%. That compares with the Canadian average of 22.2% with a university degree and 31.7% with a college and trade education, for a total of 53.4%. As the immigrant cohort has become more racialized, the immigration selection process has ensured that the group's educational attainment is greater than that of the Canadian-born group.

This educational advantage has not translated into a superior or even equivalent income position. There is a decline in income attainment over the last 10 years among

Table 6.3. Population Showing Representation by Highest Levels of Schooling Geography: Canada

Educational Attainment	Males		Females		Visible Minorities	
	No.	%	No.	%	No.	%
Total—Highest Levels of Schooling	11,626,700	48.6	12,274,500	51.4	3,041,650	12.7
Less Than Grade 9	1,103,985	47.0	1,246,505	53.0	285,305	12.1
Grade 9–13 Without Secondary Certificate	2,558,290	49.9	2,568,120	50.1	567,665	11.1
Grade 9–13 With Secondary Certificate	1,520,080	45.1	1,847,820	54.9	379,235	11.3
Trades Certificate or Diploma	1,643,455	63.2	955,470	36.8	201,830	7.8
Some Other Non-university Without Certificate	714,270	46.5	823,350	53.5	186,210	12.1
Other Non-university With Trades or Certificate	1,166,035	40.1	1,742,155	59.9	287,855	9.9
Some University Without Univ. Cert./Degree	813,835	47.2	908,920	52.8	299,210	17.4
University Certificate, Degree or Diploma	2,106,840	49.1	2,182,230	50.9	834,350	19.5
University Cert./Diploma Below Bachelor Level	242,160	40.3	359,260	59.7	117,490	19.5
Bachelor's Degree(s)	1,150,585	47.7	1,260,890	52.3	471,415	19.5
Degree in Medicine, Dentistry, Veterinary ...	79,970	65.3	42,570	34.7	28,605	23.3
University Cert./Diploma Above Bachelor Level	180,660	47.2	202,295	52.8	59,055	15.4
Master's Degree(s)	359,520	56.0	282,535	44.0	128,790	20.1
Earned Doctorate	93,945	73.0	34,680	27.0	28,995	22.5

Source: Human Resources and Skills Development Canada. Based on 1996 and 2001 Census.

university-educated immigrants, for both the most recent as well as the 10-year resident, relative to a similarly educated Canadian population, which conversely had an increase of 7% in income over the same period.

Numerous studies have suggested that the failure to translate internationally obtained training into Canadian equivalency is due to barriers in the licensing and accreditation processes, employers' risk-averse attitudes toward internationally obtained skills and experience and demands for Canadian experience that are unrelated to the core competencies of the job. This characterization of the problem

Table 6.4. Degree in Medicine, Dentistry, Veterinary Science, Canada

	1996	2001	Percentage Change
Total Population	105,050	122,535	16.64
Male Population	73,790	79,970	8.38
Female Population	31,255	42,570	36.20
Visible Minority Population	20,760	28,605	37.79

Source: Human Resources and Skills Development Canada based on 1996 and 2001
Census.

Table 6.5. Doctorate, Canada

	1996	2001	Percentage Change
Total Population	103,860	128,625	23.5
Male Population	79,560	93,945	18.1
Female Population	24,300	34,680	42.7
Visible Minority Population	19,385	28,995	49.5

Source: Human Resources and Skills Development Canada based on 1996 and 2001
Census.
Educational attainment patterns are similarly high among the recent immigrant group.

Table 6.6: Post-secondary Education among Immigrants and Canadian-Born (%)

Group	University	College	Trades	Total
Immigrated since 1970	22.5	12.1	14.0	48.4
Immigrated since 1980	25.5	12.5	10.9	48.6
Immigrated since 1990	40.7	12.7	7.57	60.9
Total Canada, 2001	22.2	17.9	12.9	53.4

Source: Statistics Canada, *Education in Canada: Raising the Standard*, 2001 Census analysis
series, March 11, 2003.

is consistent with the finding from the qualitative study done by Teelucksingh and
Galabuzi (2005) focusing on key informants in the Canadian settlement sector. They
conclude that this represents a form of anti-immigrant discrimination that adversely
impacts access to employment for those in the immigrant class. Racialized immigrants
face structural barriers to accreditation of their imported skills and job experience,
and denial of access to trades and professions by provincially regulated licensing
bodies.[38]

Myth Busting No.3: Discrimination in Employment, Not Human Capital, Explains Differences in Economic Performance

As discussed above, human-capital explanations suggest that gender and race differences in job placement arise from individual differences in productivity acquired through education, labour-force experience, and job tenure (Becker, 1957; Arrow, 1998). The assumption is that the labour market is relatively efficient at sorting individuals into jobs that are commensurate with human-capital characteristics. Human-capital explanations for gender and race wage inequality have a long history of providing useful insight into the job allocation process. We don't argue here that education, training, and experience are not linked to job requirements; the point to be made is that they are not the sole determinants of the differentials in economic performance, because they don't operate in a "free" market. Particularly in the case of race inequality in the labour process, race differences in human-capital acquisition reflect historical discrimination and class disadvantages, and provide a partial explanation for employment and income inequality.

In 1984, the Abella Commission on Equality in Employment stated that the differences in unemployment rates and incomes between racialized group members and other Canadians should be understood as "social indicators" of job discrimination and that, furthermore, such discrimination can be characterized as systemic.[39] The report led to the *Employment Equity Act* of 1986, one of whose goals was to remove inequalities in income and occupational status between racialized and non-racialized groups. Henry and Ginsberg's (1985) study, using an experimental technique called "correspondence testing," showed how one could measure the incidence of racial discrimination in employment in Toronto in 1984, and also proved the prevalence of such discrimination.[40]

Various other studies arrive at a similar conclusion, among them Gosine (2000); Hou and Balakrishnan (1996); Pendukar and Pendukar (1998); Harvey, Sui, and Keil (1999); Boyd (1992); Das Gupta (1994); Galabuzi (2001); Kunz et al. (2001); Li (1988); Preston and Giles (1995); Reitz and Sklar (1997); Wanner (1998); Anderson and Lynam (1987); Grant and Oertel (1998); Li (1988); Lian and Matthews, (1991). A number of these have attempted cross-sectional studies of racialized group and immigrants' incomes and the gender or specific ethnic differentials, using as variables education and ethnicity, length of stay, and income and occupational status returns to education. In all cases, they identify a residual effect that one can at least speculate to be a discriminatory factor. However, they do not discount the impact of some of the other factors such as change in the economy, immigration lag, and language. What is clear is that they do not attribute the same weight to low human-capital quality as do those from the diminishing-returns school.

Two studies are more specific about attributing discrimination as an important factor. Howland and Sakellariou's (1993) study of wage discrimination and the occupational segregation of racialized groups also found a significant discriminatory impact across occupations, one that was reflected in the wage differentials they encountered. While their examination indicates a divergence in the relative labour-market experience of the groups studied, they concluded that employment discrimination explained wage differentials, although to relatively different degrees. The earnings gap was as high as 21% for Black men within the same occupation, though lower for Black, South East Asian, and South Asian women. But they observed that these differentials mask dramatic earnings differences across occupational categories. According to them, within-occupation pay differences for men appear to explain the greater part of the ethnic earnings gap. Within the intra-occupational differential, "wage discrimination" was consistently the largest component. For women, intra-occupational earnings differentials appear to explain the greater part of the ethnic earnings gap. Wage discrimination was the largest factor explaining the earnings disadvantage of South and South East Asian women. Differences in various characteristics determining the levels of occupation between White and Asian women played a significant role in the earnings disadvantage of these Asian women. They concluded that for all groups, policies aimed at reducing discrimination within occupational categories would be effective. For racialized women, it would appear that anti-discrimination policies should have a twofold thrust, first to reduce the within-occupation earnings discrimination, and second to provide training programs to extend the career ladders of ethnic minority women.[41]

Howland and Sakellariou's conclusions are consistent with the finding of Christofides and Swidinsky (1994), whose research suggests that productivity differentials alone do not account for the economic performance differential. With the help of Ordinary Least Squares (OLS) wage regression analysis, and using Employment and Immigration data from 1990 and Statistics Canada Labour Market Activity Survey (LMAS) data from 1989, they were able to demonstrate that "substantial portions of the observed differentials cannot be explained by productivity differences alone." According to Christofides and Swidinsky, these differences, including age, education, language, marital status, province, occupation, and weeks worked, account for less than 30% of the wage gap.[42] They attribute the unexplained residuals (70%) to labour-market discrimination and confirm that racialized group members were more likely, on average, to be paid less than other comparable employees.[43]

Based on the studies reviewed above, it is apparent that recent immigration is increasingly used as a proxy for race, colour, and place of origin in evaluating productivity in the Canadian labour market. The outcome is a convergence of the experiences of recent immigrants and other racialized group members in the labour market.

Myth Busting No. 4: Questions about Methodology
Lastly, the diminishing human capital quality arguments are susceptible to methodological flaws that call their reliability into question. The neo-classical approach that economists use to discuss differentials in the earnings of immigrants is based on assumptions of perfect competition in the labour market. Such assumptions are clearly not sustainable. The Canadian labour market is distorted by, among other factors, racism on the part of employers, as well as numerous barriers to access, which have been widely documented. Barriers such as narrow recruitment channels (for example, overreliance on word-of-mouth hiring that tends to reproduce the composition of the

workplace), subjective employment practices and procedures, biased testing, racial stereotyping in the interview processes (using race as proxy for evaluating future job performance) all reduce access to workplaces and mobility within them.[44] The other is denial because of the conflict between the ideals of quality and the reality of racism that Henry and Tator (2000b) have referred to as democratic racism.Yet analysts, economists, and researchers persistently ignore any causal attribution of systemic racial and gender discrimination, which is widely documented elsewhere, as a factor in the differences in income and economic performance. It is hard to believe that the persistence of racial discrimination in all aspects of Canadian life, which is the subject of government and civil society campaigns, would not translate into barriers to economic opportunity. How this fails to register for many doing research on the economic impacts of immigration may after all not be such a mystery, given the pervasiveness of racism in Canadian culture. A common explanation is the orientation of the economic discipline, although the proponents of these arguments are not exclusively economists.[45] While it is true that economic models that discern discrimination in employment on the basis of race or gender have not been the subject of much of the research in the area, there are research methods like the residual method, which has become widely used.[46] One is left with questions about the subjective nature of the choices that researchers make and the extent to which these choices are informed by the social environment of the researchers.

As well, the proponents of the mainstream arguments tend to rely on limited actual data to draw inferential conclusions, especially about immigrant income differentials. However, this methodological shortcoming does not prevent their work from disproportionately driving public policy. When these studies expressed concerns about the quality of immigrants to Canada, in the early 1990s, the government responded by shifting the focus away from family- and refugee-class immigrants, and toward independent-class and business-class immigrants. It is an argument's power of resonance with social attitudes, not its validity, that prevails. The early 1990s advocacy also led to a process of revamping the immigration legislation that has culminated in the recent tabling of Bill C-31 in Parliament. A key aim of the new legislation, as stated by the Minister of Citizenship and Immigration, is to attract "the best and brightest" to Canada.[47]

Akbari (1999) zeroed in on the paucity of actual data with which studies support their conclusions about differentials in economic performance.[48] This is especially important given the extent to which competing explanations are dismissed out of hand on empirical grounds. Akbari has argued that many of the conclusions that suggest a decline in skills levels among post-1967 immigrants, the group with the most racialized members, are largely inferential. He points out that only two studies have actually analyzed relevant data to support the stated conclusions. One is Coulson and DeVoretz's (1994) study of the human capital (skills) content of immigrants who arrived in Canada during the periods 1967–1973, 1974–1979, and 1979–1987, looking at the intended occupations of immigrants at the time of entry and the corresponding levels of education.[49] The other is Green and Green's study (1995) of the occupational composition of immigration.[50]

Table 6.7: Refugees in Professional/Management Occupations in the Country of Origin and Occupations in Canada When Interviewed

Occupations in Country of Origin	Occupation in Canada
Accommodation services manager	Machine operator
Banking manager	Accounting clerk/Taxi driver
Computer systems analyst	Property administrator
Dentist	Welder
Economist	Truck driver
Editor	Sales assistant
Engineers	Labourer/Cleaner/Drafting technician/Dispatcher Delivery driver/Gas worker/Drywaller
Financial accountants	Foodservice /Cleaner/ Hairdresser/Courier/ Accounting clerk/Nursing aide/Mechanical assembler/Machine operator
Graphic artist	Sales clerk
Journalists	Labourers
Judge	Secretary
Land surveyor	Survey technician
Lawyer	Paralegal/Labourer
Librarian	Labourer/landscaping
Manufacturing manager	Labourer
Musician	Retail supervisor
Armed forces officer	Meat cutter/Mechanical assembly
Pharmacist	Health services aide
Registered nurses	Nursing assistants/Social service workers/Cleaner/ Sales clerk/Decorator/Food service
Retail/Sales manager	Labourer/Flight attendant/ Early childhood educator/ Tailor/Metal contractor/Purchasing agent
Scientist	Service station attendant
Social worker	Food server
Specialist physicians	Nursing aides/Cleaner/Medical lab technician
School teachers	Cleaner/Social service workers/Early childhood educator/Kitchen helper/Accounting clerk/Labourer
College lecturers	Customer service clerk/Electrical mechanic/Meat cutter/Welder
Veterinarian	Nursing aide

Source: H. Krahn, et al. "Educated and Underemployed: Refugee Integration into the Canadian Labour Market," *Journal of International Migration and Integration* 1, no. 1 (Winter 2000): 59–84.[51]

Coulson and DeVoretz's study concludes that the values of skills transfers to Canada have been declining since 1974, with the largest decline occurring over the 1979–1987 period. They attributed the decline to the 1978 *Immigration Act*, which further eased entry restrictions on family reunification and refugee classes. Coulson and DeVoretz's study used actual educational attainment data for each intended occupational group of immigrants who had arrived since 1978. Earlier immigrants listed educational attainment only as either a university degree or no degree held. For the pre-1978 arrivals, they made assumptions regarding the levels of university education attained, which made the accuracy of their conclusions open to question. Their conclusions also depended on the assumption that an immigrant's stated intention at the time of arrival to work in a particular occupation matched the educational qualifications normally required for that occupation in Canada, even though some might hold higher and others lower qualifications.

The Green and Green (1995) study covers similar ground. Green and Green found a negative trend in the inflow of professional immigrants into Canada. Assuming a high correlation between educational attainment and intended occupations, the study implies a corresponding decline in the educational trends of new immigrants in the post-1967 period. The Green and Green study also based its conclusion on the intended occupations reported by the immigrants at the time they acquired landed immigrant status. However, the authors were careful to note that the listed occupations may have been purposeful misrepresentations of actual intentions in order to get the required number of points for entry.[52]

Conclusion

It is clear that the conventional arguments advanced to explain the economic performance of racialized group members are inadequate. The argument about the low-quality human capital of racialized groups cannot fully explain their performance. Nor does the assumed lower educational attainment. The immigration lag has been growing longer and raises new questions. In the final analysis, Table 6.8 captures the key evidence. The answer may lie in the undervaluing and misallocation of racialized labour in the Canadian labour market.

Notes

1. A. Akbari, "Immigrant Quality in Canada: More Direct Evidence of Human Capital Content, 1956–1994," *International Migration Review* 3 (Spring 1999): 156–175; D. De Voretz, *Diminishing Returns: The Economics of Canada: Recent Immigration Policy* (Toronto: CD Howe Institute, 1995).
2. A. Brouwer, *Immigrants Need Not Apply* (Ottawa: Caledon Institute, 1999); G. Galabuzi, "Racializing the Division of Labour: Neo-Liberal Restructurings and Economic Segregation of Canada's Racialized Groups" 2004a.
3. Basran and Zong (1998); Bloom, Grenier, Gunderson (1995).
4. DeVoretz (1995); Collacott (2002); Stoffman (1993).

5. In varying degrees, some have tended to address the changing nature of the economy as a contributing factor.

6. See A. de Silva, *Earnings of Immigrants: A Comparative Analysis* (Ottawa: Economic Council of Canada, 1992); D.J. DeVoretz (ed.), *Diminishing Returns: the Economics of Canada's Recent Immigration Policy* (Toronto: C.D. Howe Institute, 1995); M. Baker and D. Benjamin, "The Performance of Immigrants in the Canadian Labour Market," *Journal of Labour Economics* 12 (1994): 369–405; K. Arrow, "What Has Economics to Say about Racial Discrimination?" *Journal of Economic Perspectives* 12, no. 2 (Spring 1998): 91–100; M. Reich, *Racial Inequality: A Political Economy Analysis* (Princeton: Princeton University Press, 1981); B. Chiswick and P. Miller, "Earnings in Canada: The Roles of Immigrant Generation, French Ethnicity and Language," *Research in Population Economics* 6 (1988): 183–228; M. Abbott and C. Beach, "Immigrant Earnings Differentials and Birth-Year Effects for Men in Canada: Post-war–1972," *Canadian Journal of Economics* 26 (1993): 505–524; A. Akbari, *The Economics of Immigration and Racial Discrimination: A Literature Survey, 1970–1989.* (Ottawa: Multiculturalism and Citizenship Canada, 1989).

7. R. Abella, *Commission on Equality in Employment* (Ottawa: Supply and Services Canada, 1985); See also Henry and Ginsburg (1985); Henry (1999); Reitz (1988); Parliament of Canada, *Equality Now: Report of the Parliamentary Task Force on the Participation of Visible Minorities in Canada* (Ottawa: Queens Printer, 1984); P. Boyer, *Equality for All: Report of the Parliamentary Committee on Equal Rights* (Ottawa: Supply and Services, Canada, 1985).

8. See captions on debate by Mississauga Mayor Hazel McCallion, Winnipeg School Trustee Granger, and Markham Deputy Mayor Bell.

9. M. Collacott, *Canada's Immigration Policy: The Need for Major Reform* (Vancouver: Fraser Institute, 2002); D.J. DeVoretz (ed.), *Diminishing Returns: The Economics of Canada's Recent Immigration Policy* (Toronto: C.D. Howe Institute, 1995); D. Stoffman, *Who Gets In: What's Wrong with Canada's Immigration Program, and How to Fix It* (Toronto : Macfarlane Walter and Ross, 2002).

10. Abbott and Beach (1993); Baker and Benjamin (1994); Chiswick and Miller (1988); De Voretz (1995); DeVoretz and Fagnan (1990); da Silva (1992); Stoffman (1993); Tandon (1978); Beach and Worswick (1993). The central argument of the Diminishing Returns Approach is that the changes in source countries in the 1970s/1980s combined with the preponderance of the family-class immigrants and the high numbers of refugee admissions to lower the quality of the human capital of immigrants. This explained their lower economic performance.

11. E. Smith and A. Jackson, *Does the Rising Tide Life All Boats?*; Akbari (1999); P. Anisef, R. Sweet, and G. Frempong, *Labour Market Outcomes of Immigrant and Racial Minority University Graduates in Canada.* CERIS Working Paper No. 23 (Toronto: CERIS, 2003).

12. CIC (2003).

13. DeVoretz (1995); R.G. Coulson and D.J. DeVoretz, "Human Capital Content of Canadian Immigrants: 1967–87," *Canadian Public Policy* 19 (1994): 357–366; See also Abbott and Beach (1993:505–524); D. Stoffman, *Towards a More Realistic Immigration Policy for Canada* (Toronto: C.D. Howe Institute, 1993).

14. G.J. Borjas, "Immigration Policy, National Origin, and Immigrant Skills: A Comparison of Canada and the United States," in *Small Differences That Matter*, edited by D. Card and R.B. Freeman (Chicago: University of Chicago Press, 1993); See also literature reviews by

A. de Silva, *Earnings of Immigrants: A Comparative Analysis* (Ottawa: Economic Council of Canada, 1992); M. Baker and D. Benjamin, "The Performance of Immigrants in the Canadian Labour Market," *Journal of Labour Economics* 12, no. 3 (1994): 369–405.

15. A. de Silva, *Earnings of Immigrants: A Comparative Analysis* (Ottawa: Economic Council of Canada, 1992) contains a good literature review of some of these arguments; P. Kuch and W. Heassel, *An Analysis of Earnings in Canada: 1971 Census* (Ottawa: Statistics Canada, 1979); A. Richmond and W. Kalback, *Factors in the Adjustment of Immigrants and Their Descendants* (Ottawa: Statistics Canada, 1980); G. Carliner, "Wage Differences by Language Group and the Market for Language Skills in Canada," *Journal of Human Resources* 16, no. 3 (1981): 384–399; B. Chiswick and P. Miller, "Earnings in Canada: The Roles of Immigrants' Generation, French Ethnicity and Language," *Research in Population Economics* 6 (1988): 183–228; A. Green and D. Green, "Canadian Immigration Policy: The Effectiveness of the Point System and Other Instruments," *Canadian Journal of Economics* 28 (November 1995): 1006–10041; D. DeVoretz and S. Fagnan, "Some Evidence on Canadian Immigrant Quality Decline: Foreign-Born Versus Resident-Born Earnings Functions for 1971–86," in mimeo (July 27, 1990).

16. D. Hiebert, "The Colour of Work: Labour Market Segregation in Montreal, Toronto and Vancouver, 1991," Working Paper No. 97-02 Burnaby: Simon Fraser University (Vancouver, Centre of Excellence: Research on Immigration and Integration in the Metropolis, 1997). See also V. Preston and N. Giles, "Ethnicity, Gender and Labour Markets in Canada: A Case Study of Immigrant Women in Toronto," *Journal of Urban Research* 6 (1995): 150–159.

17. Human capital refers to the skill and knowledge base necessary for labour market participation, e.g., professional/vocational qualification, language skills, and other "merits."

18. Green and Green (1995:1006–10041); de Silva (1992); Stoffman (1993); Baker and Benjamin (1994); R. Wright and P. Maxim, "Immigration Policy and Immigrant Quality: Empirical Evidence from Canada," *Journal of Population Economics* 6 (1991): 337–352.

19. See Abbot and Beach (1993), DeVoretz (1989), Akbari (1989), and Chiswick and Miller (1988).

20. D.E. Bloom, G. Grenier, and M. Gunderson, "The Changing Labour Market Position of Canadian Immigrants," *Canadian Journal of Economics* 28, no. 4b (November 1995): 987–1005; M. Frenette and R. Morisette, "Will They Ever Converge? Earnings of Immigrants and Canadian-Born Workers over Two Decades." Analytical Studies Paper No. 215. (Ottawa: Statistics Canada, 2003).

21. E. Herberg, "Ethno-Racial Socio-Economic Hierarchy in Canada: Theory and Analysis of the New Vertical Mosaic," *International Journal of Comparative Sociology* 31, no. 3–4 (1990): 206–221. See also, F. Henry, "Two Studies of Racial Discrimination in Employment," in *Social Inequality in Canada: Patterns, Problems and Policies*, edited by J. Curtis, E. Grabb, and N. Guppy (Toronto: Prentice-Hall, 1999): 226–235; M. Boyd, "Immigration and Occupational Attainment," in *Ascription and Attainment: Studies in Mobility and Status Attainment in Canada*, edited by M. Boyd et al. (Ottawa: Carleton University Press, 1985): 393–446.

22. Stoffman (1993). Government policy changes in 1993 focused on lowering the numbers of refugees admitted to Canada, as well as on increasing the number of business and independent-class immigrants at the expense of the family-sponsored immigrants.

23. C. Winn, "Affirmative Action and Visible Minorities: Eight Premises in Quest of Evidence," *Canadian Public Policy* 11, no. 4 (1985): 684–700.

24. Included here are D. Bloom and M. Gunderson, "An Analysis of the Earnings of Canadian Immigrants, in *Immigration, Trade, and the Market*, edited by J. Abowd and R. Freeman (Chicago: University of Chicago Press, 1991), 321–342; A. Akbari, *The Economics of Immigration and Racial Discrimination: A Literature Survey*, 1970–1989 (Ottawa: Multiculturalism and Citizenship Canada, 1989); and the Ekos/*Toronto Star* Survey, June 2000.

25. See G. Galabuzi, *Canada's Creeping Economic Apartheid: The Economic Segregation and Social Marginalization of Racialized Groups* (Toronto: Centre for Social Justice, 2001).

26. F. Henry and E. Ginsburg, *Who Gets the Job? A Test of Racial Discrimination in Employment* (Toronto: Urban Alliance on Race Relations and Social Planning Council of Metro Toronto, 1984).

27. B. Billingsley and L. Musynski, *No Discrimination Here* (Toronto: Social Planning Council of Metropolitan Toronto and Urban Alliance on Race Relations, 1985).

28. Statistical (or economic) discrimination in employment refers a situation where risk-averse employers, unable to assess the ability of members of a group, make generalized assumptions about the worth of their human capital, as may be the case when the value of qualifications from a certain country of region is unclear. On the other hand, systemic discrimination in employment occurs when members of a group are not hired or paid commensurate wages, or, once hired, are not promoted regardless of their skills and experience. The motives of the perpetuator are not primary in this consideration; rather, it is the outcome.

29. A.H. Akbari, "Immigrant 'Quality' in Canada: More Direct Evidence of Human Capital Content, 1956–1994," *International Migration Review* 33 (Spring 1999): 156–175; B. Tandon, "Earnings Differentials among Native-Born and Foreign-Born Canadians," *International Migration Review* 12, no. 3 (1978): 405–410. A fuller discussion of the issues is contained in Tandon's Ph.D. thesis, "An Empirical Analysis of Earnings of Foreign-Born and Native-Born Canadians" (Kingston: Queen's University, 1978).

30. Tandon (1978): 405–410.

31. Statistics Canada (1995): 114.

32. Citizenship and Immigration Canada, *Facts and Figures 1996: Immigration Overview* (Ottawa: Supply and Service Canada, 1997).

33. Statistics Canada, "1996 Census: Education, Mobility, and Migration," *The Daily* (April 14, 1998).

34. See also R. Pendakur, "The Changing Role of Post-war Immigrants in Canada's Workforce: An Examination across Four Census Periods," in *Strategic Research and Analysis, Social Research Unit* (Ottawa: Heritage Canada, 1995).

35. Between 1980 and 2000, male recent immigrant's full-time employment earnings fell 7% (from $40,600 to $37,900). This compares with a rise of 7% for Canadian-born cohort ($45,600 to $48,600). Among the university educated, the drop was deeper (13% — $55,300 to $48,300 versus $69,100 to $76,000). Female recent immigrant full-time employment earnings rose but less than other female full-time earnings ($23,800 to $26,800 versus $28,800 to $34, 400; 32,7000 to 34,7000 versus 45,200 to 50,000). See Statistics Canada (2003b).

36. See, for example, Statistics Canada, *2001 Census Analysis Series, Earnings of Canadians: Making a Living in the New Economy* (March 11, 2003).

37. Statistics Canada, "Longitudinal Survey of Immigrants to Canada, 2001," *The Daily* (September 4, 2003): 4; see discussion on Access to Professions and Trades above.

38. Interviewers with key informants from the settlement sector were contracted in 2004 for a study by C. Teelucksingh and G. Galabuzi, *Working Precariously: The Impact of Race and Immigrant Status on Income and Employment Opportunities* (Toronto: Centre for Social Justice/Canadian Race Relations Foundation, 2005).

39. R. Abella, *Equality in Employment: A Royal Commission Report* (Ottawa: Supply and Services Canada, 1985).

40. Henry and Ginsberg (1985).

41. J. Howland and C. Sakellariou, "Wage Discrimination, Occupational Segregation and Visible Minorities in Canada," *Applied Economics* 25, no. 11 (November 1993): 1413–1423.

42. L. Christofides and R. Swindinsky, "Wage Determination by Gender and Visible Minority Status: Evidence from the 1989 LMAS," *Canadian Public Policy* XX, no. 1 (1994): 34–51.

43. Ibid. de Silva (1997)suggests that the role of quality differences in education in the wage differentials is underestimated. However, given the evidence of superior educational attainment and the discriminatory factor attached to international training, de Silva's objections are not sustained. Ibid., 34. They also found that racialized group members were less likely to participate in the labour force and more likely to be unemployed. When employed, they were less likely to work in higher-paying occupations. A. de Silva, "Wage Discrimination against Visible Minority Men in Canada," *Canadian Business Economics* 5, no. 4 (1997): 25–42.

44. See Abella (1984); H. Jain, *Anti-Discriminatory Staffing Policies: Implications of Human Rights Legislation for Employers and Trade Unions* (Ottawa: Secretary of State, 1985); Henry (1999); F. Henry and E. Ginsberg, *Who Gets the Job: A Test of Racial Discrimination in Employment* (Toronto: UARR and SPC, 1984); B. Billingsley and L. Musynski, *No Discrimination Here* (Toronto: UARR and SPC, 1985); among others.

45. For instance, David Stoffman (1993), a journalist, has been an influential proponent of these views.

46. A. Akbari, *The Economics of Immigration and Racial Discrimination: A Literature Survey, 1970–1989* (Ottawa: Multiculturalism and Citizenship Canada, 1989).

47. Citizenship and Immigration Canada website, CCR website, etc.

48. Akbari (1999: 156).

49. R.G. Coulson and D.J. DeVoretz, "Human Capital Content of Canadian Immigrants: 1967–87," *Canadian Public Policy* 19 (1994): 357–366.

50. Green and Green (1995: 1006–1041).

51. This data from a survey of 500 refugees arriving in Alberta between 1992–1997. It was conducted in 1998 by Krahn, Derwing, Mulder, and Wilkinson. See "The Settlement Experience of Refugees in Alberta" (Edmonton: Prairie Centre of Excellence for Research on Immigration and Integration, 1999).

52. A. Green and D. Green, "Canadian Immigration Policy: The Effectiveness of the Point System and Other Instruments," *Canadian Journal of Economics* 28 (1995): 1006–1041.

Questions for Critical Thought

1. Describe three conventional explanations for the racial inequalities in labour-market outcomes.
2. What is the central argument in the "diminishing returns" approach to income inequality?
3. What are some of the alternative ways we can explain the differences in access to employment and employment income?
4. How do we measure the impact of racial discrimination in employment?
5. Do labour-market decisions such as hiring and promotion reflect the biases of the employers or are they basically rational, reflecting a free market for labour?
6. Are there differences in the quality of Canadian and international qualifications, and does that justify the demand for Canadian experience?
7. What does it mean for immigrant status to be used as proxy for racial status?

Recommended Readings

Billingsley, B., and L. Musynski. *No Discrimination Here*. Toronto: UARR and SPC, 1985.

A. de Silva. *Earnings of Immigrants: A Comparative Analysis*. Ottawa: Economic Council of Canada, 1992.

DeVoretz, D.J. (ed.). *Diminishing Returns: The Economics of Canada's Recent Immigration Policy*. Toronto: C.D. Howe Institute, 1995.

Henry, F., and E. Ginsberg. *Who Gets the Job: A Test of Racial Discrimination in Employment*. Toronto: UARR and SPC, 1984.

Hiebert, D. "The Colour of Work: Labour Market Segregation in Montreal, Toronto and Vancouver, 1991." Working paper No. 97-02, Burnaby: Simon Fraser University. Vancouver: Centre of Excellence: Research on Immigration and Integration in the Metropolis, 1997.

Jackson, A. *Is Work Working for Workers of Colour?* Ottawa: Canadian Labour Congress, 2002.

Kunz, J.L., A. Milan, and S. Schetagne. *Unequal Access: A Canadian Profile of Racial Differences in Education, Employment, and Income*. Toronto: Canadian Race Relations Foundation, 2001.

Li, P. "The Market Worth of Immigrants' Educational Credentials." *Canadian Public Policy* 27, no. 1 (2001): 23–38.

McDade, K. *Barriers to Recognition of Credentials of Immigrants in Canada*. Ottawa: Institute of Policy Research, 1988.

Pendakur, R. *Immigrants and the Labour Force: Policy, Regulation and Impact*. Montreal: McGill-Queen's University Press, 2000.

Government of Canada. *Report of the Taskforce on the Participation of Visible Minorities in the Federal Public Service, 2000: Embracing Change in the Federal Public Service*. Ottawa: Supply and Services Canada, 2000.

Wanner, R. "Prejudice, Profit or Productivity: Explaining Returns to Human Capital among Male immigrants in Canada." *Canadian Ethnic Studies* 30, no. 3 (1998): 25–55.

Worswick, C. *Immigrants' Declining Earnings: Reasons and Remedies*. C.D. Howe Institute, 2004.

CHAPTER 7

Social Exclusion: Socio-economic and Political Implications of the Racialized Gap

Introduction

In this chapter, we tackle the experience of exclusion and one of its most profound manifestations, racialized poverty. Social exclusion describes the structures and processes of inequality and unequal outcomes among groups in society. In industrialized societies, social exclusion arises from uneven access to the processes of production, wealth creation, and power. In the Canadian context, social exclusion refers to the inability of certain groups or individuals to participate fully in Canadian life due to structural inequalities in access to social, economic, political, and cultural resources arising out of the often intersecting experiences of oppression relating to race, class, gender, disability, sexual orientation, and immigrant status. Social exclusion is a form of alienation and denial of full citizenship experienced by particular groups of individuals and communities; among its characteristics are high levels of poverty, uneven access to employment and employment income, segregated neighbourhood selection leading to racialized enclaves, disproportionate contact with the criminal justice system, and low health status.

Social exclusion is both process and outcome. In the late 20th and early 21st centuries, social exclusion is a by-product of a form of unbridled accumulation whose processes commodify social relations, and validate and intensify inequality along racial and gender lines (Byrne, 1999; Madanipour et al., 1998). Processes of social exclusion intensified in the late 20th and early 21st centuries. This intensification can be traced to the restructuring of the global and national economies, which emphasized deregulation and re-regulation of markets, the decline of the welfare state, the commodification of public goods, demographic shifts leading to increased global South-North migrations, changes in work arrangements toward flexible deployment and intensification of labour through longer hours, work fragmentation, multiple jobs, and increasing non-standard forms of work. Not only have these developments intensified exploitation in the labour market, but also they have also engendered urban spatial segregation processes, including the gendered and racialized spatial concentrations of poverty.

The impact of a neo-liberal globalized political economic order and the retreat of the state from social provision means that the social exclusion analysis focuses equally on the commodification of public goods such as health care services, social services, education arising out of the dismantling of the welfare state, and the emergence of market-oriented responses to the resulting marginalization. Bryne (1999) has suggested that there are those from the possessive individualist school who have characterized this marginalization as self-inflicted, the failure of individuals to utilize their opportunities in the marketplace.[1] However, Yepez Del Castillo has noted that:

> The many varieties of exclusion, the fears of social explosions to which it gives rise, the dangers of social disruption; the complexity of the mechanisms that cause it, the extreme difficulty of finding solutions, have made it the major social issue of our time. (1994:614)

Canadian discourse on social exclusion has borrowed from the use of the concept in Europe, where analysts have used it to address the existence of their societies faced with intergenerational poverty and social alienation. Like the European, the Canadian approach has tended to focus on the exclusions experienced by those living on low incomes (Guildford, 2000). Until recently, social exclusion discourses generally overlooked the multiple dimensions of social exclusion as well as its subgroup variation; experiences of social exclusion are differentiated by oppression based on such factors as race, class, gender, disability, sexual orientation, and immigrant status.

In Canada, four groups have been identified as particularly at risk for processes of exclusion: women, new immigrants, racialized group members and Aboriginal peoples (CIHR, 2002). In this chapter, we use the social-exclusion framework to shift the focus back to the structural inequalities that determine the intensity and extensiveness of marginalization in early 21st society, and also focus on some of the groups highly vulnerable to the processes of social exclusion. The conceptual shift moves the burden of social inequality from the individual back to society, recognizing it as an outcome of social relations and raising the possibility of the reassertion of welfare state-type social rights based on the concept of social protection as the responsibility of society. The liberal conception of social inclusion, as presently constituted in policy discourse, promises equal opportunity for all without a commitment to dismantling the historical structures of exclusion; in contrast, the discourse of social exclusion seeks to unravel the structures and processes of marginalization and alienation.

In this book, we acknowledge the intellectual debt owed to the Europeans for developing the discourses and framework of social exclusion based on poverty as the primary form of alienation and exclusion. However, we see the need to broaden the concept to allow for an exploration of the other dimensions of exclusion relating to multiple forms of oppression. In a very vivid way, racism, sexism, and poverty intersect to creating specific forms of exclusion in Canada today. Here we will discuss the racialization of poverty as a specific expression of social exclusion in the early 21st century. The racialization of poverty refers to the disproportionate and persistent experience of low income among racialized groups in Canada. We embrace the now fairly well-established holistic view of poverty as encompassing not only low income and consumption but also low achievement in education, health, nutrition, and other forms of human deprivation. Among others, the experience of poverty includes powerlessness, marginalization, voicelessness, vulnerability, and insecurity. This understanding of poverty and its causes suggests that the different dimensions of the experience of poverty interact in important ways. Anti-poverty strategies must therefore target poverty in all its various dimensions. It is this idea and the approach that can be effectively articulated using the discourse and framework of *social exclusion*.

Social exclusion as a framework is increasingly used by social justice advocates as well as decision-makers because it gets at the root causes of the structural disadvantages experienced by racialized groups and other marginalized groups in society. It also puts the burden of addressing marginalization on the society and not the individuals who are its victims. By so doing, it represents a critique of the neo-liberal notion that the market should be the primary organizing principle of society. It also suggests possibilities for the transformation of the conditions of exclusion that have come to define the experience of racialized groups in Canada.

Distinguishing Social Exclusion from Social Inclusion Discourses

Social exclusion as an idea and discourse has often been confused with *social inclusion*, because it is assumed that, in a linear thought process, the remedy to exclusion is inclusion. However, social inclusion has its own meaning and application as well as ideological foundation, which don't necessarily connect to social exclusion. There is no continuum of experience that runs from exclusion to inclusion in a linear fashion. There are weak and strong versions of the social inclusion discourse. Much of the official policy discourse is of the weak variety, advocating a process similar to assimilation. The focus is on reconciling the "excluded" and the "included," on the terms of those who are included, by changing the excluded and integrating them into the predetermined structures of society. Social inclusion essentially means bringing the excluded into the tent, but likely allowing the persistence of the processes and structures of exclusion and so damning them to the periphery or the margins of the tent. However, there are strong versions that suggest a structural approach, acknowledging the historical processes that continually reproduce oppression, discrimination, and exclusion.[2] But they still don't commit to the need for transformative action, choosing instead to focus on addressing the unequal outcomes.

In practice, social inclusion has emerged as a top-down policy framework used in a very partial way to respond to the extreme manifestations of social exclusion that threaten social cohesion, while masking the structural causes of exclusion and so leaving them to reproduce alienation, powerlessness, and marginalization. Social exclusion draws from traditions that emphasize conflict in understanding society, and acknowledges the fact that society is stratified by hierarchies based on class, race, and gender. In contrast, social inclusion tends to de-emphasize the existence of hierarchies, preferring to assume the ideal of a level playing field where inequalities can be erased by some state intervention to address instances of market failure without interrogating the inherent inequality of the market. In that way, social inclusion is rooted in the liberal tradition that assumes common and equal citizenship as not socially constructed. In so doing, it seeks to erase difference in matters of public policy and suggests the ideal of a colour-blind, gender-blind, classless society as the policy objective. It fits well with the project of official multiculturalism.[3]

So as currently conceived and advocated, social inclusion has limited promise when it comes to addressing social exclusion, partly because it operates within a liberalized market framework, validating the commodification of public goods and settling for the integration of social exclusion's victims into the margins of society. It has emerged as a mechanism of pacification without providing the transformative imperative to change society; it seeks to placate those demanding that the state address social exclusion by resorting to a rhetorical device that appropriates the language of their claim. Social-inclusion discourse does not engage the historical assertion of certain forms of economic, political, social, and cultural privilege, or the generalization of certain ethnocultural norms by some groups, which occurs at the expense of others. Historically in Canada, the dominance of Eurocentric culture has granted non-racialized populations privileged access to resources while first decentring Aboriginal culture, and then marginalizing other ethnic cultures. In key institutions like the labour market, school system, health care system, and criminal justice system, this devaluation of racialized experiences has become a key source of exclusion.

There is some growing concern among Canadian policy-makers and advocates about the emergence of differentiated experiences of social exclusion. But while they acknowledge that marginal subgroups pose a threat to social cohesion in industrial societies, they still see the discourse of social inclusion and resultant policy framework as an appropriate response.[4]

Defining Social Exclusion

Social exclusion is used broadly to describe both the structures and the dynamic processes of inequality among groups in society that, over time, structure access to critical resources that determine the quality of membership in society and ultimately produce and reproduce a complex of unequal outcomes (Room, 1995; Byrne, 1999; Littlewood, 1999; Madanipour et al., 1998). Social exclusion is both process and outcome. The idea of social exclusion has attracted the attention of scholars as well as of mainstream policy-makers concerned about the emergence of marginal subgroups who may pose a threat to social cohesion in industrial societies. Madanipour et al. (1998) have suggested that social exclusion in industrialized countries such as Canada is a by-product of a form of unbridled accumulation whose processes commodify social relations, and validate and intensify inequality along racial and gender lines (Madanipour et al., 1998).[5]

According to White (1998) there are four aspects of social exclusion.

1) Social exclusion from civil society through legal sanction or other institutional mechanisms, as often experienced by status and non-status migrants. This conception may include substantive disconnection from civil society and political participation, because of material and social isolation, created through systemic forms of discrimination based on race, ethnicity, gender, disability, sexual orientation, and religion. In the post-September 11 era, racial profiling and new notions of national security have exacerbated the experience of this form of social exclusion.

2) Social exclusion refers to the failure to provide for the needs of particular groups—the society's denial of (or exclusion from) social goods to particular groups such as accommodation for persons with disability, income security, housing for the homeless, language services, sanctions to deter discrimination.

3) Exclusion from social production, a denial of opportunity to contribute to or participate actively in society's social, cultural activities.

4) Economic exclusion, a topic very much in line with this book's. The experiences of structures and processes of exclusion that condition access to economic resources and opportunities represent a form of economic exclusion from social consumption and ultimately unequal access to normal forms of livelihood and economy.

Box 7.1: Social Exclusion

- Describes the structures and processes of inequality and unequal outcomes among groups in society.
- In industrialized societies, arises from uneven access to the processes of production, wealth creation, and power.
- Is a form of alienation and denial of full citizenship experienced by particular groups of individuals and communities.
- Its characteristics occur in multiple dimensions.

Social exclusion can be experienced by individuals and communities, whether communities of common bond or geographical communities. The characteristics of social exclusion tend to occur in multiple dimensions and are often mutually reinforcing. Thus groups living in low-income areas are likely to also experience inequality in access to employment, substandard housing, insecurity, stigmatization, institutional breakdown, social service deficits, spatial isolation, disconnection from civil society, discrimination, and higher health risks. Wilson has characterized the resulting condition as one of an underclass culture (Wilson, 1987).

Box 7.2: Key Aspects of Social Exclusion

- Denial of participation in civil affairs of society through legal sanction and other institutional mechanisms.
- Denial of access to social goods—health care, education, housing.
- Denial of opportunity to participate actively in society.
- Economic exclusion.

Social Exclusion and Citizenship

In order for the social exclusion framework to be effective, it assumes a community or a society from which the process of exclusion is affected. The multiple dimensions of exclusion may suggest different ways of drawing the boundaries, and here the discourse on citizenship is helpful in demarcating the boundaries of the community or polity that provides the context within which the discussion on social exclusion takes place. The primary assumption is that the boundaries are along nation-state lines and represent the assertion of claims of belonging to a collective on the basis of agreed-upon notions of citizenship, first on the national scale, but potentially on the local or global scales. Citizenship is understood here as a:

relationship between the individual and the state as well as among individuals, it is the concrete expression of the fundamental principle of equality among members of the political community. (Jenson and Papillon, 2001)

This notion of citizenship invokes the state as guarantor of the principle of equality among members. Citizenship and equality are time- and space-specific concepts. Kymlicka and Norman (1995) have argued that the "return of the citizen" in popular political and academic discourse is the result of major transformations in modern polities and political economies brought about by neo-liberal globalization. It is both a signal and a symptom of profound changes in industrial societies. This follows a trajectory of liberal democratic conceptions of citizenship that began with the connection between civic participation and access to political power, an idea of nationhood and popular citizenship that led to the replacement of divine authority with the secular institutions of self-government following the Treaty of Westphalia in 1648.

Jenson and Papillon (2001) have observed that over time the connection to political power was broadened to cover social and economic dimensions as claims based on social mobilization forced the recognition of additional categories of the population, which merited full inclusion in the polity. Thus the shift from "free men" to "all men," from "property owners" to "non-propertied men," from White men to racialized men, from men to women, from native-born to naturalized, from heterosexual to homosexual, from adult to youth, from able-bodied to disabled, was a time-long march as full political rights were nominally gradually extended. In North America, these rights were substantiated through the emergence of the labour movement, the civil rights movement, the feminist revolution, the Aboriginal rights movement, and more recently the disabled movement and the gay and lesbian rights movements.

Jenson (2002) has discussed the notion of citizenship in terms of three key dimensions. The first dimension is one of rights and responsibilities, the second relates to equal access, and the third speaks to a sense of belonging or identity.

The first dimension of citizenship, *rights and responsibilities,* is founded on liberal conceptions of citizenship as guaranteeing political and civil rights in exchange for certain responsibilities such as paying taxes, participating in an informed manner, and defending the polity when called upon.

The second dimension of citizenship corresponds to *equal access* and is fundamental to any claims of equality. It is built on the civic recognition that basic levels of material well-being are essential to sustaining meaningful access to full citizenship and to fostering participation. The degree of access varies within and across political communities, depending on institutional design, and according to the support given by the state and the community to the groups excluded by the social, economic, or cultural structures within the society.

The third dimension of citizenship is that of *belonging.* At least nominally, citizenship defines the boundaries of belonging, giving specific recognition and status to members who participate in and benefit from the political community. To be a citizen presupposes being part of a specific political community, participating in its economic and social life, and enjoying its support in case of need. Some have referred to this dimension as a form of social citizenship, which together with the second dimension helps define the contours or boundaries of social exclusion (Byrne, 1999).

As the central institution through which the solidarity of citizenship is expressed, the state plays an essential role in determining the boundaries of belonging and the creation of political identities, making the distinction between members and non-members. The socially constructed common identity then becomes the basis for maintaining social solidarity despite important cultural, economic, and social differences among people, which often translate into competing interests.

These processes are dynamic, and neither equal access nor belonging is automatically achieved. Societies require agency to foster equality and improve access in the same way they need strategies to ensure meaningful participation in the democratic process and the full exercise of citizenship rights, all of which vary over time and place. Moreover, given the nature of power relations and unequal social relations in societies, various social forces engage in struggles to gain better access to political, economic, and social resources. These seek to upgrade their citizenship on the one hand, and to transform oppressive structures and institutional practices, and change the boundaries of access on the other. That is why the boundaries of social exclusion vary from society to society, as well as over time within any given society (Jenson and Papillon, 2001).

In the late 20th and early 21st centuries, social justice advocates and other political actors are increasingly using inclusive notions of citizenship to resist exclusion. In Europe, for instance, where the concept of social exclusion has its roots, France's *Le mouvement social*, a broad-based aggregation of associations and actors seeking to address social inequalities and exclusion, has been making claims for inclusion on the basis of equal citizenship (Helly, 1999).

Canada and the Experience of Social Exclusion

Historically in Canada, structural inequalities in access to social, economic, political, and cultural resources have arisen out of the often intersecting experiences of oppression relating to race, class, gender, disability, sexual orientation, and immigrant status; these inequalities have defined social exclusion. More recently, the demands for labour-market flexibility in the urban "globalized" economy have disproportionately exposed racialized groups to precarious employment and higher levels of poverty than other Canadians. So, for the historically vulnerable groups in the labour market, globalization exacerbates the impact of racial and gender discrimination in employment. Economic restructuring has not only polarized the labour market through labour-market segmentation, but also created employment structures that have altered the traditional workplace relationships and intensified the working experience of racialized communities through longer working hours and multiple part-time or contract jobs. The characteristics of the various forms of precarious work on offer are low pay, no job security, poor and often unsafe working conditions, intensive labour, excessive hours, and low or no benefits. Social exclusion defines the inability of certain subgroups to participate fully in Canadian life. Along with the socio-economic and political inequalities, social exclusion is also characterized by processes of group or individual isolation within and from such key Canadian societal institutions as the school system, criminal justice system, and health care system. Spatial isolation or neighbourhood segregation also characterize social exclusion.

These various forms of exclusion and isolation engender experiences of social and economic vulnerability, powerlessness, voicelessness, a lack of recognition and sense of belonging, limited options, diminished life chances, despair, opting out, suicidal tendencies, and increasingly community or neighbourhood violence. Aside from numerous health implications, the emergence of the institutional breakdown and normlessness characterized by such phenomena as the resort to the informal economy and community violence represents a threat to social cohesion and economic prosperity.

Box 7.3: Precarious Forms of Work

- contract
- temporary
- part-time
- piecework
- shift work
- self-employment

Racialized workers are disproportionately represented in this form of work as a consequence of their vulnerability to the restructuring in the economy. These developments represent characteristics and causes of social exclusion.

Box 7.4: Social Exclusion in the Canadian Context

- Historically, Canada was conceived as a White-settler colony.
- The colonization of Aboriginal peoples and marginalization of non-European groups contributed to their social exclusion.
- Social exclusion is manifested through structural inequalities in access to social, economic, political, and cultural resources.
- Structural inequalities persist on the basis of race, gender, disability, sexual orientation, and immigrant status, etc.

Though groundbreaking, Guildford's (2000) work on social exclusion in Canada is somewhat limited because of its focus on the generic experience of social exclusion defined by low income attainment. We need to interrogate the multiple dimensions of exclusion and identify subgroups in the victims of social exclusion, for the victims' experiences are differentiated by the nature of the oppressions they suffer. While some concern has been expressed about this approach leading to fragmentation, approaching exclusion through targeting its differentiated victims does not prevent us from identifying the points of convergence as a basis for solidarity and common struggles against marginalization.[6]

Box 7.5: Recent Patterns of Exclusion

- Post-September 11 legislative and administrative measures have limited the freedom of movement of racialized groups—such as members of Muslim, Arab, and Asian communities targeted
- Canadian citizenship increasingly defined by place of origin
- Lack of representation in political institutions
- Contact with the criminal justice system
- Neighbourhood selection
- Exposure to various forms of violence
- Poor health status
- Racialization of poverty

The experience of racialized groups is that certain forms of economic, political, social, and cultural privilege occur at the expense of those lower in the hierarchy of power. This is especially true in a market-regulated society where the impetus for state intervention to reduce the reproduction of inequality is minimal, as is increasingly the case under the neo-liberal regime. As we will see below, social exclusion has a dimension of time and space. Important aspects of social exclusion are manifested in the economy, in the experience of poverty, in the contact with the criminal justice system, in health status, in education, in housing and neighbourhood selection, in the way major cultural institutions such as the mainstream media depict the group, and in access to political processes. Below, we briefly outline some of the representative experiences in the Canadian context as they relate to racialized groups, beginning with the racialization of poverty.

Box 7.6: Racialized Groups and New Immigrants Experience Differential Life Chances

Characteristics include:
- A double-digit racialized income gap
- Deepening levels of poverty
- Differential access to housing and neighbourhood segregation
- Disproportionate contact with the criminal justice system
- Higher health risks

Box 7.7: The Racialization of Poverty in Canadian Urban Centres

The *2000 World Development Report* defines poverty as an unacceptable deprivation in human well-being that can comprise both physiological and social deprivation. Physiological deprivation involves the non-fulfillment of basic material or biological needs, including inadequate nutrition, health, education, and shelter. A person or family can be considered to be poor therefore if s/he or they are unable to secure sufficient amounts of goods and services to meet these basic material needs. The concept of physiological deprivation is closely related to, and extends beyond, low monetary income and consumption levels. Social deprivation widens the concept of deprivation to include risk, vulnerability, lack of autonomy, powerlessness, and lack of self-respect. Given that local definitions of deprivation often go beyond physiological deprivation and sometimes give greater weight to social deprivation, local populations (including poor communities) should be engaged in the dialogue that leads to the most appropriate definition of poverty in a country.

"Poverty is not knowing where your next meal is going to come from, and always wondering when the landlord is going to put your furniture out"

"Poverty is always praying that your husband must not lose his job. To me that's poverty" — participant at an anti-poverty forum, Toronto 2002

A most significant development in the last two decades is the *racialization of poverty*. The term refers to the emergence of structural features that pre-determine the disproportionate incidence of poverty among racialized group members. These trends are due to structural changes in the Canadian economy that conspire with historical forms of racial discrimination in the Canadian labour market to create social and economic marginalization, the result of which is the disproportionate vulnerability to poverty of racialized group communities. Racialized groups are often immigrant communities, and also suffer the impact of the immigration effect. However, current trends indicate that the economic inequality between immigrants and native-born Canadians is becoming greater and more permanent. That was not always the case. In fact, according to the historical trajectories of immigration settlement, immigrants tended to outperform native-born Canadians because of their high educational levels and age advantage.

The racialization of poverty is linked to the deepening oppression and social exclusion of racialized and immigrant communities on one hand, and to the entrenchment of privileged access to economic opportunity for an elite section of the majority population on the other. Economic exclusion takes the form of labour-market segregation, unequal access to employment, employment discrimination, disproportionate vulnerability to unemployment, and underemployment. These are both characteristics and causes of social exclusion. Attachment to the labour market is essential to both livelihood and the production of identity in society. It determines not only the ability to meet material needs, but also a sense of belonging, dignity, and self-esteem. Labour-market-related social exclusion involves income inequality as well as poor working conditions, lack of or limited mobility in workplaces, intensive work assignments, often requiring multiple shifts or multiple jobs and long hours, unequal distribution of opportunities, failure to utilize acquired skills, all of which contribute to the intensification of poverty among racialized groups.

The neo-liberal restructuring of Canada's economy and labour market towards flexible labour markets has increasingly stratified labour markets along racial lines, with the disproportionate representation of racialized group members in low-income sectors and low-end occupations, and underrepresentation in high-income sectors and occupations. It is these broader labour market processes that are responsible for the emergence of the phenomenon of the racialization of poverty in the late 20th century. Its dimensions are identifiable by such indicators as disproportionate levels of low income and racialized spatial concentration of poverty in key neighbourhoods.

The concentration of economic, social, and political power that has emerged as the market has become more prominent in social regulation in Canada helps explains the growing gap between rich and poor as well as the racialization of that gap (Yalnizyan, 1998; Kunz et al., 2001; Galabuzi, 2001; Lee, 2000; Dibbs et al., 1995; Jackson, 2001). Racialized groups and Aboriginal peoples are twice as likely to be poor as other Canadians because of the social and economic exploitation they suffer. Members of these communities have had to endure historical racial and gender inequalities accentuated by the restructuring of the Canadian economy, and more recently by racial profiling. In the midst of the socio-economic crisis that has resulted, the different levels of government have responded by retreating from anti-racism programs and policies that would have removed the barriers to economic equity. The resulting powerlessness and loss of voice has compounded the groups' inability to put issues of social inequality, and particularly the racialization of poverty, on the political agenda.

Racialized Group Members Twice as Likely as Other Canadians to Live in Poverty

In 1995, 35.6% members of racialized groups lived under the low income cut off (poverty line) compared with 17.6% in the general Canadian population. The numbers that year were comparable in urban areas—38% for racialized groups and 20% the rest of the population, a rate twice as high (Lee, 2000). In 1996, while racialized groups members accounted for 21.6% of the urban population, they accounted for 33% of the urban poor. That same year, 36.8% of women and 35% of men in racialized communities were low-income earners, compared to 19.2% of other women and 16% of other men. In 1995, the rate for children under six living in low-income families was an astounding 45%—almost twice the overall figure of 26% for all children living in Canada. The improvements in the economy have not dented the double-digit gap in poverty rates. Family poverty rates were similar—in 1998, the rate for racialized groups was 19% and 10.4% for other Canadian families (Lee, 2000; Jackson, 2002).

According to 1996 data, racialized group members experienced higher rates of poverty than other Canadians, with a rate in 1995 twice that of other Canadians (35.9% compared to 17.6%). While poverty among racialized communities varies from province to province—ranging from 24.3% in Newfoundland to a high of 52.2% in Quebec—these groups consistently face higher average rates of poverty than other Canadians in all provinces. In the three provinces with the highest concentration of racialized group members, the situation was as follows: In Ontario, with the highest population of racialized communities, the rate was 34.3% compared to 14.6%; in British Columbia, it was 32% compared to 16.9%; while in Quebec, it was 52.2% compared to 21.5% in the rest of the population.

Looking at the social economic status of racialized groups in the city of Toronto, Ornstein (2000) revealed that high rates of poverty are concentrated among certain groups such as Latin Americans, Africans Blacks and Caribbeans, and Arabs and West Asians—with rates at 40% and higher in 1996, or roughly three times the Toronto rate. This research is confirmed by accounts in the popular press, which reveal a dramatic increase in the use of food banks by highly educated newcomers (Quinn, 2002).

A United Way of Greater Toronto (2004) study looking at the geography of neighbourhood poverty between 1981–2001 found that poverty had increased dramatically, especially in neighbourhoods dominated by racialized people and immigrants.[7]

Racialization of Poverty among Immigrants

Another way to look at the experience of poverty among racialized groups is to look at the incidence of poverty among recent immigrants. As documented above, racialized groups compose the disproportionate number of recent immigrants (post-1970s). According to 1996 data, two-thirds of racialized group members were immigrants (68%). The data also showed that both racialized group members and immigrants earned less than their counterparts.[8] Immigrants were more likely to be poor than Canadian-born—on average 30% living in poverty as opposed to 21% of Canadian-born. The population of immigrants that arrived in the last 25 years, 1980 to present, are particularly vulnerable to high rates of poverty. This population is a highly racialized population group. Studies of urban areas where this group is concentrated show both the incidence of racialized group's immigration to Canada's cities and their experience with poverty rising.[9]

Immigration studies show that former waves of immigrants (pre-1970s) were subject to a short-term "immigration factor," which over time—not longer than 10 years for the unskilled and as low as two years for the skilled—they were able to overcome and either catch up to their Canadian-born counterparts or even surpass them in their performance in the economy. Their employment participation rates were as high or higher than the Canadian-born, and their wages and salaries rose gradually to the level of the Canadian-born. Today, 10 years after arriving, the average immigrant earns on average 80% of what a Canadian-born worker takes home, and recent immigrants—those living in Canada for less than five years—are much more likely to be unemployed than the Canadian-born.

While immigrant men are arriving with much more education than their predecessors, their inflation-adjusted earnings fell an average of 7% between 1980 and 2000. Male recent immigrant full-time employment earnings fell 7% between 1980 and 2000. This decline was evidently not the product of a poor economy since the earnings of Canadian-born men improved by 7% during the same time.

Research also shows low-income rates have been rising steadily among immigrants during the past two decades while falling among the Canadian-born. The trend is most pronounced in Canada's largest cities where over 76% of immigrants live (Toronto, Vancouver, and Montreal).

Kevin Lee's CCSD study (2000) documented the prevalence of poverty among immigrants, newcomers, and refugees. While the most recent arrivals were most disadvantaged, suffering 52.1% poverty, the rate for those in the country for 15 years was also high, at 35%, compared to a Canadian-born rate of 21%. The rate for immigrant populations arriving before 1986 is slightly lower than that of the Canadian-born group.[10]

Lee's study has been updated by M. Frenette and R. Morissette's study looking at low-income among immigrants between 1980 to 2000 (Frenette and Morissette, 2003). Their analysis shows that post-1980s immigrants experienced some of the highest increases in low-income rates in Canada in the last two decades. Low-income rates among successive groups of immigrants almost doubled between 1980 and 1995, peaking at 47% before easing up in the late 1990s. In 1980, 24.6% of immigrants who had arrived during the previous five-year period lived below the poverty line. By 1990, the low-income rate among recent immigrants had increased to 31.3%. It rose further to 47.0% in 1995 but fell back somewhat to 35.8% in 2000 (Frenette and Morissette, 2003).

In 1998, the annual wages of racialized immigrants were up to one-third less those of other Canadians, partly explaining why the poverty rate for racialized immigrants arriving after 1986 ranged between 36% and 50% (Jackson, 2001). This was happening at a time when average poverty rates had generally been falling in the Canadian population. Among the university-educated the drop was deeper (13%). Earnings rose for female recent immigrant full-time employment, but by less than other female full-time. More alarming are the low-income trends among highly educated immigrants. While low-income rates among recent immigrants with less than high school graduation increased by 24% from 1980 to 2000, low income rates increased by 50% among high school graduates and a whopping 66% among university-educated immigrants (Frenette and Morissette, 2003).[11]

Recent immigrants' rates of employment declined markedly between 1986 and 1996. The result is that Canada's immigrants exhibit a higher incidence of poverty and greater dependence on social assistance than their predecessors, in spite of the fact that the percentage of university graduates among them is higher in all categories of immigrants, including family class and refugees as well as economic immigrants, than it is for the Canadian-born (CIC, 2002).

This raises the question of whether it is simply the period of stay that is responsible for the differences in levels of poverty. Arguably, it is to some extent; however, the racial composition of the immigration pool has changed dramatically over the last 25 years, and even more intensely over the last 15 years. Given the previous patterns that documented income parity and in many cases an advantage for immigrants during the pre-1980s period, period of stay cannot be the only explanation. Another possible explanation is educational attainment differentials. However, most of the immigrants in the post-1991 group gained entry through a strictly enforced point system, which favoured those in the economic class.

However, as we have indicated throughout this book, in the post-1980s period, there are persistent and growing difficulties in the labour-market integration of immigrants, especially recent immigrants. Rates of unemployment and underemployment are increasing for individual immigrants, as are rates of poverty for immigrant families (Galabuzi, 2001; Ornstein, 2000; Pendakur, 2000; Reitz, 1998, 2001; Shields, 2002). The traditional trajectory that saw immigrants catch up with other Canadians over time seems to have been reversed in the case of racialized immigrants. The irony is that over that period of time, the level of education, usually an indicator of economic success, has been growing.

Table 7.1: Poverty Rate by Racialized Group Status, by Province, 1995

Province	Poverty Rate Racialized Groups	Poverty Rate Members of Other Groups
Newfoundland	24.3%	21.3%
P.E.I	28.0%	15.1%
Nova Scotia	37.9%	18.1%
New Brunswick	34.2%	18.9%
Quebec	52.2%	21.5%
Ontario	34.3%	14.6%
Manitoba	31.3%	19.7%
Saskatchewan	29.9%	18.0%
Alberta	31.9%	16.9%
British Columbia	32.0%	16.9%
Canada	35.9%	17.6%

Source: D. Ross, K. Scott, and P. Smith, *The Canadian Fact Book on Poverty* (Ottawa: Canadian Council on Social Development, 2000). Based on Statistics Canada 1996 Census data.

Finally, the poor are also increasingly exposed to homelessness in urban areas. A recent taskforce report in Ontario's Peel region investigated homelessness among a number of racialized communities, including Punjabi, Vietnamese, Tamil, Spanish-speaking, and Caribbean. Its findings suggest that the problem of homelessness is growing in these communities, especially among refugees. It was particularly concerned about the levels of displaced seniors, abused women, the unemployed, and those with mental illness and substance-abuse problems.[12]

Table 7.2: Population of Immigrants in Canadian Cities by Arrival Period and Poverty Status

	Total Population		Proportion of Population		Percentage Rate of Poverty
	Total	Poor	Total	Poor	
Canadian-born	12,147,000	2,972,200	70%	62%	21.6%
Immigrants and refugees	3,627,000	1,129,500	29.8%	38%	30.0%
Immigrants	3,627,000	1,129,500	100%	100%	30%
Pre-1986	2,094,000	411,700	59.8%	39.1%	19.7%
1986–1990	551,400	193,300	15.7%	18.4%	35.1%
1991–1996	981,800	510,500	27.0%	45.1%	52.1%

Source: D. Ross, K. Scott, and P. Smith, *The Canadian Fact Book on Poverty* (Ottawa: Canadian Council on Social Development, 2000). Based on Statistics Canada 1996 Census data.

Racialization and Neighbourhood Selection: Poor Neighbourhoods and Racialized Groups

Since the 1980s, there has been significant research in both the United States and Canada focusing on the extent to which concentrations of neighbourhood poverty are increasingly identified with racialized communities. Included here are studies by Hajnal (1995), Massey and Denton (1993), Ley and Smith (1997), Murdie (1998), and Kazemipur and Halli (1997, 2000), among others.[13]

A 1988 Quebec Human Rights Commission study matched pairs of White and Black actors in a search for housing. Of the 73 cases tested, 31 showed blatant, overt discrimination. Discrimination was confirmed when the Black actors were told there were no vacancies and the White actors given the apartment soon after. Discrimination also took the form of differential rental fees and conditions.

In Vancouver, a study in the early 1990s, a time of increased immigration from Hong Kong, found that Chinese immigrants were blamed for the increases in house prices and often faced accusations of unneighbourliness. Attempts by local residents and councils to use zoning by-laws and regulations to limit the expansion of mostly Chinese neighbourhoods showed how even affluent groups can be racialized.[14]

Research shows that the quality of a neighbourhood significantly affects the life chances of its residents.[15] In Canada, studies show that people of European heritage live in neighbourhoods with superior social qualities, while Asians and Blacks experience inferior social qualities, despite the high relative costs of the housing. Fong and Gulia's study, using the 1991 Census data and Statistics Canada special tabulation (1996), considered the effects of socio-economic resources on neighbourhood qualities among racial and ethnic groups. Conventional notions suggest the existence of perfect competition in the housing market, claiming that economic resources translate into equal access to housing. However, as Hulchanski and Mwarigha show, the market is racialized.[16]

Studies by Fong (1997) and Balakrishnan and Selvanathan (1990) show a relationship between neighbourhood quality and socio-economic status. The studies show that locational stratification varies along racial lines. Balakrishnan et al. show that racialized groups experienced higher levels of residential segregation, even when their economic status improved. Fong and Gulia's 1996 study shows that groups with lighter skin colour reside in better neighbourhoods than groups with darker skin colour. The differences relate to differential abilities to convert both socio-economic resources into neighbourhood qualities as well as differential access to resources and information. Fong and Gulia conclude that differences in the neighbourhood qualities of racial groups are influenced by resources, acculturation, and locational stratification that reflect the discriminatory experiences of some of the groups in the housing market.[17]

The study also shows that the overrepresentation of the mostly racialized group and immigrants in poor neighbourhoods acts as a barrier to economic success, hampers children's education opportunities, and raises overall health risks. The study concludes that the overrepresentation of racialized groups in poor neighbourhoods compromises the quality of their living conditions and civil services like education, health care, and recreational services. The overrepresentation may lead to a subculture that impedes the opportunities of future generations by limiting access to networks in which, for instance, job opportunities are routinely presented through word of mouth. Finally, the overrepresentation may lead to a breakdown in social institutions, increased unemployment, over-policing and contact with the criminal justice system, teenage pregnancy, family disruption, family violence, and crime.

More recently, a 2000 study by Fong and Shibuya using 1991 Census data found a high level of racialized neighbourhood segregation, especially for poor racialized group members. It found a high segregation of Blacks, and moderate to high segregation of South Asians. The findings show a close relationship between neighbourhood segregation along racial and low-income lines. The groups also became vulnerable to the process of gentrification in major cities, leading to their displacement and exposure to homelessness.[18] Fong and Shibuya suggest that racial and ethnic segregation reflects not only the social economic status of racialized groups but also patterns of social relations, in the sense that minority group members are labelled undesirable as neighbours, leading to "spatial distance" between the majority population and the minorities. This is often intensified by fears that undesirables in a neighbourhood depress property values.

Fong and Shibuya's study concludes that residential racial segregation occurs due to discriminatory practices against racialized group members, especially the poor, in the housing market. They are then left to inhabit marginal housing stock in segregated neighbourhoods. It found that Blacks were the most residentially segregated group of the racialized groups studied, and also that there was a clear correlation between race and poverty status as a function of segregation.[19]

Studies by Hou and Balakrishnan (1996), Kazemipur and Halli (2000), Fong (2000), Ley and Smith, (1997), Hou and Picot (2003), and Myles and Hou (2003) suggest that these areas show characteristics of "ghettoization" or spatial concentration of poverty, concentration in urban cores, overrepresentation, tight clustering, and limited exposure to majority communities. Increasingly these geographical areas represent racialized enclaves subject to the distresses of low-income communities.

Table 7.3: Toronto Area Racialized Enclaves and Experience of High Poverty Rates

	University Degree	Unemployment	Low Income	Single Parent
Chinese	21.2%	11.2%	28.4%	11.7%
South Asian	11.8%	13.1%	28.3%	17.6%
Black	8.7%	18.3%	48.5%	33.7%

Source: Statistics Canada, 2003, as reported in Hou and Picot (Catalogue No. 11F0019M1E—
     no. 204).

These studies show a growing tendency in urban Canada toward residential segregation that is reinforced by the low-income status of many racialized groups. The implications are higher social risks, and further social exclusion and economic marginalization. The proliferation of racialized neighbourhoods with high poverty levels coincides with a growing racialization of the housing market in Canada's urban areas. These concentrations in turn correlate to social isolation and the attendant social ills identified by a recent investigation of 1996 Canada Census data by Kazemipur and Halli (2000).[20] Kazemipur and Halli's study, which focused on racialized groups and immigrants, found correlation between neighbourhood poverty and such racialized groups as Chinese, Black, Vietnamese, and Spanish-speaking. The only other groups with equally high correlation were Aboriginal peoples and Poles. In fact, they found mostly negative correlation for those of European origin like Germans, British, Dutch, Swedish, Finnish, and Jewish. On the other hand, they found a positive correlation among immigrants arriving since 1970, when Canadian immigration began to shift substantially toward source countries predominated by racialized groups.

In Canada's urban centres, the spatial concentration of poverty or residential segregation is intensifying along racial lines. Immigrants in Toronto and Montreal are more likely than non-immigrants to live in neighbourhoods with high rates of poverty as Table 7.3 above shows. Social exclusion is increasingly manifest in urban centres where racialized groups are concentrated through the emergence of racially segregated neighbourhoods. In a segregated housing market, racialized groups are disproportionately relegated to substandard, marginal, and often overpriced housing. These growing neighbourhood inequalities act as social determinants of health and well-being, with limited access to social services, increased contact with the criminal justice system, social disintegration, and violence engendering higher health risks.

Globalization-generated pressures have led to the retreat by the state from its social obligations, leading to social deficits that impact racialized communities disproportionately. This diminishing commitment by the state toward income redistribution and income supports, social services, and adequate funding for health care and education are juxtaposed with racial inequality in access to work and in employment income, the racially unequal incidence of low income, the shift toward flexible labour deployment and precarious forms of work in the urban economies, and the marked increase in South–North immigration. Some of the resulting isolated, racially defined, low-income neighbourhoods are vulnerable to disintegrating social institutions and violence.

When racialized spatial concentration of poverty leads to racialized group members living in neighbourhoods that are heavily concentrated and "hypersegregated" from the rest of society, these neighbourhoods become characterized by social deficits such as inadequate access to counselling services, life-skills training, child care, recreation, and health care services (Kazemipur and Halli, 1997, 2000; Lo et al., 2000).

Young immigrants living in low-income areas often struggle with alienation from their parents and community of origin, and from the broader society. The social services they need to cope with dislocation are lacking, the housing on offer is often substandard, and public housing is often poorly maintained because of cutbacks. Young immigrants face a crisis of unemployment, despair, and violence. They are disproportionate targets of contact with the criminal justice system.

Finally, a word about homelessness and the recent immigrant and racialized groups. Homelessness is said to be proliferating among racialized group members and immigrants because of the incidence of low income and the housing crises in many urban areas (Lee, 2000; Peel, 2000; ISSRA, 2003). Homelessness is an extreme form of social exclusion that has many causes and factors. Recent immigrants and racialized people are more likely to be homeless in Canada's urban centres than they were 10 years ago. A recent study by the Islamic Social Services and Resource Association (ISSRA, 2003) in Toronto, titled *Living on the Ragged Edges: Absolute and Hidden Homelessness among Latin Americans and Muslims in West Central Toronto,* captured much of these emerging realities.[21] It echoed the findings of the Toronto Mayor's Homelessness Action Taskforce report that identified immigrants and refugees as a high-risk group for homelessness.[22] The report identified a range of social, economic, cultural, and political factors that interact with the various oppressions these groups face based on race, gender, sexuality, mental health, religion, and disability to increase the vulnerability of racialized and immigrant communities to homelessness.

Homelessness compounds other sources of stresses. It has been associated with early mortality, substance abuse, mental illness, infectious diseases, and difficulty accessing health services. The complex interactions between homelessness and access to health services have not received enough study, and represent a key gap in both the anti-racism and social determinants of health discourses.

Box 7.8: Quotations from the Field

"You will never be able to get any of my clients in there ... I've been there with many people and, miraculously, the vacancies disappear every time."
—Amina Ahmed, housing help worker, Toronto, 2000

"More recent immigrants, particularly those from the developing world residing in Ontario and Quebec, have substantially lower rates of home ownership even when age and period of immigration are controlled "
—Ray and Moore (1991:19)

Social Exclusion in the Canadian Educational Systems

The educational system is a key institution of socialization, especially for young people. Education has often produced and reproduced racist ideology, attitudes, and structures of inequality. There is substantial literature detailing the experiences of racialized students and workers in Canadian educational institutions at the elementary, secondary, and post-secondary levels as ones of differential treatment, denial of access and opportunities, and marginalization. The various curricula have also been identified as alienating to racialized groups, in most cases presenting the reality of racialized groups in Canada as invisible or inconsequential.

Racialized students are subjected to discriminatory educational practices that often undermine them intellectually, emotionally, and morally. Educators' attitudes and low expectations combine with the invisibility of racialized groups' contributions to Canadian history to negatively influence many racialized students. Studies show that in many racialized communities, these experiences often negatively impact student performance. In many educational institutions, young racialized group members are streamed toward non-academic programs that lead to low-paying vocations. Many young people drop out rather than continue participating in an increasingly alienating experience. The relationship between educational institutions and racialized parents and communities has also been described as dysfunctional, as some educators routinely disparage the role and contributions of racialized parents in the schools.[23]

While many racialized group members look to the educational system to help level past inequalities, they often have to contend with institutions that help perpetuate forms of racial socialization. Studies show that while both racialized and non-racialized students tend to have similar career aspirations at the beginning of their educational experience, these diverge by the time they leave the institutions.[24]

Children are routinely subjected to racist images and negative stereotypes in the books they use, in visual media, in the stories they are told, in toys, in music, in mainstream media; such images deepen their perceptions of racial differences. For non-racialized youth, these images reinforce negative stereotypes of their racialized peers, while for racialized youth, they strongly influence their social development and self-perception. The absence of portrayals of racialized peoples, in textbooks, and from the curricula further exacerbates their alienation, undermines the learning environment, and compromises performance potential. These factors speak to a history of exclusion that dates back to the days when Blacks were officially segregated from schools in Ontario.[25]

Racialized communities have often raised concerns about issues of curriculum development and knowledge production in both the school system and post-secondary institutions. The concerns centre around the Eurocentric nature of both the formal and hidden curricula, and the extent to which particular forms of knowledge are universalized and transmitted by singular perspectives in the educational process. Critics also address what's in and what's left out, as well as the choice of materials used and the overwhelmingly non-racialized personnel.[26]

Carl James (1994) has written about the impact of Black children not seeing themselves in the ranks of authority figures in the educational system. R. Patrick

Solomon (1992) and George Dei (1995) have documented the experiences of alienation that lead high school racialized students to resist by dropping out. Razack (1998) has discussed the interlocking experiences of gender and race and their impact on the education system, and numerous community organizations have appeared before government commissions to discuss their communities' experiences with the educational system. A recent report on the Ontario government's safe schools policy in the Toronto district school board addressed the issue of racial profilings in the educational system, especially with regard to the disproportionate impact of suspensions and expulsions on racialized students.[27]

The immigration system has also imposed its burdens, especially on children of non-status migrants who are denied access to some of Canada's educational system because their parents' immigration status is not regularized. The delays in the system often lead to long periods without formal education.

Issues of exclusion and discrimination are similarly prevalent in the post-secondary system, where both curriculum concerns and discrimination in employment have been the subject of many studies. This is particularly important because of the growing demands for higher education in more forms of employment. There are issues of course misrepresentation (universalizing Eurocentred areas of study), absence of anti-racism curricula, low representation of racialized group members in faculty, lack of expertise in race and ethnic studies among faculty, lack of interdisciplinary programs that reflect the experiences of racialized group members, and a general response of denial when issues of race and ethnicity are raised.[28]

The experience of racialized group members continues to be one of alienation and confronting barriers. Roxanne Ng's (1994) account of her experience in academe exemplifies these struggles. Ng calls attention to the need for opening up spaces for previously silenced or marginalized voices to be heard. Others like Carty (1991), Bannerji (1991), Bramble (2000), and James (1994) have also documented the experiences of voice appropriation and silencing that occur in post-secondary institutions. Some of the most prominent post-secondary institutions in Canada's urban centres exhibit the inequalities found in other sectors: increasingly racialized students populations face teaching faculties that are disproportionately and in many cases almost exclusively non-racialized.[29] Henry and Tator's (1994) review of post-secondary institutions under the Federal Contractors Employment Equity program reveals the extent of underrepresentation of racialized group members in Canada's university faculty. In 1992, 40% of the enrolled student population at Canada's largest university, the University of Toronto, was racialized, while 10% of the faculty was racialized, and these individuals were concentrated in a few fields. At the influential University of Toronto's Ontario Institute of Studies in Education (OISE), over the period of a decade, beginning with the late 1980s, out of a faculty of 120, the number of racialized group members did not exceed four. At York University, another of Canada's bigger post-secondary institutions, racialized faculty represented an even lower number, 6.4%, while over 30% of the parking and security staff at the university were racialized group members.[30]

"Including African and non-White scholars in one's intellectual cosmos does not necessarily mean a lowering of standards. When this university finally opens its gates and minds to non-White intellectuals, ideas and personnel, then visiting professors like me will cease to be one-year stands, interesting exotica or simple white elephants" (Ogundipe-Leslie, 1991)[31]

Social Exclusion and the Health Status of Racialized Group Members

Universal access to health care is now a core Canadian value, espoused broadly by all segments of the political elite as defining Canadian society. But beyond the policy articulation of universality of coverage lies the reality of unequal access to health service utilization; factors such as income, gender, race, immigrant status, and geography determine access to health care. A review of the limited available literature indicates that the processes of social exclusion affect the health status of racialized and recent immigrant communities. There is a gap between the promise of universal health care and the differential health status arising from inequalities in the social determinants of health. This is one form of the gap between the promise of citizenship and the reality of exclusion for racialized groups and immigrants in Canada. There is limited empirical research to draw on, perhaps because the health system has neglected this as an area of appropriate research. Anderson and Kirkham (1998) have suggested that Canada's health care system is "enmeshed in a racialized and gendered construction of nation and capitalist world view that organizes women's everyday lives."[32]

Social determinants of health, a health framework based on a synthesis of diverse public health and social scientific literature, suggests that the most important antecedents of human health status are not medical care inputs and health behaviours (smoking, diet, exercise, etc.), but rather social and economic characteristics of individuals and populations. In short, there is a significant convergence between social exclusion and health status (Evans et al., 1994; Frank, 1995; Hayes and Dunn, 1998). For racialized groups and recent immigrants, power relations, identity, status, and life chances are influenced by the processes of immigration and integration, and they in turn influence the health status of the groups (Dunn and Dyck, 1998).

International studies have long established a relationship between economic status and the life chances and health status of groups and communities. The social inequalities associated with racial discrimination in North America have also been related to health status. The World Health Organization has stated clearly that "the state of economic development is a strong determinant of the health situation of a country." The same is true of inequality in socio-economic status—the scale of social and economic differences among groups in the population. The more equal the society is, the healthier it is. Social inequality translates into health inequality.[33] Social inequality particularly affects the social fabric. Health status tells us about the differentials in the quality of life enjoyed by different groups in society.

The implications for racialized groups are obvious. Such social causes of health deterioration as depression, anxiety, alcoholism, and drug dependency are related to differences in social status, as are mortality causes such as suicides, homicides, and accidents. Material inequality is a major determinant of the social welfare. Its impact on health is but one of the social costs it imposes on the victims of this inequality; others are access to basic needs such as shelter, nutrition, and clothing. Beyond that, education and social participation also become less accessible, meaning that the level of citizenship is compromised. According to Coburn (2000), higher income inequality and lower social cohesion induced by neo-liberalism has had the effect of generating poor health status. Given the disproportionately adverse impact of globalization on racialized groups as discussed previously, there is little doubt that the health status of the group has declined.[34]

One of the more significant studies of immigrants and health was done by Dunn and Dyck (1998) using the "social determinants of health" approach. Dunn and Dyck's study investigated the social determinants of health in Canada's immigrant population using Canada's National Population Health Survey (NPHS). Specifically, they looked at the differences in health status and health-care utilization between immigrants and non-immigrants, immigrants of European and non-European origin, and immigrants of less than 10 years' and greater than 10 years' residence in Canada. They adopt a perspective which suggests that the most important determinants of human health status are not medical care inputs and health behaviours (smoking, diet, exercise, etc.). Rather, the focus is on social and economic characteristics of individuals and populations. Although their investigation was not conclusive, they strongly suggest, based on a reading of varied literature, that mechanisms related to societal power relations, social identity, social status, and control over life circumstances are highly influential on the differential distribution of health status across social strata.[35]

Other literature on social inequalities in health demonstrates a positive correlation between social status and health status. For instance, Hyman (2001) has observed that the Dunn and Dyck study did not find evidence to contradict the assertion that immigrant health status is negatively impacted by their social economic status. However, a study by Laroche (2000) that compared the health status of immigrants and the Canadian-born population discovered no difference between the two groups. There is now a wealth of other empirical research by mainstream and critical social scientists that supports the argument that growing income inequality leads to social and economic instability, which then leads to health status.[36]

Impact of Racialization on Health Status

It is now generally agreed that racism is a primary source of stress and hypertension in racialized group communities. Everyday forms of racism, often compounded by low income, sexism, xenophobia, and the related conditions of underemployment, non-recognition of prior accreditation, low-standard housing, residence in low-income neighbourhoods with significant social deficits, violence against women, other forms of domestic and neighbourhood violence, targeted policing, and disproportionate criminalization and incarceration, impose a tremendous burden on the health status of racialized group members. Everyday forms of racism define the existence of those on the margins of society, an existence of exclusion from the full participation in the social, economic, cultural, and political affairs of Canadian society. They are also important socio-economic and psycho-social determinants of health. Canadian research is underdeveloped in this area. But while empirical evidence is scarce, there is significant qualitative evidence, collected from group members, service providers, and community-based research, to suggest that these forms of racism act as determinants of the health status of socially marginalized groups such as racialized groups, immigrants, and Aboriginal peoples (Agnew, 2002). The research suggests that these conditions induce feelings of powerlessness, hopelessness, and despair, harming the emotional and physical health of group members (Chakraborty and McKenzie, 2002; Thompson, 2002; Zayas, 2001; Beiser et al., 1993).[37] These conditions in turn negatively impact attempts by affected individuals, groups, and communities to achieve full citizenship because of their inability to claim social and political rights enjoyed by other Canadians — including residents' right to physical and mental well-being (*Canada Health Act*, 1984).

International research clearly shows the connection between race and health. For instance, research in the United States correlates racism and health status (Randall, 1993). Wilkinson has investigated the processes of racialization, which result in the social and economic marginalization of certain social groups, and has shown that "racial" differences in health status can largely be accounted for by differences in individuals' social and economic circumstances (Wilkinson, 1996; Anderson, 1987, 1991).

There are other dimensions of the question with which we are more familiar. Institutionalized racism in the health care system — characterized by language barriers, lack of cultural sensitivity, absence of cultural competencies, barriers to access to health service utilization, and inadequate funding for community health services — has been identified as impacting the health status of racialized group members. Mainstream health-care institutions are Eurocentric, imposing European and White cultural norms as standard and universal. This cultural hegemony imposes a burden on racialized and immigrant communities. Insights from critical race discourses help us understand that the cumulative burden of subtle, ordinary but persistent everyday forms of racism, compounded by experiences of marginalization, also determine health status. The psychological pressures of daily resisting these and other forms of oppression add up to a complex of factors that undermines the health status of racialized and immigrant group members. They are compounded by the low occupation status, low housing and neighbourhood status, high unemployment, and high levels of poverty. Racist stereotypes by health practitioners impact health status, as does the way the health care system deals with health crises within racialized communities. Below are a few examples.

Social Exclusion and HIV/AIDS

Reports on HIV/AIDS and racialized groups suggest that discrimination against people with HIV/AIDS is compounded by their racial status. A study by the Alliance for South Asian AIDS Prevention (ASAP, 1999) found that the cultural, religious, language, and racial barriers the communities face in accessing health care services led to differential treatment for South Asian communities and people from the majority community living with HIV/AIDS. While South Asians had to deal with the cultural stigma imposed on those living with HIV/AIDS in the community, they were also vulnerable to racism and marginalization, which led to withdrawal, silencing, and higher health risks.[38]

In a study of African Canadian Women and HIV/AIDS done by Toronto's Women's Health in Women's Hands, respondents said that racist experiences with the health-care system was one of the reasons African Canadian women reported a reluctance to access health services like HIV/AIDS treatment, education, and care (Tharoa and Massaquoi, 2001).[39]

Many racialized group members and immigrants with mental health issues and mental illnesses identify racism as a critical issue in their lives. A study by Across Boundaries found that the magnitude of the association between these racism and poverty and mental health status was similar to the association by low-income racialized group members between racism and other commonly studied stressful life events such as death of a loved one, divorce, or job loss (Across Boundaries, 1999).[40]

Everyday experiences of racism generate as much stress as family separation through immigration, the intensification of work, devaluation of one's worth through de-credentialism, and the other experiences of inequality and injustice. Stress in turn is a major cause of a variety of health problems. It has been observed that one of the reasons the health status of immigrants declines is because of their experiences of discrimination and racism (Hyman, 2001). State-imposed barriers to family reunification through an immigration policy that favours independent-class immigration lead to extended period of family separation. Family separation and failure to effect reunification rob family members of their support network, but also engender separation anxiety, thoughts of suicide, and even death.

Racism and discrimination based on immigrant status intensify processes of marginalization and social exclusion, compounding the experiences of poverty and its impacts on mental health status. The everyday darts and put-downs diminish self-esteem, undermining the mental health of racialized group members.

The stigma of mental illness often bars members from seeking treatment, with some afraid that that status would compound their marginalization. The Canadian Task Force on Mental Health Issues Affecting Immigrants identified a mental-health gap between immigrants and the Canadian-born population. Concluding that the socio-economic status of immigrants was a determinant of mental health, it called for increased access to mental health services for immigrants, and more appropriate culturally sensitive and language-specific services to help close the gap (Beiser, 1988).

Beiser et al. (1993) identify the persistent gap in health-care utilization between immigrants and native-born Canadians, its impact on the mental health status of immigrants, and the need for research to better understand the phenomenon. The serious gap in research on health and racialization in the research on the mental health of immigrants can be addressed using a framework that recognizes the impact of racism and immigrant status on the process of social exclusion and social determination of health.

Racialization and Mental Health: The Discrimination-Depression Relationship

A study by Noh and Beiser on the perceived racial discrimination, depression, and coping of Southeast Asian refugees in Canada found that the refugees who reported discrimination experienced higher depression levels than their counterparts who reported none. The findings confirm the impact of discrimination on health status, but also suggest that forms of societal identification help reverse the impact of social exclusion. Perceived racial discrimination is defined as a minority group's subjective perception of unfair treatment based on racial prejudice. The focus on the perceived nature of discrimination accommodates the reality of the subtle and elusive nature of certain forms of racism in the Canadian context (Noh et al., 1999).

According to a study by Anderson et al. (1993) on chronic illness among immigrant women, for immigrant women living on meagre incomes from marginal employment, the daily struggles and the desire to hold on to their low-paying jobs tend to take precedence over the need to disclose chronic illness to ensure its active management by health professionals. In essence, these women are balancing health risks with livelihood concerns. Along with such livelihood considerations, they often face the daunting prospect of navigating the mainstream health-care system, with its barriers to access, lack of culturally appropriate services, and inability of health-care professionals to understand the choices that the poor and marginalized must make to survive.

Many skilled immigrants are barred from making full use of their skills and talents in both the economic sphere and in public life. Increasingly they are dealing with frustration at the barriers they face. Such a strong sense of inequality and injustice has implications for their mental health (Beiser, 1988). Research also shows that immigrant youth sometimes find the stresses of integration on top of the challenges of adolescence overwhelming. Their feelings of isolation and alienation are linked to perceptions of cultural differences and experiences of discrimination and racism. While these are often complicated by intergenerational issues, support from friends, family and institutions is key to overcoming the challenges—in essence it presents them with a recreated community in response to the exclusion they face in mainstream institutions like the school system (Kilbride, 2000).

All these are conditions that are related to the experience of a racialized existence and its challenges. They speak to the impact it has on the health status of racialized and immigrant populations. In a significant way, the racialized experience may partly explain why health status among immigrants tends to decline with longer period of stay (Hyman, 2001).[41]

Racialization and Canada's Mainstream Media

The media is one of the most powerful institutions in Canadian society. It has the power to socialize young and old alike, define communities, and influence the behaviour of those who make decisions that affect racialized group members daily. Canadian mainstream media is not immune to its own cultural racism, as many studies have shown. Media determines the significance of a group by whether or not it includes it in its coverage, and whether or not it represents its members on its pages or screens. A Media Watch study of women and racialized group members in the media concluded that in the two weeks of newscasts monitored in the winter of 1993, racialized group reporters appeared only 3.9% of the time (2.6% for males and 1.35% for females).[42]

The media is a key institution in the creation of the images that soon become realities defining racial minorities and their place in Canada. It perpetuates racial ideologies, and in spite of many criticisms, largely continues to treat racialized groups in one of two ways: either rendering them invisible when it comes to advertising and positive roles, or presenting sensationalized, excessive coverage of crimes that involve them.

Henry and Tator's recent study (2000), *Racist Discourse in Canada's Print Media*, uses case studies to examine links between racism, popular discourse, and the media. It concludes that racialized group members are underrepresented and largely invisible in the media, that when they appear they are often misrepresented and stereotyped, and that despite claims of objectivity and neutrality, media personnel routinely allow their values, beliefs, and interests to impact the production of news and images. Similarly, Fleras and Kunz (2001) have pointed to mass media as central to institutionalizing cultural hierarchies that privilege Whiteness; mass media uses its power and access to the Canadian population to defend and peddle racist ideologies, shaping the public consciousness by "mis/under/over/representing" racialized group communities' experiences and realities.[43]

Other researchers have tied the persistent misconceptions and misrepresentations of racialized group communities to mainstream media's systemic lack of fair, balanced, or informed reporting on immigrant and refugee issues. The reporting is too often negative and stereotypical, focusing on crime, poverty, and aberrant behaviour. Racialized group members are overrepresented in crime stories, sports, and entertainment, and underrepresented in business, politics, and public service. The reporting tends to swing from the almost always sensational to the at times non-existent (Goldfarb, 1995; Siddiqui, 1993; Ginsberg, 1985).[44] The lack of racialized personnel in the workforces at major media outlets has been identified as a contributing factor to the biased representation of immigrant experiences (Miller, 1998; Canadian Islamic Congress, 1999).[45] The effect of the inaccurate portrayals of racialized groups and immigrants in the media is to heighten xenophobic and racist tendencies, and to entrench prejudices against immigrants and racial minority groups. These attitudes have been identified as influencing public opinion, public debate, and policy-making.

More recently, the debate on the nature of Canada's immigration and refugee policy in the new millennium, initiated by the federal Minister of Immigration, has highlighted the need to disseminate accurate information about the immigrant experience to provide. Such information will provide a basis for informed public debate and policy development. Assumptions that immigrants pose a criminal threat have been widely discussed as part of the reforms of Canada's immigration legislation; these assumptions have shaped the way immigrants and refugees are evaluated, processed, and settled in Canada, including the way they are received in the country's workplaces. Such misconceptions and misrepresentations impose an undue burden on racialized groups and immigrants, and adversely impact their participation in the public, social, and economic life of the country.

Social Exclusion and the Criminal Justice System

> We must put people before beautification, crisis before gentrification. As more and more of our young people end up in superjails, we need to resolve that our young will not just be fodder for the correctional-industrial complex, but candidates for jobs in their neighbourhoods and beyond. If the different levels of government are prepared to commit 12 billion dollars for the waterfront, it can afford billions for the transformation of the neighbourhoods. Or it will pay much more later. (Galabuzi, 2002)

The available literature on the experience of racialized groups, immigrants, and the criminal justice system indicates unequal treatment at the various points in the justice process. The differential treatment begins with police use of discretion when stopping, arresting, and charging, and continues on through bail hearings, sentencing, and incarceration. The disparities are most glaring when one looks at the different points of discretion in the system, whether it is police stopping cars to determine whether the driver may be committing a crime — like trafficking in small quantities of drugs, carrying a gun — or justices of the peace granting or denying bail, or judges sentencing.

Many studies have produced overwhelming evidence of the differential treatment of racialized groups in the criminal justice system.[46] Numerous Royal Commissions, taskforces, and studies confirm the systemic nature of racial discrimination in the administration of justice as manifest through the overrepresentation of racialized group members in arrests by police, imprisonment before trial, differential management of charges by crown attorneys, differential sentencing by judges, overrepresentation in prison admissions, and differential treatment while incarcerated. Policies such as targeted policing impact the poor and racialized communities disproportionately, becayse they largely target poor and marginalized neighbourhoods.

Recently, some institutions in the criminal justice system have been accused of racial profiling, and research is underway to establish the extent to which racial profiling is employed by police and prisons. The overrepresentation of racialized group members in the penal system contrasts sharply with their underrepresentation in the ranks of lawyers, crowns, judges, and police officers. Employment equity in the criminal justice system remains a major challenge for Canadian society, even as Canada's urban areas, with their disproportionate racialized populations, become hotbeds of confrontations between racialized groups and those responsible for the administration of justice.

Minorities and poor people regularly encounter discrimination in their contact with the criminal justice system. The Ontario Commission on Systemic Racism in the Criminal Justice System surveyed the views of Blacks, Aboriginal peoples, Chinese, and Vietnamese people, and found that many believed that they were treated differently in the criminal justice system. These sentiments mirror findings by numerous reports on policing and racial minorities in Ontario, as well as reports in Nova Scotia, Manitoba, Law Reform Commission of Canada, dealing with racism in the criminal justice system.

In Canada's urban centres, differential treatment has led to tensions between minorities and Police. Blacks and Aboriginal peoples can be found in the criminal justice system (jails, courts) in disproportionate numbers. Esmeralda Thornhill, holder of the Dalhousie University Law School Black Studies chair, notes that "[b]y some unspoken societal consensus, a generalized negativity towards Blackness persistently links Black skin with criminality... All too frequently, Black skin colour becomes the initiating catalytic factor which jettisons Black people into the criminal justice system" (Thornhill, 1988).[47]

Thornhill is talking about the disproportionate incarceration of Blacks in Canada's prisons. The Ontario Commission on Systemic Racism in the Criminal Justice System found that while Blacks were 3% of Ontario population in 1995, they were 15% of the jail population; that Black imprisonment increased 204% between 1986 and 1992; and that Whites on drug offences were twice as likely as Blacks to be released, while Blacks were three times more likely to be denied bail. The commission also found that Whites found guilty were less likely to serve time, and that they got lighter sentences for similar infractions.

Racialized groups, low-income, and marginal communities bear the brunt of the law-and-order agenda of the neo-liberal era mostly through targeted policing, racial profiling, and criminalization. Persistent discriminatory practices in the criminal justice system lead to higher levels of incarceration of racialized youth, a phenomenon referred to as the criminalization of racialized youth. A young Black participant at the 1990 Jamaican Canadian Association Conference notes, "A black youth faces a white-dominated system with a white police, white lawyers, and a white judge and often white crown attorney defending him or her."

Racialized group members in the urban centres face issues of overpolicing such as targeted policing and racial profiling. To express the prevalence of unexplained police stops, racialized communities referring to a charge called "DWB": driving while Black. In the context of traffic stops by police officers, racial profiling should be defined broadly as officers' *use of race or ethnicity as a factor* in deciding to stop, question, search, or arrest someone.

Recently a *Toronto Star* investigation concluded that African Canadians are stopped more frequently by police than are other Torontonians. According to the *Toronto Star*, between 1993–1995, Black residents of Toronto were more likely to be stopped (28%) than White residents (18%) or Chinese residents (15%). Among men aged 25–40, Black men (48%) were more likely to report being stopped by police than White men (29%) or Chinese men (19%).[48]

Other indicators of systemic racism include disproportionate police shootings and killings of racialized group members, as documented in Montreal, Toronto, Calgary, as well as differential treatment in arrests. Does racial profiling aid or undermine the administration of justice? The widespread perception among people of colour is that they are unfairly targeted by the police because of their race. The police mistrust of racialized persons harms both the police and communities of colour by impeding effective police work. Racialized communities need effective policing because racialized people are more likely than Whites to be victims of crime. They need the protection offered by effective police work, and the police want to do their job effectively. Mistrust of the police frustrates this goal because it makes people less likely to cooperate with the police by reporting crimes and aiding police investigations. The investigation and eradication of racial profiling serve the common interests of police and communities of colour.

Racism is also manifest in racially biased decisions by judges, lawyers, jurors, court officials, police officers, and prison officials, as well as in biased jury-selection processes, differential sentencing, and widespread lack of representation. Police forces play the role of sentinels for dominant culture. They are the oppressive instruments responsible for keeping the marginal populations in line. Policing is the entry point into the criminal justice system. Systemic racism plays out in these encounters between members of marginal populations and the police. Society tends to support the police force. Few are convicted of crimes against minorities. Police display racist attitudes in their interaction with racial minorities. A recent police association advertisement in the Toronto subway before a municipal election stereotyped Latin American community members as gangsters.

Racism is implicitly manifest at different points in the decision-making process in the criminal justice system. These include arrest, charging, bail, jury selection, trial, sentencing, and incarceration. The Law Reform Commission of Canada has acknowledged the problem of racism in the criminal justice system as exemplified by the actions of those in positions of power who hold the positions of power, lack of access to police protection in some neighbourhoods, police harassment, and differential treatment in sentencing. In a 1992 report, the Law Reform Commission says:

> Racism in the justice system is a consistently expressed and central concern to Canada's minorities, [further,] the racism of which these groups speak mirrors attitudes and behaviours found in Canadian society as a whole.[49]

As a powerful institution in Canadian society, the criminal justice system often stands accused of perpetuating racism and disempowering racialized group members through a process referred to as criminalization. Racial profiling of group members often leads to their contact with the system and its differential outcomes. The criminal justice system is yet another important institution in Canadian society that continues to reinforce the racialized tendencies in Canadian culture.[50]

Post-September 11 and the Emergence of the National Security Regime as a Racialized Regime

In the post-September 11 period, national security has been constructed in ways that have led to the racial profiling and targeting of certain racialized groups in the workplace and in the community. This is especially the case for Canadians of Muslim, Arab, West Asian, and South Asian origin. In the aftermath of September 11, they have been the subject of undue attention from police and immigration officials. Their right to privacy has been routinely violated in the name of national security. They have become the victims of increased deportations, detentions, and vigilante attacks. Their places of worship have been desecrated, and some firebombed. There has also been an increase in attacks on non-documented workers whose vulnerability has been intensified by the dominance of security concerns.

In response to the threat posed by terrorism, the Canadian government introduced Bill C-36, which aimed to enhance the security of the Canadian population. As was common during this period, the Canadian state was simply mirroring what the American state had done. The legislation sought powers that normalized the arbitrary, contradictory, and frankly dangerous actions of the security forces. This represented an overreaction to the threat posed by terrorism, but more importantly, it compromised the rights and liberties of minorities. It became synonymous with the curtailing of civil liberties and the removal of transparency in government. The Immigration Canada department issued directives that led to the racial profiling of people at ports of entry, with the effect that law-abiding citizens who just happen to have certain superficial features were targeted, thrown off airplanes, and detained for days. A composite of a potential terrorist was developed to simplify the work of immigration officials: Middle Eastern or Muslim male in his 20s and 30s, with a science background. Arab and Muslim Canadians and landed immigrants were targeted. Pakistani students were arrested and detained in a highly sensational case in Toronto called Project Ploughshare, with allegations that they represented a clear and immediate threat to Canada's security. Some even speculated that they belonged to a terrorist cell. When all was said and done, the RCMP could not bring itself to acknowledge that this was a case full of mistakes, and the shame of failure was resolved by deporting the students whose visas had expired. It was a time when immigrants were detained because their neighbours had levelled baseless accusations at them. Islamophobia became normalized.

Racialized people were thrown off aircraft because they looked at someone the wrong way, or because they were disabled and they could only express themselves through sign language. The different levels of government become captive to irrational fears about the security threat that non-status immigrants posed. In Ontario, the Harris government endorsed racial profiling, and ironically put the project in the charge of a military general who had served in the Balkans as part of Canada's effort to stop ethnic cleansing. A federal Minister declared that students from the Middle East would be deterred from taking science classes at university for a period of time. Police forces compiled lists of hundreds of activists whose only crime was raising questions about the way the government was responding to these events. If you had mused publicly about the failures of the security apparatus, in essence holding government agencies accountable, you would be branded a terrorist sympathizer and were subject to surveillance.

Bill C-36 Means Minorities are Defined as Dangerous Subjects

At issue in the limited debate on Bill C-36, which led to the passing of the *Anti-terrorism Act*, was the conception of a form of national security that marginalized some in order to protect others. We were told that we had to accept that our security could be guaranteed only by putting the security of others among us at risk. While some felt more secure because of the government's actions, many people of Arab descent, many Muslims, many new Canadians, immigrants and refugees, many Canadians of South Asian and African origin, felt isolated by the way boundaries were drawn by Bill C-36 and other anti-terrorist state policies. For many, as for Japanese Canadians during World War II, the sense of insecurity was heightened by the "defensive" actions of the government.

The Bill benefited from the continuous public bombardment of the gruesome images of the September 11 attacks on American cities on CNN and CBC Newsworld. The images had the effect of terrorizing an already frightened population, and creating an environment in which long-standing agendas to limit civil liberties could be furthered; in this environment, public debate was a "luxury" in the "war against terrorism." The room for dissent grew frighteningly narrow as the public was stampeded into supporting policies that limited their rights.

Many in the non-racialized communities took some comfort in not being in the immediate line of fire. They abandoned the victims of the abuses of civil and political rights because they were largely members of racialized groups, outsiders, mostly from the global South. Some saw it as an opportunity to slow the pace of immigration from Asian and Middle Eastern countries.

Social Exclusion, Social Inequality, and Violence

In the summer of 2001, Toronto's African Canadian community was engulfed in an undeclared crisis of internecine violence. The community learned that it could not count on the leadership of the city, the province, or the country to respond to the crisis. Over 18 Black youths lost their lives in violence over a period of four months, adding to 100 such deaths in a five-year period and 200 in a 10-year period. Reasonable people assumed that someone should take notice in much the same way that the different levels of government, the media, and civil society rose to the challenge of Walkerton, a south-western Ontario town whose water was contaminated by the E. coli virus, leading to the death of eight people earlier that year. The media had been saturated with stories about the plight of the community, families who had lost loved ones, and charges that government restructuring had caused the gaps in service and regulation responsible for the failure to detect the virus in the water system. The government responded by providing water, sending the premier and other high-ranking officials to meet with families of the dead, and appointing a commission of inquiry into the Walkerton affair. Emergency resources were provided for the families and community, and provincial health, environmental, and social agencies went to work to help the community recover.

This contrasted sharply with the official silence that greeted the deaths of 18 Black youths over a four-month period in Toronto's summer of discontent. While the victims of violence were mourned by their families, relatives, friends, and the community, the leadership of the city and the province remained curiously silent, prompting some in the Black community to suggest that Canadian society's mainstream institutions — the police, City Council, the Legislature, Parliament, the media, the business community, the labour movement, the faith communities, and even institutions seeking social justice — were complicit in the loss of Black life. Some described it as deliberate institutional neglect of the community — a sort of "if they want to kill themselves, let 'em" attitude. The mayor had recently referred to Africans as cannibals, and doubtless felt that dealing with the Black community was not worth the aggravation. The premier's most informed comments were to imply that he would rather they died than be dependent on the state.

The wave of gun violence spread through the Toronto low-income neighbourhoods of Regent Park, Rexdale, Lawrence Heights, Scarborough-Malvern, and Jane-Finch, claiming over 125 Black youths in six years — representing one-third of Toronto's homicides. Deeply troubling was the fact that 75% of these cases went unsolved by Toronto's police, whose standard claim was that although many of the victims and their families knew the perpetrators, there was a code of silence that allowed the perpetuators remain at large. The police department was not self-critical enough to recognize that its poor relations with the community, after years of police brutality, contributed to the lack of confidence in them.

Most of the youths lost to gun violence in Toronto in 2001 were African Canadian, many of them members of low-income communities left behind by the retreat of the welfare state from social protective responsibilities, and by the breakdown in the institutional supports in many of these communities. In Toronto, where 50% of the documented African Canadian population in Canada lives, African Canadian university graduates have the same rate of unemployment as White high-school dropouts. The crisis of violence, hopelessness, and despair in the African Canadian and poor communities represents the intensification of a historical process of marginalization leading to social exclusion, some of whose characteristics we have outlined above. Thanks to the new economy, the fastest-growing form of work is casual, part-time, contract, low-paying, low-skill, dead-end work with poor working conditions and no job security. This is where a disproportionate number of African Canadians are employed. According to a recent study by Gartner and Thompson (2004), between 1992–2003 the rate of homicides among Blacks was 10.1 per 100,000, almost five times the overall rate of 2.4 per 100,000.[51]

The community has attempted to fight back, but with mixed results. The violence has escalated and will likely persist for as long as the conditions that precipitated it are not addressed. A community coalition called the Building Hope Coalition was organized to respond to the crisis. The coalition's approach was to organize a series of community meetings in the most geographically affected areas of the city, providing Black youth with an opportunity to discuss the crisis with the communities. The coalition also produced and disseminated anti-violence posters and literature as part of an anti-violence campaign that involved the mass media. It advocated a multi-sector development of a comprehensive community action plan to guide a more systematic response by what was described as the four levels of government: federal, provincial, city, and community. It also called for services focusing on the immediate well-being of the bereaved, notably grievance counselling for the parents, relatives, and friends dealing with the trauma of the violent loss of their loved ones. To that end, the coalition organized a mass memorial service.

Perhaps the most significant part of the process was the community meetings, which served as public therapy sessions for many in the low-income communities. These meetings presented a picture of the depth of social exclusion low-income racialized groups suffer in the midst of Toronto's plenty.

The meetings heard from mothers who had lost their children and were struggling to cope without counselling or psychological services. They heard from young people who were struggling to deal with the loss of their friends and their own innocence; some of these dismissed adults and politicians because they felt no one cared. They heard from community workers struggling because of cuts to the programs they once used as a buffer against the hopelessness and despair that have now gripped the youth in many of the neighbourhoods.

They heard from single mothers struggling with cuts in income supports, as well as from Toronto City Parks and Recreation workers whose facilities are either inadequate or closed, or for which they now have to demand fees, effectively driving young people into the hands of dealers. From parents they heard about struggles to maintain their rental apartments or having to fight landlords seeking to evict them so that they can hike the rents. Staff at the Toronto Housing Authority said they could no longer maintain the housing because of cuts to their maintenance budgets.

Many questions were raised about the conditions in the communities. Why, if politicians and the public cared, would conditions in the neighbourhoods continue to deteriorate during a period of economic boom? Why are so many public housing buildings so short on maintenance staff? Why was staff so long in coming to fix the elevators, the leaking water pipes, holes in the apartments, the stench in the fire escapes, the squalor in the backyards? If rent control works, why do so many people in low-income neighbourhoods increasingly spend time appealing evictions by landlords? Why is it that in almost five years, not a single unit of affordable housing had been build by any level of government, and only 80 units a year by the private sector? Why were there are 60,000 families on waiting lists for public housing? Why were homeless shelters increasingly taking in families with children? Why did politicians and the media ignore the intersection between low-income communities, low-cost and substandard housing, the concentrations of Black communities, and the incidence of violence? Why was there a reluctance to acknowledge that the city is being segregated along racial lines? Why were there so many people juggling part-time, low-paying jobs and struggling with child care at the same time? Where are the anger-management programs for at-risk youth?

In the end there were consistent calls are for action in the form of job creation, skills training, recreational programming, community development workers, affordable housing, and an educational system that does not too quickly expel and simply induce drop-outs. These calls are yet to be heeded.

Box 7.9: Violence in the Black Community in Toronto

- Since 1996, 125 Black youth have been killed in Toronto at the hands of other Black youth. Average age of the victims is 26.
- 52% of all murders in Toronto involve handguns, up from 23% in 1998.
- 45% of Toronto's Black community live below the poverty line. In single-parent homes, that rate is as high as 60%.
- Unemployment in Toronto's Black community is at 20% (two to three times higher than the city average), and 32% for Black youth.
- In 2000, the Canadian Centre for Justice Statistics reported that the violent crime rate among youth in Ontario had increased by 11.8% over 1999. Incarceration rates among Black youth rose 203% from 1986 to 1993.
- Black youth are three times more likely to be stopped by police than other youth.
- They are twice as likely to be detained and also denied bail on drug-trafficking offences than White youth.
- 28% more violent crime is committed by Black youth relative to their numbers in the Toronto population.
- Black youth have been subjected to criminalization at earlier ages.

Civic and Political Participation

The majority of immigrants who settle in Canada obtain Canadian citizenship, usually within three to four years of immigrating to Canada. Of all immigrants eligible to become Canadian citizens, 83% had done so by 1996.[52] Yet this has not translated into active participation in the civic and political life of Canada. Many factors explain this reality, not least of which are barriers that exist in the political processes at the different levels of government. Racialized group members are underrepresented in the public service sector, accounting for only 5.4% of employees in the federal government (compared to 11.4% in the population), in spite of legislation aimed at increasing the numbers of group members in the service and their mobility within it.[53] These socio-economic, political, and cultural barriers translate into a form of exclusion that extends beyond the lack of representation in the decision-making bodies of the country. Socio-economic exclusion impairs societal (economic, political, and civic) participation and undermines the objective of full citizenship. This in turn lessens the ability of these communities to make claims on the decision-making institutions, meaning that issues of inequality go unaddressed and their condition simply deteriorates. While the average levels of participation are low for most racialized communities, they vary from community to community, and also break down along gender lines.

The process of integration is one in which immigrants become part of the social, cultural, and institutional fabric of society.[54] Societal participation here is used in a holistic way to refer to processes of engagement by individuals and groups in the economic, socio-cultural, and civil/political spheres, and the deployment of social capital in the formal and informal institutional spheres of the society.[55] These processes are partially overlapping, and include labour-market participation and related activity (e.g., educational), social interaction, acculturation, and electoral and civil activism.

Because of the structures of social exclusion, for many of the racialized communities, integration has not achieved the central goal of empowering them to participate fully in Canadian society. While the communities have articulated empowerment goals based on three institutional imperatives — access (openness to visible minorities), representation (proportionate to numbers in the population), and equity (equality of opportunity and removal of systemic barriers) — it remains to be seen if they have partners in dismantling the structures of social exclusion and creating processes of inclusion that would eventually lead to full participation.[56]

Social Exclusion and Instability

Numerous studies have investigated the claims made here that (1) increased income inequality leads to increased social and political instability, and that (2) the increase in social and political instability negatively affects economic progress. Most have been done in the world's developing areas, mostly between states. They suggest that income inequality is strongly and systematically related to the character of social relations and to the nature of the social environment in a society.[57] More recently, though, some studies have made comparisons between industrialized countries. Lester Thurow's work considers the relationship between inequality and instability in the ties between Western countries. He claims that "free markets [also] tend to produce levels of income inequality over the nation's history that are politically incompatible with democratic governments."[58] Putman has also argued recently that "[e]quality is an essential feature of the civic community."[59]

Even more relevant are recent articles by William Dugger, Christopher Niggle, and Caroline Rodriguez, which examine the issue within the United States.[60] Caroline Rodriguez's work has empirically tested the relationship between income inequality and social and political instability, as well as the relationship between this instability and economic progress in different regions of the United States. The results show that there is a strong relationship between income inequality and the amount of property and violent crimes, which she uses as proxies for social and political instability. Her work also shows that there is an inverse relationship between instability and economic growth, meaning that inequality limits the levels of economic growth a country can attain. Niggle's survey of empirical literature finds that economic, social, and political institutions influence the relationship between income inequality and economic progress. More importantly, Dugger's research shows that economic inequality in the United States is (a) a product of social processes involving racism, sexism, and nationalism, and (b) has a cumulative effect on the level of social stability and cannot be addressed simplistically by either federal or state governments.

Conclusion

Social exclusion describes the structures and processes of inequality and unequal outcomes among groups in society. In industrialized societies such as Canada, social exclusion arises from uneven access to the processes of production, wealth creation, and power. It represents a form of alienation and denial of full citizenship experienced by racialized groups or individuals. Its characteristics occur in multiple dimensions, with racialization being a major one in early 21st-century Canada. Manifestations of social exclusion include high levels of poverty, uneven access to employment and employment income, segregated neighbourhood selection leading to racialized enclaves, disproportionate contact with the criminal justice system, and low health status. Social exclusion is different from social inclusion because the former seeks to identify and transform the root causes of exclusion, while the latter in practice seeks to reconcile the excluded to the existing societal institutions without changing them.

Of particular concern is the racialization of poverty as an expression of social exclusion. The racialization of poverty refers to the emergence of disproportionate incidence of poverty among racialized group members on a structural level. It tends to compound the dimensions of exclusion; it creates further alienation and detachment from the body politic, ultimately leading to actions that engender social instability. Some of those we have detailed above, while others will inevitably intensify if these processes of economic exclusion, exclusion from civil society, exclusion from social goods, and exclusion from social production are not addressed. The exclusions manifested in declining health status, differential access to education, neighbourhood selection, social services, differential experiences with the criminal justice system and the national security regime all contribute to a situation in which racialized groups increasingly live in the same cities with non-racialized Canadians, but lead separate existences. The experience of economic apartheid may move beyond the economy to the neighbourhoods and the institutions that define Canada as a liberal democratic state.

Notes

1. D. Byrne, *Social Exclusion* (London: Open University Press, 1999).
2. A. Saloojee, *Social Inclusion, Anti-racism and Democratic Citizenship* (Toronto: Laidlaw Foundation, 2003); J. Veit-Wilson, *Setting Adequacy Standards* (Bristol: The Policy Press, 1998).
3. A. Saloojee, *Social Inclusion, Citizenship and Diversity: Moving beyond the Limits of Multiculturalism* (Toronto: The Laidlaw Foundation, 2002).
4. Recently the Laidlaw Foundation commissioned a series of papers on social inclusion (www.laidlawfdn.org): P. Barata, *Social Exclusion: A Review of the Literature* (Toronto: Laidlaw Foundation, 2000); Saloojee (2003); R. Omidvar and T. Richmond, *Immigrant Settlement and Social Inclusion in Canada* (Toronto: Laidlaw Foundation, 2003); Z. Hajnal, "The Nature of Concentrated Urban Poverty in Canada and the United States," *Canadian Journal of Sociology* 20 (1995): 497–528; B. Baklid, *The Voices of Visible Minorities – Speaking Out on Breaking Down Barriers* (Ottawa: Conference Board of Canada, 2004); J. Guildford, *Making the Case for Economic and Social Inclusion* (Ottawa: Health Canada, 2000).

5. For a further discussion of social exclusion and racialized groups, see G. Galabuzi, "Social Exclusion," in *Social Determinants of Health: Canadian Perspectives*, 233–251, edited by D. Raphael (Toronto: Canadian Scholars' Press, 2004).

6. R. Labonte, "Social Inclusion/Exclusion and Health: Dancing the Dialectic," in *Social Determinants of Health:Canadian Perspectives*, edited by D. Raphael (Toronto: Canadian Scholars Press, 2004), 253–266.

7. While in 1981, Toronto's rate of poverty equalled that of Canada at 13% and 13.3% respectively, by 2001 Toronto's was at 19.4% compared to 12.8% for Canada. A key contributing factor was poverty increases among highly racialized low-income neighbourhoods where poverty rose from 17.8% in 1981 to 43.1% in 2001. These findings are also supported by a study Khosla (2003) on low-income women in Toronto, which found that racialized single families led by women experienced over 60% rates of low income. United Way of Greater Toronto, *Poverty by Postal Code: The Geography of Neighbourhood Poverty 1981–2001* (Toronto: UWGT/CCSD, 2004); P. Khosla, *If Low Income Women of Colour Counted in Toronto: Breaking Isolation, Getting Involved* (Toronto: Community Social Planning Council, 2003).

8. Statistics Canada, "1996 Census: Ethnic Origin, Visible Minorities," *The Daily* (February 17, 1998).

9. A study by M. Ornstein, *Ethno-racial Inequality in Toronto: Analysis of the 1996 Census* (Toronto: City of Toronto, 2000) documents poverty levels for racialized groups that are three times those for non racialized groups. It also points to deep pockets of poverty among segments of the racialized communities as high as 70%, with single women with children especially affected.

10. K. Lee, *Urban Poverty in Canada: A Statistical Profile* (Ottawa: Canadian Council on Social Development, 2000).

11. M. Frenette and R. Morissette, *Will They Ever Converge? Earnings of Immigrants and Canadian-Born Workers over the Last Two Decades*, Analytical Studies paper No. 215 (Ottawa: Statistics Canada, 2003); F. Hou and G. Picot, *The Rise in Low-Income Rates among Immigrants in Canada*, catalogue no. 11F0019M1E–No. 198 (Ottawa: Statistics Canada, 2003); G. Schellenberg, *Immigrants in Canada's Census Metropolitan Areas*, Catalogue no. 89-613-MIE-No. 003 (Ottawa: Statistics Canada: 2004); E. Smith and A. Jackson, *Does a Rising Tide Lift All Boats? The Labour Market Experiences and Incomes of Recent Immigrants, 1995 to 1998* (Ottawa: CCSD, 2002).

12. Peel Regional Taskforce on Homelessness, 2000 (Region of Peel): http://www.region.peel.on.ca/housing/homeless/

13. Z. Hajnal, "The Nature of Concentrated Urban Poverty in Canada and the United States," *Canadian Journal of Sociology* 20 (1995): 497–528; A. Kazemipur and S. Halli, "The Plight of Immigrants: The Spatial Concentration of Poverty in Canada," *Canadian Journal of Regional Science* 20, no. 1, 2 (1997): 11–28; H. Krahn, "Social Stratification," in *New Society: Sociology for the 21st Century*, edited by R. Brym (Toronto: Harcourt Brace, 1995), 1–29; D. Ley and H. Smith, "Immigration and Poverty in Canadian Cities, 1971–1991," *Canadian Journal of Regional Science* 20, no. 1, 2 (1997): 29–48; I. MacLachlan and R. Sawada, "Measures of Income Inequality and Social Polarization in Canadian Metropolitan Centres," *Canadian Geographer* 41 (1997): 377–397; D. Massey and N. Denton, *American Apartheid: Segregation and the Making of the Underclass* (Cambridge: Harvard University Press, 1993); W.J. Wilson, *When Work Disappears: The World of the New Urban Poor* (New York: Vintage Books, 1996);

R. Murdie, "The Welfare State, Economic Restructuring and Immigrant Flows: Impacts of Spatial Segregation in Greater Toronto," in *Urban Segregation and the Welfare State: Inequality and Exclusion in Western Cities*, edited by S. Muster and W. Ostendorf (New York: Routledge, 1998), 64–93.

14. P. Li, "Unneighbourly Houses or Unwelcome Chinese: The Social Construction of Race in the Battle over 'Monster' Homes in Vancouver," *International Journal of Race and Ethnic Studies* 1–2 (1994): 47–66.

15. W. Wilson, *The Truly Disadvantaged: The Inner City, the Underclass and Public Policy* (Chicago: University of Chicago, 1987); R. Sampson and W. Wilson, "Towards a Theory of Race, Crime and Urban Inequality," in *Crime and Inequality*, edited by J. Hagen (Stanford: Stanford University Press, 1995), 37–54.

16. Hulchanski, 1993; Mwarigha, 2002.

17. T. Balakrishnan and K. Selvanathan, "Ethnic Residential Segregation in Metropolitan Canada," in *Ethnic Demography*, edited by S. Hilli, F. Trovato, and L. Driedger (Ottawa: Carleton University Press, 1990), 399–413; E. Fong and M. Gulia, "Differences in Neighbourhood Qualities among Racial and Ethnic Groups in Canada," *Sociology Inquiry* 69, no. 4 (Fall 1999): 575–598; E. Fong and M. Gulia, "The Attainment of Neighbourhood Qualities among British, Chinese, and Black Immigrants in Toronto and Vancouver," *Research in Community Sociology* 6 (1996): 123–145; E. Fong, "A Systemic Approach to Racial Residential Segregation," *Social Science Research* 26 (1997): 465–486.

18. E. Fong and K. Shibuya, "The Spatial Separation of the Poor in Canadian Cities," *Demography* 37, no. 4 (November 2000): 449–459.

19. Ibid., 450.

20. A. Kazemipur and S. Halli, "The Invisible Barrier: Neighbourhood Poverty and Integration of Immigrants in Canada," *Journal of International Migration and Integration* 1, no. 1 (2000): 85–100; see also A. Kazemipur and S. Halli, *The New Poverty in Canada: Ethnic Groups and Ghetto Neighbourhoods* (Toronto: Thompson Educational Publishing, 2000).

21. Islamic Social Services and Resource Association (ISSRA), *Living on the Ragged Edges: Absolute and Hidden Homelessness among Latin Americans and Muslims in West Central Toronto* (Toronto: CERIS, 2003).

22. Toronto Mayor's Homelessness Action Task Force Report, *Taking Responsibility for Homelessness: An Action Plan for Toronto* (Toronto: City of Toronto, 1999).

23. G. Dei, *Anti-Racism Education: Theory and Practice* (Halifax: Fernwood, 1996); R. Ng, P. Staton, and J. Scane (eds.), *Anti-Racism, Feminism and Critical Approaches to Education* (Toronto: OISE Press, 1995); C. James, *Seeing Ourselves: Exploring Race, Ethnicity and Culture* (Toronto: Thompson Educational Publishing, 1999); B. Troyna, *Racial Inequality in Education* (London: Routledge, 1987); S. Lewis, *Report on Racism: Letter to the Ontario Premier* (Toronto: Queen's Printer, 1992).

24. R. Hatcher and B. Troyna, "Racialization and Children," in *Race, Identity and Representation in Education*, edited by C. McCarthy and W. Crichlow (New York: Routledge, 1993), 109–125; F. Rizvi, "Children and the Grammar of Popular Racism," in *Race, Identity and Representation in Education*, edited by C. McCarthy and W. Crichlow (New York: Routledge, 1993), 126–139; A. Ijaz and H. Ijaz, "The Development of Ethnic Prejudice in Canada," *Guidance and Counselling* 2, no. 1 (September 1986): 28–39; S. Lewis, *Report on Racism: Letter to the Ontario Premier* (Toronto: Queen's Printer, 1992); C. James, "Distorted Images of African Canadians: Impacts, Implications and Responses," in *Globalization and Survival in the Black Diaspora*, edited by C. Green (Albany: State University of New York Press, 1997),

307–330; P. Grayson, T. Chi, and D. Rhyne, *The Social Construction of 'Visible Minority' for Students of Chinese Origin* (Toronto: Institute for Social Research, York University, 1994); G. Dei, "Race and the Production of Identity in the Schooling Experiences of African Canadian Youth," *Discourse* 18, no. 2 (1997): 241–257.

25. P. Essed, *Everyday Racism: Reports from Women of Two Cultures* (Claremont: Hunter House, 1990); K. Brathwaite and C. James, *Educating African Canadians* (Toronto: James Lorimer and Company Publishers, 1996); Toronto Board of Education Consultative Committee on the Education of Black Students in Toronto Schools, *Report* (Toronto: Board of Education for the City of Toronto, 1987); C. Sleeter, "How Teachers Construct Race," in *Race, Identity and Representation in Education*, edited by C. McCarthy and W. Crichlow (New York: Routledge, 1993), 157–171; P. Kakembo and R. Upshaw, "The Emergence of the Black Learners Advisory Committee in Nova Scotia," in *Re/Visioning: Canadian Perspectives on the Education of Africans in the late 20th Century*, edited by V. D'Oyley and C. James (Toronto: Captus Press, 1998), 140–158; Black Learners Advisory Committee, *Report on Education: Redressing Inequality – Empowering Black Learners* (Halifax: Black Learners Advisory Committee, 1994); S. Razack, *Looking White People in the Eye: Gender, Race and Culture in Courtrooms and Classrooms* (Toronto: University of Toronto Press, 1998); A. Rattansi, "Changing the Subject? Racism, Culture and Education" in *Race, Culture and Difference*, edited by J. Donald and A. Rattansi (London: Sage Publications, 1992), 11–48; P. Essed, *Everyday Racism: Reports from Women of Two Cultures* (Claremont: Hunter House, 1990).

26. F. Henry et al., *The Colour of Democracy* (Toronto: Harcourt Brace, 2000); A. Calliste, "Blacks' Struggle for Education Equity in Nova Scotia," in *Innovations in Black Education in Canada*, edited by V. D'Oyley (Toronto: Umbrella Press, 1994), 25–41; G. Dei, *Drop Out or Push Out? The Dynamics of Black Students Disengagement from School*, Report to the Ontario Ministry of Education (Toronto: Queen's Printer, 1995); Ontario Royal Commission on Learning, *For the Love of Learning: Report of the Royal Commission on Learning* (Toronto: Queen's Printer, 1994).

27. C. James, *Seeing Ourselves: Exploring Race, Ethnicity and Culture* (Toronto: Thompson Educational Publishing, 1999); Dei (1995); R.P. Solomon, *Black Resistance in High School: Forging a Separation Culture* (Albany: State University of New York Press, 1992); Razack (1998); Black Learners Advisory Committee, *BLAC Report on Education: Redressing Inequality – Empowering Black Learners* (Halifax: Black Learners Advisory Committee, 1994); Ontario Parents of Black Children (OPBC), *Tenth Anniversary Celebration Booklet: Ten Years of Involvement, Struggle, Achievement* (Toronto: OPBC, 1990). Report of the Task Force on Safe and Compassionate Schools in the Toronto District School Board (Toronto: TDSB, 2004).

28. Queen's University, "Towards Diversity and Equity at Queens's: A Strategy for Change," Final Report of the Principal's Advisory Committee on Race Relations." *Queen's Gazette Supplement* (April 8, 1991); York University, *Report of the President's Committee on Race and Ethnic Relations* (Toronto: York University, 1989); F. Henry and C. Tator, "Racism and the University," *Canadian Ethnic Studies* 26, no. 3 (1994), 74–90.

29. R. Ng, "Sexism and Racism in the University: Analysing a Personal Experience in the University," *Racism and Gender* 14, no. 22 (Spring 1994): 41–46; L. Carty, "Black Women in Academia: A Statement from the Periphery," in *Unsettling Relations: The University As a Site of Struggle*, edited by H. Bannerji, L. Carty, S. Heald, and K. Himmanji (Toronto: Women's Press, 1991); H. Bannerji, "But Who Speaks for Us? Experience and Agency," in *Unsettling Relations: The University as a Site of Struggle*, edited by H. Bannerji, L. Carty, S.

Heald, and K. Himmanji (Toronto: Women's Press, 1991), 67–107; M. Bramble, "Being in the Academy" in *Experiencing Difference*, edited by C. James (Halifax: Fernwood Publishing, 2000).

30. University of Toronto, *Employment Equity Annual Report, 1992–93* (Toronto: University of Toronto, 1993); S. Razack, *Looking White People in the Eye: Gender, Race and Culture in Courtrooms and Classrooms* (Toronto: University of Toronto Press, 1998).

31. M. Ogundipe-Leslie, "Forum," *University of Toronto Bulletin* 16 (September 9, 1991), as quoted in Henry et al. (2000b).

32. J. Anderson and S.R. Kirkham, "Constructing a Nation: The Gendering and Racializing of the Canadian Health Care System," in *Painting the Maple: Essays on Race, Gender, and the Construction of Canada*, edited by V. Strong-Boag, A. Eisenberg, and J. Anderson (Vancouver: UBC Press, 1998): 243–261.

33. R.G. Wilkinson, *Unhealthy Societies: The Affliction of Inequality* (London: Routledge, 1996); W.M. Dugger, "Against Inequality," *Journal of Economic Issues* 32 (1998): 287–304; C.J. Niggle, "Equality, Democracy, Institutions, and Growth," *Journal of Economic Issues* 32 (1998): 523–530.

34. D. Coburn, "Income Inequality, Social Cohesion and the Health Status of Populations: The Role of Neo-liberalism," *Social Science and Medicine* 51 (2000): 135–146.

35. J. Dunn and I. Dyck, *Social Determinants of Health in Canada's Immigrant Population: Results from the National Population Health Survey, #98-20* (Vancouver: The Metropolis Project, 1998).

36. See D. Raphael (ed.), *Social Determinants of Health: Canadian Perspectives* (Toronto: Canadian Scholars' Press Inc., 2004); V. Agnew, *Gender, Migration and Citizenship Resources Project: Part II: A literature Review and Bibliography on Health* (Toronto: Centre for Feminist Research, York University, 2002); I. Hyman, *Immigration and Health*, Health Canada Working Paper No. 01-05 (Ottawa: Queen's Printer, 2001); Across Boundaries, *Healing Journey: Mental Health of People of Colour Project* (Toronto: Across Boundaries, 1999); D. Adams, *Health Issues of Women of Colour: A Cultural Diversity Perspective* (Thousand Oaks, London: Sage Books, 1995); J.M. Anderson, "Gender, Race, Poverty, Health and Discourses of Health Reform in the Context of Globalization: A Post-Colonial Feminist Perspective in Policy Research," *Nursing Inquiry* 7, no. 4 (2000): 220–229; J.R. Dunn, "Inequalities in Health and the Housing Question," in *Proceedings, 7th International Symposium in Medical Geography*, edited by G. Moon et al. (Portsmouth, U.K., July 29–Aug. 2, 1996); J.R. Dunn, "Social Inequality, Population Health, and Housing: Towards a Social Geography of Health," Ph.D. dissertation (Vancouver: Simon Fraser University, 1998); T. Bhatti and N. Hamilton, *Population Health Promotion* (Ottawa: Health Canada, 1996); R.G. Evans, M.L. Barer, and T.R. Marmor (eds.), *Why Are Some People Healthy and Others Not? The Determinants of Health of Populations* (New York: Aldine DeGruyter, 1994); M.V. Hayes and J.R. Dunn, *Population Health in Canada: A Systematic Review* (Ottawa: Canadian Policy Research Networks, 1998); C. Hertzman and M. Weins, "Child Development and Long-Term Outcomes: A Population Health Perspective and Summary of Successful Interventions," *Social Science and Medicine* 43, no. 7 (1996): 1083–1095; National Forum on Health, *Canada Health Action: Building on the Legacy*, Final Report of the National Forum on Health (Ottawa: Minster of Public Works and Government Services, 1997); M. Laroche, "Health Status and Health Services Utilization of Canada's Immigrant and Non-Immigrant Populations," *Canadian Public Policy* 26, no. 1 (2000): 51–73.

37. A. Chakraborty and K. McKenzie, "Does Racial Discrimination Cause Mental Illness?" *British Journal of Psychiatry* 180 (2002): 475–477; V.S. Thompson, "Racism: Perceptions of Distress among African Americans," *Community Mental Health Journal* 38, no. 2 (2002): 111–117; L. Zayas, "Incorporating Struggles with Racism and Ethnic Identity in Therapy with Adolescents," *Clinical Social Work Journal* 29, no. 4 (2001): 361–372; M. Beiser, K. Gill, and G. Edwards, "Mental Health Care in Canada: Is It Accessible and Equal?" *Canada's Mental Health*, Summer (1993): 2–7.

38. Alliance for South Asian AIDS Prevention, *Discrimination and HIV/AIDS in South Asian Communities* (Toronto: Health Canada/ASAP, June 1999).

39. E. Tharoa and N. Massaquoi, "Black Women and HIV/AIDS: Contextualizing Their Realities, Their Silence and Proposing Solutions," *Canadian Women Studies* 22, no. 2 (2001): 72–80.

40. Across Boundaries, *Healing Journey: Mental Health of People of Colour Project Report* (Toronto: Across Boundaries, 1999).

41. Hyman (2001).

42. Media Watch report, "Front and Centre: Minority representation in the media," Toronto: Media Watch, 1994.

43. F. Henry and C. Tator, *Racist Discourse in Canada's English Print Media* (Toronto: Canadian Race Relations Foundation, 2000); A. Fleras and J.L. Kunz, *Media and Minorities: Representing Diversity in a Multicultural Canada* (Toronto: Thompson Education Publishing, 2001).

44. M. Goldfarb, *Tapping into a Growing Readership: Visible Minorities Research Project*, Research Report for Canadian Daily Newspaper Association (1995); H. Siddiqui, "Media and Race: Failing to Mix the Message," *The Toronto Star* (April 24, 1993): D1, D5; E. Ginsberg, *Power without Responsibility: The Press We Don't Deserve* (Toronto: Urban Alliance on Race Relations, 1985).

45. Canadian Islamic Congress, *Anti-Islam in the Media: A Six-Month Study of the Six Top Canadian Newspapers*, http://www.cicnow.com/docs/media-report/1999/anti-islam.html; J. Miller, *Yesterday's News: Why Canada's Daily Newspapers Are Failing Us* (Halifax: Fernwood Publishing, 1998).

46. National Council of Welfare, *Justice and the Poor* (Ottawa: National Council of Welfare, 2000); K. Lee, *Urban Poverty in Canada: A Statistical Profile* (Ottawa: Canadian Council on Social Development, 2000); Public Inquiry into the Administration of Justice and Aboriginal People, *Report of the Aboriginal Justice Inquiry of Manitoba* (Winnipeg: Province of Manitoba, 1991); M. Gittens and D. Cole, *Report of the Ontario Commission on Systemic Racism in the Criminal Justice System* (Toronto: Queen's Printer, 1995); M. Gittens and D. Cole, *Racism behind Bars: The Treatment of Black and Racial Minority Prisoners in Ontario Prisons* (Toronto: Queen's Printer, 1994; *Report of the Royal Commission on the Donald Marshall Jr. Prosecution* (Halifax: Province of Nova Scotia, 1989); *Report of the Taskforce on the Criminal Justice System and Its impact on the Indian and Metis People of Alberta* (Edmonton: Province of Alberta, 1991); J. Tarnopolsky, J. Whitman, and M. Ouellette (eds.), *Discrimination in the Law and the Administration of Justice/La discrimination dans le droit et l'administration de la justice Canadian Institute for the Administration of Justice/Institut Canadien d'administration de la justice* (Montreal: Editions Themis, 1993).

47. E. Thornhill, "Presentation to the Donald Marshall Inquiry," in *Proceedings of Consultative Conference on Discrimination against Natives and Blacks in the Criminal Justice System and the Role of the Attorney General* (Halifax: Province of Nova Scotia, 1988): 68.

48. S. Wortley and J. Tanner, "Data, Denials and Confusion: The Racial Profiling Debate in Toronto," *Canadian Journal of Criminology and Criminal Justice* (July 2003): 367–389; F. Henry and C. Tator, *Racial Profiling in Toronto: Discourses of Domination, Mediation, and Apposition* (Toronto: Ontario Race Relations Foundation); Ontario Human Rights Commission, *Paying the Price: The Human Cost of Racial Profiling: Inquiry Report* (Toronto: OHRC, 2003).

49. Law Reform Commission of Canada, *Consultative Document* (Ottawa: The Commission, 1992): 10.

50. C. Aylward, *Canadian Critical Race Theory: Racism and the Law* (Halifax: Fernwood Publishing, 1999).

51. R. Gartner and S. Thompson, *Community Safety: From Enforcement and Prevention to Civic Engagement* (Toronto: University of Toronto Centre for Criminology, 2004).

52. Statistics Canada, *The Daily* (November 4, 1997).

53. A recent study by a federal taskforce found the federal government's performance woeful. See note 51, Chapter 2.

54. R. Breton, *Report of the Academic Advisory Panel on the Social and Cultural Impacts of Immigration Canada: Research Division, Strategic Planning and Research* (Ottawa: Immigration Policy Group, Employment and Immigration, 1992).

55. Social capital refers to the capacity for deploying, and utilizing to advantage, acquired human capital, e.g., the skill of "orienteering" in the social structure, and using networks of contacts that serve as channels to participation.

56. J.L. Elliot and A. Fleras, "Immigration and the Canadian Ethnic Mosaic," in *Race and Ethnic Relations in Canada*, edited by P.S. Li (Toronto: Oxford University Press, 1990); M. Siemiatycki and A. Saloojee, *Ethno-cultural Political Representation in Toronto: Patterns and Problems* (Unpublished, 2003); T. Richmond and R. Omdivar, *Immigrant Settlement and Social Inclusion in Canada* (Toronto: Laidlaw Foundation, 2003).

57. R. Wilkinson, "Income Inequality, Social Cohesion and Health: Clarifying the Theory. A Reply to Muntaner and Lynch," *International Journal of Health Services* 29, no. 3 (1999): 525–543; R.G. Wilkinson, *Unhealthy Societies: The Afflictions of Inequality* (London: Routledge, 1996).

58. L. Thurow, *Head to Head: The Coming Economic Battle among Japan, Europe, and America* (New York: William Morrow and Company, 1992).

59. R.D. Putnam, R. Leonardi, and R.Y. Nanetti, *Making Democracy Work: Civic Traditions in Modern Italy* (Princeton: Princeton University Press, 1993), 105.

60. W.M. Dugger, "Against Inequality," *Journal of Economic Issues* 32 (1998): 287–304; C.J. Niggle, "Equality, Democracy, Institutions, and Growth," *Journal of Economic Issues* 32 (1998): 523–530; C.B. Rodriguez, "An Empirical Test of the Institutionalist View on Income Inequality: Economic Growth within the United States," *The American Journal of Economics and Sociology* 59 (April 2000): 303.

Questions for Critical Thought

1. Describe the concept of social exclusion. How does it differ from social inclusion?

2. What are some of the key aspects of social exclusion and why are they relevant in the early 21st century?

3. How does social exclusion help explain the inequalities that racialized groups face in Canada?
4. What is the relationship between social exclusion and citizenship?
5. What is the racialization of poverty and how does it impact the life chances of racialized group members?
6. What are the implications of social inequality on social cohesion and social stability?
7. How does exclusion based on racialization impact the health status of some groups?

Recommended Readings

Beiser, M. *After the Door Has Been Opened: Mental Health Issues Affecting immigrants and Refugees in Canada.* Report of the Canadian Taskforce on Mental Health Issues Affecting Immigrants and Refugees. Ottawa: Health and Welfare Canada, 1998.

Bolaria, B., and R. Bolaria. "Immigrant Status and Health Status: Women and Racial Minority Immigrant Workers." In *Racial Minorities, Medicine and Health,* edited by B.S. Bolaria and R. Bolaria. Halifax: Fernwood Press, 1994. 149–168.

Byrne, D. *Social Exclusion.* Buckingham: Open University Press, 1999.

Galabuzi, G. "Social Exclusion." In *Social Determinants of Health: Canadian Perspectives,* edited by D. Raphael, 233–251. Toronto: Canadian Scholars' Press, 2004.

Guidford, J. *Making the Case for Economic and Social Inclusion.* Ottawa: Health Canada, 2000.

Hyman, I. *Immigration and Health. Health Canada.* Working Paper No. 01-05. Ottawa: Queen's Printer, September 2001.

Jackson, A. *Is Work Working for Workers of Colour?* Ottawa: Canadian Labour Congress, 2002.

James, C. *Seeing Ourselves: Exploring Race, Ethnicity and Culture.* Toronto: Thompson Educational Publishing, 1999.

Kazemipur, A., and S. Halli. *The New Poverty in Canada.* Toronto: Thompson Educational Publishing, 2000.

Laidlaw Foundation. Working papers on social inclusion (workingpapers@laidlawfdn. org).

Lewis, S. *Report on Racism: Letter to the Ontario Premier.* Toronto: Queen's Printer, 1992.

National Anti-racism Council of Canada. *Racial Discrimination in Canada: The Status of Compliance by the Canadian Government with the International Convention on the Elimination of All Forms of Racial Discrimination.* Toronto: NARC, 2002.

Picot, G., and F. Hou. *The Rise in Low-Income Rates among Immigrants in Canada.* Ottawa: Statistics Canada, 2003.

Razack, S. *Looking White People in the Eye: Gender, Race and Culture in Courtrooms and Classrooms.* Toronto: University of Toronto Press, 1998.

Schellenberg, G. *Immigrants in Canada's Census Metropolitan Areas.* Catalogue no. 89-613-MIE-No. 003. Ottawa: Statistics Canada, 2004.

CHAPTER 8

The Role of the State

The state has responded to issues of racial discrimination and inequality in a variety of ways (see Box 8.1). Much of the response has focused on mechanisms to deal with individual incidents of racial discrimination. However, responses that aim at systemic forms of discrimination and that target disadvantages experienced by groups have become increasingly prevalent.

Box 8.1: Chronology of Federal Action Relating to Racial Inequality

1960 Passage of the *Canadian Bill of Rights*

1963 Establishment of the Royal Commission on Bilingualism and Biculturalism

1969 Book IV of the Bilingualism and Biculturalism Commission Report emphasizes the bilingual and multicultural nature of Canada

1971 Introduction of Canada's Multiculturalism Policy

1977 Passage of the *Canadian Human Rights Act*

1982 Adoption of the *Canadian Charter of Rights and Freedoms*

1984 Special Parliamentary Committee Report, *Equality Now*, calls for a *Multiculturalism Act* and establishment of a national research institute on multiculturalism and race-relations issues

1985 Royal Commission Report on Employment equity, the *Abella Report*, calls for employment equity legislation

1986 Passage by Parliament of the *Employment Equity Act*

1988 Passage of the *Canadian Multiculturalism Act*

1996 Government establishes the Canadian Race Relations Foundation

1996 New *Employment Equity Act* passed

1998 Government tables Bill 69, *An Act to Amend the Canadian Citizenship Act*

1999 Government announces renewed Multiculturalism Program

At the federal level, key initiatives include the *Bill of Rights*, *Charter of Rights and Freedoms*, Multiculturalism Policy, *Canadian Human Rights Act*, *Federal Employment Equity Act*, Federal Service Employment Equity Program.

The *Multiculturalism Act* represents the federal government's definitive statement on the changing nature of the country. However, the Act and the policy it mandates have not addressed issues of racial discrimination, instead implying a form of neutral diversity and harmony among equals.

The *Federal Employment Equity Act*, introduced in 1986, has had mixed results. Successive Annual Employment Equity reports show that the progress made after 15 years has not matched the growth in the numbers of racialized group members in the Canadian population. Most experts have suggested that the weak enforcement regime is to blame.[1]

In fact, the report of the Taskforce on the Participation of Visible Minorities in the Federal Public Service shows clearly that the federal employment equity program has performed even more poorly than a number of the employers the federal government regulates. The report, which looked at current levels of representation, current rates of hires and promotions, and current separation rates, found that representation of racialized group members has increased only marginally, from 4.1% in 1990–1991 to 5.9% in 1998–1999, even though representation in the population had increased to nearly 12% by 1996. Some of the largest departments—Department of National Defence (3rd largest), Correctional Services (4th), and Fisheries and Oceans (6th)—have the lowest representation at 2.8%, 2.8%, and 2.6% respectively. The report found low representation of racialized group members in the executive category at 3%, and low rates of progress over the eight-year period. The representation in the key feeder groups was 3.7%. The report also found low rates of external recruitment of racialized group members and identified this as the most significant barrier to improved representation. The report concluded that at the current rate of hires, the federal service would not achieve equity until after 2023; to meet its goal of parity by 2005, one in every five recruits would have to be from the racialized group population.[2]

At the provincial level, the focus has been on Human Rights Commissions. Some provinces have introduced employment equity programs and anti-racism programs. Ontario introduced a comprehensive employment equity legislation in 1994, which was subsequently repealed by the Conservative government in 1995.

Box 8.2: *State Responses to Racism in Canada* by Frances Henry, Carol Tator, Winston Mattis, and Tim Rees

In many ways, the role of the State in responding to issues of racism and inequality has had to fit within the context of an imagined national culture consisting of a unique blend of English and French cultures, and an identity built on English and French values. As a result, three categories of citizens were recognized: English Canadians, French Canadians, and "others" (Fleras and Elliott, 1992). Only the first two groups had constitutional rights. The construction of undesirable "otherness" has persisted as Canadians have continued to struggle for a national identity (Mackey, 1996). This notion of "otherness" can be seen from three interlocking perspectives:

- "Otherness" provides the dominant White culture with unmarked, invisible privilege and power;
- Issues are deflected in a way which suggests that these "others" threaten the democratic fabric of Canadian society;
- There is a reassertion of individual rights and identity over collective identity and group rights.

Those in privileged positions, intent on maintaining their power, lay claim to the liberal values of individualism, equal opportunities, tolerance, and so on. In so doing, they construct a view of ethno-racial minorities who do not share these values and therefore are outside the boundaries of the common culture of the state. Anglo-European cultural dominance asserts its entitlement and authority, defining all others as "ethnics," "minorities," "immigrants," and "visible minorities," who are then marginalized and rendered subordinate to its unmarked centre. The power elite determines which differences and which similarities are allowed in the public domain (Suvendrini and Pugliese, 1997; Mackey, 1996). That authority "to define crucial homogeneities and differences" is defended within the liberal discourse of equality and progress (Asad, 1979:627).

For many Canadians, the increasing pluralism of Canadian society poses a threat to the way they have imagined and constructed Canadian identity. They hold on to an image of Canada distinguished from other countries, particularly the United States, by its French-English duality.

Many Anglo-Canadians and others fear that multiculturalism will never provide a solution to the issue of national identity. Canadians want to resolve French-English tensions without having to address the multicultural issue of identity. One scholar argued that Canada is a nation in which "state-sanctioned proliferation of cultural difference itself is seen to be its defining characteristic" (Mackey, 1996:11).

Multiculturalism as state policy embraces, in theory, the notion of cultural and racial diversity. Ethno-racial minorities are declared to be part of the "imagined" community of Canada (Anderson, 1983). However, in reality, the policy and practice of multiculturalism continue to position certain ethno-racial groups at the margins rather than in the mainstream of public culture and national identity.

The "symbolic multiculturalism" of state policy does not consider the need to restructure or reconceptualize the power relations between cultural and racial communities based on the premise that communities and societies do not exist autonomously but are deeply woven together in a web of interrelationships.

Liberal pluralist discourse is unable to move beyond "tolerance," "sensitivity," or "understanding" of the "others." The state's construction of symbolic multiculturalism as a mechanism for maintaining the status quo can be seen in many forms of public discourse around issues of race, culture, difference, politics, and identity. This discourse is not restricted to the public declarations of policy-makers, legislators, and bureaucrats. It is also reflected in the language and practices employed by the state through its institutions and systems, including justice and law enforcement, print and electronic media, cultural and educational institutions, and public-sector corporations (Tator et al., 1998).

Minorities are seldom invited into the mainstream discourse of Canadian public-core-common culture. The select few are considered to be models and are imagined as being different from others of their kind. In contrast, the airing of diverse perspectives by people of colour on issues related to multiculturalism and racism is commonly dismissed, deflected, or ignored. In a liberal democracy, justice and equality are assumed to already exist. Therefore, ethno-racial minorities' demands for access and inclusion are seen as "radical," "unreasonable," "undemocratic," and a threat to cherished democratic, liberal values. The small gains made by minorities and women are seen by the dominant groups as being "too expensive" economically and ideologically. Dissent by the oppressed is considered disruptive and dangerous.

The "symbolic multiculturalism" of state policies holds to a paradigm of pluralism premised on a hierarchical order of cultures that under certain conditions "allows" or "tolerates" non-dominant cultures to participate in the dominant culture. Such an approach imagines minority communities as "special-interest groups," not as active and full participants in the state and part of its shared history. This paradigm represents notions of tolerance and accommodation, but not of equity and justice. It holds to a unified and static concept of identities and communities as fixed sets of experiences, meanings, and practices rather than of identities as dynamic, fluid, multiple, and historically situated. In summary, state policies continue to be largely centred on maintaining the status quo.

References
Anderson, B. *Imagined Communities*. London: Verso, 1983.
Asad, T. "Anthropology and the Analysis of Ideology." *Man* 14 (1979): 607–627.
Fleras, A., and J.L. Elliott. *Multiculturalism in Canada: The Challenge of Diversity*.Toronto: Nelson, 1992.
MacKey, E. "Managing and Imagining Diversity: Multiculturalism and the Construction of National Identity in Canada." Unpublished thesis, D. Phil. Social Anthropology, University of Sussex, 1996.
Suvendrini, P., and J. Pugliese. "Racial Suicide: The Re-licensing of Racism in Australia." *Race and Class* 39, no. 2 (October–December, 1997): 1–19.
Tator, C., et al. *Racism in the Arts: Case Studies of Controversy and Conflict*. Toronto: University of Toronto Press, 1998.

Source: F. Henry et al., *The Colour of Democracy: Racism in Canadian Society*, 347–348. Toronto: Harcourt Brace, 2000.

Employment Equity

State responses to racism and racial discrimination in employment have been varied and inconsistent at best. Key legislative instruments, such as the *Charter of Rights and Freedoms*, the *Multiculturalism Act*, and various provincial human rights legislation and commissions, have provided a basis for a culture of tolerance by imposing sanctions on certain forms of racial expression. What is still elusive, however, is a systematic commitment to building an anti-racism culture in the workplace, schools, other state and social institutions, and key cultural institutions, such as the media, that are central to intervening in public debates and discourses that determine public policy.

Employment equity is a uniquely Canadian-designed response to discrimination in employment, which also involves a legislative response at the federal level and affirmative action programs at the provincial level.

Arresting the "Brain Waste"

A key area where timely state policy action can make a difference is in dealing with the disconnect between regulators of professions and trades, employers, and skilled immigrants. Governments are the regulators of last resort as well as being leaders in policies and programs. Immigration falls under federal jurisdiction, and the federal government has some responsibility for human resource development. However, most of the regulated and unregulated professions fall under provincial jurisdiction. Federal government immigration, weak provincial government labour-market policies, and a lack of federal-provincial coordination contribute to the persistence of inequality in access to professions and trades for those with international qualifications.

The federal government's most forceful response to concerns about the failure of the internationally trained to integrate into their fields of expertise has been to make the selection process more stringent. This policy direction is contradictory.

It implies that the problem will be solved if the state successfully attracts the "perfect immigrant," so validating the sterotype that immigrant human-capital quality has diminished with the shift to immigration from the global South. The onus is shifted onto the individual as the state embraces an essentially laissez-faire approach to the labour market. Yet as the data increasingly show, the more highly educated the immigrant pool gets, the greater the gap between skill utilization and the reality of skill depreciation in the post-immigration period, suggesting a structural problem within the labour market.[3] Moreover, by the department of immigration's own admission, individuals who are in occupations excluded from the skilled-worker category but who arrive as family members or refugees can be successful in integrating into the labour market.[4] The socio-class-specific approach to immigration, aside from reversing the tradition of Canadian immigration, de-emphasizes social skills that are key to integration while not fixing what ails the labour market.

As part of the immigration process, the Canadian government's "General Occupations List" is used to assign points to prospective immigrants by occupation. The number of points assigned to various occupations is intended to reflect demand in the Canadian labour market. The federal government assigns up to 25 points for education obtained abroad, up to 21 points for experience, and up to 24 points for official languages. Until 2003, applicants required a minimum of 75. Since 2003, applicants need 67 points to qualify for permanent residency. Other point categories include age (10 points), arranged employment (10 points), and adaptability (10 points). The objective is to provide an advantage to educated immigrants, who are assumed to be in demand in the Canadian economy. Ironically, skewing the selection process in favour of highly educated immigrants de-emphasizes the very "soft skills" such as adaptability and communication that employers claim are key to a successful job search. No points are awarded for Canadian experience, yet for many regulators and employers, this seems to be the most important attribute. Since 2001, over 60% of immigrants, including their dependants, had at least a university degree or a trade certificate (CIC, 2003). While labour-market shortages persist or are projected in a number of areas of the economy, such as health care, education, and construction, this has not translated into ready jobs for this highly educated group.

Addressing Unequal Access to Professions and Trades

Recently, the growing level of skills shortages, especially in the health and education sectors, the growing numbers and advocacy of IEPs, global labour-market competition, and pressure from employers, have combined to call unprecedented attention to the issue of credential recognition. Those pressures occur within the context of requirements in international and internal trade agreements for labour mobility.[5] Over the years, governments have made mostly symbolic responses to the concerns expressed by employers and communities. Recently, however, governments have mandated assessment agencies and supported a range of pilot projects addressing the occupational language needs of IEPs: job shadowing and mentoring, profession-based career counselling, etc. Governments have begun to increase residency positions for international medical graduates. They are also paying some attention to the coordinating function: a federal-provincial Working Group on Access to Professions and Trades was established in the late 1990s.

In 1991, the federal government established the Canadian Information Centre for International Credentials (CICIC) to act as a clearing house for information about regulated trades and professions. Provincial governments in British Columbia, Quebec, and Ontario have mandated credential assessment agencies.[6] Most of the regulation of trades and professions falls under provincial jurisdiction, but many self-regulating bodies act independently of the governments to secure the public interest. They are under no obligation to accept the credential assessments of the mandated agencies, and most do not. This puts a premium on both federal-provincial coordination and government action to ensure that the self-regulating bodies open up to the newcomers. Many internationally trained immigrants charge that the regulatory bodies' gatekeeping function too often translates into barriers to access when the interests of existing members come into conflict with those of international graduates. To solve the problem, they are calling for an appeal process to review their decisions.

In response to concerns about inadequate language training, federal and provincial governments are supporting some employment-related training or occupational and sector-specific language training.[7] However, funding for this training is far outweighed by funding for low-level language training for immigrants in English or French as a second language, appropriate for beginners rather than for those seeking occupation- or sector-specific language training. The governments have also committed to funding some training and upgrading for immigrants, notably by funding innovative pilot projects run by settlement sector agencies. However, these pilot projects do not seem to mature into permanent programming. Some soft-skills training has focused on better preparing IEPs for the Canadian labour market through job placement training, mentoring, and job shadowing. Much of this is under the initiative of settlement agencies, in some cases partnering with employers or regulatory bodies. Non-governmental organizations have also shown resourcefulness and innovation by establishing loan programs to cover the cost of licensing exams and upgrading.[8]

Regulators are also involved in some pilot projects aimed at providing experience in the workplace, including mentorships and job-shadowing programs. They are also increasingly organizing across professions to discuss more appropriate ways of evaluating international skills and developing tools for competency assessment. That said, there are other positive signs arising out of pressure from some employers dealing with skill shortages and regulators, some of whom are involved in dialogue with IEPs and governments. These discussions are making some progress in encouraging the governments to abandon the passive laissez-faire approach and become more engaged in the IEP integration process. But some of the policy responses can compound the problem. For instance, to respond to the concern about communication skills, the federal government has made immigrant selection more stringent with regard to language requirements. Moreover, despite some sector-specific career planning, most of the newcomers are forced to take any low-wage job available as a condition of public assistance, short-circuiting the possibility of going through the credential assessment and accreditation process.

Box 8.3: Successful Anti-racism Strategies

- Raising race consciousness—addressing race as a social relation
- Reviewing policies and practices for racial bias and resistance
- Developing an anti-racism, anti-oppression vision and programs
- Developing reflective skills and practices—challenging White power and privilege, rhetoric and symbolism, deconstructing everyday forms of racism in all walks of life
- Responding to allegations of racism in an organization
- Empowering racialized groups and individuals—organizational resources, legitimacy, expertise, leadership, political representation, and representation in decision-making
- Monitoring anti-racism initiatives
- Emphasizing the role of institutions in combatting racism

Most of the issues identified are within the purview of public policy and can be addressed by governments in partnership with regulators, educational institutions, assessment agencies, trade unions, employers, and service providers. There is a need to define the public interest as including a focus both on equity and economic efficiency. This need has never been greater than it is in the current globalized labour market environment.

Notes

1. A. Bakran and A. Kobayashi, *Employment Equity Policy in Canada: An Interprovincial Comparison* (Ottawa: Status of Women Canada, 2000).
2. Government of Canada, *Report of the Taskforce on the Participation of Visible Minorities in the Federal Public Service, 2000: Embracing Change in the Federal Public Service* (Ottawa: Supply and Services Canada, 2000).
3. In the first three years of the millennium, due to the stringent selection process, over 60% of the immigrants admitted to Canada were admitted under the "independent" or "skill-based" class. Many of these immigrants also came with highly educated spouses and dependants. This occurred because the selection process was skewed in favour of a certain type of migrant with education and experience, attributes that don't seem to translate into

value in the Canadian labour market because of the low regard in which that education and experience is held by regulators and employers. In fact, many informants in the interviews suggested that to be successful in the job search process, many newcomers are advised to under-report their education.

4.   See Citizenship and Immigration Canada, *Skilled Worker Immigrants: Towards A New Model of Selection* (Ottawa: Economic Policy and Programs Division: Selection Branch, 1998).

5.   Advocacy groups for internationally trained engineering graduates, international medical graduates, teachers, and accountants have sprung up along with ethno-specific IEP associations, in British Columbia, Ontario, Quebec, Alberta, and they have become active in the public debate. The Framework for the Social Union, signed in 1999, requires provincial governments to comply with the mobility provisions of the Agreement on Internal Trade. The Red Seal Program was established to facilitate the mobility of skilled workers across provincial borders. Canada is also a signatory to NAFTA and the WTO, both of which contain some provisions relating to skilled labour mobility.

6.   Along with the Canadian Centre for International Credentials, provinces have mandated a variety of agencies for credential assessment. This is the case in Quebec, Ontario, and Western Canada, but not in the Maritimes, where they rely largely on Ontario's mandated service provider, WES.

7.   An example is the Sector Specific Training Information and Counselling (STIC) program that is a partnership of the federal and Ontario governments along with settlement sector partners. It began running in four sectors: Engineering, Health Care, Accounting, and Auto Mechanics.

8.   Maytree Foundation in Toronto, AMSSA, and a Vancouver Credit Union ran loan funds for IEPs to help them cover the high cost of processing their accreditation.

Questions for Critical Thought

1.   What is the role of the state in meeting the challenges of racial discrimination in employment?
2.   Describe and evaluate the effectiveness of some of the policies and programs aimed at eliminating racial discrimination.
3.   How effective are human rights laws in eliminating racial discrimination in employment?
4.   What were the key findings of the report of the Taskforce on the Participation of Visible Minorities in the federal government?
5.   What is employment equity and why does it represent a solution to the problem of discrimination in employment?
6.   How has the dismantling of the welfare state impacted the fight against racism?
7.   In what ways can government do more to end discrimination in employment?

Recommended Readings

Abella, R. *Equality Now: Report of the Commission on Equality in Employment*. Ottawa: Supply and Services Canada, 1984.

Bakan, A., and A. Kobayashi. *Employment Equity Policy in Canada: An Interprovincial Comparison*. Ottawa: Status of Women Canada, 2000.

Canadian Charter of Rights and Freedoms. http://canada.justice.gc.ca/Loireg/charte/const_en.html

Employment Equity Reports. www.tbs-sct.gc.ca/report/empequi/2003/ee14_e.asp

Government of Canada. *Report of the Taskforce on the Participation of Visible Minorities in the Federal Public Service, 2000: Embracing Change in the Federal Public Service*. Ottawa: Supply and Services Canada, 2000.

PROMPT. *In the Public Interest: Immigrant Access to Regulated Professions in Ontario* (July 2004). www.prommptinfo.com.

Siemiatycki, M., and E. Isin. "Immigration, Ethno-racial Diversity and Urban Citizenship in Toronto." *Canadian Journal of Regional Sciences* Special Issue XX, no. 1, 2 (Spring-Summer 1997): 73–102.

Toronto Region Immigrant and Employment Council. www.triec.ca

CHAPTER 9

A Program for Action

Introduction

To address the crisis of racial discrimination and social exclusion in Canadian society, we need a multi-sector approach in which the different levels of government and other institutions in society would work with racialized communities as partners. Such initiative requires a level of political will well beyond what has been demonstrated to this point. Any adequate response must aim at dismantling the structures that make racial inequalities inevitable. This has become more critical as racialized group members increase in number in Canadian society, and the implications for the Canadian economy grow. The response must address issues of social exclusion from equal citizenship that lie at the heart of what has been described as democratic racism.

In the final analysis, the assaults of everyday racism, the threat posed by routine workplace decisions informed by racial assumptions, by biased service delivery, and by the government have greater impact on the lives of racialized people than do the harangues of the self-proclaimed White supremacist Heritage Front. Canadian society, its cultural institutions like the media, its economic institutions such as the labour market, and its political institutions have got to confront the spectre of racial inequality before it confounds the nation.

More specifically, the response to the problem of social exclusion falls on society's most dominant institution — the state. Canadian governments share this responsibility with key institutions in society, including labour unions, business, and social justice organizations. They have to invest in a creative, multi-sector coalition that would provide an inclusive way to both interrogate the structures of exclusion that have given rise to these conditions, and to empower their victims to be part of a process of dismantling them and creating new possibilities based on a socially just future.

As the representative institutions that Canadians look upon to mobilize support for action, the federal, provincial, and municipal governments, along with major business, labour, and cultural institutions, need to make a commitment to real and meaningful action to address social exclusion, through processes that empower those who are socially excluded to transform their lives and the communities. They must commit to an approach that puts the experiences of racialized groups front and centre when addressing the needs of urban Canada. This would involve undertaking community programs that seek to identify structures of inequality, barriers to access and equity, and barriers to full participation; a multidimensional approach is needed to confronting the multiple dimensions of social exclusion.

Below is an agenda for the new millennium outlining ways of confronting the social exclusion of racialized groups:

- Naming the processes that perpetuate structures of inequality and social exclusion
- Focusing on communities in distress and on the needs of all excluded groups
- Empowering excluded groups to become active participants, reversing exclusion
- Creating a multi-agency response that mobilizes all relevant actors

- Structuring policy interventions around a life-cycle approach to meet both individual and community development needs
- Fighting discrimination and oppression in their various, often intersecting dimensions
- Using community-based research as a basis for policy formulation[1]

We have attempted to sketch out a program for action that may be the basis for discussion and debate about how to move forward. Many of the ideas, while not new, have not been effectively tried or implemented, and in any case require a multi-sector, multi-level of government and social justice community approach. What is outlined below is a starting position of a process that should involve all sectors of society, not just racialized groups. It should involve governments, key institutions in civil society, the labour movement, and the business community. But it should also aim to empower racialized group members to participate actively in setting the agenda and in dismantling the barriers that deny them the experience of full citizenship. There is also a need for a sense of urgency to arrest the situation before its outcomes become inevitable.

Key Elements of a Program for Action: Royal Commission on Racial Inequality in Canadian Society

Royal Commissions have focused the attention of the Canadian population on issues of vital importance. Racial inequality is one such issue in the 21st century. It demands the resources of some of Canada's best minds, as well as an openness of mind to ensure that it is discussed by as many people as possible in both passionate and dispassionate tones. Above all, racialized group members must have the right to speak, and not be marginalized even in this endeavour.

Employment Equity
The problem of discrimination in employment lies at the heart of access to the workplace for many racialized group members. The need to remove barriers to access to employment has been identified by many reports, but the responses have lacked the necessary commitment. The federal *Employment Equity Act* remains poorly enforced and needs new attention. The enforcement mechanisms in the federal *Employment Equity Act* need to be strengthened. At the provincial level, the mistakes of the federal act should not be repeated. Mandatory employment equity programs should be introduced to deal with the failure of the marketplace to equitably allocate employment opportunities and incomes.

Strengthening Employment Standards Legislation
Precarious work is becoming a key feature of the Canadian labour market. Because of the disproportionate exposure of racialized group members to precarious forms of work, these groups stand to benefit from the strengthening of labour and employment standards by provincial governments. This is ever more urgent as globalization intensifies employer demands for flexibility. The protections against abuse by

unscrupulous employers and employment agencies can contribute to improving the lives and economic performance of racialized group members.

A National Urban Strategy

Most racialized group members live and work in Canada's urban centres. The crisis of racial inequality is likely to first manifest itself in tensions in these communities. Because urban centres are the engines of Canada's economy and because many racialized group members' cheap labour subsidizes them, we imperatively need a National Urban Strategy within an anti-racism framework. A national urban forum would focus attention on the condition of Canada's urban centres and bring together for debate the different levels of government with civil societal organizations, including organizations representing racialized groups. These groups could prepare a strategy that would guide the development of Canada's urban centres. The call for a national forum recognizes the urgency of the issues of racialized poverty, a segregated labour market, and increasingly segregated neighbourhoods, and their implications for Canada's social stability and economic growth. It also recognizes the multi-layered complexity of the challenge we face. Central to these discussions should be the issues of persistent inequality in the labour market, urban poverty, and racialized poverty in particular.

Dismantling Barriers to Access to Professions and Trades

The Canadian economy is attracting some of the world's best and brightest only to disappoint them by failing to streamline the processes of accrediting their qualifications. Some are choosing to leave their families here so that they can maintain their professional careers. Increasingly, others are choosing to return to the country of origin or move to the United States of America. If they are to make a commitment to Canada, Canada needs to reciprocate by allowing them the opportunity to practice their trades and professions. It is clear that for Canada to continue to attract the best and the brightest from around the world, immigrants' skills must be utilized. That means that the barriers to access to regulated professions and trades must come down. Provincial and federal legislative and program initiatives are necessary to deal with the inability of many racialized group members to convert their educational attainment into comparable compensation and employment. The federal government is responsible for immigration, human resources, and skills development; it therefore needs to concern itself more with what is happening to the "star" immigrants for which it competes.

Increasing the Supply of Affordable Housing

Canada is the only country in the industrialized world without a national housing program. Research shows that Canada's racialized groups have difficulty accessing the limited stock of housing in very tight housing markets in the major urban centres. The role of the state in providing affordable housing is indispensable. It is imperative that a national affordable housing program be re-established and that its elements address specifically the segregationist nature of the housing market in Canada's urban centres.

Strengthening Access to Child Care

A national child care program with national standards has been publicly debated for the past decade. Yet jurisdictional wrangling and bureaucratic inertia have been cited as impediments to delivering child care to the many who need it. Addressing the demand for child care is a key element in dealing with the low levels of earnings, especially among racialized women, and the resulting disproportionate level of poverty. Action by the federal government and provincial governments is urgently required. Some provinces have established superior practices that need to be studied. Quebec is a leader in this field: its five-dollar-a-day child care program acknowledges the social value of providing affordable, accessible, good-quality care for Canadian children in a safe and nurturing environment.

Anti-racism Programs

The level of provincial and national support for anti-racism programs diminished significantly over the 1990s. Moreover, its starting point was barely adequate to meet the need for anti-racism action in cities and neighbourhoods. The federal Department of Multiculturalism has an important role in mobilizing support from all levels of government to this end. A federal urban strategy must include support for anti-racism initiatives at the local, provincial, and national levels.

Community Economic Development

Increased participation in Canadian life for racialized groups depends on the level of development in the communities. Community institutions are essential to ensuring that institutions in racialized communities mature into strong organs for community empowerment. Federal, provincial, and municipal programs aimed at successful integration have tended to be restricted to the newest members of the racialized communities, often at the expense of support for fledgling institutions and service agencies. Increased federal, provincial, and municipal funding is needed for ethno-cultural organizations involved in community development as well as for ethno-specific service delivery organizations. Adequate funding would acknowledge the fact that these are safe zones for racialized peoples, and incubators of ideas and social innovations on which other mainstream institutions can draw.

Canadian Social Justice Movements

Labour unions and other progressive agents of change in society need to recognize the implications of the changing demographical landscape of Canada. They need to open up leadership channels for racialized groups so that the organizations that fight for social justice reflect, in their leadership and their membership, the changing reality of Canada. They need to become vehicles of mobilization to address the issues of social exclusion. The labour movement needs to commit itself to organizing workers in the new sites of precarious employment and investing in new forms of labour organization that may extend beyond the standard work arrangements with which it is most familiar. Racism is a cultural phenomenon to which change agencies are not immune. Adopting an anti-racism stance, undertaking anti-racism programs, and empowering those for whom they fight will require self-assessment for many such organizations. Social justice groups must be at the forefront of a new progressive coalition against racial inequality. They must show the other sectors in society that it is possible to empower racialized members and draw on their resources to re-establish a progressive agenda for Canada, one that responds to all forms of oppression.

Notes

1. See T. Richmond and R. Omdivar, *Immigrant Settlement and Social Inclusion in Canada* (Toronto: Laidlaw Foundation, 2003).

Questions for Critical Thought

1. Describe why a political strategy is essential in responding to the socio-economic crisis that faces racialized groups.
2. What approach should such a strategy take regarding the issue of White privilege?
3. What is the "brain drain" and what role can different levels of government play to end it?
4. What is the role of social justice organizations in dealing with social exclusion, and how can social justice organizations better prepare for that role?
5. How can a multi-agency approach be organized to respond to social exclusion?
6. What role can the trade unions play in fighting racial discrimination in the workplace?

CHAPTER 10

Conclusion

In this book, we have sought to explore the experience of racialized and immigrant populations in the Canadian labour market, and the implications of life changes for these groups. The processes of economic restructuring and demographic change underway in late 20th- and early 21st-century Canada have created a more multicultural, multiracial society. Yet because of the neo-liberal restructuring of Canada's economy, the massive deregulation of the labour market, and the dismantling the welfare state that have coincided with increased immigration from the global South, racialized groups have become increasingly vulnerable. While racialized immigrants are becoming the primary source of new labour for the Canadian economy, this is occurring within the context of a broader restructuring of the global economy, which has imposed such features as a flexible mode of accumulation and greater economic inequality in Canada. Their impacts are uneven and have intensified existing inequalities along racial and gender lines.

These processes are rooted in Canada's unique history. Traditionally, Canada's search for the appropriate immigrant pool has occurred within the framework of an assimilation policy aimed at maintaining a "White society." Hence the official categories of "desirables" and "undesirables" that dominated immigration policy until recently, leading to the dominance of immigrants from Europe. Canada's labour-market policies have always corresponded to the demands for population stabilization. The complex dynamics of immigration policies aimed to maintain a viable capitalist economy and a White society. Racial hierarchies in the Canadian economy became more prominent in the 1970s as the numbers of racialized immigrants became more significant, with the sheer numbers of "new" immigrants from the South giving new significance to the familiar tensions.

Race is a social construct based principally on superficial differences in physical appearance. While always an important part of Canada's population-economy complex, it has acquired new significance in determining access to economic, social, and political resources. In some ways, this is consistent with the historical existence of structures of racial discrimination that determined the incorporation of racialized immigrants into the Canadian labour market, leading to a racially (and gender) stratified labour market. Many potential immigrants from the South worked only as domestics and labourers in earlier periods of immigration, despite their professional and other qualifications. While selected for their skills, today's racialized immigrants often end up with similar labour-market participation patterns. They work largely in precarious employment: low-end, low-paying jobs in low-income sectors with minimal mobility.

Examples of labour-market displacement and exclusion of racialized group members, especially during tough economic times, are widely documented.[1] They fit into a hierarchy of capitalist deployment of labour that imposed differential levels of exploitation to ensure capital a racial dividend from labour-market differentiation. This dividend also contributed to nation building.

These historical experiences are being reproduced in the workplaces of many of Canada's urban areas, where precarious employment is becoming the dominant form of organization of work. In essence, this points to a reproduction of the racial segmentation in the labour market. The congruence of the emergence of precarious forms of work as a dominant phenomenon of neo-liberal restructuring and the growth of the size of racialized communities in Canada's urban areas represents a qualitative departure in the process of racial stratification of Canada's labour market. It amplifies the racial segmentation of the labour market as a prominent feature of the Canadian economy.

We have presented evidence to suggest that racist conceptions of the value of immigrant human capital continue to degrade its earning potential and equal access to employment in the Canadian labour market.[2] While far outpacing the general Canadian population growth, and contributing a majority of new entrants into the labour market, racialized groups and immigrants continue to experience discrimination and economic exclusion in the labour market. There is a double-digit income gap between racialized and non-racialized populations in the Canadian labour market. Racialized groups and recent immigrants, a highly racialized category, experience higher unemployment and lower participation rates, and occupational concentrations in the low-income occupations.

Racialized group members and recent immigrants are not able to translate their educational attainment into comparable occupational status and compensation. This is partly explained by the experience of internationally educated professionals who face barriers to converting their skills into skilled occupations. There are variations in the size of the income gap among subgroups such as racialized youth and women. There is an income gap between racialized men and women, suggesting a gendered dimension to the inequality identified.

The unequal unemployment rates, the inability of racialized group members to convert their educational attainment advantage into commensurate occupational status and income, the differential experience of internationally trained racialized group members, and the sectoral concentrations are all dimensions of the racial inequality and social exclusion that have become typical of too many racialized lives. The impact of racialization is amplified in the early 20th century because of the conditions of globalization and the demands for flexibility brought on by neo-liberal restructuring. These new conditions have combined with the historical processes of racial discrimination to intensify structures of social exclusion and make the lives of racialized group members more precarious. Their health status is diminished, they are more likely to live in poor neighbourhoods, and they exist in tension with the criminal justice system.

Looking at key social and economic indicators like income inequality, differential levels of unemployment and underemployment, differential sectoral participation, and differential access to professional and trades, we are able to draw some conclusions with regard to how the process of globalization and the persistent legacy of racism have resulted in the prevalence of low incomes among the racialized groups, and the decline in neighbourhood, housing, and health status of racialized groups. The intensification of racial stratification in the labour market and the reversal of state anti-discriminatory policies and programs mean that despite higher levels of educational attainment, disproportionate numbers of racialized workers, confined to precarious forms of work in certain sectors of the economy, cannot utilize their skills and are condemned to low-status occupations and low-wage jobs.

These developments point directly to the emerging racialization of poverty. Racialized group families are twice as likely to be poor as White families. In some urban areas and among some groups of racialized group members, the rate is three to four times. The situation is particularly adverse with single-parent families, most of which are led by women. In urban centres like Toronto, Vancouver, Montreal, and Calgary, where racialized group populations are statistically significant, the racial segmentation of labour markets leads not just to the racialization of poverty, but also to other social patterns such as sustained school drop-out rates, the racialization of the penal system, the criminalization of youth, and the racial segregation of urban low-income neighbourhoods. The latter are socially precarious environments that foster various forms of violence, including gun violence and violence against women. These conditions further deepen social marginalization and exclusion as the processes of immiseration, desperation, hopelessness, and disempowerment become normalized.

Work is central to livelihood, to the creation of identity, and to a sense of belonging to a community. Racialized groups are increasingly likely to work in precarious work environments — in part-time, temporary, and casualized employment with low wages, little or no job security, and no benefits. This is particularly true of racialized women, who suffer the double burden of gendered racism, even as they are called upon to bear the disproportionate burden of social reproduction.

These developments have coincided with the growing size of the racialized population. Despite the fact that this population's contribution to the Canadian economy has grown exponentially over the last two decades, it is vulnerable to what we term the racialization of poverty. Race continues to be a major factor in the distribution of opportunities in the Canadian labour market and by extension in determining the life chances of racialized peoples and immigrants in Canada. The major difference is that this disadvantage will now translate into a drag on the Canadian economy and the Canadian population as a whole.

Empowering and Organizing Racialized Workers: The Union Advantage

Perhaps no institution represents as much promise in empowering racialized workers to overcome their oppression in the labour market as does organized labour. The role of unions in improving the lives of working people is well documented. The major improvements in the lives of workers in the post-war period were not a gift from employers or capital, but rather the outcome of workplace and political struggles waged by organized workers in Canada. For Canada's racialized group members to make significant progress in the labour market, they need the union advantage — the power of collective bargaining. The leadership and members of Canada's organized labour must seize the opportunity and meet the challenge of empowering an increasingly marginalized and socially excluded segment of our society. Unions can bargain employment equity provisions as well as organize drives in the sectors of the economy in which racialized groups are overrepresented. They can improve the lives of racialized workers in precarious environments by organizing part time and temporary workers, putting them in a stronger bargaining position, especially with bad bosses.

Organized labour has not always seen a benefit in this approach, sometimes succumbing to competitive racism in its own ranks. But given that the racialized population is on average younger than the rest of the Canadian population, the labour movement needs to pay attention to this growing source of entrants into the labour force. This is not a paternalistic mission. Rather it is a defensive one and one of solidarity. Labour cannot afford to sit out the struggle against economic apartheid. Organizing those in precarious employment does not undermine workers in standard employment relationships, as alleged by those who have counselled organized labour to consolidate its gains by focusing on organizing better-paid workers in the private sector, and workers with stable employment in the public sector. Rather, it provides the labour movement with a defensive position against creeping precariousness before it overruns those secure jobs in the private and public sectors.

By extending the union advantage to workers in sectors with precarious employment and by strengthening the bargaining capacity of marginalized workers, one establishes a safety net against the deployment of the reserve army of labour against the ranks of today's securely employed. These measures establish common cause and solidarity among organized and non-organized workers so as to protect against the assaults on labour power. Ironically, the class shifting imposed by precariousness and global forces of migration has meant that among the ranks of the unorganized racialized workers are many with skills that would be of benefit to organized labour. Many were professionals and tradespeople who now find themselves in lines of employment unrelated to their training, but who possess skills that can be utilized to build a strong movement. They make for very resourceful working-class allies. Labour should take advantage of them, not shun them.

A Political Response to Social Exclusion

Finally, no response to social exclusion will be adequate to the task until its victims are an integral part of the process of transformation. That includes empowering them to be central political actors in the systems and structures that drive the process. What is required is an approach that breaks the cycles of victimization and exclusion. In order to respond effectively to social exclusion, a new, more assertive political approach to racism is imperative, one that locates racism within the broader context of the social and economic exploitation responsible for the racialization of poverty. The approach needs to link racism with power and the politics of class and group interest. It should expose the connection between majority privilege and minority oppression, showing that racial oppression is often necessary to sustain privilege. With a changing global and Canadian economy creating fewer jobs, and mostly precarious jobs, racialized groups can escape alienation only by forcefully asserting their citizenship, rather than accepting the position that marginalizes them as the "other."

The political backlash of the 1990s does to some extent account for the loss of ground in the socio-economic conditions of racialized group members. This was a political process that created winners and losers. It consolidated the gains of the dominant group, especially its elite sections, at the expense of racialized and other marginalized groups. The rewards of the economy clearly show this, and the concentration of economic and political power in fewer hands proves it. In the backlash, not only was employment equity repealed in Ontario, but also it lost momentum in other jurisdictions. Even at the federal level where the legislation was maintained, it did not translate into the lowering of barriers to access to employment and mobility. The political backlash ensured that members of the dominant group essentially asserted their interests through the mainstream Canadian institutions, especially the state, by the process of deregulation, state non-intervention in social crises, and substantial cuts to public services. The impacts were disproportionately felt by racialized groups.

The backlash manifested the intersection of White privilege and racial oppression; hence the persistence of racism and the emergence of racialization of poverty today are the fruit of a political struggle. In the same way that we now understand the male privilege as dependent on the oppression of women, racial oppression can only be confronted by acknowledging its connection to an unearned but deep-rooted White privilege, one that is differentiated by class and gender, but still generalizable.

Racialized group members, whether oppressed by police, employers, governments, or institutions, have tended to perceive power as inherently evil; they therefore view its pursuit, possession, and application as corrupting. That attitude needs to change because power alone offers racialized people protection against inequality, even in a liberal democratic society such as Canada. The claim to full participation in the economic, political, social, and cultural life of the nation can be sustained only through the pursuit of power. Racialized groups need to confront the disproportionate representation in governing institutions, especially in the geographic communities in which they live. In urban centres with large racialized communities like Vancouver, Abbotsford, Toronto, Markham, and Montreal, the governing institutions need to be challenged or transformed to reflect issues that concern the large communities of racialized peoples.

Because of their growing numbers, racialized group members can potentially mobilize to take control of the liberal democratic institutions by electing a critical mass of representatives in them. Such a critical mass can then help force a shift in the political agenda toward anti-racism priorities. The call is to transform the marginality of racialized existence into a basis for political, social power, which will advance the agenda for job creation, employment equity, access to professions and trades, labour regulation, minimum wage, child care, educational reform, affordable housing, income support, culturally appropriate health care services, and equal access to social services and other public resources. Coalitions with other marginalized peoples are essential, and are possible if the agenda addresses the concentration of power and privilege in the hands of fewer and fewer people.

In the end, this book speaks to the material realities of the racialized experience in Canada. It seeks to understand how their labour market experience, the disproportionate concentration of racialized populations, particularly women, in part-time, temporary, and home work, and the intensification of precarious employment through long hours and multiple jobs with low pay and few benefits, exposes them to higher levels of poverty, higher mental and other health risks, increases tensions between communities and the criminal justice system, and heightens social exclusion.

Notes

1. T. Das Gupta, *Racism and Paid Work* (Toronto: Garamond Press, 1996); "The Political Economy of Gender, Race and Class: Looking at South Asian Immigrant Women in Canada," *Canadian Ethnic Studies* XXVL, no. 1 (1994): 59–73; D. Brand, "Black Women and Work: The Impact of racially Constructed Gender Roles on the Sexual Division of Labour," *Fireweed* 25 (1987): 28–37; I. Zeytinoglu and J. Muteshi, "Gender, Race and Class Dimensions of Non-Standard Work," *Industrial Relations* 55, no. 1 (Winter 2000): 133–166; A. Calliste, "Canada's Immigration Policy and Domestics from the Caribbean: The Second Domestic Scheme," in *Race, Class, Gender: Bonds and Barriers*, edited by J. Vorst et al. (Toronto: Garamond Press/Society of Socialist Studies, 1991), 136–168; P. Daenzer, *Regulating Class Privilege: Immigrant Servants in Canada, 1940–1990s* (Toronto: Canadian Scholars' Press, 1993); T. Schecter, *Race, Class, Women and the State: The Case of Domestic Labour* (Montreal: Black Rose Books, 1998); J. Anderson and J. Lynam, "The Meaning of Work for Immigrant Women in the Lower Echelons of the Canadian Labour Force," *Canadian Ethnic Studies* XIX, no. 2 (1987): 67–90; J. Reitz, *Ethnicity and Inequality and Segregation in Jobs* (Toronto: University of Toronto, 1981); M. Ornstein, *Ethno-Racial Inequality in Toronto: Analysis of the 1996 Census* (Toronto: City of Toronto Access and Equity Unit, 2000); A. de Wolff, *Breaking the Myth of Flexible Work: Contingent Work in Toronto* (Toronto: Contingent Worker's Project, 2000); G. Galabuzi, *Canada's Creeping Economic Apartheid: The Economic Segregation and Social Marginalization of Racialized Groups* (Toronto: Centre for Social Justice, 2001).

2. R. Abella, *Report of the Royal Commission on Equality in Employment* (Ottawa: Supply and Services Canada, 1985); A. de Silva, *Earnings of Immigrants: A Comparative Analysis* (Ottawa: Economic Council of Canada, 1992); T. Das Gupta, *Racism and Paid Work* (Toronto: Garamond Press, 1996); A.H. Akbari, "Immigrant 'Quality' in Canada: More Direct Evidence of Human Capital Content, 1956–1994," *International Migration Review* 33 (Spring 1999): 156–175; J. Howlett and C. Sakellariou, "Wage Discrimination, Occupational Segregation and Visible Minorities in Canada," *Applied Economics* 25, no. 11 (November, 1993): 1413–1422; D. Hiebert, "The Colour of Work: Labour Market Segregation in Montreal, Toronto and Vancouver, 1991," working paper no. 97-02, Research on Immigration and Integration in the Metropolis, Burnaby, B.C.: Simon Fraser University (Vancouver, Centre of Excellence, 1992); M. Boyd, "At a Disadvantage: The Occupational Attainment of Foreign Born Women in Canada," *International Migration Review* 18, no. 4 (1985): 1091–1119; L. Christofides and R. Swindinsky, "Wage Determination by Gender and Visible Minority Status: Evidence from the 1989 LMAS," *Canadian Public Policy* XX, no. 1 (1994): 34–51; I. Zeytinoglu and J. Muteshi, "Gender, Race and Class Dimensions of Non-standard Work," *Industrial Relations* 55, no. 1 (Winter, 2000): 133–166; J. Anderson and J. Lynam, "The Meaning of Work for Immigrant Women in the Lower Echelons of the Canadian Labour Force," *Canadian Ethnic Studies* XIX, no. 2 (1987): 67–90; A. Calliste, "Resisting Exclusion and Marginality in Nursing: Women of Colour in Ontario," in *Race and Ethnicity in Canada*, edited by M. Kalbach and W. Kalbach (Toronto: Harcourt Brace, 2000), 308–328; J. Reitz, *Ethnicity and Inequality and Segregation in Jobs* (Toronto: University of Toronto Press, 1981); Ornstein (2000); de Wolff (2000); Galabuzi (2001).

APPENDIX A

Universal Declaration of Human Rights (United Nations, 1948)

On December 10, 1948, the General Assembly of the United Nations adopted and proclaimed the Universal Declaration of Human Rights, the full text of which appears in the following pages. Following this historic act, the Assembly called upon all member countries to publicize the text of the Declaration and "to cause it to be disseminated, displayed, read and expounded principally in schools and other educational institutions, without distinction based on the political status of countries or territories."

PREAMBLE

Whereas recognition of the inherent dignity and of the equal and inalienable rights of all members of the human family is the foundation of freedom, justice and peace in the world,

Whereas disregard and contempt for human rights have resulted in barbarous acts which have outraged the conscience of mankind, and the advent of a world in which human beings shall enjoy freedom of speech and belief and freedom from fear and want has been proclaimed as the highest aspiration of the common people,

Whereas it is essential, if man is not to be compelled to have recourse, as a last resort, to rebellion against tyranny and oppression, that human rights should be protected by the rule of law,

Whereas it is essential to promote the development of friendly relations between nations,

Whereas the peoples of the United Nations have in the Charter reaffirmed their faith in fundamental human rights, in the dignity and worth of the human person and in the equal rights of men and women and have determined to promote social progress and better standards of life in larger freedom,

Whereas Member States have pledged themselves to achieve, in co-operation with the United Nations, the promotion of universal respect for and observance of human rights and fundamental freedoms,

Whereas a common understanding of these rights and freedoms is of the greatest importance for the full realization of this pledge,

Now, Therefore THE GENERAL ASSEMBLY proclaims THIS UNIVERSAL DECLARATION OF HUMAN RIGHTS as a common standard of achievement for all peoples and all nations, to the end that every individual and every organ of society, keeping this Declaration constantly in mind, shall strive by teaching and education to promote respect for these rights and freedoms and by progressive measures, national and international, to secure their universal and effective recognition and observance, both among the peoples of Member States themselves and among the peoples of territories under their jurisdiction.

Article 1.

All human beings are born free and equal in dignity and rights. They are endowed with reason and conscience and should act towards one another in a spirit of brotherhood.

Article 2.

Everyone is entitled to all the rights and freedoms set forth in this Declaration, without distinction of any kind, such as race, colour, sex, language, religion, political or other opinion, national or social origin, property, birth or other status. Furthermore, no distinction shall be made on the basis of the political, jurisdictional or international status of the country or territory to which a person belongs, whether it be independent, trust, non-self-governing or under any other limitation of sovereignty.

Article 3.

Everyone has the right to life, liberty and security of person.

Article 4.

No one shall be held in slavery or servitude; slavery and the slave trade shall be prohibited in all their forms.

Article 5.

No one shall be subjected to torture or to cruel, inhuman or degrading treatment or punishment.

Article 6.

Everyone has the right to recognition everywhere as a person before the law.

Article 7.

All are equal before the law and are entitled without any discrimination to equal protection of the law. All are entitled to equal protection against any discrimination in violation of this Declaration and against any incitement to such discrimination.

Article 8.

Everyone has the right to an effective remedy by the competent national tribunals for acts violating the fundamental rights granted him by the constitution or by law.

Article 9.

No one shall be subjected to arbitrary arrest, detention or exile.

Article 10.

Everyone is entitled in full equality to a fair and public hearing by an independent and impartial tribunal, in the determination of his rights and obligations and of any criminal charge against him.

Article 11.

(1) Everyone charged with a penal offence has the right to be presumed innocent until proved guilty according to law in a public trial at which he has had all the guarantees necessary for his defence.

(2) No one shall be held guilty of any penal offence on account of any act or omission which did not constitute a penal offence, under national or international law, at the time when it was committed. Nor shall a heavier penalty be imposed than the one that was applicable at the time the penal offence was committed.

Article 12.

No one shall be subjected to arbitrary interference with his privacy, family, home or correspondence, nor to attacks upon his honour and reputation. Everyone has the right to the protection of the law against such interference or attacks.

Article 13.

(1) Everyone has the right to freedom of movement and residence within the borders of each state.

(2) Everyone has the right to leave any country, including his own, and to return to his country.

Article 14.

(1) Everyone has the right to seek and to enjoy in other countries asylum from persecution.

(2) This right may not be invoked in the case of prosecutions genuinely arising from non-political crimes or from acts contrary to the purposes and principles of the United Nations.

Article 15.

(1) Everyone has the right to a nationality.

(2) No one shall be arbitrarily deprived of his nationality nor denied the right to change his nationality.

Article 16.

(1) Men and women of full age, without any limitation due to race, nationality or religion, have the right to marry and to found a family. They are entitled to equal rights as to marriage, during marriage and at its dissolution.

(2) Marriage shall be entered into only with the free and full consent of the intending spouses.

(3) The family is the natural and fundamental group unit of society and is entitled to protection by society and the State.

Article 17.

(1) Everyone has the right to own property alone as well as in association with others.

(2) No one shall be arbitrarily deprived of his property.

Article 18.

Everyone has the right to freedom of thought, conscience and religion; this right includes freedom to change his religion or belief, and freedom, either alone or in community with others and in public or private, to manifest his religion or belief in teaching, practice, worship and observance.

Article 19.

Everyone has the right to freedom of opinion and expression; this right includes freedom to hold opinions without interference and to seek, receive and impart information and ideas through any media and regardless of frontiers.

Article 20.

(1) Everyone has the right to freedom of peaceful assembly and association.

(2) No one may be compelled to belong to an association.

Article 21.

(1) Everyone has the right to take part in the government of his country, directly or through freely chosen representatives.

(2) Everyone has the right of equal access to public service in his country.

(3) The will of the people shall be the basis of the authority of government; this will shall be expressed in periodic and genuine elections which shall be by universal and equal suffrage and shall be held by secret vote or by equivalent free voting procedures.

Article 22.

Everyone, as a member of society, has the right to social security and is entitled to realization, through national effort and international co-operation and in accordance with the organization and resources of each State, of the economic, social and cultural rights indispensable for his dignity and the free development of his personality.

Article 23.

(1) Everyone has the right to work, to free choice of employment, to just and favourable conditions of work and to protection against unemployment.

(2) Everyone, without any discrimination, has the right to equal pay for equal work.

(3) Everyone who works has the right to just and favourable remuneration ensuring for himself and his family an existence worthy of human dignity, and supplemented, if necessary, by other means of social protection.

(4) Everyone has the right to form and to join trade unions for the protection of his interests.

Article 24.

Everyone has the right to rest and leisure, including reasonable limitation of working hours and periodic holidays with pay.

Article 25.

(1) Everyone has the right to a standard of living adequate for the health and well-being of himself and of his family, including food, clothing, housing and medical care and necessary social services, and the right to security in the event of unemployment, sickness, disability, widowhood, old age or other lack of livelihood in circumstances beyond his control.

(2) Motherhood and childhood are entitled to special care and assistance. All children, whether born in or out of wedlock, shall enjoy the same social protection.

Article 26.

(1) Everyone has the right to education. Education shall be free, at least in the elementary and fundamental stages. Elementary education shall be compulsory. Technical and professional education shall be made generally available and higher education shall be equally accessible to all on the basis of merit.

(2) Education shall be directed to the full development of the human personality and to the strengthening of respect for human rights and fundamental freedoms. It shall promote understanding, tolerance and friendship among all nations, racial or religious groups, and shall further the activities of the United Nations for the maintenance of peace.

(3) Parents have a prior right to choose the kind of education that shall be given to their children.

Article 27.

(1) Everyone has the right freely to participate in the cultural life of the community, to enjoy the arts and to share in scientific advancement and its benefits.

(2) Everyone has the right to the protection of the moral and material interests resulting from any scientific, literary or artistic production of which he is the author.

Article 28.

Everyone is entitled to a social and international order in which the rights and freedoms set forth in this Declaration can be fully realized.

Article 29.

(1) Everyone has duties to the community in which alone the free and full development of his personality is possible.

(2) In the exercise of his rights and freedoms, everyone shall be subject only to such limitations as are determined by law solely for the purpose of securing due recognition and respect for the rights and freedoms of others and of meeting the just requirements of morality, public order and the general welfare in a democratic society.

(3) These rights and freedoms may in no case be exercised contrary to the purposes and principles of the United Nations.

Article 30.

Nothing in this Declaration may be interpreted as implying for any State, group or person any right to engage in any activity or to perform any act aimed at the destruction of any of the rights and freedoms set forth herein.

Declaration on the Rights of Persons Belonging to National or Ethnic, Religious and Linguistic Minorities (United Nations, 1992)

The Universal Declaration of Human Rights provides the framework within which a variety of convenants, connections, and declarations have been developed to implement the key human rights principles it embodies. The Declaration on the Rights of Minorities is one such.

Adopted by General Assembly resolution 47/135 of 18 December 1992

The General Assembly,
Reaffirming that one of the basic aims of the United Nations, as proclaimed in the Charter, is to promote and encourage respect for human rights and for fundamental freedoms for all, without distinction as to race, sex, language or religion,

Reaffirming faith in fundamental human rights, in the dignity and worth of the human person, in the equal rights of men and women and of nations large and small,

Desiring to promote the realization of the principles contained in the Charter, the Universal Declaration of Human Rights, the Convention on the Prevention and Punishment of the Crime of Genocide, the International Convention on the Elimination of All Forms of Racial Discrimination, the International Covenant on Civil and Political Rights, the International Covenant on Economic, Social and Cultural Rights, the Declaration on the Elimination of All Forms of Intolerance and of Discrimination Based on Religion or Belief, and the Convention on the Rights of the Child, as well as other relevant international instruments that have been adopted at the universal or regional level and those concluded between individual States Members of the United Nations,

Inspired by the provisions of article 27 of the International Covenant on Civil and Political Rights concerning the rights of persons belonging to ethnic, religious and linguistic minorities,

Considering that the promotion and protection of the rights of persons belonging to national or ethnic, religious and linguistic minorities contribute to the political and social stability of States in which they live,

Emphasizing that the constant promotion and realization of the rights of persons belonging to national or ethnic, religious and linguistic minorities, as an integral part of the development of society as a whole and within a democratic framework based on the rule of law, would contribute to the strengthening of friendship and cooperation among peoples and States,

Considering that the United Nations has an important role to play regarding the protection of minorities,

Bearing in mind the work done so far within the United Nations system, in particular by the Commission on Human Rights, the Subcommission on Prevention of Discrimination and Protection of Minorities and the bodies established pursuant to the International Covenants on Human Rights and other relevant international human rights instruments in promoting and protecting the rights of persons belonging to national or ethnic, religious and linguistic minorities,

Taking into account the important work which is done by intergovernmental and non-governmental organizations in protecting minorities and in promoting and protecting the rights of persons belonging to national or ethnic, religious and linguistic minorities,

Recognizing the need to ensure even more effective implementation of international human rights instruments with regard to the rights of persons belonging to national or ethnic, religious and linguistic minorities,

Proclaims this Declaration on the Rights of Persons Belonging to National or Ethnic, Religious and Linguistic Minorities:

Article 1

1. States shall protect the existence and the national or ethnic, cultural, religious and linguistic identity of minorities within their respective territories and shall encourage conditions for the promotion of that identity.

2. States shall adopt appropriate legislative and other measures to achieve those ends.

Article 2

1. Persons belonging to national or ethnic, religious and linguistic minorities (hereinafter referred to as persons belonging to minorities) have the right to enjoy their own culture, to profess and practise their own religion, and to use their own language, in private and in public, freely and without interference or any form of discrimination.

2. Persons belonging to minorities have the right to participate effectively in cultural, religious, social, economic and public life.

3. Persons belonging to minorities have the right to participate effectively in decisions on the national and, where appropriate, regional level concerning the minority to which they belong or the regions in which they live, in a manner not incompatible with national legislation.

4. Persons belonging to minorities have the right to establish and maintain their own associations.

5. Persons belonging to minorities have the right to establish and maintain, without any discrimination, free and peaceful contacts with other members of their group and with persons belonging to other minorities, as well as contacts across frontiers with citizens of other States to whom they are related by national or ethnic, religious or linguistic ties.

Article 3

1. Persons belonging to minorities may exercise their rights, including those set forth in the present Declaration, individually as well as in community with other members of their group, without any discrimination.

2. No disadvantage shall result for any person belonging to a minority as the consequence of the exercise or non-exercise of the rights set forth in the present Declaration.

Article 4

1. States shall take measures where required to ensure that persons belonging to minorities may exercise fully and effectively all their human rights and fundamental freedoms without any discrimination and in full equality before the law.

2. States shall take measures to create favourable conditions to enable persons belonging to minorities to express their characteristics and to develop their culture, language, religion, traditions and customs, except where specific practices are in violation of national law and contrary to international standards.

3. States should take appropriate measures so that, wherever possible, persons belonging to minorities may have adequate opportunities to learn their mother tongue or to have instruction in their mother tongue.

4. States should, where appropriate, take measures in the field of education, in order to encourage knowledge of the history, traditions, language and culture of the minorities existing within their territory. Persons belonging to minorities should have adequate opportunities to gain knowledge of the society as a whole.

5. States should consider appropriate measures so that persons belonging to minorities may participate fully in the economic progress and development in their country.

Article 5

1. National policies and programmes shall be planned and implemented with due regard for the legitimate interests of persons belonging to minorities.

2. Programmes of cooperation and assistance among States should be planned and implemented with due regard for the legitimate interests of persons belonging to minorities.

Article 6

States should cooperate on questions relating to persons belonging to minorities, inter alia, exchanging information and experiences, in order to promote mutual understanding and confidence.

Article 7

States should cooperate in order to promote respect for the rights set forth in the present Declaration.

Article 8

1. Nothing in the present Declaration shall prevent the fulfilment of international obligations of States in relation to persons belonging to minorities. In particular, States shall fulfil in good faith the obligations and commitments they have assumed under international treaties and agreements to which they are parties.

2. The exercise of the rights set forth in the present Declaration shall not prejudice the enjoyment by all persons of universally recognized human rights and fundamental freedoms.

3. Measures taken by States to ensure the effective enjoyment of the rights set forth in the present Declaration shall not prima facie be considered contrary to the principle of equality contained in the Universal Declaration of Human Rights.

4. Nothing in the present Declaration may be construed as permitting any activity contrary to the purposes and principles of the United Nations, including sovereign equality, territorial integrity and political independence of States.

Article 9

The specialized agencies and other organizations of the United Nations system shall contribute to the full realization of the rights and principles set forth in the present Declaration, within their respective fields of competence.

Glossary of Terms

After-tax income: Net market income plus transfers.

Anti-racism: Process by which racism is identified and eradicated in its various forms in organizations, institutions, and society.

Average income: The income of the person or family derived by adding up all incomes and divided by the total number of families. It tends to be skewed to higher levels due to the fact that at the high end, many people earn hundreds of times the income of low earners.

Colour-coded mosaic: Refers to a system of racial stratification in Canada. Canadian society is structured into social, economic, and political hierarchies along racial lines, with racialized minorities and Aboriginal peoples at the bottom; these groups find themselves socially excluded from political, economic, and social resources.

Contract compliance: Refers to a voluntary affirmative action or employment equity program used by the federal government and other levels of government to encourage those with government contracts to meet equity objectives. The principle has been embraced by governments seeking to influence the behaviour of companies in the private sector. Under the program, any firm bidding on government contracts has to comply with equity-based conditions such as implementing employment equity programs.

Discrimination: Refers to acts or practices toward members of a particular group that impose a disadvantage on the basis of unsubstantiated assumptions about that group's shared physical or cultural characteristics.

Dominant/subordinate relations: Refer to relations between groups with majority and minority status in society. Race, ethnicity, class, or gender are often the basis for the majority/minority status.

Economic apartheid: The use of the term here denotes the structuring of the Canadian economy such that a segregated labour market has evolved. Historically, this market consigned first Aboriginal peoples and then racialized group members to particular types of work, occupations, and sectors of the economy. The resulting system of racialized exploitation is dependent on the persistent structures of racialized undervaluing of human capital, racialized undercompensation for labour, and racialized income inequalities to benefit capital accumulation. The growing social exclusion — evidenced in segregation in housing and neighbourhoods, higher poverty rates, above-average contact with the law — also contributes to the characterization of separate development or "aparthood."

Economic power: Refers to the accumulation and concentration of the means of production and material resources such as wealth, property, income, and access to well-paying occupations and education.

Employment equity: Refers to policies and programs aimed at creating fairness in employment. The policies and programs seek to ensure that all qualified individuals have equal access to positions and that their qualifications are assessed in relation to the requirements of the job. The policies and programs also seek to eliminate barriers in the recruitment, selection, promotion, or training practices that have a discriminatory effect on designated groups.

Employment income: Income from wages, salaries, and self-employment.

Equity groups: In the Canadian context, women, visible minorities, people with disabilities, Aboriginal peoples.

Ethnicity: Refers to arbitrary classifications of human populations based on the biological factor of common ancestry and such cultural factors as language and religion. Ethnicity tends to have biological and cultural dimensions, referring to bloodlines as well as shared geographical history.

Ethnocentrism: Refers to the tendency to view all the peoples and cultures of the world from a single, central point of view defined by the practices, values, and standards of one's ethnic culture.

Formal equality: Prescribes identical treatment of all individuals regardless of their actual circumstances or majority/minority status.

Income gap: The difference between the average incomes of two identifiable groups, e.g., racialized groups and other Canadians.

Individual discrimination: Refers to individual acts of discrimination stemming from personal prejudice and often based on stereotypes.

Institutional discrimination: Refers to acts of discrimination carried out by representatives of institutions in conformity with the policies and practices of the institutions.

Intersecting (multiple) oppressions: Experiences of multiple oppressions that some groups of racialized group members face. Among these oppressions are racism, sexism, and discrimination against people with disabilities and those with diverse sexual orientations.

Islamophobia: Islamophobia is a form of racism that involves expression of hostility toward those of the Muslim faith and people from what is referred to as the Islamic world. It has intensified in the late 20th century and early 21st century. Islamophobia manifests itself as intolerance and stereotypical views of Islam communicated through verbal/written abuse, as well as discrimination at schools and workplaces, psychological harassment/pressure, and outright violent attacks on mosques and individuals. Islam is seen as a monolithic bloc, static and unresponsive to change. Islam is seen as separate and "other." It does not have values in common with other cultures, is not affected by them, and does not influence them. Islam is seen as inferior to the West. It is seen as barbaric, irrational, primitive, and sexist. Islam is seen as violent, aggressive, threatening, supportive of terrorism, and engaged in a "clash of civilizations."

LICO (Low Income Cut Off): Statistics Canada's generally accepted poverty line.

Majority status: Refers to a dominant social category whose members wield the greatest degree of structural, economic, social, cultural, and political power in society.

Majority/minority relations: Refers to the inter-group power relations that generate and/or reinforce social, economic, cultural, and political inequalities. These relations are not necessarily predicated on disparities in numerical strength but reflect differential access to social, economic, and political power.

Marginalization: Refers to a long-term, structural process of systemic discrimination that creates a class of disadvantaged minorities. These groups become permanently confined to the margins of society; their status is continually reproduced because of the various dimensions of exclusion particularly in the labour market, but also from full and meaningful participation in society.

Median income: The income of the middle person when one arranges all income earners in a row. Half the earners earn more, and half earn less.

Minority status: Refers to a subordinate status or social category whose members have a lower degree of political, economic, and social power than do those of the majority status.

Multiculturalism: Refers to a doctrine and corresponding set of practices, as well as to a Canadian policy. Multiculturalism acknowledges, describes, and promotes the existence of diverse ethnic groups; it also manages relations between and among them without demanding assimilation into the dominant culture.

Multiple minority status: Refers to the existence of multiple experiences of minority status. The experience of gendered racism is an example.

Neo-racism (New racism): Refers to the shift in the basis for racial differentiation from a belief that inherent biological differences exist to the belief that cultural differences are fixed and immutable, thereby determining the ability and social behaviour of individuals who belong to certain groups. New racism is expressed in neutral language that disguises its negative intent with the use of such concepts as common sense, democracy, and even social justice.

Race: A socially constructed category used to classify humankind according to such physical characteristics as skin colour, hair texture, and facial features. Race is also used to differentiate groups based on common ancestry.

Racial profiling: Action by administration-of-justice officials that identifies an individual as potentially criminal based on his/her race, ethnicity, or national origin, rather than based on individual behaviour or on information incriminating him/her.

Racial segmentation: Refers to patterns of racial majority/minority relations often operating in the labour market. The majority closes access to occupational and sectoral opportunity, leading to concentrations of minority members in sectors and occupations that tend to be low-wage, low-mobility, highly insecure, and largely precarious.

Racialization: Process by which racial categories are constructed as different and unequal in ways that have social, economic, and political consequences.

Racialization of poverty: Refers to the emergence of structural features that pre-determine the disproportionate incidence of poverty among racialized group members.

Racialized group members: Persons other than Aboriginal peoples who are non-Caucasian in race or non-White in colour. The federal *Employment Equity Act* defines visible minorities as Chinese, South Asian, Black, Arab/West Asian, South East Asian, Filipino, Latin American, Japanese, Korean, and Pacific Islanders. The use of the term *racialized group members* here and elsewhere suggests a discomfort with the official use of the term *visible minority* because of the connotation of permanent minority status imposed on the population being described. "Racialized" denotes that process of imposition, the social construction of the category, and the attendant experience of oppression as opposed to the seemingly neutral use of the terms *visible minorities* or *racial minorities* which have the effect of masking the oppressions.

Racism: A system in which one group of people exercises power over another or others on the basis of socially constructed categories based on distinctions of physical attributes such as skin colour.

Social construction: Refers to the ideologically motivated creation of social categories that reproduce social, political, and economic inequalities as normal. The outcome is to generate social relevance for the classifications in a way that naturalizes differential treatment.

Social exclusion: Describes the structures and processes of inequality and unequal outcomes among groups in society. It is a process through which a group or groups are disempowered, degraded, or disenfranchised by oppressive, discriminatory practices or attitudes. Social exclusion arises from uneven access to the processes of production, wealth creation, and power. It is a form of alienation and denial of full citizenship experienced by particular groups of individuals and communities, and its characteristics occur in multiple dimensions. Social exclusion is also used to refer to the inability of certain groups or individuals to participate fully in Canadian life due to structural inequalities in access to social, economic, political, and cultural resources. This inability arises out of the often intersecting experiences of oppression relating to race, class, gender, disability, sexual orientation, and immigrant and refugee status.

Social inclusion: A public-policy approach aimed at reconciling segments of society that are excluded from full citizenship. In its current application, it seeks to change the excluded and integrate or re-integrate them into the existing structures of society.

Stereotype: Refers to a generalized, oversimplified characterization of a group based on preconceived notions or pre-judgments used to perpetuate unequal treatment and disadvantage.

Substantive equality: Requires that differences among social groups be acknowledged and accommodated in policies and laws to avoid adverse impacts on individual group members. This approach evaluates the fairness of apparently neutral laws, policies, and practices to ensure that their outcomes strengthen rather than undermine equality. The approach may sometimes require positive measures that involve different but equivalent treatment.

Systemic discrimination: Refers to unequal treatment based on system-wide policies and practices. System-wide policies and practices have unintended consequences of discriminatory effects on disadvantaged groups and reproduce structures of discrimination and marginalization.

Systemic racism: In the Canadian context, refers to social processes that tolerate, reproduce, and perpetuate judgments about racial categories that produce racial inequality in access to life opportunities and treatment. In discussing the impact of such forms of discrimination, the Supreme Court has established the standard for unequal treatment as based on impact on the victim, not on the motive or intent of the perpetrator.

Vertical mosaic: Refers to Canada's system of ethnic classification as defined by John Porter. He described Canadian society as structured by social, economic, and political hierarchies along ethnic lines. The following are his three broad social categories from top to bottom: the charter group including the English and French as founding peoples; other European immigrants, especially from Eastern and Southern Europe; and finally Aboriginal peoples.

Bibliography

Abbott, C., and C. Beach. "Immigrant Earnings Differentials and Birth-Year Effects of Men in Canada: Post-War–1972." *Canadian Journal of Economics* (August 26, 1993): 505–524.

Abella, R. *Equality Now: Report of the Commission on Equality in Employment*. Ottawa: Supply and Services Canada, 1984.

Across Boundaries. *Healing Journey: Mental Health of People of Colour Project*. Toronto: Across Boundaries, 1999.

Adachi, K. *The Enemy That Never Was: A History of the Japanese-Canadians*. Toronto: McClelland and Stewart, 1976.

Adams, D. *Health Issues of Women of Colour: A Cultural Diversity Perspective*. Thousand Oaks, London: Sage Books, 1995.

Agnew, V. *Gender, Migration and Citizenship Resources Project: Part II: A Literature Review and Bibliography on Health*. Toronto: Centre for Feminist Research, York University, 2002.

Agocs, C., and C. Burr. "Employment Equity, Affirmative Action and Managing Diversity: Assessing the Differences." *International Journal of Manpower* 17 (1991): 4–5.

Akbari, A. "The Benefits of Immigrants to Canada: Evidence on Tax and Public Services." *Canadian Public Policy* 15, no. 4 (Dec 1989): 424–35.

Akbari, A. *The Economics of Immigration and Racial Discrimination: A Literature Survey (1970–1989)*. Ottawa: Multiculturalism and Citizenship Canada, 1992.

Akbari, A. "Immigrant 'Quality' in Canada: More Direct Evidence of Human Capital Content, 1956–1994." *International Migration Review* 33, no. 1 (Spring 1999): 156–175.

Akbari, A., and D. DeVoretz. "The Substitutability of Foreign-Born Labour in Canadian Production: circa 1980." *Canadian Journal of Economics* 25 (1992): 604–614.

Alboim, N., R. Finnie, and M. Skuterud. *Immigrants' Skills in the Canadian Labour Market: Empirical Evidence and Policy Issues*. Mimeo 2003.

Alliance for Employment Equity. "Charter Challenge — The Case for Equity." Toronto. Spring, 1998).

Alliance for South Asian AIDS Prevention (ASAP). *Discrimination and HIV/AIDS in South Asian Communities: Legal, Ethical and Human Rights Challenges: An Ethnocultural Perspective*. Toronto: ASAP/Health Canada, 1999.

Anderson, J.M. "Gender, Race, Poverty, Health and Discourses of Health Reform in the Context of Globalization: A Post-Colonial Feminist Perspective in Policy Research." *Nursing Inquiry* 7, no. 4 (2000): 220–229.

Anderson, J., C. Blue, A. Holbrook, and M. Ng. "On Chronic Illness: Immigrant Women in Canada's Workforce — A Feminist Perspective." *Canadian Journal of Nursing Research* 25, no. 2 (1993): 7–22.

Anderson, J., and R. Kirkham. "Constructing Nation: The Gendering and Racializing of the Canada Health Care System." In *Painting the Maple: Essays on Race, Gender, and the*

Construction of Canada, edited by Veronica Strong-Boag, Sherill Grace, et al. Vancouver: UBC Press, 1998.

Anderson, J., and M. Lynam. "The Meaning of Work for Immigrant Women in the Lower Echelons of the Canadian Labour Force." *Canadian Ethnic Studies* 19, no. 2 (1987): 67–90.

Anderson, J. Migration and Health: Perspectives on Immigrant Women. *Sociology of Health and Illness*, 94, no. 4 (1987): 410–438.

Anderson, J. "Health Care in a Multicultural Society: Future Directions." Manitoba Council for Multicultural Health Conference, *Building Bridges to Improve Access to Health Care. Conference Proceedings Newsletter* 2, no. 1 (1991): 7–16.

Anderson, J. "Notes on Visible Minorities and the Income Gap." Unpublished paper. Toronto: Centre for Social Justice, 2000.

Anisef, P., R. Sweet, and G. Frempong. *Labour Market Outcomes of Immmigrant and Racial Minority University Graduates in Canada.* Ceris Working Paper No. 23. Toronto: Ceris, March 2003.

Arrow, K. "Models of Job Discrimination." In *Racial Discrimination in Economic Life*, edited by Anthony Pascal, 187–203. Lexington: D.C. Heath, 1972.

Arrow, K. "What Has Economics to Say about Racial Discrimination?" *Journal of Economic Perspectives* 12, no. 2 (Spring 1998): 91–100.

Aylward, C. *Canadian Critical Race Theory: Racism and the Law.* Halifax: Fernwood Publishing, 1999.

Badets, J., and L. Howatson-Leo. "Recent Immigrants in the Workforce." *Canadian Social Trends* 52 (Spring 1999): 16–22.

Bakan, A., and A. Kobayashi. *Employment Equity Policy in Canada: An Interprovincial Comparison.* Ottawa: Status of Women Canada, 2000.

Baker, M. and D. Benjamin. "Labour Market Outcomes and the Participation of Immigrant Women in Canadian Transfer Programs." In *Diminishing Returns: The Economics of Canada's Recent Immigration Policy*, Policy Study 24 (Toronto: C.D. Howe Institute, 1995). 209–42.

Baker, M., and D. Benjamin. "The Performance of Immigrants in the Canadian Labour Market." *Journal of Labour Economics* 12 (1994): 369–405.

Balakrishnan, T., and K. Selvanathan. "Ethnic Residential Segregation in Metropolitan Canada." In *Ethnic Demography*, edited by S. Hilli, F. Trovato, and L. Driedger. Ottawa: Carleton University Press, 1990. 393–413.

Balibar, E. "Is There a Neo-Racism?" In *Race, Nation, Class: Ambiguous Identities*, edited by E. Balibar and I. Wallerstein. London: Verso, 1991.

Bannerji, H. "But Who Speaks for Us? Experience and Agency." In *Unsettling Relations: The University as a Site of Struggle,* edited by H. Bannerji, L. Carty, S. Heald, and K. Himmanji. Toronto: Women's Press, 1991.

Banton, M. *Racial Theories.* London: Cambridge University Press, 1987.

Basavarajappa, K., and R. Verma. "Asian Immigrants in Canada: Some Findings from the 1981 Census." *International Migration* 23, no. 1 (1985): 97–121.

Basran, G.S., and L. Zong. "Devaluation of Foreign Credentials as Perceived by Visible Minority Professional Immigrants." *Canadian Ethnic Studies* 30, no. 3 (1998): 7–23.

BC Internationally Trained Professionals Network. *Internationally Trained Professionals in BC: An Environmental Scan.* Prepared by CB Mercer and Associates (2002).

Beach, C., and C. Worswick. "Is there a Double-Negative Effect on the Earnings of Immigrant Women?" *Canadian Public Policy* 19, no. 1 (1993): 36–53.

Becker, G. *The Economics of Discrimination.* Chicago: University of Chicago Press, 1957.

Beiser, M. *After the Door Has Been Opened: Mental Health Issues Affecting immigrants and Refugees in Canada. Report of the Canadian Taskforce on Mental Health Issues Affecting Immigrants and Refugees.* Ottawa: Health and Welfare Canada, 1998.

Beiser, M., K. Gill, and G. Edwards, "Mental Health Care in Canada: Is It Accessible and Equal?" *Canada's Mental Health* (Summer 1993): 2–7.

Billingsley, B., and L. Musynski. *No Discrimination Here.* Toronto: Social Planning Council of Metropolitan Toronto and Urban Alliance on Race Relations, 1985.

Black Learners Advisory Committee (BLAC). *Report on Education: Redressing Inequality – Empowering Black Learners.* Halifax: Black Learners Advisory Committee, 1994.

Bloom, D., G. Grenier, and M. Gunderson. "The Changing Labour Market Position of Canadian Immigrants." *Canadian Journal of Economics* 28 (1995): 987–1005.

Bloom, M., and M. Grant. *Brain Gain: The Economic Benefits of Recognizing Learning Credentials in Canada.* Ottawa: Conference Board of Canada, 2001.

Bolaria, B., and R. Bolaria. "Immigrant Status and Health Status: Women and Racial Minority Immigrant Workers." *Racial Minorities, Medicine and Health*, edited by B.S. Bolaria and R. Bolaria, 149-168. Halifax: Fernwood Press, 1994.

Bolaria, B.S., and P. Li. *Racial Oppression in Canada.* Toronto: Garamond Press, 1985.

Bonacich, E. "Advanced Capitalism and Black/White Relations in the United States: A Split Labour Market Interpretation." *American Sociological Review* 41 (1976): 34–51.

Borjas, G.J. "Assimilation, Changes in Cohort Quality, and the Earnings of Immigrants." *Journal of Labour Economics* 3, no. 4 (Oct 1985): 463-489.

Borjas, G.J. "The Economics of Immigration." *Journal of Economic Literature*, 32 (December 1994): 1667-717.

Boyd, M. "At a Disadvantage: The Occupational Attainment of Foreign-Born Women in Canada." *International Migration Review* 18 (1984): 1091–1119.

Boyd, M. "Gender, Visible Minority and Immigrant Earnings Inequality: Reassessing and Employment Equity Premise." In *Deconstructing a Nation: Immigration, Multiculturalism and Racism in the 1990s Canada*, edited by V. Satzewich, 229–321. Toronto: Garamond Press, 1992.

Bramble, M. "Black Education: Past, Present, and Future." In T. Goldstein & D. Selby (Eds.). *Weaving Connections: Education for Peace, Environmental and Social Justice.* Toronto: Second Story Press, 2000.

Brand, D. "Black Women and Work: The Impact of Racially Constructed Gender Roles on the Sexual Division of Labour." *Fireweed* 25 (1987).

Broad, D. *Hollow Work, Hollow Society? Globalization and the Casual Labour Problem in Canada.* Halifax: Fernwood, 2000.

Brouwer, A. *Immigrants Need Not Apply.* Ottawa: Caledon Institute of Social Policy, 1999.

Brym, R.J. and B. Fox. *From Culture to Power: The Sociology of English Canada.* Toronto: Oxford University Press, 1989.

Byrne, D. *Social Exclusion.* Buckingham: Open University Press, 1999.

Calliste, A. "Sleeping Car Porters in Canada: An Ethnically Submerged Split Labour Market." *Canadian Ethnic Studies* 19, no. 1 (1987): 1-20.

Calliste, A. "Canada's Immigration Policy and Domestics from the Caribbean: The Second Domestic Scheme." In *Race, Class, Gender: Bonds and Barriers*, edited by J. Vorst et al., 136–168. Toronto: Garamond Press/Society of Socialist Studies, 1991.

Calliste, A., and G. Sefa Dei. "Anti-racist Feminism: Critical Race and Gender Studies." In *Anti-Racist Feminism*, edited by A. Calliste and G. Sefa Dei, 11–18. Halifax: Fernwood Publishing, 2000.

Canadian Human Rights Commission. *Employment Equity Annual Reports 1996–1999*. Ottawa: Supply and Services Canada.

Canadian Institute of Health Research. *Charting the Course: Canadian Population Health Initiative – A Pan-Canadian Consultation on Population and Public Health Priorities*. Ottawa: Canadian Institute for Health Research, 2002.

Canadian Islamic Congress. *Anti-Islam in the Media: A Six-Month Study of the Six Top Canadian Newspapers*. http://www.cicnow.com/docs/media-report/1999/anti-islam.html

Carty, L. "Black Women in Academia: A Statement from the Periphery." In *Unsettling Relations: The University as a Site of Struggle*, edited by H. Bannerji, L. Carty, S. Heald, and K. Himmanji, 13–44. Toronto: Women's Press, 1991.

Chard, J., J. Badets, and L. Howatson-Leo. "Immigrant Women," *Women in Canada, 2000: A Gender-Based Statistical Report*. Ottawa: Statistic Canada, 2000.

Chen, J., R. Wilkins, and E. Ng. "Life Expectancy of Canada's Immigrants from 1986 to 1991." *Health Report* 8, no. 3 (1996): 29–38.

Chiswick, Barry R. "The Effect of Americanization on the Earnings of Foreign-Born Men," *Journal of Political Economy* 86 (1978): 897-922.

Chiswick, B., and P. Miller. "Earnings in Canada: The Roles of Immigrant Generation, French Ethnicity and language." *Research in Population Economics* 6 (1988): 183–228.

Christofides, L., and R. Swindinsky. "Wage Determination by Gender and Visible Minority Status: Evidence from the 1989 LMAS." *Canadian Public Policy* 20, 1 (1994): 34–51.

Citizenship and Immigration Canada. *Skilled Worker Immigrants: Towards a New Model of Selection*. Ottawa: Economic Policy and Programs Branch, 1998.

Citizenship and Immigration Canada. *The Economic Performance of Immigrants: Education Perspective, Strategic Policy, Planning and Research*. Ottawa: Government of Canada, 2000.

Citizenship and Immigration Canada. *The Economic Performance of Immigrants: Immigration Category Perspective, 1998*. Ottawa: CIC Strategic Policy and Planning Research Branch, 2000.

Citizenship and Immigration Canada. *Facts and Figures 2000*. Ottawa: CIC, 2001.

Citizenship and Immigration Canada. *Facts and Figures 2001*. Ottawa: CIC, 2002.

Citizenship and Immigration Canada. *Facts and Figures 2002*. Ottawa: CIC, 2003.

Collacott, M. *Canada's Immigration Policy: The Need for Major Reform*. Vancouver: Fraser Institute, 2002.

Committee to Stop Targeted Policing. *Who's the Target? An Evaluation of Community Action Policing*. Toronto, 1 Aug 2000. www.tdrc.net/ReportList.htm 13 Oct 2005.

Conference Board of Canada. *Making a Visible Difference: The Contributions of Visible Minorities to Canadian Economic Growth*. Ottawa: Economic Performance and Trends, April 2004.

Creese, G. "Organizing against Racism in the Workplace: Chinese Workers in Vancouver before World War II." In *Racism in Canada*, edited by O. McKague, 33–44. Saskatoon: Fifth House, 1991.

Creese, G. *Contracting Masculinity: Gender, Class, and Race in a White-Collar Union, 1944-1994*. Toronto: Oxford University Press Canada, 1999.

Cummings, P., et al. *Access! Report of the Taskforce on Access to Trades and Professions*. Toronto: Ontario Ministry of Citizenship, 1989.

Daenzer, P. *Regulating Class Privilege: Immigrant Servants in Canada, 1940–1990s.* Toronto: Canadian Scholars' Press, 1993.

Darroch, G.A. "Another Look at Ethnicity, Stratification and Social Mobility in Canada." *Canadian Journal of Sociology* 4 (1979): 1-25.

Das Gupta, T. "Political Economy of Gender, Race, and Class: Looking at South Asian immigrant Women in Canada." *Canadian Ethnic Studies* 26, no. 1 (1994): 59–73.

Das Gupta, T. *Racism and Paid Work.* Toronto: Garamond Press, 1996.

Das Gupta, T. "Anti-Black Racism in Nursing in Ontario." *Studies in Political Economy* 51 (Fall 1996): 97-116.

Dei, G. *Drop Out or Push Out? The Dynamics of Black Students' Disengagement from School.* Report to the Ontario Ministry of Education. Toronto: Ontario Ministry of Education, 1995.

Dei, G. *Anti-Racism Education: Theory and Practice.* Halifax: Fernwood, 1996.

de Silva, A. *Earnings of Immigrants: A Comparative Analysis.* Ottawa: Economic Council of Canada, 1992.

de Silva, A. *Wage Discrimination against Visible Minorities Men in Canada.* Ottawa: Human Development Canada, 1997.

DeVoretz, D., and S. Fagnan. "Some Evidence on Canadian Immigrant Quality Decline: Foreign Born Versus Resident Born Earnings Functions for 1971–1986." Presented at Canadian Economics Association Meetings, Victoria, BC, 1990.

DeVoretz, D. *International Metropolis Seminar on Barriers to Employment. Some Conclusions.* Vancouver: RIIM, 1998.

DeVoretz, D.J. (ed.). *Diminishing Returns: The Economics of Canada's Recent Immigration Policy.* Toronto: C.D. Howe Institute, 1995.

de Wolff, A. *Breaking the Myth of Flexible Work: Contingent Work in Toronto.* Toronto: Contingent Worker's Project, 2000.

de Wolff, A. "Guide to Fair Employment Contracts." Informational Booklet. Toronto: Alliance on Contingent Employment, 2001.

Dibbs, R. and T. Leesti. *Survey of Labour and Income Dynamics: Visible Minorities and Aboriginal Peoples.* Ottawa: Statistics Canada, 1995.

Doeringer, P.B. and Piore, M.J. *Internal Labor Markets and Manpower Analysis.* Lexington, MA: Heath, 1971.

Dossa, P. *The Narrative Representation of Mental Health: Iranian Women in Canada.* Vancouver: RIIM, 1999.

Driedger, L. and J. Peters. "Identity and Social Distance: Towards Understanding Simmel's *The Stranger.*" *Canadian Review of Sociology and Anthropology* 14 no. 2 (May 1977): 158-173.

Dua, E. "The Hindu Woman's Question: Canadian National Building and the Social Constraints of Gender for South Asian Canadian Women." In Calliste, A. and S. Dei (2000): 55-72.

Dugger, W.M. "Against Inequality." *Journal of Economic Issues* 32 (1998): 287–304.

Dunn, J., and I. Dyck. "Social Determinants of Health in Canada's Immigrant Population: Results from the National Population Health Survey, #98-20. Vancouver: The Metropolis Project, 1998.

Eboe-Osuji, C. "Ferrel and Others v. Attorney General of Ontario, Factum." Toronto: Alliance for Employment Equity, 1996.

Economic Council of Canada. *Economic and Social Impacts of Immigration.* Ottawa: Supply and Services Canada, 1991.

Edwards, T. *Contested Terrain.* New York: Basic Books, 1979.

Elliot, J.L., and A. Fleras. "Immigration and the Canadian Ethnic Mosaic." In *Race and Ethnic Relations in Canada,* edited by P.S. Li. Toronto: Oxford University Press, 1990.

Essed, P. *Everyday Racism: Reports from Women of Two Cultures.* Claremont: Hunter House, 1990.

Evans, R.G., M.L. Barer, and T.R. Marmor, eds. *Why Are Some People Healthy and Others Not?: The Determinants of Health of Populations.* New York: Aldine DeGruyter, 1994.

Fellegi, I. "'Brain Drain' — What We Know and What We Don't." Presentation to a Joint Seminar of the Toronto Association for Business and Economics and the C.D. Howe Institute, Toronto, September 23, 1999.

Feng, H. and T.R. Balakrishnan. "The Integration of Visible Minorities in Contemporary Canadian Society." *Canadian Journal of Sociology* 21 (1996): 307-326.

Fernando, T., and K. Prasad. *Multiculturalism and Employment Equity: Problems Facing Foreign-Trained Professionals and Trades People in British Columbia.* Vancouver: Affiliation of Multicultural Societies and Services of British Columbia, 1986.

Fleras, A., and J.L. Kunz. *Media and Minorities: Representing Diversity in a Multicultural Canada.* Toronto: Thompson Educational Publishing, 2001.

Fong, E. "A Systemic Approach to Racial Residential Patterns." *Social Science Research* 26 (1997): 465-486.

Fong, E. and M. Gulia. "The Attainment of Neighborhood Qualities Among British, Chinese, and Black Immigrants in Toronto and Vancouver." *Research in Community Sociology* 6 (1996): 123-45.

Fong, E., and K. Shibuya. "The Spatial Separation of the Poor in Canadian Cities." *Demography* 37, no. 4 (November 2000): 449–459.

Fong, E. "Spatial Separation of the Poor in Canadian Cities." *Demography* 37, no. 4 (2000): 449-459.

Fox, B. and P. Sugiman. "Flexible Work, Flexible Workers: The Restructuring of Clerical Work in a Large Telecommunications Company." *Studies in Political Economy* 60 (Autumn 1999): 59-84.

Frank, J. "Why Population Health?" *Canadian Journal of Public Health* (May-June 1995): 162-164.

Frenette, M., and R. Morissette. *Will They Ever Converge? Earnings of Immigrants and Canadian-Born Workers over the Last Two Decades.* Analytical Studies Paper No. 215. Ottawa: Statistics Canada, 2003.

Galabuzi, G. *Canada's Creeping Economic Apartheid: The Economic Segregation and Social Marginalization of Racialized Groups.* Toronto: CJS Foundation for Research and Education, 2001.

Galabuzi, G. "Racializing the Division of Labour: Neo-liberal Restructuring and the Economic Segregation of Canada's Racialized Groups." In *Challenging the Market: The Struggle to Regulate Work and Income,* edited by J. Stanford and L. Vosko, 175–204. Montreal/Kingston: McGill-Queen's University Press, 2004a.

Galabuzi, G. "Social Exclusion." In *Social Determinants of Health: Canadian Perspectives,* 235–251. Toronto: Canadian Scholars' Press Inc, 2004b.

Galabuzi, G. "We Need to Build Hope in Black Communities." *Toronto Star* (August 26, 2001): A23.

Gittens, M., and D. Cole. *Racism Behind Bars: The Treatment of Black and Racial Minority Prisoners in Ontario Prisons.* Toronto: Queen's Printer, 1994.

Gittens, M., and D. Cole. *Report of the Ontario Commission on Systemic Racism in the Criminal Justice System.* Toronto: Queen's Printer, 1995.

Globerman, S. *Immigration and Health Care Utilization Patterns in Canada.* Vancouver: Research on Immigration and Integration in the Metropolis, 1998.

Goldfarb, M. *Tapping into a Growing Readership: Visible Minorities Research Project. A Research Report for Canadian Daily Newspaper Association.* Toronto: Canadian Daily Newspaper Association, 1995.

Gosine, K. "Revisiting the Notion of a 'Recast' Vertical Mosaic in Canada: Does a Post Secondary Education Make a Difference?" *Canadian Ethnic Studies* 32, no. 3 (2000): 89-104.

Grant, H., and R. Oertel. "Diminishing Returns to Immigration? Interpreting the Economic Experience of Canadian Immigrants." *Canadian Ethnic Studies* 30, no. 3 (1998): 57–76.

Government of Alberta. *Report of the Taskforce on the Criminal Justice System and Its Impact on the Indian and Metis People of Alberta.* Edmonton: Province of Alberta, 1991.

Government of Canada. *White Paper on Immigration: Canadian Immigration Policy.* Ottawa: Department of Manpower and Immigration, 1966.

Government of Canada. *Report of the Taskforce on the Participation of Visible Minorities in the Federal Public Service, 2000: Embracing Change in the Federal Public Service.* Ottawa: Supply and Services Canada, 2000.

Government of Manitoba. *Public Inquiry into the Administration of Justice and Aboriginal People, Report of the Aboriginal Justice Inquiry of Manitoba.* Winnipeg: Province of Manitoba, 1991.

Government of Nova Scotia. *Report of the Royal Commission on the Donald Marshall Jr. Prosecution.* Halifax: Province of Nova Scotia, 1989.

Green, A. and D. Green. "Canadian Immigration Policy: The Effectiveness of the Point System and Other Instruments." *Journal of Economics* 28 (1995): 1006–1041.

Guildford, J. *Making the Case for Economic and Social Inclusion.* Ottawa: Health Canada, 2000.

Harvey, E.B. and B. Siu."Immigrants' Socioeconomic Situation Compared, 1991–1996." Ottawa: *INSCAN* 15, no. 2 (Fall 2001).

Harvey, E.B., B. Siu, and K. Reil. "Ethnocultural Groups, Periods of Immigration and Social Economic Situation." *Canadian Ethnic Studies* 30, no. 3 (1999): 95–103.

Hayes, M.V. and J.R. Dunn. *Population Health in Canada: A Systematic Review.* Ottawa: Canadian Policy Research Networks (CPRN), Health Network Report H-01, 1998.

Health Canada. *Metropolis Health Domain Seminar, Final Report.* Ottawa: Supply and Services Canada, 1998.

Helly, D. "An Injunction: Belong, Participate. The Return of Social Cohesion and the Good Citizen." *Lien Social et Politiques – RIAC* 41, no. 81 (Spring 1998): 35-46.

Henry, F. "Two Studies of Racial Discrimination in Employment" in James Curtis, Edward G. Grabb, and Neil Guppy (eds) (3rd. ed.), *Social Inequality in Canada: Patterns, Problems, and Policies,* Toronto, ON: Prentice-Hall, 1999: 226-235.

Henry, F., and E. Ginsberg. *Who Gets the Job: A Test of Racial Discrimination in Employment.* Toronto: Urban Alliance on Race Relations/Social Planning Council of Metro Toronto, 1985.

Henry, F., and C. Tator. *Racist Discourses in Canada's English Print Media.* Toronto: Canadian Race Relations Foundation, 2000a.

Henry, F., and C. Tator. "The Theory and Practice of Democratic Racism in Canada." In *Perspectives on Ethnicity in Canada*, edited by M.A. Kalbach and W.E. Kalbach, 285–302. Toronto: Harcourt Canada, 2000b.

Henry, F., C. Tator, W. Mattis, and T. Rees. *The Colour of Democracy: Racism in Canadian Society*. Toronto: Harcourt Brace, 2000.

Herberg, E. "The Ethno-racial Socio-Economic Hierarchy in Canada: Theory and Analysis of the New Vertical Mosaic." *International Journal of Comparative Sociology* 31, no. 3–4 (1990): 206–221.

Hickman, T. A. *Royal Commission on the Donald Marshall, Jr. Prosecution: Commissioners' Report: Findings and Recommendations*. Halifax, N.S.: The Commission, 1989.

Hiebert, D. "The Colour of Work: Labour Market Segregation in Montreal, Toronto and Vancouver, 1991." Working Paper No. 97-02. Burnaby: Simon Fraser University, Centre of Excellence, Research on Immigration and Integration in the Metropolis, 1997.

Hou, F. *Recent Immigrants and the Formation of Visible Minority Neighbourhoods in Canada's Large Cities*. Research Paper Series. Catalogue no. 11f0019MIE2004221. Ottawa: Statistics Canada, 2004.

Hou, F., and T. Balakrishnan. "The Integration of Visible Minorities in Contemporary Canadian Society." *Canadian Journal of Sociology* 21, no. 3 (1996): 307–326.

Hou, F. and J. Myles. *Neighbourhood Attainment and Residential Segregation among Toronto's Visible Minorities*. Ottawa: Statistics Canada, 2003.

Hou, F. and G. Picot. "Visible-Minority Neighbourhood Enclaves and Labour Market Outcomes of Immigrants." *Analytical Studies Branch Research Paper Series*. Ottawa: Statistics Canada, 2003.

House of Commons. *Equality Now! Report of the Special Committee on the Participation of Visible Minorities in Canadian Society*. Ottawa: Government of Canada, 1984.

Hulchanski, J.D. *Barriers to Equal Access in the Housing Market: The Role of Discrimination on the Basis of Race and Gender*. Centre for Urban and Community Studies, University of Toronto, November 1993.

Hum, D., and W. Simpson. *Wage Opportunities for Visible Minorities in Canada*. Ottawa: Statistics Canada, 1998.

Human Resources and Skills Development Canada. *Knowledge Matters: Canada's Innovation Strategy* (February, 2002). www.hrdc.gc.ca/stratpol/sl-ca/doc/summary.shtml

Human Resources Development Canada. "Recent Immigrants Have Experienced Unusual Economic Difficulties." *Applied Research Bulletin* 7, no. 1 (Winter/Spring, 2001). Ottawa: HRDC, 2001.

Human Resources Development Canada. *Knowledge Matters: Skills and Learning for Canadians – Canada's Innovation Strategy*. Ottawa: HRDC, 2002. http://www.hrdc-drhc.gc.ca/sp-ps/sl-ca/doc/summary.shtml

Hutchinson, J. "Urban Policy and Social Exclusion." In *Policy Responses to Social Exclusion: towards Inclusion?* edited by J.Percy-Smith, 164–183. Buckingham: Open University Press, 2000.

Hyman, I. *Immigration and Health*. Health Canada Working Paper No. 01-05 (September 2001). Ottawa: Queen's Printer, 2001.

Isajiw, W. *Understanding Diversity: Ethnicity and Race in the Canadian Context*. Toronto: Thompson, 1999.

Islamic Social Services and Resource Association (ISSRA). *Living on the Ragged Edges: Absolute and Hidden Homelessness among Latin Americans and Muslims in West Central Toronto*. Toronto: CERIS, 2003.

Jackson, A. "Poverty and Immigration." *Perception* 24, no. 4 (Spring 2001).

Jackson, A. *Is Work Working for Workers of Colour?* Ottawa: Canadian Labour Congress, 2002.

Jain, H. *Anti-Discrimination Staffing Policies: Implications of Human Rights Legislation for Employers and Trade Unions*. Ottawa: Secretary of State, 1985.

Jain, H. *Employment Discrimination against Visible Minorities and Employment Equity*. Hamilton: McMaster University, 1988.

James, C. "Distorted Images of African Canadians: Impacts, Implications and Responses." In *Globalization and Survival in the Black Diaspora*, edited by C. Green. Albany: State University of New York Press, 1997.

James, C.E. *Talking about Difference: Encounters in Culture, Language and Identity*. Toronto: Between the Lines, 1994.

James, C. *Seeing Ourselves: Exploring Race, Ethnicity and Culture*. Toronto: Thompson Educational Publishing, 1999.

Jenson, J. "Citizenship: Its Relationship to the Canadian Diversity Model." Canadian Policy Research Networks (CPRN), 2002. www.cprn.org

Jenson, J., and M. Papillon. "The Changing Boundaries of Citizenship. A Review and a Research Agenda." Canadian Policy Research Networks (CPRN), 2001. www.cprn.org

Kallen, E. *Ethnicity and Human Rights in Canada*. Toronto: Oxford University Press, 2003.

Kawachi, I.R., and B. Kennedy. *The Health of Nations: Why Inequality is Harmful to Your Health*. New York: The New Press, 2002.

Kawachi, I., R. Wilkinson, and B. Kennedy. "Introduction." In *The Society and Population Health Reader. Volume I: Income Inequality and Health*, edited by I. Kawachi, B. Kennedy, and R. Wilkinson. New York: The New Press, 1999.

Kazemipur, A., and S. Halli. "Plight of Immigrants: The Spatial Concentration of Poverty in Canada." *Canadian Journal of Regional Sciences Special Issue* 20, nos. 1, 2 (Spring–Summer, 1997): 11–28.

Kazemipur, A., and S. Halli. *The New Poverty in Canada*. Toronto: Thompson Educational Publishing, 2000.

Kilbride, K.M., P. Anisef, E. Baichman-Anisef, and R. Khattar. *Between Two Worlds: The Experiences and Concerns of Immigrant Youth in Ontario*. Toronto: CERIS and CIC-OASIS, 2000. www.settlement.org

King, W.L. Mackenzie. C.M.G. *On the Need for the Suppression of the Opium Traffic in Canada*. Microfiche. Ottawa: S. E. Dawson, 1908.

Krahn, H., et al. "Educated and Underemployed: Refugee Integration into the Canadian Labour Market." *Journal of International Migration and Integration* 1, no. 1 (Winter 2000): 59-84.

Kunz, J.L., A. Milan, and S. Schetagne. *Unequal Access: A Canadian Profile of Racial Differences in Education, Employment, and Income*. Toronto: Canadian Race Relations Foundation, 2001.

Kymlicka, W., and W. Norman. "Return of the Citizen: A Survey of Recent Work on Citizenship Theory." In *Theorizing Citizenship*, edited by Ronald Beiner, 283-322. Albany: State University of New York Press, 1995.

Labonte, R. "Social Inclusion/Exclusion and Health: Dancing the Dialectic." In *Social Determinants of Health: Canadian Perspectives*, edited by D. Rapheal, 253-266. Toronto: Canadian Scholars' Press Inc., 2004.

Lautard, H. and N. Guppy. "The Vertical Mosaic Revisited — Occupational Differentials among Canadian ethnic groups." In P. Li, *Race and Ethnic Relations in Canada*, Toronto: Oxford University Press, 1990. 189-208.

Lee, K. *Urban Poverty in Canada: A Statistical Profile*. Ottawa: Canadian Council on Social Development, 2000.

Lee, Y. "Social Cohesion in Canada: The Role of the Immigrant Service Sector." *OCASI Newsletter* 73 (Summer/Autumn, 1999).

Lewis, C. *The Report of the Race Relations and Policing Task Force*. Toronto: The Task Force, 1989.

Lewis, S. *Report on Racism: Letter to the Ontario Premier*. Toronto: Queens Printer, 1992.

Ley, D. and H. Smith. "Immigration and Poverty in Canadian Cities, 1971-1991." *Canadian Journal of Regional Science* 20, no. 1-2 (Spring-Summer 1997): 29-48.

Li, Peter S. "A Historical Approach to Ethnic Stratification: The Case of the Chinese in Canada, 1858-1930." *Canadian Review of Sociology and Anthropology* 16, no. 3 (Aug 1979): 320-332.

Li, P. *Ethnic Inequality in a Class Society*. Toronto: Wall and Thompson, 1988.

Li, P. "Unneighbourly Houses or Unwelcome Chinese: The Social Construction of Race in the Battle over 'Monster' Homes in Vancouver." *International Journal of Race and Ethnic Studies* 1–2 (1994): 47–66.

Li, Peter S. *The Chinese in Canada*. London: Oxford University Press, 1998.

Li, Peter S. "The Market Value and Social Value of Race," in *Racism and Social Inequality in Canada: Concepts, Controversies and Strategies of Resistance*, ed. V. Satzewich. Toronto: Thompson Educational Publishing, 1998.

Li, Peter S. "Race and Ethnicity." In *Race and Ethnic Relations in Canada*, edited by P. Li. London: Oxford University Press, 1999: 3-20.

Li, Peter S. "Earning Disparities Between Immigrants and Native-Born Canadians." *Canadian Review of Sociology and Anthropology* 37, no. 3 (August 2000): 288-311.

Li, P. "The Market Worth of Immigrants' Educational Credentials." *Canadian Public Policy* 27, no. 1 (2001): 23–38.

Li, P. *Destination Canada: Immigration Debates and Issues*. Toronto: Wall and Thompson, 2003.

Lian, J., and D. Matthews. "Does a Vertical Mosaic Really Exist? Ethnicity and Income in Canada, 1991." *Canadian Review of Sociology and Anthropology* 35, no. 4 (1998): 461–481.

Littlewood, P. *Social Exclusion in Europe: Problems and Paradigms*. Aldershot: Ashgate, 1999.

Lo, L. and S. Wang. "Economic Impacts of Immigrants in the Toronto CMA: A Tax-Benefit Analysis." *Journal of International Migration and Integration* 1, no. 3 (Summer 2000): 273-303.

Loomba, A. *Colonialism/Postcolonialism*. London: Routledge, 1998.

Lundahl, M., and E. Wadensjo. *Unequal Treatment: A Study in the Neo-classical Theory of Discrimination*. New York: New York University Press, 1984.

Lynch, J. "Income Inequality and Health: Expanding the Debate." *Social Science and Medicine* 51 *(2000): 1001–1005.*

Madanipour, A. "Social Exclusion and Space." In *Social Exclusion in European Cities*, edited by A. Madanipour, G. Cars, and J. Allen, 75–94. London: Jessica Kingley, 1998.

Madanipour, A., G. Cars and J. Allen [eds.] *Social Exclusion in European Cities*. London: Jessica Kingsley Publishers in conjunction with the Regional Studies Association, 1998.

Manitoba. *Report of the Aboriginal Justice Inquiry*. Aboriginal Justice Implementation Commission. Winnipeg, MB: The Inquiry, 1991.

Marmot, M. *Explaining Socioeconomic Differences in Sickness Absence: The Whitehall II Study.* Toronto: Canadian Institute for Advanced Research, 1993.

Marmot, M., and R. Wilkinson (eds.). *Social Determinants of Health..* Oxford: Oxford University Press, 1999.

Mata, F. "The Non-Accreditation of Immigrant Professionals in Canada: Societal Impacts, Barriers and Present Policy Initiatives." Paper presented at Sociology and Anthropology Meetings, University of Calgary, June 3, 1994.

Mata, F. "Intergenerational Transmission of Education and Socio-economic Status: A Look at Immigrants, Visible Minorities and Aboriginals." Ottawa: Statistics Canada 1997.

Maytree Foundation. *Brain Drain, Brain Gain. Session Proceedings.* Toronto: Maytree Foundation, May 25, 2000.

McDade, K. *Barriers to Recognition of Credentials of Immigrants in Canada.* Ottawa: Institute of Policy Research, 1988.

Miles, R. *Racism and Migrant Labour.* London: Routledge and Kegan Paul, 1982.

Miles, R. *Racism.* London: Routledge, 1989.

Miller, J. *Yesterday's News: Why Canada's Daily Newspapers Are Failing Us.* Halifax: Fernwood, 1998.

Murray, C.A. *In Pursuit of Happiness and Good Government.* New York: Simon and Schuster, 1988.

Murray, S. "Presentation to the Brain Drain, Brain Gain Session Proceedings." Maytree Foundation, Toronto, May 25, 2000.

Mwarigha, M.S. *Towards a Framework for Local Responsibility: Taking Action to End the Current Limbo in Immigrant Settlement.* Toronto: The Maytree Foundation, January 2002.

National Anti-racism Council of Canada. *Racial Discrimination in Canada: The Status of Compliance by the Canadian Government with the International Convention on the Elimination of All Forms of Racial Discrimination.* Toronto: NARC, 2002.

Ng, R. "Racism, Sexism and Canadian Nationalism." In R. Ng, *Race, Class and Gender: Bonds and Barriers.* Toronto: Between the Lines, 1988.

Ng, R. "Sexism and Racism in the University: Analysing a Personal Experience in the University." *Racism and Gender* 14, no. 2 (Spring 1994): 41–46.

Noh, S., M. Beiser, V. Kaspar, F. Hou, and J. Rummens. "Perceived Racial Discrimination, Discrimination, and Coping: A Study of South East Asian Refugees in Canada." *Journal of Health and Social Behaviour* 40 (1999): 193–207.

Omi, M., and H. Winant. "On the Theoretical Status of the Concept of Race." In *Race, Identity and Representation in Education,* edited by C. McCarthy and W. Crichlow. New York: Routledge, 1993.

Ontario. *Report of the Commission on Systemic Racism in the Ontario Criminal Justice System.* Toronto: Queen's Printer, 1995.

Ontario Advisory Council on Women's Issues. *Women and Mental Health in Ontario. Immigrant and Visible Minority Women.* Ottawa: Ministry of Health, 1990.

Ontario Ministry of Training, Colleges and Universities. *The Facts Are In: A Study of the Characteristics and Experiences of Immigrants Seeking Employment in Regulated Professions in Ontario.* Toronto: Queen's Printer, 2002.

Ontario Regulators for Access. "Proceedings from the Regulators Forum," Toronto, June 7, 2004.

Ornstein, M. *Ethno-racial Inequality in the City of Toronto: An Analysis of the 1996 Census.* Toronto: City of Toronto, 2000. http://ceris.metropolis.net

Palmer, D. "Determinants of Canadian Attitudes towards Immigration: More Than Just Racism?" *Canadian Journal of Behavioural Sciences* 28 (1996): 190-192.

Palmer, D. "Canadians' Attitudes Towards Immigration: November and December 1996, and February 1997 Surveys." Ottawa: Citizenship and Immigration Canada, 1997.

Parkin, F. *Marxism and Class Theory: A Bourgeois Critique.* New York: Columbia University Press, 1979.

Peel Region. *Report of the Peel Regional Taskforce on Homelessness.* Region of Peel. 2000. www.region.peel.on.ca/housing/homelessness

Pendakur, R. *The Changing Role of Post-War Immigrants in Canada's Labour Force: An Examination Across Four Census Periods.* PhD Thesis. Ottawa: National Library of Canada. 1995.

Pendakur, R. *Immigrants and the Labour Force: Policy, Regulation and Impact.* Montreal: McGill-Queen's University Press, 2000.

Pendakur, K., and R. Pendakur, "The Colour of Money: Earnings Differentials among Ethnic Groups in Canada." *Canadian Journal of Economics* 31, no. 3 (1998): 518–548.

Pendakur, R. and K. Pendakur. *Earnings Differentials Among Ethnic Groups in Canada.* Hull, PQ: Strategic Research and Analysis, Corporate and Intergovernmental Affairs, 1996.

Picot, G., and F. Hou. *The Rise in Low-Income Rates Among Immigrants in Canada.* Research Paper Series. Catalogue no. 11F0019MIE2003198. Ottawa: Statistics Canada, 2003.

Pitman, W. *Now is Not too Late.* Toronto: Task Force on Human Relations, November 1977.

Porter, J. *The Vertical Mosaic: An Analysis of Social Class and Power in Canada.* Toronto: University of Toronto Press, 1965.

Preston, V., and W. Giles. "Ethnicity, Gender and Labour Markets in Canada: A Case Study of Immigrant Women in Toronto." *Canadian Journal of Urban Research* 6 (1995): 15–159.

Preston, V., and G. Man. "Employment Experiences of Chinese Immigrant Women: An Exploration of Diversity." *Canadian Woman Studies/Cahiers de la femme* 19 (1999): 115–122.

Price Waterhouse. *Foreign Academic Credential Assessment Services Business Assessment.* Final Report. Toronto, 1998.

PROMPT. "In the Public Interest: Immigrant Access to Regulated Professions in Ontario." Toronto: PROMPT, July 2004.

Quinn, J. "Food Bank Clients Often Well-Educated Immigrants." *The Toronto Star* (March 31, 2002): A12.

Randall, V. R. "Racist Health Care: Reforming an Unjust Health Care System to Meet the Needs of African-Americans." *Health Matrix* 3 (1993).

Ranumgo, R. (ed.) *South Asians in the Canadian Mosaic.* Montreal: Kala Bharati, 1984.

Raphael, D. "Health Effects on Economic Inequality: Overview and Purpose." *Canadian Review of Social Policy* 44 (1999): 25–40.

Raphael, D. "From Increasing Poverty to Societal Disintegration: How Economic Inequality Affects the Health of Individuals and Communities." In *Unhealthy Times: The Political Economy of Health and Care in Canada,* edited by H. Armstrong, P. Armstrong, and D. Coburn, 223–246. Toronto: Oxford University Press, 2001.

Ray, B.K. and E. Moore. "Access to Homeownership among Immigrant Groups in Canada." *Canadian Review of Sociology and Anthropology* 28 (Feb 1991): 1-29.

Razack, S. *Looking White People in the Eye: Gender, Race and Culture in Courtrooms and Classrooms.* Toronto: University of Toronto Press, 1998.

Reitz, J.G. "Immigrant Skill Utilization in the Canadian Labour Market: Implications of Human Capital Research." *Journal of International Migration and Integration* 2, no. 3 (Summer, 2001): 347–378.

Reitz, J., L. Calzavara, and D. Dasko. *Ethnic Inequality and Segregation in Jobs.* Toronto: Centre for Urban and Community Studies, University of Toronto, 1981.

Reitz, J., and M. Sklar. "Culture, Race and the Economic Assimilation of Immigrants." *Sociological Forum* 12, no. 2 (1997): 233–277.

Reitz, J.G. "The Institutional Structure of Immigration as a Determinant of Inter-racial Competition: A Comparison of Britain and Canada." *International Migration Review* 22, (Spring 1988): 117-46.

Reitz, J.G. "Ethnic Concentrations in Labour Markets and Their Implications for Ethnic Inequality." In *Ethnic Edentity and Equality – Varieties of Experience in a Canadian City.* Ed. R. Breton. Toronto: University of Toronto Press, 1990: 135-195.

Reitz, J.G. *Warmth of the Welcome: The Social Causes of Economic Success for Immigrants in Different Nations and Cities.* Boulder, CO: Westview Press, 1998.

Reitz, J.G. *Immigrant Success in the Knowledge Economy: Insititutional Change and the Immigrant Experience in Canada, 1970-1995.* Toronto: Centre for Industrial Relations and Department of Sociology, University of Toronto, March 2000.

Reitz, J. and R. Breton. *The Illusion of Difference: Realities of Ethnicity in Canada and the United States.* Toronto: C. D. Howe Institute, 1994.

Richmond, A.H. *Aspects of the Absorption and Adaptation of Immigrants.* Ottawa: Manpower and Immigration, 1974.

Richmond, A.H. *Global Apartheid: Refugees, Rcism, and the New World Order.* Toronto: Oxford University Press, 1994.

Room, G. "Conclusions." In *Beyond the Threshold: The Measurement and Analysis of Social Exclusion,* edited by G. Room. Bristol: The Polity Press, 1995.

Saloojee, A. *Social Inclusion, Citizenship and Diversity: Moving Beyond the Limits of Multiculturalism.* Toronto: The Laidlaw Foundation, 2002.

Samuel, J. "Racial Equality in the Canadian Work Force: The Federal Scene." *Journal of Intergroup Relations* (Summer, 1991).

Sangster, D. *Assessing and Recognizing Foreign Credentials in Canada – Employers' Views.* Prepared for Citizenship and Immigration Canada and Human Resources Development Canada. Toronto: Canadian Labour and Business Centre, January 2001. www.clbc.ca/files/Reports/Fitting_In/Credentials_paper.pdf

Sassen, S. "Whose City Is It? Globalization and the Formation of New Claims." International Sociological Association (ISA) Conference paper, 1998.

Schecter, T. *Race, Class, Women and the State: The Case of Domestic Labour.* Montreal: Black Rose Books, 1998.

Schellenberg, G. *Immigrants in Canada's Census Metropolitan Areas.* Catalogue no. 89-613-MIE-No. 003. Ottawa: Statistics Canada, 2004.

Shadd, A. "Dual Labour Markets in 'Core' and 'Periphery' Regions of Canada: The Position of Black Males in Ontario and Nova Scotia." *Canadian Ethnic Studies* 19, 2 (1987).

Shaw, M., D. Dorling, and G.D. Smith. "Poverty, Social Exclusion, and Minorities." In *Social Determinants of Health,* edited by M. Marmot, and R. Wilkinson, 211–239. Oxford: Oxford University Press, 1999.

Shields, J. "No Safe Haven: Markets, Welfare and Migrants." Paper presented to the Canadian Sociology and Anthropology Association, Congress of the Social Sciences and Humanities, Toronto, June 1, 2002.

Siddiqui, H. "Immigrants Subsidize Us by $55 Billion Per Year." *The Toronto Star* (January 14, 2001).

Siemiatycki, M., and E. Isin. "Immigration, Ethno-racial Diversity and Urban Citizenship in Toronto," *Canadian Journal of Regional Sciences Special Issue* XX, no. 1, 2 (Spring—Summer, 1997): 73–102.

Smith, E. and A. Jackson. *Does a Rising Tide Lift All Boats? The Labour Market Experiences and Incomes of Recent Immigrants, 1995 to 1998*. Ottawa: CCSD, 2002.

Solomon, R.P. *Black Resistance in High School: Forging a Separatist Culture*. Albany: State University of New York Press, 1992.

Stasiulis, D. "Affirmative Action for Visible Minorities and the New Politics of Race in Canada." In *Canada 2000: Race Relations and Public Policy*, edited by O.P. Dwivedi et al. Guelph: University of Guelph, 1989.

Stasiulis, D., and R. Jhappan. "The Fractious Politics of a Settler Society: Canada." In *Unsettling Settler Societies*, edited by D. Stasiulis and N. Yuval-Davis, 55–131. London: Sage Publications, 1995.

Statistics Canada. "1996 Census: Education, Mobility and Migration." *The Daily*. (April 14, 1998).

Statistics Canada. "1996 Census: Ethnic Origin, Visible Minorities." *The Daily*. (February 17, 1998).

Statistics Canada. "1996 Census: Immigration and Citizenship." *The Daily*. (November 4, 1997).

Statistics Canada. "1996 Census: Sources of Income and Earnings." *The Daily* (February 17 1998).

Statistics Canada. *2001 Census Analysis Series. The Changing Profile of Canada's Labour Force*. Catalogue No. 96F0030XIE2001009, February 2003.

Statistics Canada. *Earnings of Canadians*. Ottawa: Statistics Canada, 2003.

Statistics Canada. "The Daily." *Longitudinal Survey of Immigrants to Canada, 2001* (September 4, 2003): L4.

Stoffman, Daniel. *Pounding at the Gates: A Study of Canada's Immigration System*. The Atkinson Charitable Foundation, 1992.

Stoffman, D. *Towards a More Realistic Immigration Policy for Canada*. Toronto: C.D. Howe Institute, 1993.

Stoffman, D. *Who Gets In : What's Wrong with Canada's Immigration Program, and How to Fix It*. Toronto : Macfarlane Walter and Ross, 2002.

SUCCESS. *Enhancing the Participation of Immigrants in British Columbia's Economy and Labour Market: A Chinese Canadian Workforce Strategy*. Prepared by Kerry Jothen, Human Capital Strategies, 2002.

Tandon, B. "Earnings Differentials among Native Born and Foreign Residents of Toronto." *International Migration Review* 12 (Fall 1978): 405–410.

Teelucksingh, C. and G. Galabuzi. "Working Precariously: The Impact of Race and Immigrants' Status on Employment Opportunities and Outcomes in Canada." *CRRF/CSJ* 2005.

Treasury Board Secretariat. *Employment Equity in the Public Service: Annual Reports 1996–2001*. Ottawa: Supply and Services Canada, various.

Ujimoto, K. "Racial Discrimination and Internment: Japanese in Canada." In *Racial Oppression in Canada*, edited by S. Bolaria and P. Li, 126–160. Toronto: Garamond Press, 1988.

Vosco, L. *Temporary Work: The Gendered Rise of a Precarious Employment Relationship*. Toronto: University of Toronto Press, 2000.

Walker, J. *The History of Blacks in Canada*. Ottawa: Minister of State for Multiculturalism, 1980.

Wanner, R. "Prejudice, Profit or Productivity: Explaining Returns to Human Capital among Male Immigrants in Canada." *Canadian Ethnic Studies* 30, no. 3 (1998): 25–55.

Weber, Max. *Economy and Society: An Outline of Interpretive Sociology* (1922). New York: Bedminster Press, 1968.

White, P. "Ideologies, Social Exclusion and Spatial Segregation in Paris." In *Urban Segregation and the Welfare State: Inequality and Exclusion in Western Cities*, ed. S. Musterd and W. Ostendorf, London: Routledge, 1998: 148-67.

Wilkinson, R. *Unhealthy Societies: The Afflictions of Inequality*. New York: Routledge, 1996.

Wilkinson, R., and M. Marmot. *Social Determinants of Health: The Solid Facts*. Copenhagen: World Health Organization, 1998. www.who.dk/healthy-cities

Wilson, W.J. *The Truly Disadvantaged. Inner City, the Underclass and Public Policy*. Chicago: University of Chicago Press, 1987.

Winant, H. *Racial Conditions*. Minneapolis: University of Minnesota Press, 1994.

Winks, R. *Blacks in Canada*. New Haven: Yale University Press, 1971.

Worswick, C. *Immigrants Declining Earnings: Reasons and Remedies*. Toronto: C.D. Howe Institute, 2004.

Wright, R.E. and P. Maxim . "Immigration Policy and Immigrant Quality: Empirical Evidence from Canada." *Journal of Population Economics* 6, no. 4 (Nov 1993): 337-52.

Yalnizyan, A. *The Growing Gap: A Report on Growing Inequality Between the Rich and Poor in Canada*. Toronto: Centre for Social Justice, 1998.

Yanz, L., B. Jeffcoat, D. Ladd, and J. Atlin. *Policy Options to Iimprove Standards for Women Garment Workers in Canada and Internationally*. Toronto: Maquila Solidarity Network/Status of Women Canada, 1999.

Yepez Del Costello, I. "A Comparative Approach to Social Exclusion: Lesson from France and Belgium." *International labour Review* 133, no. 5–6 (1994): 613–633.

Copyright Acknowledgements

Photos

Chapter 1 photo from Health Canada web site and Media Photo Gallery, Health Canada, http://www.hc-sc.gc.ca. Reproduced with the permission of the Minister of Public Works and Government Services Canada, 2004.

Chapter 2 photo reprinted by permission of Tina Lorien from the stock.xchng web site, http://www.sxc.hu.

Chapter 3 photo reprinted by permission of David Stowell from the stock.xchng web site, http://www.sxc.hu.

Chapter 4 photo from Health Canada web site and Media Photo Gallery, Health Canada, http://www.hc-sc.gc.ca. Reproduced with the permission of the Minister of Public Works and Government Services Canada, 2004.

Chapter 5 photo from Health Canada web site and Media Photo Gallery, Health Canada, http://www.hc-sc.gc.ca. Reproduced with the permission of the Minister of Public Works and Government Services Canada, 2004.

Chapter 6 photo from Health Canada web site and Media Photo Gallery, Health Canada, http://www.hc-sc.gc.ca. Reproduced with the permission of the Minister of Public Works and Government Services Canada, 2004.

Chapter 7 photo reprinted by permission of John Pring from the stock.xchng web site, http://www.sxc.hu, http://www.johnpringphotography.com.

Chapter 8 photo from Health Canada web site and Media Photo Gallery, Health Canada, http://www.hc-sc.gc.ca. Reproduced with the permission of the Minister of Public Works and Government Services Canada, 2004.

Chapter 9 photo from Health Canada web site and Media Photo Gallery, Health Canada, http://www.hc-sc.gc.ca. Reproduced with the permission of the Minister of Public Works and Government Services Canada, 2004.

Chapter 10 photo from Health Canada web site and Media Photo Gallery, Health Canada, http://www.hc-sc.gc.ca. Reproduced with the permission of the Minister of Public Works and Government Services Canada, 2004.

Tables and Boxes

Table 1.1: "Total Population 15 Years and Over by Racialized Population, 2001 Census, Geography: Canada" from 2001 Census. Reprinted by permission of Statistics Canada.

Table 1.2: "Racialized Groups, 2001 Count and Percentage Change 1996-2001" from 2001 Census. Reprinted by permission of Statistics Canada.

Table 1.3: "Total Population in the Labour Force (15 Years and Over by Racialized Groups) – Male" from 2001 Census. Reprinted by permission of Statistics Canada.

Table 1.4: "Total Population in the Labour Force (15 Years and Over by Racialized Groups) – Female" from 2001 Census. Reprinted by permission of Statistics Canada.

Table 1.5: "Racialized Group Members Proportion of Population by City, 2001" from 2001 Census. Reprinted by permission of Statistics Canada.

Table 1.6: "Immigrant Proportion of Population by Census Metropolitan Area, 2001" from 2001 Census. Reprinted by permission of Statistics Canada.

Table 1.7: "After-Tax Income of Racialized Persons, Canada, 1996" from Statistics Canada, Income Statistics Division, Survey of Labour and Income Dynamics, Custom Tables, 1999-2002. Reprinted by permission of Statistics Canada.

Table 1.8: "After-Tax Income of Racialized Persons, Canada, 2000" from Statistics Canada, Income Statistics Division, Survey of Labour and Income Dynamics, Custom Tables, 1999-2002. Reprinted by permission of Statistics Canada.

Table 1.9: "After-Tax Income of Racialized Persons with University Degree, Canada, 2000" from Statistics Canada, Income Statistics Division, Survey of Labour and Income Dynamics, Custom Tables, 1999-2002. Reprinted by permission of Statistics Canada.

Table 1.10: "After-Tax Income of Racialized Persons with Less Than High School Education, Canada, 2000" from Statistics Canada, Income Statistics Division, Survey of Labour and Income Dynamics, Custom Tables, 1999-2002. Reprinted by permission of Statistics Canada.

Box 1.1: "Emergence of Visible Minorities in Canada" from Peter S. Li, *Destination Canada: Immigration Debates and Issues*, 2003. Reprinted by permission of Oxford University Press.

Box 2.1: "The Social Value of Race" from Peter S. Li, *Racism and Social Inequality in Canada*, 1998. Reprinted by permission of Thompson Educational Publishing.

Box 2.2: "Everyday Racism" from Frances Henry, *The Colour of Democracy: Racism in Canadian Society*, 2000. Reprinted by permission of Harcourt Brace.

Box 2.4: "The Market Value of Race" from Peter S. Li, *Racism and Social Inequality in Canada*, 1998. Reprinted by permission of Thompson Educational Publishing.

Box 2.5: "The Concept of Democratic Racism" from Frances Henry, *The Colour of Democracy: Racism in Canadian Society*, 2000. Reprinted by permission of Harcourt Brace.

Table 3.1: "Racialized Group Population as Percentage of Total Canadian Population, 2001" from 2001 Census. Reprinted by permission of Statistics Canada.

Table 3.2: "Racialized Group Population as Percentage of Total Census Metropolitan Areas (CMA), 2001" from 2001 Census. Reprinted by permission of Statistics Canada.

Table 3.3: "Distribution of Immigrant Landings by Class, 1970-1993" from Akbari, "Immigrant 'Quality' in Canada: More Direct Evidence of Human Capital Content, 1956-1994" *International Migration Review* 33, no. 1 (Spring 1999): 156-175; de Silva, *Earnings of Immigrants: A Comparative Analysis*, 1992. Reprinted by permission of Statistics Canada.

Box 3.1: "Starting Life Poor" from Margaret Philip, *The Globe and Mail*, June 26, 2003, p. A6. Reprinted by permission of *The Globe and Mail*.

Box 3.2: "Biases in Public Discourse on Immigration" from Peter S. Li, *Destination Canada: Immigration Debates and Issues*, 2003. Reprinted by permission of Oxford University Press.

Table 4.1: "Canada: Income of Racialized Group Individuals, 1995" from Statistics Canada, Centre for Social Justice Special Run of Data, Survey of Labour and Income Dynamics, 1999-2000. Reprinted by permission of Statistics Canada.

Table 4.2: "Canada: Income of Racialized Persons, 1996, before Tax" from Statistics Canada, Centre for Social Justice Special Run of Data, Survey of Labour and Income Dynamics, 1999-2000. Reprinted by permission of Statistics Canada.

Table 4.3: "Canada: Income of Racialized Persons, 1996, after Tax" from Centre for Social Justice Special Run of Data, Statistics Canada, Survey of Labour and Income Dynamics, 1999-2000. Reprinted by permission of Statistics Canada.

Table 4.4: "Canada: Income of Racialized Persons, 1997, before Tax" from Centre for Social Justice Special Run of Data, Statistics Canada, Survey of Labour and Income Dynamics, 1999-2000. Reprinted by permission of Statistics Canada.

Table 4.5: "Canada: Income of Racialized Persons, 1997, after Tax" from Centre for Social Justice Special Run of Data, Statistics Canada, Survey of Labour and Income Dynamics, 1999-2000. Reprinted by permission of Statistics Canada.

Table 4.6: "Canada: Income of Racialized Persons, 1998, before Tax" from Centre for Social Justice Special Run of Data, Statistics Canada, Survey of Labour and Income Dynamics, 1999-2000. Reprinted by permission of Statistics Canada.

Table 4.7: "Canada: Income of Racialized Persons, 1998, after Tax" from Centre for Social Justice Special Run of Data, Statistics Canada, Survey of Labour and Income Dynamics, 1999-2000. Reprinted by permission of Statistics Canada.

Table 4.8: "Canada: Average Income of Persons by Education Levels, 1998" from Centre for Social Justice Special Run of Data, Statistics Canada, Survey of Labour and Income Dynamics, 1999-2000. Reprinted by permission of Statistics Canada.

Table 4.9: "Canada: Median Income of Persons by Education Levels, 1998" from Centre for Social Justice Special Run of Data, Statistics Canada, Survey of Labour and Income Dynamics, 1999-2000. Reprinted by permission of Statistics Canada.

Table 4.10: "Canada: Income of Racialized Persons by Select Deciles, 1996" from Centre for Social Justice Special Run of Data, Statistics Canada, Survey of Labour and Income Dynamics, 1999-2000. Reprinted by permission of Statistics Canada.

Table 4.11: "Canada: Income of Racialized Persons by Select Deciles, 1996, after Tax" from Centre for Social Justice Special Run of Data, Statistics Canada, Survey of Labour and Income Dynamics, 1999-2000. Reprinted by permission of Statistics Canada.

Table 4.12: "Canada: Income of Racialized Persons by Select Deciles, 1996, before Tax" from Centre for Social Justice Special Run of Data, Statistics Canada, Survey of Labour and Income Dynamics, 1999-2000. Reprinted by permission of Statistics Canada.

Table 4.13: "Canada: Income of Racialized Persons by Select Deciles, 1998, before Tax" from Centre for Social Justice Special Run of Data, Statistics Canada, Survey of Labour and Income Dynamics, 1999-2000. Reprinted by permission of Statistics Canada.

Table 4.14: "Employment Income of Full-Year/Full-Time Racialized Persons in Unionized Workplaces before Taxes, 1998" from Centre for Social Justice Special Run of Data, Statistics Canada, Survey of Labour and Income Dynamics, 1999-2000. Reprinted by permission of Statistics Canada.

Table 4.15: "After-Tax Income of Racialized Persons, Canada, 2000" from Statistics Canada, Income Statistics Division, Survey of Labour and Income Dynamics, Custom Tables, 1999-2002. Reprinted by permission of Statistics Canada.

Table 4.16: "After-Tax Income of Racialized Persons, University Degree, Canada, 2000" from Statistics Canada, Income Statistics Division, Survey of Labour and Income Dynamics, Custom Tables, 1999-2002. Reprinted by permission of Statistics Canada.

Table 4.17: "After-Tax Income of Racialized Persons, Less Than High School, Canada, 2000" from Statistics Canada, Income Statistics Division, Survey of Labour and Income Dynamics, Custom Tables, 1999-2002. Reprinted by permission of Statistics Canada.

Table 4.18: "After-Tax Income of Racialized Persons by Select Deciles, Canada, 2000" from Statistics Canada, Income Statistics Division, Survey of Labour and Income Dynamics, Custom Tables, 1999-2002. Reprinted by permission of Statistics Canada.

Table 4.19: "After-Tax Income of Racialized, Female Persons, Canada, 2000" from Statistics Canada, Income Statistics Division, Survey of Labour and Income Dynamics, Custom Tables, 1999-2002. Reprinted by permission of Statistics Canada.

Table 4.20: "After-Tax Income of Racialized, Male Persons (Ages 16-24), Canada, 2000" from Statistics Canada, Income Statistics Division, Survey of Labour and Income Dynamics, Custom Tables, 1999-2002. Reprinted by permission of Statistics Canada.

Table 4.21: "After-Tax Income of Racialized Male Persons, Age 65 or Over, Canada, 2000" from Statistics Canada, Income Statistics Division, Survey of Labour and Income Dynamics, Custom Tables, 1999-2002. Reprinted by permission of Statistics Canada.

Table 4.22: "After-Tax Income of Racialized, Female Persons, Age 16-24, Canada, 2000" from Statistics Canada, Income Statistics Division, Survey of Labour and Income Dynamics, Custom Tables, 1999-2002. Reprinted by permission of Statistics Canada.

Table 4.23: "After-Tax Income of Persons with Full-Year/Full-Time Unionized, Canada, 2000" from Statistics Canada, Income Statistics Division, Survey of Labour and Income Dynamics, Custom Tables, 1999-2002. Reprinted by permission of Statistics Canada.

Table 4.24: "Average Earnings of Immigrants and Canadian-Born with University Degree" from Statistics Canada, 2001 Census Analysis Series, Earnings of Canadians: Making a Living in the New Economy. Reprinted by permission of Statistics Canada.

Table 4.25: "Canada: Number and Average Earnings of Racialized and Non-Racialized Immigrants by Period of Immigration" from Statistics Canada, *The Daily*, May 12, 1998. Copyright © Statistics Canada, 2003. Reprinted by permission of Statistics Canada.

Table 4.26: "After-Tax Income of Families, Canada, 2000" from Statistics Canada, Income Statistics Division, Survey of Labour and Income Dynamics, Custom Tables, 1999-2002. Reprinted by permission of Statistics Canada.

Table 4.27: "Unemployment Rates for Immigrants, Non-Immigrants, and Racialized Groups (%)" from Statistics Canada, 2001 Census Analysis Series. *The Changing Profile of Canada's Labour Force*, February 11, 2000 and 2001 Employment Equity Act Report, Human Resources and Development Canada. Reprinted by permission of Statistics Canada and Human Resources and Development Canada.

Table 4.28: "Labour Force Participation Rates for Immigrants, Non-Immigrants, and Visible Minorities (%)" from Statistics Canada, 2003: *The Changing Profile of Canada's Labour Force* and The Conference Board of Canada, April 2004, *Making a Visible Difference: The Contribution of Visible Minorities to Canadian Economic Growth*. Reprinted by permission of Statistics Canada and The Conference Board of Canada.

Table 4.29: "Population Showing Representation by Highest Levels of Schooling, Geography: Canada" from Human Resources and Skills Development Canada. Reprinted by permission of Statistics Canada.

Table 4.30: "Degree in Medicine, Dentistry, Veterinary, Canada" from Human Resources and Skills Development Canada, based on 1996 and 2001 Census. Reprinted by permission of Statistics Canada.

Table 4.31: "Doctorate, Canada" from Human Resources and Skills Development Canada, based on 1996 and 2001 Census. Reprinted by permission of Statistics Canada.

Table 4.32: "Post-secondary Education among Immigrants and Canadian-Born (%)" from Statistics Canada, 2001 Census Analysis Series, *Education in Canada: Raising the Standard*. Reprinted by permission of Statistics Canada.

Table 4.33: "Racialized Group Population Aged 15+ Lowest Representation in Occupation Groups and Unit Groups, 2001, Geography: Canada" from Human Resources and Skills Development Canada. Reprinted by permission of Statistics Canada.

Table 4.34: "Racialized Group Population Aged 15+ Highest Representation in Occupation Groups and Unit Groups, 2001" from Human Resources and Skills Development Canada. Reprinted by permission of Statistics Canada.

Table 4.35: "Workforce Population Showing Representation by Employment Equity Occupational Groups (2001 NOC) in Canada by Employment Equity Occupational Groups"

Box 8.2: "State Responses to Racism in Canada" from Frances Henry, *The Colour of Democracy: Racism in Canadian Society*, Harcourt Brace, 2000. Reprinted by permission of Harcourt Brace.

Appendix A: "Universal Declaration of Human Rights (United Nations 1948)." Reprinted by permission of the United Nations.

Appendix B: "Declaration on the Rights of Persons Belonging to National or Ethnic, Religious and Linguistic Minorities." Reprinted by permission of the United Nations.

Index